DIMENSIONS·
DIMENSIONS·

DIMENSIONS:

AGING, CULTURE, AND HEALTH

CHRISTINE L. FRY
and
Contributors

PRAEGER SPECIAL STUDIES • PRAEGER SCIENTIFIC
A J.F. BERGIN PUBLISHERS BOOK

Library of Congress Cataloging in Publication Data
Main entry under title:
Dimensions: aging, culture, and health.

  Bibliography: p.
  Includes index.
  1. Aging—Addresses, essays, lectures.
2. Aged—Care and hygiene—Addresses, essays,
lectures. 3. Cross-cultural studies— Addresses,
essays, lectures. I. Fry, Christine L.
GN 485.D55   305.2'6   80-28607
ISBN 0-03-052971-9

Published in 1981 by Praeger Publishers
CBS Educational and Professional Publishing
A Division of CBS, Inc.
521 Fifth Avenue, New York, New York 10017 U.S.A.

0123456789   056   987654321

Printed in the United States of America

Foreword

Whether we see gerontology as returning to anthropology, or anthropology as maturing in its relationship with gerontology, the combination is very good. Corrine Nydegger's outline of challenges to gerontology and anthropology, given at the end of this volume, proves that this relationship can continue to produce important results along many lines. As a sociologist who looks at the adult development and transition crises of human beings, I have gained insights through the use of anthropological analyses of events, such as widowhood and retirement in national cultures other than America. The Human Relations Area Files and the work of such pioneers as Clark, Simmons, Cowgill, and Holmes have advanced our understanding of how these events affect men and women in different ages who are involved in different role clusters. However, we need more of such works. There is still a shortage of anthropological, in-depth, analyses of transitions and processes as experienced in different cultures, historical periods and social systems. Unfortunately, comparative work of this type is still far too rare.

American society and social gerontology can benefit immensely from anthropological analyses of older people, the culture in which they live, and the problems they must negotiate. Ethnocentrism leads our society to definitions of problems and to policy formulations which often do not alleviate human misery or which have unanticipated and unwelcome consequences. For example, our definitions of nursing homes as inevitably infantilizing and depriving people of dignity can be modified by the knowledge that other societies have organized such homes along more satisfying lines.

The White House Conferences on the Family of 1980 and on Aging in 1981 consistently brought out the inadequacies of our policies in the public and private sectors affecting family members and people of all ages, especially the very young and the old. The limitations of social policies that have not been adequately dealt with include: our social security program; our failure to protect people's economic security in illness; the inflexibility of our work schedules and career lines; our unwillingness to create adequate child-care resources; discrimination against women and minorities; our outdated values concerning families; and the penalizing of women who stay home to care for children. In her presidential address for the Midwest Sociological Society, Joan Huber documented that such policies could lead outside observers to assume our society is "anti-family" or at least anti-children. It is unfortunate that the kind of knowledge which anthropology

iii

could provide to policy (i.e., showing how other societies experience and solve some of the problems of the life course) is usually absent from the information base out of which policy is formed.

Of course, it is not the only function of a discipline to provide policy makers with knowledge; rather, the broad scope of studies subsumed under the rubric of anthropology certainly provides space for such contributions. Another way in which anthropology can relate to societal needs is by reminding its sister disciplines and fields of inquiry—such as sociology and gerontology—to look outside of the here and now; back into history and out to other nations. All too often we need to be freed from assumptions of the "naturalness" of our way of life. To someone born in another society, as I was, this society appears very different. It differs in its heterogeneity, values and methods of dealing with life's problems, and assisting members to a full life over its whole course. I am not saying that sociologists looking at the social relations, social roles and social persons of adults and older people, are not making important contributions (a little ethnocentrism and loyalty to one's discipline is not inappropriate). In actuality, sociologists benefit from work done by other disciplines. Other fields of inquiry, such as gerontology, are excellent places for cross-fertilization. I am always excited when I see the concept "support systems" spreading so rapidly across social gerontology from different perspectives. Anthroplogists contributing to this volume have obviously dipped in to the literature of related fields. It is refreshing to see that more attention is being given by anthropologists to the life course of women beyond the childbearing years in a variety of societies and times. It has been frustrating in the past to hunt for bits and pieces of data about widowers (who are assumed to remarry without difficulty), but even more exasperating to learn nothing about widows except what the culture forbade them to do.

Thus, as a sociologist trying to contribute to social gerontology and benefiting from the contribution of others, I am pleased to see the blooming of anthropological interest in adult and old age stages of the life course. I have learned a lot from this book.

Helen Znaniecka Lopata

Contents

Part 2 AGE, HEALTH, AND MEDICINE

Part 3 ANTHROPOLOGY AND GERONTOLOGY

Introduction
Anthropology
And Dimensions
Of Aging

Christine L. Fry

Ask an anthropologist and you will find another dimension. What dimension we cannot say since that is dependent upon the question and the expertise of the anthropologist. However, if you want a pet theory challenged, take it to the laboratory of Anthropology. This laboratory is unlike other labs in that it is global in nature, encompassing the total range of human cultural experiments at all times and all places. With a lab so grand, is it not filled with uniqueness and chaos? . . . No, no more so than the Astronomer's lab! It is the task of the anthropologist to identify and measure the dimensions which structure the human world. Dimensions of complex problems are what anthropologists analyze in our search for the universal in the diversity of human culture. Universals, on the other hand, are difficult to find when it comes to human behavior. Anthropological reports often effectively veto theories supported by data from cultures representative of one or a few cultural types. Theories are continually honed and refined as the search proceeds for other variables and the charting of other dimensions salient to the problem. In a laboratory as vast as the 3000 + human cultures, the dimensions are innumerable and often unsuspected; new ones are always on the horizon.

New dimensions enter our knowledge via the diversity inherent in cross-cultural analysis, but these variables are also incorporated by the way in which anthropologists approach the data in a particular culture. There are many ways to study a culture, but one canon anthropologists maintain is that of "holism." Holism refers to an emphasis upon context and the understanding of a context in its entirety. Hence, one of the first tasks of ethnography is to map the socio-cultural dimensions of an ethnographic setting. Obviously, by holistically investigating a culture, the anthropologist is seaching for (1) dimensions which are salient to people in that culture and (2) salient to anthropological theory.

Anthropology and Gerontology are well suited for each other. Although Anthropology is a discipline, its interests are catholic, being limited only to anything which furthers our understanding of *Homo sapiens sapiens*. Gerontology, too, is broad. It is an area of study which is based in phenomena and problems, rather than being bounded by the perspective and methodology of a discipline. Its focus, all aspects of aging, encourages cooperative, interdisciplinary research. Since aging is not a simple matter, we find researchers in the biological, psychological, and social sciences, as well as the humanities, investigating the phenomena. Anthropology is "pre-adapted" for gerontological research. Age is a dimension of *Homo sapiens sapiens*. It is inherent in the human biological being. It is an ingredient in individuals' personality development, self concepts and mental life. It shapes social interaction, group formation and social structure. It is a component of the cultural codes people use to negotiate each other and their environment. Thus, with the dimensionality of age and Anthropology's concern for dimensions and complex interactions, we are seeing an encounter between Anthropology and Gerontology which is enriching both through comparative and holistic research.

Dimensions structuring age and the human world are not infinite, although at one time we suspected they might be. In this book the dimensions are restricted to aging, culture and health. This is a book about ethnology. It deals with the cultural and social organization of age; the consequences for the old; and cultural solutions to social and health-created dependencies. Obviously, each dimension, in and of itself, is complex and readily leads to other dimensions. In the sections which follow, we will examine age and culture, and age, social supports and health, within the anthropology of aging.

Aging and Culture

A decade ago it was possible to cite the literature in anthropology of aging by naming two monographs (Simmons 1945, Clark and Anderson 1967), along with a handful of scattered articles. Today, it is a different story. Not only has there been an exponential growth in published research, but the issues have become increasingly differentiated. The origin and development of the anthropology of aging has been documented elsewehre (Clark 1973, Fry 1980b, Holmes 1976, Keith 1980b). The anthropology of aging is a comparatively young specialization with an expanding body of knowledge. As is characteristic of most emergent areas of study, there is no established paradigm guiding and organizing the entire field. However, major currents or issues are sufficiently crystallized, with hypotheses and theories ripening for harvest. These I identify as: (1) cultural comparisons and regularities; (2) the effects of cultural change upon the old; (3) strategies and opportunity structures available to the elderly; and (4) the social organization of age differences.

Cultural Comparisons and Regularities. A basic problem in cross-cultural research is comparability. If we are to evaluate a theory using data from many cultures, then this data should be obtained using similar methodologies and measurements. To accomplish this, integrated and coordinated fieldwork with research protocols (i.e., Whiting and Whiting 1975) is ideal. The ideal, however, is not always attainable. Alternatively, comparative analysis is possible through (1) the use of published ethnographic reports, or (2) a re-examination of anthropologist's fieldnotes in the light of new research questions. Analysis of secondary materials is fraught with pitfalls. In the 1930s George Peter Murdock rectified some of these problems by systematizing the accumulating wealth of ethnographic reports into the Human Relations Area Files (HRAF). These files have had a continuing evolution, especially with respect to the addition of current research and methodological problems. A distinct variety of comparative research has emerged. Holocultural research (Rohner et. al. 1978, Naroll 1970) is methodologically distinct in that (1) it relies on secondary materials in the HRAF files; (2) it pays attention to sampling; and (3) it is concerned with coder reliability. (See Chapter 1 of this book for a more thorough discussion of holocultural analysis.) Other comparative research using either coordinated fieldwork, re-analysis of fieldnotes or examination of ethnographic cases, not selected by an explicit sampling procedure, is conventionally referred to as cross-cultural research.

Most of the comparative research on old age has focused on status, prestige or treatment of older adults as the dependent variables. The now classic work of Simmons (1945) blazed the trail. Working with the then-new HRAF files, Simmons massed a large quantity of data to be analyzed in an era before computers. His work is now an often cited reference volume for Anthropology and Gerontology with his insights pointing to a wide variety of factors shaping the experiences of the aged. What factors affect esteem or prestige? The holocultural research of Maxwell and Silverman (1970) reveals that control of useful knowledge by the old is positively related to esteem. Cross-cultural research has suggested that modernization is detrimental to the prestige of the elderly (Cowgill and Holmes 1972b, Cowgill 1974) except in mature industrialized nations (Palmore and Manton 1974). This and other research demonstrates that prestige is not a simple variable produced by single factors. Using data from Mesoamerican peasant communities, Press and McKool (1972) isolate four prestige generating components of roles and statuses for older people: (1) advisory; (2) contributory; (3) control; and (4) residual. In this book, the work of Anthony Glascock and Susan Feinman (Chapter 1) furthers this tradition. Using a holocultural methodology, they conceptually clarify the issues by searching for explicit definitions of old and the determinants for the category "old." Also they sharpen the main dependent variable by analytically separating prestige (attitudes) from treatment (behavior). Their discovery of the prevalence of non-supportive behavior and its being directed toward the decrepit old, mirrors the lessons from Simmons (1960) concerning the "over aged" and our increasing concern of "death with dignity."

Consequences of Change for Older People. A near universal is that change produces adverse effects upon the position of the elderly. This is especially true if change is rapid and involves the social and economic transformations associated with modernization (Cowgill and Holmes 1972b). Knowledge controlled by older people is no longer relevant to solve transformed problems (Maxwell and Silverman 1970) and the prestige generating components of roles and statuses are eroded to the detriment of the elders (Press and McKool 1972). One of the immediate effects of modernization has been a major demographic disruption and population explosion. Although we know very little about the demographic profiles of small populations, our available evidence indicates they may have been remarkably similar to those of maturing industrial societies with approximately 10 percent in the older category (Underwood n.d.). We do know that those societies experiencing industrialization are demographically young, and that this can have profound effects upon that society's opportunity structure and system of rewards. These effects are clearly seen in New Guinea among the Asmat (as reported in Chapter 2 by Peter Van Arsdale). With a larger decline in infant and lesser decline in adult mortality, the population becomes younger. Simultaneously, the opportunity structure changes, with the former system of ritually reinforced roles of importance being replaced by state-enforced rules rewarding those who have acquired some formal education and can speak a *lingua franca*. It is the young and not the old who are rewarded to articulate with the "new way." Thus the old, especially males, are left in a void, both ritually and socially.

Common sense should tell us that change is not always negative, even for the old. Also change does not occur in jerks and halts, but is a continous process that sometimes gallops, other times crawls, but is always happening. In Chapter 3, written by Pam Amoss, we see another dimension of change—among the Coast Salish. Here, contact and modernizing influences have been of longer duration. Indians have rejected Anglo society with its limited opportunities for them. The new is bad and the old—Indian roots—must be rejuvenated. Coast Salish Indians turned to the curators of the old way: the elders who had some experience and contact with an earlier time and another culture. This is not an isolated case. As ethnic groups try to counter the forces of assimilation or discrimination by forging an ethnic identity, it is the old who often benefit with valued contributions to make (see Cool 1980). On the other hand, the old may not always benefit by renewed interest in roots on the part of the young. To respond to the demands for the old way, the elders must have some requisite knowledge of the former culture to be the curators and (as Amoss argues) the creators of tradition. If they did not experience this by being born too late or by living off the reservation, a sense of frustration will be the result (i.e., Williams 1980).

Culture, Strategies and Solutions. Humans use culture to size up situations in negotiating the business of everyday living. Cultures set parameters on action, but they also create alternative solutions to basic problems. Older people are prone to problems related to security and role attrition. Although strategies vary in each cultural context (i.e., see Guemple 1976 for the Eskimo, Kerns 1980 for the Black Carib, Hamer 1972 for the Sidamo, Shelton 1972 for the Ibo, and Ikels 1980 for urban China), it is kin and the cultivation of filial piety which usually provides for security in old age in traditional cultures. What happens if the old person has no relatives, or if that person has chosen to violate the cultural norms by not marrying and having children? Alternative solutions are created, as is demonstrated by Andrea Sankar in Chapter 4, in her study of elderly Chinese spinsters. In traditional China it is one's religiously sanctioned duty to marry and procreate, perpetuating one's own or one's husband's lineage. For those who could not achieve this ideal, a number of substitute paths were acceptable, including adoption, uxorilocal marriage, concubinage, prostitution, nunneries, *etc.* One alternative, developed primarily on the Canton Delta among silk workers, was a sisterhood of both a secular and sacred nature. These sisterhoods were later adapted to urban Hong Kong. Sisterhoods do provide security in old age for their members, but, as Sankar's study reveals, this is often precarious, especially for the smaller sisterhoods lacking community supports. Nevertheless, even in a kin-dominated society, non-kin or fictive kin can and do form bonds granting mutual security into old age.

Role attrition is a problem which is more acute for those older adults in industrialized societies. Family and work roles go through their cycles, only to be exited in old age with few and ambiguous roles remaining and little opportunity for socialization to new statuses (Rosow 1974). If this is a problem, then what's its solution? Rosow suggests that through peer groups and age homogenous settings with roles, norms and sanctions which are either distinctive or isolative, positive old age or new roles can be created and socialization can occur. Indeed, ethnographic research in retirement communities points to the positive effects of such homogenous environments for their members (e.g., Ross 1977, Keith 1979, 1980a, Boyer 1980, Jonas and Wellin 1980, Byrne 1971, Johnson 1971, Myerhoff 1978). Doris Francis, in her cross-cultural study of the experience of two remarkably similar populations in Leeds and Cleveland, raises new questions about the community creation process. A community is not always formed as the case of Cornell Arms demonstrates. Francis (Chapter 5) argues that homogeneity in ethnicity, class, and income are insufficient to trigger the process resulting in community. Homogeneity in cultural expectations about parent-child relationships and the prior opportunity and experience in forming peer bonds is also essential. In addition, communities must be fostered in the early planning phases of both (1) the physical layout, to encourage opportunities for interaction; and (2) in the sociological design, to permit leaders to emerge, to permit internal status differentiation to occur, and to encourage the participation in community-wide events by residents. Community did not form in Cleveland because of these factors. On the other hand, in Leeds we find a developed community which has flourished and continues to flourish. Creative solutions involve the search for alternatives. With increased ethnographic and cross-cultural analysis of alternate strategies for older people, we are able to isolate the factors which make them work or those which inhibit the ameliorating effects.

Social Organization and Age Differences. Age is clearly a principle of social organization, but it seldom stands alone. There is no such thing as a pristine age role or status: young, middle, old. These are age grades or categories. Age, along with sex, is an ascribed characteristic shaping the allocation of roles and statuses within the institutions of a society (e.g., kinship, economics, politics, religion). Although age and sex may appear to be masked by other criteria of role differentiation, both remain primary and omnipresent, but may be of varying significance. Thus age differentiation, the basic questions of the structure of age strata, the effects of age differences in interaction and group formation, and transitions throughout the life course, can only be understood in the holistic context of other principles of social organization.

Interlinkages between age and sexual stratification are explored by David Kertzer and Oker Madison (Chapter 6) in societies where age is an explicit and emphasized principle of differentiation: age-set or generation-set societies. Age sets are predominately a male phenomena, regulating relations within and between generations of males and collectivizing transitions. Of the ethnographically documented cases, Kertzer and Madison found only three societies to have age sets for women, and these sets are different than the equivalent men's age sets. With the dual focus on sex and age stratification, we find that the sexual differences in productive and reproductive domains point to advantages that accrue for males—but not females—from collective transitions and formalized relations between sets. This, of course, raises fascinating questions about the collectivization of rites of passage and the ritualization of social life for males and females in cultures where age is not as explicit.

Age and sex constitute points of social solidarity reflected in the aphorism, "Birds of a feather, flock together." At least this is true when relationships are by choice or are voluntary. Valerie Fennell (Chapter 7), in her study of age relations in a Southern retirement town, found that an age difference of not more than 5-8 years constituted age homophily. However, she also found that age heterogenous relationships are formed when a person, known to one of the parties, serves as an age-intermediary or as an age-bridge. These linkages may either be a relative (familial peer linkage) or a peer (peer linkage). Linkages are important in that they either introduce or legitimize a relationship that otherwise would probably not exist. The effects of the operation of peer and familial peer linkages is seen in the recruitment of new members to Women's Clubs in the town studied by Fennell. All of these clubs were age homogenous in spite of the fact that only one had explicit age restrictions (and, ironically, it was the least age homogenous). Even though age is not the paramount criterion defining the roles and statuses of these women (choice, co-residence, and sex are), age does have a profound effect upon network and group formation.

Just as age differentiation is understood in the context of the social arena in which it operates, it also must be seen through the life cycle and the transitions shaping the life course. Discontinuities and transitions, especially the abrupt and individualized transitions characteristic of industrialized societies, have been seen as posing problems for individuals and intensifying generational conflict in a society. Recent research (Foner and Kertzer 1978, 1979) has demonstrated that transitions are not always smooth and conflict-free in simpler societies. Jack Weatherford (Chapter 8) further shatters this myth through his research in Kahl, West Germany. Here he found—in a highly industrial region—life cycles in both the economic and kinship institutions to be characterized by gradual, finely graded transitions for both men and women. Transitions entailing changes and transferal of wealth, responsibility, power and prestige, contain the seeds of conflict. Such tensions are reduced, as is documented in the German community studied by Weatherford, by the gradual and continous rehearsing of the next transition and shift in activities with explicit, yet flexible age norms.

Age and Health

The coming of old age poses problems for both individuals and their society. Some of these issues are age related, others are exascerbated by age, and even others are a product of earlier life-long patterns. "Dependency" is usually associated with "old," with both young and old striving to maintain independence. Fortunately most older adults maintain a high degree of interdependence in their interactions and exchanges with others in their social networks. Yet real problems are there. Ethnographic probing of target populations often reveal differing definitions of the problem, the presence of a non-problem, or factors contributing to the problem. The issues anthropologists in this volume have investigated that are relevant to social and medical services are: (1) social support and nutrition (inclusive of alcohol abuse); (2) institutionalization; and (3) the responses of medical services to the demands of larger cohorts of older people.

Social Support and Nutrition. Of all the heterogenous populations of older adults, it is the elderly of the inner city of most metropolitan areas in the United States who are considered to be the most at risk. Until recently, the scant research we had available indicated many older Americans were leading a marginal existence in single-room-occupancy hotels with very little income, in near complete social isolation, and in poor health. Ethnographic research in both New York and San Diego now gives us a more complete picture of this population. Using a network profile to map and analyze social networks and the qualities of social relationships, Jay Sokolovsky and Carl Cohen (Chapter 9) demonstrate that the fierce independence and image of loner is, in fact, built upon a network of support. These networks are small and their structure camouflages their existence from the probes of social scientists, social workers, and other outsiders. For the SRO dwellers these networks are of great cultural significance, enabling them to negotiate and find strength in an environment which planners will "urban renew" out of existence.

The impression of isolation is also erased in Paul Bohannan's study of the food habits of SRO elderly in San Diego (Chapter 10). Commensality rituals are of social and symbolic importance in all cultures, including the restaurants and cafes of SRO dwellers. Nutrition is viewed as a major problem of these inner city dwellers precisely because of isolation and poverty. Bohannan shatters yet another myth. It is not meager resources which determine the quality of diet, but cultural factors in shaping food preferences and structuring the choice of where to eat. Ironically, it is the middle class SRO resident who eats a poorer diet and pays more for it.

Alcohol abuse is also an issue which many practitioners have seen as a problem in older populations. This too, could be an outsider's view or one biased by working with selective populations in which alcohol is abused. Barry Bainton's study of alcohol use among older adults in Arizona (Chapter 11) confirms earlier studies indicating that alcohol consumption declines with age. In fact, in his sample individuals curtailed their consumption by an average of a little over a shot a day as compared with the pre-retirement pattern. Although Bainton's research points to a potential non-problem, his analysis indicates the complexities in the different patterns of the young-old and old-old, the factors shaping drinking habits, and the potential costs of heavy alcohol consumption.

Institutionalization. Non-supportive behavior of incapacitated older adults is not a universal feature to be found in all cultures. With advances in medical technology, industrialized cultures have been able to prolong life through long-term care. Sophisticated medical services, however, are beyond the capabilities of the average family to administer, and consequently hard decisions must often be made about insitutional care. With increases in the over-65 cohorts and changes in state mental hospitals, the use of extended care facilities has correspondingly increased. Our statistics reveal that only 5 percent of the older population is institutionalized, but the probability of dying in a nursing home is one in four. The prospects of institutionalization, with the associated negatives of custodial care, are a dismal prospect for the last days of life.

American medical services have made remarkable advances in the past 30 years, and the delivery capabilities of those services has simultaneously expanded. With the increase in scale we also find changes in social organization. Entry into an extended care facility has been affected by this expansion, which has enlarged the influence of the physician's role in the decision to institutionalize. Margaret Faulwell and Rhoda Pomerantz (Chapter 12) examine the factors shaping institutionalization rates of physicians in two acute care hospitals in Chicago. Of all significant factors affecting the physician's rate of institutionalizing elderly patients, it is the opportunity to know patients, the similarity in cultural backgrounds, and the increased ability to empathize with patients, which results in markedly lower rates of referral to and admission to a nursing home. Communication and cooperation between physician and patient are clearly essential for the optimal decision about care. With more older adults seeking care for chronic problems, the authors encourage expanded training in geriatrics to increase physician awareness and empathy.

Nursing homes in the United States have a bad reputation. The ethnography of Jeanie Kayser-Jones (Chapter 13) indicates that the reputation is deserved, but goes on to place these homes in the context of the cultural and social organization of health care services in the United States. Nursing homes don't have to be that way, as is demonstrated in her comparative ethnography of a nursing home in Scotland. Patients in Scotland are not infantilized, dehumanized, depersonalized or victimized as are their counterparts in the United States. Because of differences in social organization, patients in Scotland are able to maintain themselves as valued persons through meaningful exchange with the staff. If we are to improve the conditions in our nursing homes, then this ethnographic lesson should be heeded.

Medical Services. With demographic change and shifts in the demand structure, the medical profession is responding to these older cohorts. Should medical services be designed along age stratification lines? Should we have a geriatric specialty in the medical profession? In England and Europe, geriatrics and geriatricians are a part of the system of medical care. But in America, the answer is by no means clear. Otto von Mering and Angela O'Rand, in their review of gerontologic services (Chapter 14), argue yes. Health care delivery should be based upon a behavioral-medical model which incorporates life cycle stages, disease pattern and health risk, treatment modalities, and service types. In this model, they emphasize cultural definitions of health and encourage training in the sociocultural perspective. They see that for effective planning to take place, cultural as well as bio-medical demands should be determined on a local and regional, rather than national, level. Arnold Arluke and John Peterson, on the other hand, give us a cautionary warning (Chapter 15). They see aging increasingly defined as disease. Diseases can be cured—are to be cured—and then go away. Aging, however, is unlike other medicalized problems in that it is normal and not transitory. Medicalization of aging has extended the jurisdiction of physicians, permitted the control of behavior of older people through psychotropic drugs, and absolved the responsibility of other institutions (such as family or religion) for the elderly by individualizing the problems.

Change has, is and will continue to occur. There is much to be said for expanding training in geriatrics (Chapters 12 and 14). Geriatrics, as a specialty, contributed to the positive conditions in extended care for the elderly in Scotland (Chapter 13). The scale, the cultural assumptions, and the social organization of medical delivery systems in the United States, however, are considerably different. The cautions raised by Arluke and Peterson should be heeded as unintended consequences. As von Mering and O'Rand indicate, with continued inflation, energy shortages, and steady-state economics, changes are inevitable. It is our hope that in negotiating these changes, the findings of anthropologists and other social scientists will be incorporated. Health and disease, illness and wellness, problems and solutions, are cultural in definition. Although real physical difficulties can be resolved through technological intervention, it is culture which is paramount in the way a society collectively communicates about, organizes its resources, and tries to resolve the problem. Thus, equal attention should be paid to the cultural dimension of aging and health.

Anthropology of Aging

Anthropology of aging has come of age. In many aspects, this book is a rite of passage. As this book matured, many anthropologists committed their careers or portions of their careers to the study of aging. AAGE, the Association for Anthropology and Gerontology was founded, thereby formalizing the informal social organization which had evolved among these anthropologists. A "tradition" has emerged, a vigorous hybrid of anthropology and gerontology. Having passed through our adolescent search for identity, we are ready to address anthropology and gerontology on a more mature footing. As Jennie Keith (Chapter 16) argues, the "back to anthropology movement" has begun. Our research has increased our pool of ethnographies of old age. The return to anthropological theory can only be mutually enriching, in that new (and sometimes old) dimensions emerge with enticing hypotheses as we systematize our knowledge. Systematization triggers further growth. Full maturity, however, is still on the road ahead. One thing is clear, the anthropology of aging will be the anthropology of age (see Kertzer and Madison Chapter 6, Keith Chapter 16, and Keith 1980b).

We are also forging ahead meeting the challenges of gerontology. As Corinne Nydegger points out in Chapter 17, these challenges are many, but the opportunities are even greater. The holistic, emic, comparative and evolutionary nature of anthropology makes anthropologists ideally suited to grapple with some of the more difficult and rewarding problems in gerontology. Here, too, as we systematize our knowledge with that of our colleagues in other disciplines, we will continue to grow. Anthropology's contribution will, of course, mature both from within itself and within gerontology. Maturity here is more difficult to foresee, since sciences are noted for recombining their dimensions and shifting paradigms (Kuhn 1970). Again, the one thing that is certain is that anthropology and gerontology will have a long, productive life.

1

Social Asset or Social Burden: Treatment of the Aged In Non-Industrial Societies

Anthony P. Glascock
and
Susan L. Feinman

1. Introduction

Interest in the treatment of aged individuals within anthropological gerontology has grown steadily since 1960, but there has been a lack of
nomothetic models, generalizations and hypotheses that can be tested in
fieldwork situations. This lack of nomothetic generalizations concerning
the treatment of the aged has led to analyses that are largely descriptive and
non-comparative. It is the intention of the present work to contribute to the
analysis of aging by constructing a series of holocultural generalizations
concerning the treatment of aged individuals to be used in developing a
comparative framework within anthropological gerontology.

Holocultural analysis "is a research design for statistically measuring
the relationship between two or more theoretically defined and opera-
tionalized variables in a world sample of human societies" (Rohner et.al.
1978:128). The method relies on the analysis of previously collected
ethnographic data and in the majority of cases utilizes the Human Relations
Area Files (Naroll 1970; Rohner 1977a; 1977b). There is some confusion
as to the proper terminology to be applied to multicultural comparative
research. For many years the terms cross-cultural and holocultural were
used interchangeably, but during the 1970s a distinction came to be made
between the two terms. Cross-cultural now refers to studies of two or more
societies which do not use one of the recognized holocultural samples (Murdock and White 1969; Naroll, Michik and Naroll 1976). Some examples of
cross-cultural aging studies are Guttman 1969; Hippler 1969; Lopata

1972; Press and McKool 1972; Shanas 1973; and Townsend 1973. Holocultural now refers to studies that do use one of these samples. Examples of holocultural aging studies are Simmons 1945a, 1945b; Silverman and Maxwell 1970, 1978.

Holocultural analysis has been little used in the analysis of the treatment of aged individuals. In fact, the relationship between ethnographic, cross-cultural and holocultural analyses is little understood or appreciated by most anthropological gerontologists. Ethnographic, cross-cultural and holocultural studies are related to each other in a cyclical manner. Ethnographic monographs yield data which can be used in the construction of holocultural hypotheses. Holocultural analyses, in turn, yield new, untested propositions which can then be tested by ethnographic fieldwork and in cross-cultural studies of a limited number of societies. Through these methods of testing, a hypothesis can be refined and the cycle begun anew. The goal of the present work is to begin the cycle of suggesting a series of holocultural hypotheses concerning the aged that can be systematically tested. The lack of propositions that can be systematically tested appears to the authors to be the major weakness of the anthropological study of the treatment of the aged.

2. Anthropology of Aging: Cultural, Cross-Cultural and Holocultural

Anthropological studies investigating specific aspects of the aging process are reported in the literature (e.g., Cowgill 1971, 1972b; Cowgill and Holmes 1972a; Fry 1976; Goody 1976; Myerhoff and Simic 1978; Ross 1977), but only in rare instances have specific hypotheses seeking cross-cultural validity been tested. In these few studies little if any continuity or integration has existed; Sheehan (1976) tries to answer questions concerning social esteem, Press and McKool (1972) try to discern the structural determinants related to the status of old people, and Bengsten, et. al., (1975) try to test hypotheses concerning the inverse relationship between individual modernity, societal modernization and favorable attitudes toward aging and the aged.

Comparative or cross-cultural attempts within anthropological gerontology have also suffered from the lack of nomothetic generalizations concerning the aged (e.g., Arnhoff, Leon and Lorge 1964; Cowgill 1972b; Guttman 1969; Hippler 1969; Press and McKool 1972; Shanas 1973; Slater 1964; Townsend 1973). These studies—whether they focus on one society (as Palmore's 1975 study of Japan) or several societies (as Myerhoff and Simic's 1977 study of the life histories of the elderly in five societies)—have in common three basic features: (1) They do not test specific hypotheses which have been developed from replicable research; (2) Their selection of societies for inclusion in the studies is for convenience rather than sample validity and; (3) The results are not comparable among the various studies since different kinds of subjects were selected, different methods of data collection were utilized, and different analytical tests were employed. Consequently, the results of these cross-cultural studies are as descriptive and non-theoretical as the anthropological literature which focuses on specific aspects of aging. To correct these deficiencies we need a series of nomothetic holocultural generalizations from which testable hypotheses can be derived.

Only two previous studies attempt to develop nomothetic holocultural generalizations concerning the aged. The first is the classic work of Leo W. Simmons resulting in *The Role of the Aged in Primitive Society* (1945a) and several articles (1945b, 1946, 1960). Simmons examined the ethnographic materials available for 71 primitive societies and coded all the data dealing with the aged. In particular, he investigated the relationships among various aspects of the status and treatment of the aged and certain ecological, economic, political and social dimensions of the societies. Even though Simmons worked when the holocultural methodology was in its infancy and no standard holocultural sample of societies existed, his book provided an abundance of ideas, suggestions and unrefined hypotheses which could have been utilized by anthropological gerontologists.

Unfortunately, his work, although almost always cited in the literature, did not become a source of testable hypotheses. There appear to be two reasons for this lack of utilization of Simmons' work—one historical and the second methodological. First, there was little or no interest in the anthropological study of aged individuals until the 1960s. Margaret Clark (1967a, 1967b, 1973) has argued persuasively that old people were not studied in other societies by American anthropologists because they were not seen as being important in our own society. When anthropologists turned to the study of the aging process in the late 1960s, Simmons' work was twenty years old and apparently considered dated.

The second reason for the non-utilization of Simmons' work is found in the work itself. Though he was aware throughout his work of the importance of how "old" was being defined, Simmons did not deal directly with the issue since he perceived the development of explicit definitions as an insurmountable problem (1945a:15; 1946:436). Perhaps if he had developed valid holocultural definitions of "old," other anthropologists would have utilized his work more often. A second methodological problem with Simmons' work was that he utilized the concepts of the treatment of aged individuals and the prestige accorded to aged individuals interchangeably. This is a major error in Simmons' conceptualization. Prestige describes an attitude whereas treatment describes behavior, and the joining of them causes tremendous problems in the analysis of ethnographic materials. In addition, several critical reviews of Simmons' work, concentrating on his statistical computations, may have discouraged anthropologists from pursuing his ideas and hypotheses (see Holmes 1976).

The second major attempt to develop holocultural generalizations of the aged is the work of Maxwell and Silverman (1970; 1971a; 1971b; 1972; 1976; 1978). Maxwell and Silverman's work has led to the extensive Bakersfield Aging Study Schedule (nd), comprised of coding protocols for a wide range of variables including the aged's roles in the economic, political and religious spheres of their societies; types and extent of positive and negative treatment of the aged; types of informational processes, resource control and deference accorded the aged. Their work has resulted in the generation of a series of hypotheses which concentrate on the relationship between social isolation and social rigidity and the amount of prestige enjoyed by the aged within a given society. These hypotheses have not as yet been tested in ethnographic fieldwork, but they do provide the beginnings of comparative framework within anthropological gerontology.

The work of Maxwell and Silverman is a clear improvement over that of Simmons. They utilize a recognized holocultural sample, apply a rigorous holocultural methodology, and include within their analysis a wide range of variables. However, in two areas they appear to be unable to overcome difficulties encountered by Simmons. Maxwell and Silverman, like Simmons, recognize the importance of determining a holocultural definition of "old," but only conclude that the limits of the "old" social category vary from place to place (1970:40). In addition to not developing hypotheses concerning the definition of "old," Maxwell and Silverman, again like Simmons, fail to clearly differentiate the treatment of old people from the attitudes held by members of a society about old people. The differentiation of treatment and attitude is difficult, especially when the research relies on secondary sources, but if respect and treatment are regarded as interchangeable concepts it is hard (if not impossible) for researchers to operationalize Maxwell and Silverman hypotheses.

The present analysis attempts to both refine the two previous holocultural studies within anthropological gerontology and extend the number of variables included by concentrating on two main areas. First, the analysis answers the dual questions: (1) Do people in preliterate societies explicitly define "old age"; and (2) if they do, what criteria are utilized to mark the transition into the old age category? Secondly, the analysis separates the dimensions of treatment and esteem/respect that have been combined into a single dimension in previous holocultural analyses, and develops a series of propositions concerning the treatment of the aged in non-industrial societies.

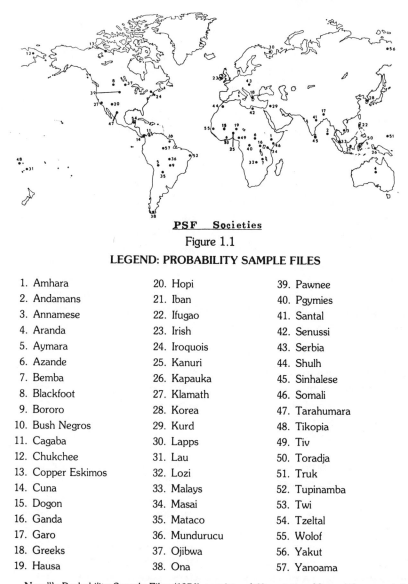

PSF   Societies

Figure 1.1

LEGEND: PROBABILITY SAMPLE FILES

1. Amhara	20. Hopi	39. Pawnee
2. Andamans	21. Iban	40. Pgymies
3. Annamese	22. Ifugao	41. Santal
4. Aranda	23. Irish	42. Senussi
5. Aymara	24. Iroquois	43. Serbia
6. Azande	25. Kanuri	44. Shulh
7. Bemba	26. Kapauka	45. Sinhalese
8. Blackfoot	27. Klamath	46. Somali
9. Bororo	28. Korea	47. Tarahumara
10. Bush Negros	29. Kurd	48. Tikopia
11. Cagaba	30. Lapps	49. Tiv
12. Chukchee	31. Lau	50. Toradja
13. Copper Eskimos	32. Lozi	51. Truk
14. Cuna	33. Malays	52. Tupinamba
15. Dogon	34. Masai	53. Twi
16. Ganda	35. Mataco	54. Tzeltal
17. Garo	36. Mundurucu	55. Wolof
18. Greeks	37. Ojibwa	56. Yakut
19. Hausa	38. Ona	57. Yanoama

Naroll's Probability Sample Files (1976) consists of 60 societies. Nine of these societies could not be used because either they had no *Ethnographic Atlas* entry or had no information within the HRAF categories searched. Possible substitute societies were suggested by Dr. Naroll and were used in six of the cases (Greeks for Bahia Brazilians, Malays for Central Thai, Tupinamba for Guaranti, Irish for Highland Scots, Annamese for Taiwan Hokkien, Mundurucu for Tucano). There were no substitutes available for the Khasi, Tlingit and Trobriands and their elimination reduced the PSF to 57 societies.

3. Methodology

A standard holocultural methodology was employed in the development and testing of the hypotheses concerning the treatment of old people (see Glascock and Feinman 1980 for a more complete discussion of the methodology utilized). Five categories from the Human Relations Area Files provided the data base from which the codes were constructed: age stratification, old age dependency, senescence, activities of the aged, and status and treatment of aged.

A pre-test composed of 36 societies chosen at random from the HRAF was utilized to develop 18 coding schemes. Six of these schemes concerned the definition of old age and 12 the treatment of old individuals. Since separate entries were made for males and females, the final coding procedure contained 36 distinct elements. Raoul Naroll's HRAF Probability Sample Files (Naroll, Michik and Naroll 1976) were selected for final analysis (see Figure 1:1) for three reasons: (1) they are a direct outgrowth of Murdock's work on holocultural sample design and the *Ethnographic Atlas* (1967); (2) the size of the sample, 60 societies, is manageable; and (3) they have a companion statistical package that allows for the application of sophisticated statistical tests.

Identical coding procedures were followed for both the pretest data and the Probability Sample Files data. Two sophisticated and one naive coder independently coded the data.[1] The intra-rater reliability for each of the sophisticated coders was .94 and .96. The inter-rater reliability for the pretest data was .85; for the Probability Sample File data .90.

The determination of the appropriate unit definition is a common problem in holocultural research, and one that usually arises before data collection takes place. In the present research, however, the issue arose both before and after data collection. Given the nature of the data it was possible to undertake analysis either in terms of societies (36 for the pre-test, 57 for the PSF) or in terms of occurrences. Analysis in terms of societies is complicated. Each society may have a different number of entries for definition and treatment, with a maximum of six each per society, which leads to fractional computations. Analysis in terms of occurrences avoids this difficulty, but also presents computational problems because of variation in the number of components for the different codings. Computations were undertaken utilizing each method, and since the results were consistent only the computations of occurrences are reported in this chapter.

4.1   Results:
Definitions of "Old"

In order to determine if and how "old age" is defined in pre-industrial societies, three hypotheses were developed. The first hypothesis—that the majority of societies in the ethnographic record have explicit ways of defining the category "old age"—was initially tested by an analysis of the pretest data. The results of the analysis showed that in 60 percent of the pretest societies it was possible to discern at least one explicit definition of old age. This figure, although substantiating the hypothesis, was lower than desired for the support of the initial and pivotal hypothesis. However, since one of the criteria utilized for selecting the societies in the PSF was bibliographic fullness (Naroll, et. al., 1970), the prospects of strongly substantiating the hypothesis by the analysis of the societies in the PSF initially appeared good. Unfortunately, although the hypothesis was again substantiated, only 62 percent of the societies in the PSF had an explicit definition of old age.

The PSF is not believed to be the source of this low figure. Instead, it appears that there is a distinct lack of concern by the majority of ethnographers with the aging process and old age. Three explanations for this paucity of data are suggested: (1) as Clark (1967a) argues, because old people have not been regarded as important actors in our society, they have not been regarded as important subjects by ethnographers; (2) many ethnographers have concentrated on the subsistence activities of societies, and as a result have paid little attention to the aged, most of whom are not directly involved in subsistence activities; and (3) when aged informants have been the focus of research, they have been utilized to reconstruct culture the way it was before contact, rather than as a source of information concerning the aging process.

The second and third hypotheses concern those societies for which at least one definition of old age was discernable. Hypothesis 2 states that if explicit definitions of old age can be determined from the ethnographic data, then these definitions should cluster into a limited number of definitional categories. Seven definitional categories emerged from the pretest data: chronology, invalid status, senility, change in work patterns, adult status of children, menopause, and change in physical characteristics[2]. For hypothesis 2 to be substantiated, there could exist no societal definition of old age in the PSF data that could not be coded within one of the seven categories. This was the case, and therefore hypothesis 2 is considered substantiated.

For the initial coding, allowance was made for the existence of primary, secondary, and tertiary definitions of old age. The original contention was that there would be a major societal definition of old age, with the possibility of secondary and tertiary definitional parameters for special individual cases. After analysis of the pretest data, the validity of this contention came into question. The results of the analysis indicate that—while a large minority of the societies with definitional information have more than one way of defining an individual as old (44 percent of the pretest definitions, 41 percent of the PSF definitions)—these definitions appear to be applied independently of each other. Consequently, it is suggested that the first definitional parameter to apply to an individual is the one used to define a man or woman as old in a particular society.

To reduce the number of cells used in the statistical computations to

TABLE 1.1

DISTRIBUTION OF DEFINITIONAL CODES
FOR THE PRETEST AND PSF SAMPLES
(PERCENTAGES-ABSOLUTE NUMBERS IN PARENTHESES)

	Pretest		PSF	
	Single	Multiple	Single	Multiple
Change in work patterns	50 (13)	32 (11)	64 (27)	35 (23)
Chronology	20 (5)	39 (14)	19 (8)	30 (20)
Adult status of children	12 (3)	9 (3)	5 (2)	8 (5)
Menopause	7 (2)	11 (4)	2 (1)	6 (4)
Invalid status	7 (2)	6 (2)	10 (4)	6 (4)
Senility	4 (1)	0 (0)	0 (0)	0 (0)
Change in physical characteristics	0 (0)	3 (1)	0 (0)	15 (10)
Total	100 (26)	100 (35)	100 (42)	100 (66)

TABLE 1.2

DISTRIBUTION OF DEFINITIONAL CLASSIFICATIONS
FOR THE PRETEST AND PSF SAMPLES
(PERCENTAGES-ABSOLUTE NUMBERS IN PARENTHESES)

	Pretest		PSF	
	Single	Multiple	Single	Multiple
Change in social role	69 (18)	50 (17)	71 (30)	46 (27)
Chronology	19 (5)	41 (14)	19 (8)	34 (20)
Change in capabilities	12 (3)	9 (3)	10 (4)	20 (12)
Total	100 (26)	100 (34)	100 (42)	100 (59)

be applied to the pretest and PSF data requires a grouping of the seven definitional codes into a smaller number of classifications. The three definitional classifications constructed are: (1) chronology; (2) change of social role—comprised of change in work patterns, adult status of children, and menopause; and (3) change in capabilities—comprised of invalid status, senility, and change in physical characteristics.[3]

Hypothesis 3—if definitional categories exist, then their distribution should be equal (14 percent for each category cell and 33 percent for each classification cell)—is not substantiated by either an analysis of the pretest or PSF data. Tables 1:1 and 1:2 indicate the extent of the variation from the predicted distribution.

Even though the distinction is made in both tables between societies which have a single definition of old age and those that have more than one definition, the patterns are consistent. When the data are divided into the seven categories, changes in work patterns and in chronology as the definition of old age occur in more societies than anticipated, and in the other five categories less than predicted. When the data are grouped into the three classifications, change in social role as a definition of old age occurs far more often than anticipated, chronology in multiple definitions occurs slightly more than anticipated, whereas chronology in single definitions is less prevalent than anticipated and change in capabilities is significantly underrepresented. These variations from the predicted distribution must be explained.

Perhaps the most surprising figure in Tables 1:1 and 1:2 is the lack of the utilization of capabilities as definitions of old age. In particular, the figures in Table 1:1 show how seldom senility, invalid status, and change in physical characteristics are used as definitions. In absolute numbers, there are only six instances in the pretest data and 16 instances in the PSF data when change of physical capabilities occur in any form. There appear to be two possible explanations for this lack of occurrence of capabilities: (1) that people in most indigenous societies just do not live long enough to become senile or incapacitated; or (2) that people in most indigenous societies are classified as old before they become senile or incapacitated.

The first possible explanation can be explored by the analysis of demographic data from the HRAF. This is currently being investigatged at the University of Wyoming, and the data is not yet available. On the other hand, there is information available from the present study to suggest that the second explanation is tenable. If people *are* defined as old before undergoing a change in physical or mental capabilities, it would therefore follow that there would be differentiation within the old age category. The existence of just such a distinction within the old age category was first suggested by Simmons (1945a:62; 1945b:42; 1960:87).

> Among all peoples a point is reached in aging at which any further usefulness appears to be over, and the incumbent is regarded as a living liability. "Senility" may be a suitable label for this. Other terms among primitive peoples are the "overaged," the "useless stage," the "sleeping period," "the age grade of the dying," and the "already dead" (1960:87).

Maxwell and Silverman also recognized that there is a distinction made by most societies between the decrepit old and the intact old, but they offer no data to support their contention (1970:40).

The data from the PSF were analyzed in order to determine if societies made allowances for the existence of more than one group of old people. Thirty-two percent of the societies in the PSF distinguished different groups of elderly people. Of these 18 societies, 15 (26 percent) of the PSF societies made the distinction between young or intact old and old or decrepit old. While this cannot be used as proof that individuals are defined as old before undergoing physical or mental deterioration, it does suggest that this may be the case. If this distinction is found in a large number of societies, then it may be of particular importance to the differences found in the treatment of old people. (This subject is discussed in detail below.)

A further look at Tables 1:1 and 1:2 suggests several interesting conclusions concerning the use of chronology in the definition of old age. First, only five of the 61 definitional codes (8 percent) and eight of the 101 PSF definitional codes (8 percent) were for chronology alone. This is an even

TABLE 1.3

FREQUENCY AND DISTRIBUTION OF MULTIPLE DEFINITIONAL CODES
FOR THE PRETEST AND PSF SAMPLES
(PERCENTAGES-ABSOLUTE NUMBERS IN PARENTHESES)

	Pretest	PSF
Chronology & change in social role	82 (14)	55 (16)
Chronology & change in capabilities	0 ( )	0 (0)
Change in social role and capabilities	18 (3)	21 (6)
Chronology & change in social role & change in capabilities	0 (0)	14 (4)
Change in social role & change in social role	0 (0)	3 (1)
Change in capabilities & change in capabilities	0 (0)	7 (2)
Total	100 (17)	100 (29)

lower figure than that for change in capabilities. The vast majority of cases where chronology is used as a definition of old age are cases where chronology occurs with another definitional category. In particular, chronology occurs with a change of social role: 14 of 17 pretest societies with multiple definitions (82 percent) and 21 of 29 PSF societies with multiple definitions (72 percent) (Table 1:3).

The final and most dramatic variation from the distribution predicted by Hypothesis 3 is the overrepresentation of the change in social role classification and change in work patterns category. The figures in Table 1:3 for the PSF data most clearly show the degree of this overrepresentation. Seventy-one percent of the occurrences for single definitions and 46 percent for multiple definitions are for change in social role. These figures appear to confirm the often-stated but seldom-substantiated assumption in anthropology that a person's social role is the most important factor in the determination of one's "place in a society."

4.2 Treatment of Those Defined as Old

In order to determine the patterns that exist in the treatment of the aged in preindustrial societies, four additional hypotheses were developed. Hypothesis 4 states that the majority of societies reported on in the ethnographic record will have explicit ways of treating old persons. The PSF data was more generous in its yield of information on the treatment of the elderly than it was on the definition of old age. While only 62 percent of the societies in the PSF had ethnographic data concerning the definition of old age, over 73 percent of the societies had ethnographic data containing information on the treatment of old people.

Hypothesis 5 states that if explicit treatment of the aged can be determined from ethnographic data, these treatments should cluster into a limited number of treatment categories. Ten treatment codes emerged from the analysis of the pretest data: (1) supportive treatment; (2) non-specific non-supportive treatment; (3) insults directed at the old; (4) old people regarded as witches; (5) old people forsaken; (6) loss of property; (7) old people living apart from the main social group; (8) abandonment of old people; (9) old people killed; and (10) no mention of treatment.[4] For Hypothesis 5 to have been substantiated, there could exist no form of treatment of the elderly in the PSF data that could not be coded as one of the ten treatment categories. This was the case, and therefore Hypothesis 5 is considered upheld.

This ten-code scale was converted from a nominal to an ordinal one by randomizing the ten codes and distributing them to introductory behavioral science classes at the University of Wyoming. The students were asked to rate the treatment from very supportive (0) to very non-supportive (10).

Supportive behavior was defined as behavior which actively maintained the existence and well-being of the aged individual. Non-supportive behavior was defined as behavior which did not contribute to the maintenance of the aged individual. The means for the treatments were determined and used to rank the treatments. The treatments were statistically grouped by t-tests: (1) supportive; (2) no mention; (3) own dwellings and non-specific; (4) insulted, loss of property and regarded as witches; (5) forsaken and abandoned; (6) killed.

These six groupings were further reduced to form three major groupings: (1) supportive treatment; (2) non-death-hastening treatment, comprised of own dwellings, non-specific, insulting, loss of property and regarded as witches, and defined as non-supportive treatment that does not lead directly to death; and (3) death-hastening treatment, comprised of forsaken, abandonment and killed and defined as non-supportive treatment that leads directly to death of the aged individual.[5] Since the pretest data were not coded utilizing the expanded and ordinal scale, only the PSF data is discussed in the following analysis.

As with the definitional codes, allowance was made for multiple treatments, three codes per sex per society. Unlike the definitional codes, the distinctions of primary, secondary and tertiary proved to be relevant. Treatments for a given sex in a given society were ranked by a combination of how often the treatment was mentioned and how much emphasis was placed upon the treatment by the ethnographers. As with all other codes, the treatment codes (and their ranked order) were subject to agreement among the sophisticated and the naive coders.

Hypothesis 6 states that if treatment categories exist, then their distribution should be equal (11 percent for each treatment category; 33 percent for each treatment classification). As Table 1:4 indicates, this hypothesis is not substantiated. Referring to the last column of Table 1:4, the categories of own dwellings, non-specific, insulting and loss of property are underrepresented, while the categories of supportive, forsaken, abandoned and killed are overrepresented. Witches occurred exactly 11 percent of the time.

Two possible explanations are suggested for own dwellings, non-specific, insulting and loss of property being underrepresented: (1) these behaviors occur infrequently because they are not separate from harsher treatments, but are instead part of a continuum of non-supportive behavior. Segregation, insult behavior, loss of property and regarding the elderly as witches may be the first steps toward forsaking, abandoning and killing of the aged; and/or (2) a sharp distinction between intact and decrepit old is made by members of many societies, with the result that only the ends of the behavior continuum — supportive for the intact aged and death hastening for the decrepit aged — are found.

TABLE 1.4

DISTRIBUTION OF TREATMENT CODES
FOR THE PSF SAMPLE
(PERCENTAGES-ABSOLUTE NUMBERS IN PARENTHESES)

	Single	Multiple	Combined
Supportive	56 (23)	26 (26)	35 (49)
Own Dwellings	0 (0)	3 (3)	2 (3)
Non-Specific	2 (1)	0 (0)	1 (1)
Insulting	2 (1)	2 (2)	2 (3)
Property	5 (2)	8 (8)	7 (10)
Witches	7 (3)	12 (12)	11 (15)
Forsaken	5 (2)	15 (15)	12 (17)
Abondoned	11 (4)	12 (12)	12 (16)
Killed	12 (5)	21 (21)	19 (26)
Total	100 (41)	99 (99)	101 (140)

Supportive treatment is the most frequent single category, occurring 35 percent of the time. However, supportive treatment alone occurred in only 16 percent of the societies in which treatment could be coded. In the remaining instances, supportive treatment was found in conjunction with at least one non-supportive treatment. Astoundingly, 84 percent of the societies with data concerning the treatment of the aged had some form of non-supportive treatment.

Killing of the aged was the second most prevalent treatment, occurring 19 percent of the time. Killing alone occurred in only five instances (4 percent); the remaining occurrences linked killing with another treatment. Killing occurred with supportive treatment in ten instances (45 percent); with loss of property in one instance (5 percent); with regarded as witches in three instances (14 percent); with forsaken in four instances (18 percent): with abandonment in four instances (18 percent). In all of these cases, gericide was either the second of two treatments or the third of three treatments.

Forsaking and abandoning the elderly are slightly overrepresented at 12 percent each, again occurring alone rarely (3 percent for abandoning and 1 percent for forsaking). These treatments are never the primary of multiple treatments and occur as the final choice of treatment except where killing also occurs. Then forsaking and abandoning the aged occurs before the most drastic act of murder.

Table 1:5 groups the treatment data into the classifications of supportive, non-death-hastening and death-hastening. Supportive treatment of the

TABLE 1.5

DISTRIBUTION OF COMBINED TREATMENT CLASSIFICATIONS
FOR THE PSF SAMPLE
(PERCENTAGES-ABSOLUTE NUMBERS IN PARENTHESES)

	Single	Multiple	Combined
Supportive	55 (23)	35 (26)	42 (49)
Non-Death Hastening	16 (7)	25 (19)	22 (26)
Death-Hastening	29 (12)	40 (3)	36 (42)
Total	100 (42)	100 (75)	100 (117)

elderly is the most common, closely followed by death-hastening, non-supportive treatment (forsaking, abandoning and killing). This contradicts the commonly held belief that old people in most societies are primarily given supportive treatment, and that the prolongation of life is sought (Cowgill 1971; 1972; Myerhoff and Simic 1978; Simmons 1960). Only Arnhoff, Leon and Lorge found that there was

> . . . a predominance of negative attitudes and beliefs about the aging and the aged (1964:41).

The simultaneous occurrences of supportive and non-supportive treatment require further investigation. Specifically, two questions are raised: (1) how societies manage to have both types of behavior without internal strain; and (2) how individuals are selected as recipients for each type of treatment.

Table 1:6 is a breakdown of the 18 PSF societies which differentiate groups within the old age category and the classification of treatment which

TABLE 1.6

TREATMENTS AND GROUPINGS OF OLD
(PERCENTAGES-ABSOLUTE NUMBERS IN PARENTHESES)

	Supportive	Non-Supportive	Supportive and Non-Supportive	No Information	Total
Intact/Decrepit	25 (1)	100 (5)	100 (6)	100 (3)	83 (15)
Chronological	75 (3)	0	0	0	17 (3)
Total	100 (4)	100 (5)	100 (6)	100 (3)	100 (18)

these old people receive. Hypothesis 7 states that a significant number of the combination supportive/non-supportive treatment will be in the intact/decrepit grouping. This was true 100 percent of the time, substantiating Hypothesis 7.

It is suggested that the following is occurring in these societies. While an aged individual is considered young or intact by the other members of the society, support for his or her existence is provided. However, once this individual passes over into the old or decrepit group of elderly, support is withdrawn dramatically, since the non-supportive treatment in all but one instance is death-hastening. Societies manage, therefore, to have both types of behavior without internal strain because the two types of behaviors are directed at different populations. Individuals are selected as recipients for each type of behavior acccording to which group of old they belong. This would also account for the overrepresentation of the supportive, forsaking, abandoning and killing categories and the supportive and death-hastening classifications.

Sumner (1940), Simmons (1945a; 1960) and Fischer (1978) all observed that the decrepit old are burdens to their societies and are often removed. Sumner (1940) states that those who become burdens are removed either by themselves or by their relatives. Simmons states that:

> . . . even in societies where the aged have possessed firmly entrenched rights, the very decrepit have faced the threat of indifference, neglect and actual abuse (1945a:177).

> Actual neglect or even abandonment of the helpless old was rather common. . . (1960:85, 86).

To prevent being labeled decrepit, many elderly people will continue to do whatever tasks they can and are allowed to do, however trivial or degrading (Simmons, 1945a; 1960). This is why segregating the elderly to dwellings of their own is threatening. Once removed from the main social body, they may come to be defined as excess baggage, no longer capable of contributing to the group's welfare, and as such are vulnerable to the more extreme forms of non-supportive behavior.

Fischer (1978) makes an interesting point when he discusses the danger of keeping senile people in the society. In a preliterate society, many old people were consulted for their wisdom and experience. Advice from a senile person could prove dangerous to one and all. Therefore he or she had to be removed. Once a society has written records, this danger is removed.

There were 26 instances in the PSF of killing, 18 instances of abandoning, and 17 instances of forsaking the elderly. In 16 (62 pecent) of the 26 killings, the decision was made by the aged individual's immediate relatives. Despite Simmons' (1945a) and Fischer's (1978) claims that suicide is common and/or encouraged, there were only two cases of it in the PSF data. In 12 (46 percent) of the 26 killings, regardless of who decided it was time to eliminate the aged person, it was the direct responsibility of the close relatives to carry out the execution. The obligations of family responsibility carry even this far.

The death-hastening treatment of the elderly appears to be accepted by everyone in the social group, including the victim. There were no cases of resistance by any of the elderly in any of the PSF societies. This goes along with Simmons' conclusion that one of the primary interests of aging persons is

> . . . to withdraw from life when necessity requires it, as timely, honorably and comfortably as possible. . . (1960:65, 66).

There has been disagreement as to whether or not all the elderly retain the respect of the other members of their society. Maxwell and Silverman (1970) and Simmons (1945a; 1960) claim that while their treatment may be harsh and even fatal, the elderly retain their society members' respect up until the end. Simmons (1945a; 1960), again, however, claims that the overaged suffer a loss of respect along with their loss of support. Results of the PSF data analysis uphold the first opinion. Of the 86 instances where there was information on respect, 76 cases (88 percent) had increased respect for the aged. Only two instances (2 percent) of diminished respect were coded.

5. Conclusions

Several of the propositions presented in this chapter are in conflict with the generally held views on the treatment of the aged in preindustrial societies. The validity of these propositions can be shown in two ways. First, anthropological gerontologists can test their validity through research in field situations. It is hoped that such testing will soon be undertaken. Second, further holocultural studies can be conducted which concentrate on: (1) the relationship between the treatment of the aged and major societal features; (2) demographic features which may influence the treatment of the aged; and (3) the relationship between the treatment of the aged and views towards death and dying. These three areas are being pursued by the authors, and should provide tests for the validity of the various propositions.

Notes

[1]One sophisticated coder was a faculty member and the other was a graduate student, both in the Department of Anthropology at the University of Wyoming. The naive coder was a University of Wyoming undergraduate anthropology major who had not been involved in the earlier phases of the research. The codings for each set were compared after all the coding for that data set were completed, and discrepencies were settled in one of two ways. If two of the three coders agreed on a particular item, the principle of majority rule was followed and the third, dissenting code was ignored. If all three coders disagreed on a particular item, the data were jointly reviewed and the discrepency subsequently resolved.

[2]*Seven Definitional Codes:*

1.   Chronology: A chronological indicator is used by the society to designate when an individual is considered old.

2.   Invalid Status: An individual is designated as old because of inability to care for oneself and/or invalid status.

3.   Senility: An individual is designated as old because of the demonstration of senility including mental weakness, mental confusion and failing memory.

4.   Change in Work Patterns: An individual is designated as old because of the inability of the individual to do work that is associated with adults of his or her sex; other work or tasks are assigned to or undertaken by the individual; the social group recognizes the changes in the individual's behavior; ceremonial, religious and/or secular activities may be involved.

5.   Adult Status of Children: An individual is designated as old because all of his or her children are grown and either married and/or have left home; as a parent this individual is no longer responsible for his or her children's behavior or well-being.

6.   Menopause: a woman is designated as old when she reaches menopause.

7.   Change in Physical Characteristics: An individual is designated as old when his or her physical characteristics change, including hair turning white, alteration in dentition and deterioration of vision.

[3]Classifying the seven definitional codes was accomplished in the following way. The codes were reviewed to see if natural groupings appeared. This led to the joining of change in work patterns and adult status of children, as well as the joining of invalid status, senility and change of physical characteristics. It seemed logical that chronology remain in a classification of its own. The remaining definition, menopause, presented a difficult problem. An argument can be made for its being included in change of capabilities or in change of social roles. No research could be found to help solve the dilemma. It was therefore decided by the authors that menopause be included with change of social roles on the basis that the cessation of reproductive capabilities for women is qualitatively different from becoming incapacitated or senile.

⁴*Treatment Codes*

1.   There is no mention of non-supportive treatment of the aged, but there is mention of the supportive treatment of the aged. Supportive behavior is behavior which actively maintains the existence and well-being of the aged individuals. Non-supportive behavior is behavior which does not contribute to the maintenance of the aged individual.

2.   There is mention of the non-supportive treatment of the aged without any detail as to the specifics of such treatments.

3.   The aged are subject to lack of respect and/or social derision, including insults and ridicule. They may be insulted to their faces or this behavior may occur behind their backs.

4.   The aged are believed to be agents of sickness, evil or death. They may be believed to be witches and/or have supernatural powers. Often the aged may be avoided or harmed because of these beliefs.

5.   The aged are forsaken by the rest of the social group. They may not be supported by members of the group; may get only scraps of food or no food at all; may receive poor or no medical care.

6.   The aged have to give up their property. They may have to give up their homes, land and/or livestock.

7.   The aged do not live with the main body of the social group. They live apart in dwellings of their own.

8.   The aged are temporarily or permanently abandoned by the rest of the social group. Harm, up to and/or including death, may come to the aged because of this abandonment.

9.   Aged are killed by members of the social group. The manner of execution may differ; as may the initiator of the murder. The aged are not simply left alone to die; rather, a member or members of the social group actively kills the aged person.

10.   There is no mention of either supportive or non-supportive treatment of the aged.

⁵*Non-Supportive Treatment Categories*
The seven specific categories of non-supportive treatment are own dwellings, insulting, loss of property, regarded as witches, forsaken, abandoned and killed. Although the categories were developed directly from the pretest data, further explanation of their non-supportive features is necessary.
Forcing the elderly into dwellings of their own is non-supportive, since separate dwellings remove the aged from the emotional and practical support of their families. Simmons (1945a) states that the family is the most secure resource of security for the aged, and Cowgill and Holmes point out that all societies provide mutual parent-child responsibilities and obligations (Cowgill 1971, 1972; Cowgill and Holmes 1972). When forced to live apart, this security must diminish, if not wholly disappear.
Insulting the elderly is also not life threatening, but it too is non-supportive. Fischer sees insult behavior as an indirect attack, reporting that elderly in Europe and colonial America were often mocked in drama: "Ridicule, we must remember, is often a

form of rage" (1978:70). Insult behavior can also be considered the opposite of Maxwell and Silverman's (1976) category of linguistic deference. If verbal deference is to be considered a positive or supportive display, then its opposite, verbal abuse, must be considered non-supportive.

Loss of property is non-supportive because it diminishes or totally denies the aged's ability to be self-supporting. In many societies, the deed to property is also the deed to family aid (Goody 1976; Simmons 1945a; 1960). Without the power of property, the aged may find themselves partially or totally without support. This situation can be viewed as the first step toward the death-hastening, non-supportive treatment of forsaking the elderly.

The most difficult of the treatments to evaluate was the elderly being regarded as witches. The attribution of supernatural powers can be seen as either supportive or non-supportive treatment. Simmons (1960:83-84, 1945a:173, 230) realized the dual nature of the attribution of the possession of witchcraft, while Maxwell and Silverman (1976) consider the belief of the control of supernatural powers to be a positive attribute.

In the present analysis, being considered a witch is considered non-supportive for two reasons: (1) the pretest data revealed instances of the accusation of the possession of the supernatural being non-supportive treatment; and (2) it was considered that, like property, this was one step toward the more extreme non-supportive treatments.

Why the categories of forsaken, abandonment and killing are considered non-supportive is self-explanatory.

2
Disintegration of the Ritual Support Network Among Aged Asmat Hunter-Gatherers Of New Guinea *

Peter W. Van Arsdale

1. Introduction

Elderly male hunter-gatherers living in the Asmat region of Indonesian New Guinea (Irian Jaya) have seen a complex ritual system developed over a period of several thousand years virtually disintegrate within a period of two decades. A majority of these men now are living in a "ritual void." Men who were important *tesmaypits* ("Big Men") in 1950—spending hours deliberating as to which war ornaments to wear and what time to strike—are now described as "idle" by curious Western observers. Headhunters who prided themselves in recounting their battle feats and the names of slain enemy now are old men, rarely listened to by the younger generation. The Asmat, once members of residentially mobile and semi-autonomous bands, are now but one subgroup of Indonesia's pluralistic society of 148 million.

The purpose of this chapter is not to point out supposedly unique aspects of this situation as compared with other primitive peoples who

* Adapted from "The Elderly Asmat of New Guinea" in *Other Ways of Growing Old: Anthropological Perspectives*, edited by Pamela T. Amoss and Stevan Harrell, with the permission of the publishers, Stanford University Press. ©1981 by the Board of Trustees of the Leland Stanford Junior University.

have experienced the impact of externally induced change, because in most respects processes here are paralleling those seen elsewhere. Rather, the intent is to demonstrate the unifying importance, to older Asmat males in particular, of ritual in society, to indicate the total sociocultural context for men and women within which daily activities and rituals exist, to indicate what happens when older persons lose their network of support, and to assess the prospects for ritual replacement—given the policies of the Indonesian national government. It will be shown that elderly hunter-gatherers in a developing country face some of the same social problems as those in industrialized countries such as the United States.

2. The Demographic Context

The initial fieldwork upon which most of this study is based was conducted in 1973 and 1974, exactly 20 years after the first permanent mission and government posts were established in coastal Asmat. Followup fieldwork was conducted in 1979. By 1974, the total Asmat population had reached nearly 42,000, indicating a relatively constant annual rate of increase of approximately 1.5 percent since 1956. Of this number, 3,167 persons were residing in the six near-coastal Bismam Asmat villages under consideration here. In these settlements—where change has been more dramatic than elsewhere—headhunting and cannibalism have been suppressed. Separate

FIGURE 2.1
**AGE-SEX STRUCTURE FOR ALL
CENSUS HOUSEHOLDS (n = 72)**

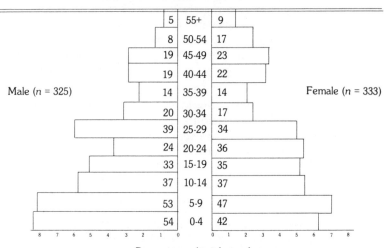

Percentage of total sample

longhouses for each major residential kin-group have been abolished, to be replaced by a single community house for people of the entire village. The irregular scattering of huts that once surrounded each longhouse has been supplanted by straight rows of houses, some of which follow a building design suggested by Indonesian officials unfamiliar with Asmat. With population growth and the imposition of new sociopolitical regulations has come a disintegration of most of the rituals described in the following section. For many elderly men in particular, a "ritual void" has been created.

Given these changes, specific data identifying aged Asmatters are needed to place them in total demographic perspective.[1] Figure 2:1 presents the age-sex structure of the coastal villages, based upon all individuals resident in 72 random sample households. Because of its wide base it is immediately apparent that the pyramid represents a "young" population: 41.0 pecent are under the age of 15. The proportion aged 15 to 50 is 53.0 percent. The proportion aged 50+ years is only 5.9 percent. Age was not reckoned in years in traditional Asmat society, but interviews with a number of informants indicate that persons over the age of about 45 are considered to be "old." For women, it appears that "old age" may be conceptualized as a partial correlate of menopause. Less than one percent of the sample were found to be 65+ years, although it must be noted that accurate estimations of extreme old age are very difficult to derive. As is the case elsewhere, more women reach "old age" than men. It is unusual for a man to live as long as 60 years, although a report substantiated by missionary cross-checking indicates that an old warrior by the name of Saati was approximately 90 years old when he died in November, 1970.

A comparison with demographic data from other New Guinea societies indicates a fairly high degree of correspondence. For example, the Tsembaga Maring (Rappaport 1968:16) and the Kepaka (Bowers 1971:15) have profiles indicating similar, relatively "young" populations. A small proportion reach "old age"—the Tsembaga show the highest percentage (13.2) in the 45+ range, with the Asmat at 12.3 percent and the Kepaka at 12.0 percent. By way of a broader comparison, 10.4 percent of the U.S. population was in what Americans consider to be the "old age" bracket of 65+ in 1975 (DHEW 1976). It is interesting to note that the average age for the Asmat, as calculated from the random household census, is about 22.1 years. Average male age is 20.9 and that for females is 23.4. The overall male-to-female ratio is 92:100 in favor of females.

Any consideration of aged persons must take life expectancy into account. Where exact birth and death registrations are unavailable, or limited to a few recent missionary records as in Asmat, complex methods of estimation must be employed. Weiss (1973a, 1973b) has developed a number of techniques in this regard, one result of their application to Asmat data being the statistics presented here. Asmat life expectancy at birth, termed E (0), is approximately 24.8 years. For those surviving the pre-adult years (0-14.9), additional life expectancy at age 15 /E (15)/ is 27.0 years. That is, those reaching 15 statistically can be expected to nearly reach "old age" (i.e., about 42 years as the projected age at death). An extremely high infant mortality rate of nearly 30 percent prevents overall life expectancy from being higher. The steady population growth described earlier is attributable, in part, to the differential between a crude birth rate of about 55 per 1000 and a crude death rate of 35 to 40 per 1000 (see Van Arsdale, 1978a). By comparison, whereas E (0) was 24.8 for Asmat in 1974, during the same year E (0) was 71.9 in the U.S. (Brotman 1977:14).

The wide demographic disparity represented in a cross-cultural comparison such as that between Asmat and the U.S. must be kept in proper perspective. First, while noting that "old age" as it is culturally and functionally defined in Asmat begins some 20 years earlier than it does in the U.S., it must be stressed that "old" is a relative term. Second, both societies use the term with a minimum of reliance upon biological criteria (q.v. Clark 1973:80). Third, when biology and physical anthropology are brought into the picture, it is seen that the actual process of human aging is relatively uniform across cultural boundaries. It is incorrect to say that Asmatters and Americans age at different rates, but rather that levels of mortality are different (e.g.) for the 25-29.9 cohort in the two societies. Different levels of mortality have their causes in the respective natural and social environments (Howell 1976:33-34).

Howell's (1976) research among !Kung-speaking hunter-gatherers of the Kalahari, for whom she derived E (0) = 30, bears upon the Asmat situation. A low life expectancy in a pre-agricultural population is achieved as a result of considerable infant and childhood mortality, a certain amount of adult mortality, and a rapidly rising rate of mortality after the age of 50 (1976:28). Those few !Kung or Asmat who avoid as they grow older the relatively large numbers of mortality-related factors in their environments will live (as did Saati) to an age as great as that attained by the most elderly Americans—the latter a people who have fewer mortality-related factors to contend with.

A detailed survey of aging and worldwide population trends was recently completed by Hauser (1976). While projecting that the proportions of older people (65 +) will increase in nearly all regions of the world between the years 1970 and 2000, he calculated the increase for Oceania would be from 7.3 to 8.6 percent. Although Asmat still is far below even the 1970 figure, it is important to recognize the demographic importance of such trends on a broad regional basis. This would place the Oceanic proportion in 2000 A.D. at a point considerably higher than those predicted for East Asia, South Asia, Africa, and Latin America (1976:75). Absolute numbers of persons aged 65 and over will be small in Oceania in

2000—perhaps no more than three million—but they may well become increasingly important in modern regional political and economic affairs.

3. The Daily and Ritual Context

Traditionally, the Asmat were a group of scattered hunting, fishing, and sago-gathering Papuan tribesmen inhabiting a portion of Irian Jaya's southwestern lowland swamp and rain forest. Early in the 20th century it is likely that their bands ranged in size from perhaps 25 to 100 or more individuals. Reconstructions based upon local oral history indicate that at least eight major Asmat subdivisions existed, being based loosely upon common ancestry, dialect, and geographic proximity. Because of the abundance of natural sago groves in the near-coastal region, where all data for the present study were collected, territorial-resource ranges were relatively well-defined. Then as now, women and children provided a majority of the food. The time required to obtain necessary foodstuffs was (and is) remarkably low—an average of only 2.0 workdays per week per person aged four and over (Van Arsdale, 1978b). Even today, work of all kinds occupies only 47.8 percent of a man's waking time and 54.4 percent of a woman's. It should be stressed that work is not conceptualized as needing continuous input, and indeed varies greatly on weekly, monthly, and seasonal bases. Time "set aside" for ritual and recreation is pre-eminent.

In the pre-contact context, time not used for work could seldom be classified as "idle." Even though swamp, mud, and rain forest provided barriers to overland travel, a complex and time-consuming pattern of ritualistic revenge warfare had evolved utilizing the intricate maze of interconnected rivers and waterways. Headhunting and cannibalism co-evolved with warfare as ritual responses to perceived spiritual imbalances and as rites of ancestor propitiation.

The roles of the *tesmaypits,* particularly those who were older, can be understood only in conjunction with the dualistic, spatially oriented social system. Briefly, territorial-resource ranges then and now reflect land (especially sago grove) and river utilization rights. Although there is a lack of extensive lineal recognition and a relative lack of recognition of descent-based segmentary principles, resource rights clearly mirror the dual segmentation found in group settlement patterns and men's longhouse (*yew*) divisions. For example, the assorted river rights of one *yew* moiety are grouped together geographically in many instances, and counterpose geographically the rights of the *yew*'s other moiety. Due to the fact that kindred are recognized in Asmat, rather than extensive lineages, the allocation of sago and river rights can change over time. This traditionally was dependent upon the decisions of elder men, new rights of resource access obtained through marriage, and an overall tendency toward patri-inheritance.

Men's longhouses served as social, spiritual, and ritual focal points. Each settlement was comprised of one or more *yew* houses surrounded by the huts of their family members. Each *yew*, being the largest stable unit of social and ritual organization, still today is equated conceptually with a men's house group (*yew mopan*) and by extension to its men's wives and children. A Catholic missionary to Asmat correctly has written of the dualistic system:

> . . . every longhouse on earth had an associated longhouse on the "other side," the spirit world where the ancestors live. Man, by continuously exchanging locations, kept membership relatively equal. If a longhouse on earth became overpopulated, some members would die. If the [moiety] on the other side became too large, some would seek out [moiety] women on earth to be reborn (Sowada 1968:192).

In most cases it was the elder men of the *yew* who, through visions, dreams, or merely consultations, informed all other Asmatters of the state of such affairs. It was the elder men who, taking the spirit and human populations into account, planned and led preparations for the rituals surrounding propitiation of *bis* pole ancestors, initiation activities, sago palm and sago grub festivals, and the organization of headhunting raids. All such activities took place at the longhouse's central fireplace, which served as the dividing line between the *yew*'s two moieties.

To understand the role of the aged male Asmatter is to understand that not all such people were revered, and that those who were revered were not necessarily afforded prestige by virtue of their "wisdom" or "knowledge of tribal mysteries." This stereotype of the wise yet wizened tribal elders, so commonly portrayed in the literature (e.g., Jung, quoted in Clark 1973:78), must be re-examined in light of indications that aged male bandsmen or tribesmen in fact represent a diverse, heterogeneous lot. Those Asmatters proficient in rituals associated with the carving of *bis* poles were afforded ritual prestige as but one type of "Big Man"; those proficient in the organization of headhunting raids were recognized as another type. Most aged males did not stand out as men of influence, but merely were recognized as "old men." This can be applied even more broadly to women.

Three brief synopses serve to illustrate this diversity. Certain elderly Asmatters interviewed in 1979 were clearly knowledgeable in some aspects of music, curing, or myth—but none proved knowledgeable in all these areas. Emermanmuk of Ewer's *yew* Darkau is a woman of about 60. Her knowledge of traditional medicine proved fairly good, but she was able to relate little of Asmat oral history, legends, or music. Our inquiries prompted her younger female friends to attempt to help her with information concerning legends, but all finally agreed that our inquiries should be directed at a man named Dopa instead. He is considered to be the "village expert."

These women concluded by telling us emphatically that many old people know very little of the lore of Asmat.

Dopa, a member of *yew* Yuwiof, indeed was a valuable informant. Aged about 55-60 years, he is the owner of a valuable song known as *pirso*, which he claimed is the original (or oldest) of Ewer's songs. Dopa was able to place the Asmat culture heros Ewer, Jumpits, and Fumiripits into both legendary and musical perspective, tying this to a discussion of the creation of mankind and the relation between earth and *safan* (the "other side"). Perhaps because of his dual role as owner of an especially valuable song and respected oral historian, he expressed confidence that *pirso* would be passed on to song owners in future generations, a process which does not necessarily follow hereditary channels. Other village elders were less confident. Indeed, during the mere five years between our visits to Asmat, interest in traditional songs and legends had declined markedly among younger people. Some of the men and women who traditionally would have been leading candidates to acquire song ownership now evidence little knowledge of the words nor interest in "taking title."

A very few old people are labeled *gila* (an Indonesian loan word meaning "crazy"). One such woman is Amember, about 50 years old, also of the village Ewer. Daily during our research in 1979 she carried a spear, sago basket, and carved wooden plaque on her rounds of the village, stopping long enough to taunt young children or make faces at teenagers. Occasionally she would aim her spear at a child, sending him away screaming. It was claimed that Amember "dances every day." Our observations indicated that she indeed was adept at dancing, and that it was frequently used as a disruptive but attention-getting activity. The large groups that gathered for recreational drumming and singing were frequently disrupted by Amember. Other elderly persons were extremely tolerant, but younger people occassionally became irritated or taunted her in return. Still others laughed at her or mocked her. Yet her place in village life is secure. She is able to draw on her "social credit." Prior to May of 1979 she had been an ordinary old woman; she had developed social relationships over her lifetime which *gila* behavior might attenuate but not destroy. It was only in May that Amember claimed to have been suddenly transformed because of a visit to a legendary river where she had spoken with a powerful spirit.

In Asmat aged men afforded the highest prestige seem to have been of four types: (1) those proficient in sago palm and sago grub rituals; (2) those renowned for headhunting exploits; (3) those who had developed expertise as woodcarvers; (4) those who were able "to arrange things." Wisdom, admittedly a difficult term to translate, does not singularly stand out as a key element; the term *tes* does. Roughly translated, *tes* is that quality which distinguishes the various types of elder "Big Men" from all others. *Tes* is a form of "wealth" which encompasses far more than material goods. It is, in part, a "wealth" of personality attributes—a form of complex charisma—by which a man demonstrates his bravery, manual dexterity, organizational ability, and/or concern for others' welfare (cf. Sahlins 1968). Thus, the *tesmaypits* was the "man possessing *tes*."

Ritual recognition of the *tesmaypits* took several forms. That involving cannibalism perhaps is the most interesting. As the victorious war party paddled back from a raid, the heads of victims were severed as junctions of important rivers were passed. After arriving at the home village the flesh of the corpse was divided in accordance with ritual (not dietary) prescriptions. Through a trephination cut in the right temporal bone the brains were extracted and, after being mixed with sago starch, were consumed by elder *tesmaypits* related to the warrior responsible for the killing (Zegwaard 1971). Less exotic, but equally as important in terms of ritually reducing disequilibrium among friend, foe, and spirit, was the practice of name acquisition. After an appropriate period of mourning following an elder *tesmaypits'* death, his name was adopted by a young man from the same settlement hoping to enhance his own prestige. (Similarly, the names of enemy slain in battle were adopted by some individuals.)

A final point needs to be made in terms of the ability of certain aged men "to arrange things." At times this was done in the ritual context, but at other times in the context of settlement relocation. Prior to the establishment of relatively permanent coastal villages in the mid-1950's, territorial-internal relocation occurred every two to five years. No formal councils existed in Asmat, but in consultation with other *yew* elders, the most prestigious *tesmaypits* determined availability of resources, enemy placements, and resettlement possibilities. The move sometimes covered no more than a few hundred meters downstream, but the ability "to arrange things" in relation to the move was crucial. Clearly, the imposition of the Indonesian political economy upon Asmat has created a controlled sociopolitical environment wherein aged men no longer can make decisions of this sort. Village moves have been terminated, as have the opportunities for *tesmaypits* to decide upon the usage of certain forest hardwoods. In 1979 we witnessed beatings being inflicted at gunpoint upon male elders (as well as younger men) by government officials dissatisfied with the reluctant participation of Asmatters in Indonesian-sponsored logging activities. The same men were forced by authorities to degrade themselves by waddling like ducks in front of women and children. They also were forced to hop like toads. Although some government officials have demonstrated genuine concern for Asmat welfare, a more prevalent theme has been concern for resource exploitation such that more populated regions of the country will benefit economically.

4. New Opportunities: A Changing Context

What, then, is happening to that 12.3 percent of the Asmat who are in the "old age" bracket? Disintegration of traditional rituals has had only an indirect impact upon elderly women, but there is one ironic aspect to the changes which have taken place. Whereas women once were excluded from core participation in rituals such as those pertaining to war prepartion, with the suppression of headhunting and the development of religiously syncretic rituals such as those surrounding Christmas, certain older women have expanded their once-limited repertoire of traditional chants. On Christmas Day in the village of Amandesep in 1973 small circles of women were observed chanting and drumming traditional lines under the leadership of the oldest, and under the watchful gaze of a catechist. An alternative was available in the transitional sociocultural environment, and was accepted by certain of the older women (cf. Clark 1973:85).

No such ritual alternative has been accepted by elderly Asmat men. In several instances missionaries have offered them the opportunity to participate as leaders in church services; those who finally accepted were younger men. At this point it must be stressed that not all traditional rituals have been eliminated; for example, *ji pok mbu* (the bringing of the sago logs to the village for ritual storage) still is enacted, and elderly men still participate. "Disintegration of Asmat ritual" is disintegration of the sociocultural context within which the enactment of rites occurs. A "ritual void" exists for aged men not merely because some rituals are no longer enacted, but because the enactment no longer takes place within the traditional framework with which it co-evolved, and because alternative sources of ritual need-satisfaction have yet to be accepted.

The complexities of this situation are best illustrated by considering the constraining parameters of ritual participation in a cargo cult which has been active in one of the six near-coastal villages under consideration here. Being but one type of millenarian movement, a cargo cult can be defined as a magico-religious attempt "to *create* something new when the old is destroyed, to *reform* when time and circumstances so demand, and to *accommodate* when cultures meet" (Oosterwal 1968:47). The first of the cult's four phases began in October of 1966, in response to a series of stressful sociopolitical and economic developments associated with the increasingly stringent demands of the Indonesian political economy, and a diminishing supply of material goods available to Asmatters upon termination of what had amounted to "tobacco Christianity" (Van Arsdale 1975:157-160). Over the course of the cult's development innovation, reform, and accommodation indeed have taken place. Alternative forms of ritual need-satisfaction indeed have been accepted by some. Aged Asmat men have not been those involved.

Asmat's cult has afforded many people an alternative to both the ritual context of pre-contact times and the ritual context presented by Catholic and Protestant missionaries. In large measure cult ritual has been a blend of both (Van Arsdale and Gallus 1974). As conceived by a 27-year-old man with the baptismal name of Marsellus, the cult relied upon Tuhan Tanah (the "Lord of the Earth") in its earliest phases. Tuhan Tanah was described to the rapidly growing faction of cult members as a combination of the traditional spirit *namer-o* and God. The prophet Marsellus claimed that a vast array of "white man's goods" would materialize, for those who believed, from a locked hole in the ground to which he held the key. Unbeknownst to the local pastor, goods were stolen from the mission warehouse to make good on the promise. Shortly thereafter, Marsellus began wearing a star-shaped pin he had stolen. Villagers began calling him "President."

Although the original prophet's influence virtually disappeared when villagers learned that the goods had been stolen, another man named Sotor rose to take his place. Asmatters were still eager for a ritual (as well as sociopolitical) alternative. The second prophet, still cargo cult leader today at the age of about 35, has cleverly maneuvered *yew* factions and used his own considerable abilities as a curer to perpetuate the cult and its rituals. Other younger men have been brought into the cult leadership structure; promises of "white man's goods" have diminished as promises of "unity" and "freedom" have intensified. People in neighboring villages claim that Sotor is the most influential person in the region. Why is it that older men did not take similar steps to secure a place of importance for themselves in transitional Asmat society? Why is it that an elder *tesmaypits* did not use his considerable influence to become involved? Why is it that older men have not played a primary role in the adaptive ritual processes of innovation, reform, and accommodation?

The answers are found by assessing opportunities afforded old versus young men in Asmat as externally induced processes of change occur. The new ritual context now developing must be understood as dependent upon rapid economic, educational, and political changes. Although the cargo cult rituals in part are reactions to perceived negative aspects of such induced change, they nonetheless must be viewed as dependent. Traditional rituals co-evolved within the framework of a diversified preagricultural economy, informal education, and low-level political leadership via elder *tesmaypits*; new rituals must (and indeed will) co-evolve within the framework of a partial cash economy, formal education, and hierarchical political leadership within the Indonesian system. As stated at the outset, the Asmat are now but one subgroup of a complex state society. Younger men are being afforded opportunities within it, older men are not. A missionary offering older men the opportunity to participate as leaders in church services (whether they accept or not) does nothing to remedy the "ritual void" because this void is a product of other societal changes in which such men have not extensively participated. It does nothing to remedy the underlying situation of prestige loss among the elderly, because while prestige may be manifested in ritual it is tied to economic, educational, and political factors.

The formulation of the above statements was aided by a series of statistical tests. A culture change questionnaire was administered in 1973-74 to 115 married Asmat men ranging in age from 17 to 55. Included were behavioral (as opposed to attitudinal) questions on economic, educational, and political factors. For example, number of years of formal education in mission or government schools was found to be inversely correlated with age at a highly significant level ($-.6283$, $p < .001$). The coefficient for age and ability to speak the Indonesian language, introduced as the standard trade tongue by change agents, shows an even stronger inverse correlation ($-.7262$, $p < .001$). In other words, 70 percent of the variation in Indonesian speaking ability can be explained merely by considering a man's age. A strong negative association also was found for age and the ability to write ($X^2 = 43.2$, df $= 7$, $p < .001$). The negative association between age and reading ability is even stronger ($X^2 = 52.8$, df $= 7$, $p < .001$).

Despite the strong influence household members traditionally exerted upon one another in Asmat, a further test was run to determine if minimal educational correlates of old age are diminished or dampened by the activities of other household members today. This was not found to be the case. From a random sample of households, 60 with one or more persons in the 10-19.9 age range were compared with 57 having one or more in the 40+ range. In 50 of the 60 representing the younger cohort (83.3 percent), all of the children in each household had received some formal education, whereas in 47 of the 57 representing the older cohort (82.4 percent) none of the children or adults in each household had ever received any education. A series of other correlations were determined for these same households (regardless of age of male residents) on variables of education and contact with change agents; the four significant ($p < .001$) results confirmed that the influence of the total household upon the change-related activities of its individual members is profound. Thus, it has been demonstrated that older men are significantly less integrated into the Indonesian system of formal education and communication, and that those households in which they reside are significantly less integrated as well. The traditional ritual context is disintegrating, but household influences remain strong (q.v. Shanas 1975).

Analysis of economic and political variables produced similar results. For example, it was found that older men who are household heads have access to a greater number of modern goods than do younger men who are household heads, a seemingly contradictory finding. However, by controlling for household size it was found that these older men tend to reside in larger households, and that degree of access to such goods is a function of the larger number of young people securing them. Political data indicate that most Asmat men being selected for local Indonesian government offices such as *Kepala desa* (subdistrict head) are less than 40 years of age. There is no trend toward the selection of men who have demonstrated the abilities of the traditional *tesmaypits* (or who, in fact, once were *tesmaypits* themselves), but a significant trend toward the selection of those who are younger and can read, write, and speak Indonesian.

5.   Conclusion

Sakarpits is still considered to be the most important headhunter-*tesmaypits* in Sotor's village. Yet Sotor, a man of 35, has far more influence than does Sakarpits, a man of 60. Sotor has "made a name for himself" as second prophet of the cargo cult, and has even consulted Sakarpits as to what strategies should be used to increase cult membership. Sakarpits has let it be known that his own influence should be greater than it is—in 1979 he took his sixth wife—but he continues to operate within a "ritual void." Sotor, on the other hand, is not only active in the Catholic church but fluent in Indonesian and conversant on problems of induced political and economic change.

In 1974 Yucemin was still considered to be one of the most important headhunter-*tesmaypits* in Owus, another of the near-coastal villages. Yet Yacobus was selected by Indonesian officials as *Kepala desa* despite a lackluster record in village political activities. Yucemin was approximately 60 years old at the time, Yacobus approximately 38. As was the case with Sakarpits, Yucemin was a vital, active man. However, whereas Yucemin spoke of traditional territorial prerogatives restricting the cutting of prized ironwood trees, Yacobus negotiated with government and military officials as to the cash value of timber near the village.

Older men are being excluded from opportunities asssociated with externally induced processes of change not because of their age, and not because of their abilities. In fact, the exclusion has not been overt or intentional on the part of change agents or on the part of older Asmatters themselves. These men are being excluded due to a total spectrum of constraining parameters associated with economic, educational, and political change. Just as in the U.S., certain of the elderly are finding it difficult to readjust a *wide enough* range of their activities. This is tied to an expansion of the scale of institutions which is not favorable to the elderly. Were there to be a resurgence in traditional forms of Asmat village life, as has been predicted for villages in some regions of the developing world (Critchfield 1979; Nusberg 1979), elderly men and women alike might be able to readjust. But this is unlikely to occur in Irian Jaya within the foreseeable future. Ritual replacement is indeed possible, especially given ritual's importance as a mechanism of social unification, but such modifications cannot occur in a void. It is probable that today's aged Asmat men in particular will be unable to solve this problem, but it is equally probable that when those growing up today reach old age they will have a better chance to successfully cope and contribute to Indonesia's development.

Notes

[1]Little demographic data was available for the Asmat prior to my first visit in 1973-74. Some had been systematically collected by Van Amelsvoort (1964). Basic census enumerations, by sex and estimated age, had been made at irregular intervals since the mid-1950s by government officials and missionaries. The age data proved to be of little statistical value. Most of the enumerators were entirely untrained, and little consistency in age estimation was found from one village to the next. (However, beyond the age of about 20, there was a significant trend toward more women than men per cohort.)

Based upon their research among the Chimbu people of Papua New Guinea's Central Highlands, Brown and Winefield (1965) found that in a demographically underdeveloped region errors are most prevalent with age estimates and mortality data. Other researchers agree (Feeney 1975; Weiss 1973a:12; Carrier and Hobcraft 1971:2). My own age estimates were based upon birth order among siblings, marital and parenthood history, event calendars, and appearance. Through practice I was able to refine this procedure to the point where my "blind estimate" of an older Asmatter's age (i.e., 40 to 50 years) came within three to five years for those few individuals whose exact year of birth had been recorded by nonresident missionaries of the pre-World War II era. In concert with household random sampling procedures conducted within the overarching framework of a village-level intraregional controlled comparison, these techniques provided me with demographic information I believe to be fairly accurate (q.v. Van Arsdale 1978a; Moore, et al. 1980).

3
Cultural Centrality and Prestige for the Elderly: The Coast Salish Case *

Pamela T. Amoss

1. Introduction

Contemporary Coast Salish Indian elders show that it is possible for old people to enjoy high prestige on the basis of strictly cultural contributions. Most comparative evidence suggests that rank is best predicted by social and economic contributions which old people make to their communities and that substantial contributions are usually correlated with positive evaluation of old age and the elderly (Press and McKool 1972; Cowgill and Holmes 1972; Amoss and Harrell 1981). The Coast Salish case is interesting because it shows that high rank for the old can be achieved on the basis of cultural contributions with a negligible economic component. There are two universal themes in the cultural definition of old age which are relevant here: it is linked on the one hand with the threat of death and on the other with the promise of cultural continuity. Both themes found expression in aboriginal Coast Salish culture and have been reinterpreted in the contemporary context to raise the evaluation of the current elderly cohort significantly.

Relatively little work has been done by anthropologists on the possible universal cultural determinants of rank for the elderly; more attention has been paid to the social, political and economic dimensions of the problem.

*This paper appears by permission of Stanford University Press, which will publish in 1981 "Coast Salish Elders," from which sections of the present paper were adapted, in *Other Ways of Growing Old: Anthropological Perspectives*, edited by Pamela T. Amoss and Stevan Harrell.

Press and McKool, for example, have suggested a universal set of criteria that will predict the rank of old people. Rank they say, will be high if the old are in a position to control, contribute, or advise (1972).[1] Although their definition of "advise" is broad enough to embrace advice on matters of history and ritual, the thrust of their argument concentrates on social relations. Similarly, Cowgill and Holmes (1972a), enlarging on Simmons' (1945a) early findings, conclude that modernization robs the old of rank because it erodes their roles and undermines their family support (ibid:11). Less attention has been given to how the meaning of old age and the cultural definition assigned to the elderly might determine high rank for the old. This neglect may be traced to the assumption that in stable societies cultural values rationalize social arrangements, and the conviction that the latter are somehow "primary." The Coast Salish Indians, however, have shown a recent rapid rise in the prestige of the elderly when the economic and social factors that caused previous cohorts of old people to lose prestige since the period of European contact over 100 years ago are, if anything, less favorable to the old.

2.   Culture and Society

The approach taken in this chapter depends on distinguishing culture and society as separate and distinct systems, each operating by its own internal rules. The distinction between culture and society is one that is difficult to specify when describing human behavior, but useful to maintain for analytical purposes. Following Parsons by way of Geertz, culture is here defined as "an ordered system of meaning and of symbols in terms of which social interaction takes place," and society as "the pattern of social interaction itself" (Geertz 1973:144) Both culture and society are systems, internally consistent and integrated. Culture is characterized by "a unity of style, of logical implication, of meaning and value," while society is held together because the "parts are united in a single causal web." Culture is logically integrated; society is functionally integrated (ibid.:145). From this view of the two systems, it is clear that cultural beliefs cannot be reduced to mere epiphenomena of social arrangements. Culture does, of course, rationalize and make palatable the facts of a set of social relationships and can be reinterpreted and rethought when they change. The converse, where social order is remade to conform to the requirements of a culture system, is less common, but does occur in the case of revitalization movements (Wallace 1956:267).[2] The more usual relationship between these two inseparable but non-isomorphic systems is a process of mutual accomodation. During periods of rapid change, however, they are very likely to lose their mutually supportive relationship because the process of internal adjustment within the two is so different. In the case we are examining here, cultural themes defining old age can be seen to have been closely correlated with social institutions in aboriginal times, but in the contemporary world to be out of joint with economic and political arrangements. Yet, on the contemporary scene cultural factors are powerful determinants of the rank assigned to the old.

3.   Cultural Factors in the Evaluation of Old Age

There are, or appear to be, two well-nigh universal cultural themes influencing the value attached to the last stage of life. First is one that usually has pejorative impact: the association between old age and death. Although most pre-industrial communities, in fact, observed more infants and young children dying than old people—simply because so few people survived childhood to become candidates for death at advanced age—it was only the old for whom death inevitably came. This inexorable connection between death, with the debility that preceeds it, and age, has created a common perception of old age as fearful and threatening.

In contrast, the other universal theme has had largely positive implications for the evaluation of the old. In comparison with the young, the old represent "culture" as opposed to "nature." Levi-Strauss has found this nature/culture distinction to be a widespread motif in myth and has pointed out how many myths celebrate the transformation of humankind from a state of nature to a state of culture by focusing on the gift of the hearth fire and the origins of cooked food (Levi-Strauss 1970). More recently Sherry Ortner has extended Levi-Strauss' insight in an attempt to fathom the reasons behind the universal devaluation of women in human culture. She suggests that the pan-cultural preference for males and things defined as male springs from the association of women with nature and men with culture (1974:73). The same argument can profitably be made for a pan-human factor influencing favorable cultural evaluation of old people. Indeed, old people are more akin to culture than to nature. The association is most apparent in pre-literate groups (and it may be reversed in modern industrialized communities). It is the old who carry cultural traditions. They remember group history and family genealogy. They are the masters of rhetoric and oral literature. They are the most proficient ritualists, sometimes specializing in the supernaturally legitimized healing arts. Furthermore, old people have lived beyond bearing and begetting children. As the embodiment of the group's cultural traditions, the aged are precious and tend to inspire the sense of Durkheimian awe aroused in ephemeral humanity contemplating "society."

These two major themes, which are reflected to some extent in the cultural evaluations of old age in all human cultures, are obviously discordant. That the old, who are the ultimate guardians of cultural systems of meaning, are also those who must soon succumb to the greatest threat to all humanly created systems of meaning—death—is surely an insoluble paradox. Under the circumstances it is not surprising that cultural representations of old age are usually janus-faced. The ambivalence is most clearly marked in those societies where the old are most revered for their wisdom and most endowed with ritual significance. There the fear of death and old age may be expressed in disguised forms. The old may be feared and even hated for the power they are believed to have to prolong their own lives at the expense of their young kinsmen (Opler 1965; Colson and Scudder 1981). The balance between the two themes will shift in different socio-cultural settings. In industrialized countries like our own, where the association between old age and death has become almost exclusive as well as inevitable, and where the aged have been largely deprived of their dominant association with the precious cultural tradition, the evaluation of old age may be very low (although older cultural themes of honoring one's elderly kinfolk may persist as ideals towards which people still strive).

These two major themes have been important in the cultural definition of old age for the Coast Salish Indians of Western Washington and British Columbia in the pre-contact period and are still evident in the present cultural understanding of old age. This chapter will show how this current cohort of Coast Salish elders is using the association between old age and culture to reestablish their central position in contemporary Indian society. In so doing I expect to demonstrate that in the case of the Coast Salish elders it has been a shift in the cultural climate, not in the conditions of economic and social life, that has opened up the opportunity for them to reestablish themselves in the prestigious position they have not occupied in Coast Salish society since the aboriginal period.

First, we need to look at what can be reconstructed of Coast Salish life in the precontact and early historic period, before massive economic and social disintegration had taken its toll of the position of the old.

4. Coast Salish Elders: The Ethnographic Past

Our picture of the position of old people during precontact times is tentative, being based on the scanty reports of early observers and the memories of old people's impressions of aboriginal life recalled from childhood or heard from their grandparents. Nevertheless, the evidence suggests that old people were honored and deferred to, both because they made real economic contributions to group survival and because they were repositories of vital information of both a practical and ritual nature. How was "old" defined in pre-white times? Apparently not chronologically, because the Coast Salish, like most pre-literate peoples, did not keep close track of age, but rather by a combination of generational position and physical functioning.

The importance of generational position can be deduced from kinship terminologies that illuminate both the kinds of relations prescribed between classes of relatives and also the native concept of the ideal human life span (Geertz 1966:20). Although information is limited, we do know that in at least one Coast Salish group, the Klahuse of mainland British Columbia, adults were named teknonymously, suggesting that generational position defined the most important roles (Barnett 1955:132). A person moved through a sequence of statuses from youth to old age. A new family cycle began again with the birth of a great grandchild. The terms for great grand-child and great grandparent are the same, suggesting that they are in some sense equivalent: one ends when the other begins (Collins 1974:88; Hess 1976:105; Smith 1940:174; Elmendorf and Kroeber 1960:347; Spier 1935:74). Following this line of reasoning, a person would have entered the final stage of life and become "old" on the birth of his or her first grandchild.

People were considered old when they could no longer perform the full range of adult tasks appropriate to their sex and station. When men could no longer fish all night or hike miles to kill game and pack it home again, and when women found it hard to butcher salmon for hours on end or bend and stoop to pick berries and dig roots, they would begin to shift the major part of these jobs to younger relatives and turn to the tasks reserved for older people. The heavy physical demands of men's work suggest that men may have become functionally "old" sooner than women, but menopause was a complicating factor. A woman was "old" for certain purposes when she could no longer bear children, even if her food producing and process-ing abilities were still in their prime. Old age did not bring leisure to either sex, but only a shift from the physically more demanding tasks to those where skill, patience, or experience were more important than strength and speed.

Old age not only brought new responsibilities, it conferred freedom from old restrictions. Among the Upper Skagit and probably elsewhere too, old age, when one's reproductive responsibilities were discharged, was the time for love affairs (Collins 1974:232). People found the prospect of an alliance between beautiful youth and experienced old age romantic. Unlike contemporary Western culture—which accepts such a relationship between an older man and a younger woman but stigmatizes the reverse—Coast Salish people found the old of either sex suitable paramours for young peo-ple.

Many of the taboos which applied to people in their youth and maturity were waived for the elderly. To phrase the transition in positive terms, when people became old they were more closely associated with culture and less with nature. Women past child-bearing age could no longer pollute hunters or their gear, nor would they contaminate the berry patches or offend the salmon. Old men no longer had to observe the discipline of sexual abstinence and fasting that were incumbent on active hunters and fishermen. Certain foods forbidden to the young were reserved for the old. With the raising of these restrictions, new avenues of spiritual power opened up to both men and women. The old were often caretakers for people in dangerous liminal states—successful spirit questors, girls at menarche, women in childbirth, warriors returned brom battle, mourners, and the bodies of the recently dead. A grandmother was an ideal attendant for a girl at first menstruation because not only was she wise, experienced, and concerned about her granddaughter, but impervious to the girl's sacred contagion (Elmendorf and Kroeber 1960:439).

In recognition of their special status, old people were always treated with deference. All elders, whether blood kin or not, were addressed with kinship terms appropriate to the age difference. Even within a sibling set there were special terms of address to express relative age (Hess 1976; Barnett 1955). This pattern reflected a cultural theme of subordination of younger to elder, but it also represented a fear that slighting old people might be dangerous. It was believed that anyone who had lived a long time must have good supernatural helpers ready to avenge any insult to their human partner. It was assumed that a person's spiritual power would increase throughout life. Although adolescents were enjoined to quest for spirit visions, mature people might also look for additional help or receive new gifts from the guardians they had encountered first in their youth. Religious specialists, whether shamans, mediums, or people who knew magical spells, were almost always old. Shamans, endowed with power to cure or to kill, often received their visions first during their pre-adolescent quests, but usually did not practice until they were at least middle-aged, because powers acquired early in life needed time to season and develop full potency. Old people took prominent roles in the winter season ceremonials, when people whose vision-quest encounters had given them a song and dance performed publicly for fellow villagers and visitors from nearby communities.

Young people of good families were trained to be helpful as well as deferential to all old people. Just as slighting the old might be dangerous, helping them might yield unsuspected benefits. Tommy Paul of Sanetch reported that his father used to send him to carry water for an impoverished old woman who lived alone near them. Whenever he helped her, she made cryptic reference to how she would thank him by sending him supernatural help when she died (Barnett 1955:142).

In pre-literate societies old people are always the repositories of cultural information. But not only do they transmit and store the cultural corpus they have received, they also contribute their own creative innovations to a growing and changing tradition. The Coast Salish elders, too, were creators and keepers of traditional lore in the form of genealogies, family histories, and myths. Although every old person probably knew all the myths told in his local group, not everyone was an equally skilled raconteur. Nor did everyone have the right to tell stories that belonged to other families. Those who had a gift for telling the stories well and the right to tell them would recite them during the long northern winter evenings in the big communal houses.

Part entertainment, part moral code, part religious dogma, the myths were one of the major devices old people used to instruct the young. The parental generation bore children and supported them, but it was the grandparent generation that made them competent members of society. The archetype of a pitiful figure in Coast Salish mythology is the child without grandparents to instruct him. Deprived of legitimate access, his only recourse was eavesdropping on instructions given more fortunate children by their grandparents. In contrast, the successful person was one who had "listened to his grandparents' words" (Barnett 1955:144). Grandparents taught the children how to prepare for the all-important spirit quest, how to conduct themselves in polite society, how to give speeches at potlatches or funerals, and even how to perform many practical tasks of everyday life. Among some groups, it was the grandparent who gave the child the first formal name.

The old led all community enterprises except warfare. Although there were no hereditary political offices, members of wealthier families dominated village politics and maintained intervillage alliances through networks of marriage and potlatch ties. Political leaders were supposed to be wise, gentle, courteous, forebearing, and old. They never traded insults with ill-bred people, but maintained a dignified silence in the face of criticism. Undoubtedly the experience gained through many years of observing and interacting with fellow villagers and the widespread network of friends and affines in other villages made it possible for such men to achieve their ends through persuasion and influence. The war leader, on the other hand, was young and often rather unpleasant. His irascible disposition testified to the ferocity of his spirit helpers. Although people feared him, he had little influence except in planning and leading raids on other villages.

Despite the cultural dictum that all old people should be deferred to, in fact real power was limited to old people backed by large and affluent kindreds. Poor old people, like poor young ones, had little influence. In a society where a person's place depended on kinship ties, an old person without grandchildren was in as pitiable a state as a child without grandparents. Nevertheless, the cultural ideal of honoring the elders probably assured even the poor elderly at least bare subsistence and public deference.

The other universal cultural theme of aging, the dread of waning strength and imminent death, also found expression in Coast Salish thinking, but only in muted form. The real power many elders exerted and the overt respect paid to all notwithstanding, there are indications that people greeted old age with mixed feelings. Twana youth, for example, were taught never to call anyone "old" in his or her hearing (Elmendorf and Kroeber 1960:431). People mourned the loss of full competence in adult roles, despite the expanded influence they would enjoy as elders. Most tellingly, in the face of inextricable linkage between death and old age, Coast Salish ideology offered little consolation to the dying. As death approached, even a person's spirits withdrew from him (Collins 1974:232). As an old person felt life ebbing away, he or she might sing the spirit songs for one last time, releasing the spirit partners. Although denied the comfort and assistance of spirit guardians in the land of the dead, a person might direct his or her former guardians to assist a relative or friend, as the old woman promised Tommy Paul. The saddest plight was reserved for elders who became mentally confused. Though supported by their families and tolerated by the community, they were neither honored nor cherished. Their loss of competence was taken as proof that their spirit helpers had left them prey to some malicious enemy who had stolen their understanding.

The close integration between social arrangements and cultural values outlined for the Coast Salish represents an example of a functionalist "ideal": cultural systems support and rationalize social systems, which in turn make the cultural beliefs seem plausible (Berger 1967:50). Although it is convenient for us to think of native society before contact as settled into a relatively unchanging mode of existence, if we probe a bit more deeply it is clear that social and ideological change generated from within was going on even before Europeans arrived (Amoss n.d.). But from what we hypothesize, the probable course of change was in the direction of more social inequality, and as such it posed no threat to the central place of the old as the incarnations of culture. It only meant that the differences between poor and rich elderly would widen.

The prophet cults reported from the period of early contact may, as Spier and Suttles have suggested, represent a religious pattern old in the region (Spier 1935:13-16; Suttles 1957). If so, they constitute another challenge to the assumption of a state of balanced equilibrium. But again, the instability implied by the rise of prophets need not have threatened the roles of the old but may, in fact, have opened the way for elders themselves to seek new sources of religious legitimation for political power (Suttles 1957:383).

5.   Coast Salish Elders After Culture Contact

Elsewhere, (Amoss 1981) I have described the historical changes in the position of old Coast Salish after contact. Briefly, after white economic and political control was established, the old Indians rapidly lost both their economic and social power base. With the wholesale defection from the old religion, their supremacy in the ritual sphere came to mean little. The early history of the Shaker Church—a revitalistic religion which began in the 1880s with the revelation of John Slocum, a Puget Sound Indian—showed young people taking the lead in religious innovation during the early historic period. At that time the old still represented "culture" but in a complex new cultural arena. Where Indian people were confronted with more than one grand system of meaning, the old represented the aboriginal culture that had come to seem both powerless and doomed. The "new" culture represented by the Shaker Church, which promised Indians a way out of their dilemma, came not from the ancestors, but by direct revelation to the young leaders of the church. Insofar as the new order demanded that the old religious ideas be rejected, it implied the rejection of the old themselves, who were the embodiment of the old cultural values and bearers of the old knowledge. In some cases the rejection of things from the old order extended beyond the symbols of sacred power to mundane items such as baskets and tools and even to the old language. In the 1950s an old Shaker woman from the Olympic peninsula—one of the few remaining fluent speakers of her language—declined to work with a linguist because she believed that the millenia would be delayed until all vestiges of the old speech had vanished. Guided by convictions acquired in her youth, she reasoned that if she helped him preserve the language in written form, she might interfere with the divine plan (Kinkade personal communication).

Although the bearers of a discredited tradition, some old people were still treasured on an individual basis, especially those whose family networks were strong and whose individual aptitudes had allowed them to adjust to the demands of the new economic situation with some degree of success. Also, there were regional variations in the extent to which aboriginal culture was denigrated. The cultural ideal of deferring to the old also persisted, but for the most part the social arrangements and cultural beliefs supporting the ideal had become inoperative.

6.   Contemporary Coast Salish Elders

In the 1970s rapid cultural change has once more reinterpreted the relationship between old people and "culture." Now, that which is defined as old is once more highly esteemed. It has become precious to the descendants of

the very people who found it hollow. The significant oppostion is still between Indian culture, which is defined as old, and white culture, which is
new, but the evaluation has been reversed. That which is old is now good;
new is now bad. Old Indian people are still judged to embody the old
culture, but they are now esteemed for what was a liability to their great
grandparents.

Although in the aboriginal world cultural evaluation of old age was linked with significant economic and social contribution, the rise in rank of contemporary elders is almost entirely due to their contributions in the cultural
sphere. There has been little change in the level of direct economic contribution by old people since the early contact period, when the drastic
changes in subsistence displaced them from both production and
managerial roles. Old people still contribute something of economic value
by taking care of children, helping with housework and the like, but, again,
this represents an old pattern whose dimensions have changed little if any
in the recent past. Some old people get pensions or welfare assistance they
can share with children and grandchildren, but this, too, probably
represents a small contribution at best (but see Goodwin 1942:517 and
Williams 1980:107 for a different evaluation of the economic contribution
of Indian elders in Arizona and Oklahoma). There is, in short, no direct
evidence to support the interpretation that contemporary old people have
risen in prestige because they are controlling any significant economic or
political resources. The shift in the evaluation of the old is clearly a cultural
phenomenon with cultural causes. Before attempting to explain the
dynamics of the cultural changes that have made it possible for this cohort
of elders to become the "cultural cynosure" (Guemple 1969), we should
look at the areas where their influence is most apparent.

7.   Ritual Roles of the Elders

Of the public settings where old people are prominent, ritual occasions are
the most important because Indian people gather there to express their own
special variety of spirituality and to encounter other Inidans who share the
same set of values and communicate according to the same ritual code. Indian elders are also prominent in another arena, the tribal cultural education
programs. Here they serve as teachers and consultants. Although their
knowledge of language and customs is valued in both settings, in the educational programs, still new and somewhat strange even to the organizers,
there is a more self-conscious attempt to draw on the presence of the elders
to legitimize the undertakings. Younger tribal officials go to some trouble to
involve the older people in these programs and to create opportunities for
them to meet old people working in similar programs on neighboring
reservations.

Before looking more closely at the ritual occasions where the cultural role of the old is most clear, I should say first that in my experience all Coast Salish people are "religiously musical." They participate in a number of institutionalized religions: Roman Catholicism, Protestant Christianity, Pentecostalism, and Mormonism. A sizeable number belong to the Indian Shaker Church. Many participate in the revived aboriginal-style winter dancing circuit. Furthermore, a number of people are active in several of these religious systems at once because they feel that they can and should take advantage of a variety of sources of help. The two avenues of religious expression that are most "Indian" and in which the elders are most important are the Winter Dancing and the Shaker Church. Both exalt knowledge of the old ways and the older people as vessels of that knowledge. Both systems maintain that a person grows in power as he or she learns how to cooperate with the spirit, whether a guardian spirit or the Holy Spirit which inspires Shakers. Since older people have been practicing this cooperation longer, they are spiritually stronger than young people. Furthermore, survival to old age is itself still taken as evidence of good spiritual connections.

Although elders are important in both, their participation is essential in the aboriginal style Winter Dancing rituals, because they are the only ones who really know how things should be done. During the earlier part of this century, when the middle-aged people were growing up, the old rites were moribund and rarely performed. Only the elders remember an earlier period when they were still lively. In the winter when the individual spirit guardians of the participants return and inspire them to perform their spirit songs and dances, big gatherings take place every weekend on reservations in British Columbia and Washington. Families who want to give names to their children, to put special dancing outfits on their young people, or memorialize their dead, act as hosts. Before the dancing begins the guests are all fed, and then the host family makes its announcements and passes out presents to thank the guests for witnessing the event. Elders are essential in all of this. They recite the history of the names, they thank the guests and make laudatory speeches for the hosts. They are acquainted with all the other important old people and know their Indian names, which must be used on formal occasions like these. If family privileges are displayed—inherited masks or the like—it is the oldest family members who know how it should be done. Old people both direct the rituals from the sidelines and take leading roles in enacting them.

Elders are important in deciding who may participate fully in the Winter Dancing. While any Coast Salish can attend, only the properly initiated actually dance at winter gatherings. Adults of all ages can be dancers, but most are in their late teens or early twenties. Almost all of these young people have been initiated, if not at the specific behest of their family elders at least with their consent. In theory, people are initiated because they are troubled by possessing spirits. The intitiation is intended to establish a cooperative relationship between the dancer and the spirit. In fact, not everyone "bothered by a song" is initiated, and not everyone who is initiated has first been troubled by a spirit.

The old dancers who specialize as initiators are believed capable of inducing spirit possession in a person who has no prior history of it. Every year some people are initiated because their parents or grandparents are concerned about their rebelliousness, depression, drinking, or self-destructive behavior (Jilek 1974; Amoss 1978). Parents are careful to select initiators with good reputations; they prefer a relative or someone they know well. Experience is at a premium in the initiation process because mismanagement can cause serious illness or even death. Although some initiators are only middleaged, the most prominent ones are elderly. In effect the old—a coalition of family elders and old ritual specialists—control entry into the dancers' sodality.

Old people have also a virtual monopoly over other ritual specialties that affect the general welfare. The few contemporary shamans are all old. Mediums, who can see ghosts and who officiate after funerals when food is burned for the deceased, are also old. Although inherited or shamanistic powers have no place in Shaker ideology, many older Shakers are believed to have special gifts for diagnosing or curing.

8. Innovative Activities of Elders

Although the old are perceived as the only source of information on the old ways, their central place in ritual depends as much on their willingness to take responsiblity for ceremonial occasions as on public confidence in their expertise. They are much more than passive transmitters of received knowledge, but are actively engaged in promoting the revival of the old ceremonies and, when necessary, the introduction of new ones. They are living examples of how old people confronted with sociocultural change can take advantage of the opportunity it offers to consolidate or improve their own position. (See also Amoss 1981).

These talented old people are the ones who have the intuitive grasp of the old systems and who are in a position to develop new rituals or revive old ones that are consistent with the traditional ideology and symbolism.[3] They have a gift for creating new forms within the asesthetic tradition, which embraces visual elements of form, color, and movement, as well as vocal and drum music. Even when young people have the talent for such innovation they need old people to put the stamp of authenticity on their efforts.

An example of the revival of ceremonies that had been abandoned in some communities for over 100 years is the First Salmon Ceremony, celebrated for the last three years at a reservation north of Seattle. Old accounts of the aboriginal ceremony (Gunther 1926, 1928) allow us to see clearly that the modern ritual is not merely a copy of the old but incorporates religious ideas that have become part of Indian spirituality during the past century. These new forms are accepted because they are congruent with contemporary Indian beliefs, and because people have confidence in the knowledge of the elders who are orchestrating the revival. In the ceremony that I witnessed, the old people were directing the proceedings, but it was the young people who brought the first salmon in from the bay in a canoe. It was treated as an honored guest and brought up ceremoniously from the beach on an astroturf and plywood tray covered with a layer of ferns. Although the First Salmon Ceremony is one in which old accounts tell us that young people—children actually—were supposed to carry the salmon from the river or beach, the practice of involving younger people in rituals is characteristic of all the ceremonies I have witnessed. The old organize, direct, and enact, but they always find jobs for younger people to do.

Although only recently reinstated, the First Salmon Ceremony is ideologically and stylistically consistent with the other rituals of the revived aboriginal tradition. Free though the elders are, they seem to have a firm grasp of acceptable limits of innovation. The same symbols appear in the First Salmon Ceremony as are found in other ritual contexts, and the new meanings assigned to them resonate comfortably with already established interpretations.

9. Ritual and Indian Identity

In becoming the designers and managers of the rituals, old people have become the arbiters of Indian identity. Coast Salish Indians themselves recognize cultural factors as the crucial determinants of Indian identity. The most important marker is commitment to some form of Indian spiritual expression. People who are Indian are, of course, assigned that identity on the basis of birth (though not necessarily of blood—the half-white daughter of an Indian woman is as "Indian" as her full-blood half sister). But their perception of what makes that identity special and desirable, despite the obvious disadvantages—a history of poverty and discrimination—is defended in cultural terms. Active participation in Winter Dancing and Shakerism are, of course, not the only symbols of Indianness, and there are local Indians who do not participate in either and whose birthright status as Indians is in no sense at risk. Shakerism and Spirit Dancing, however, signify a positive affirmation of Indian identity.

The revival and spread of Winter Dancing in the 1960s and 70s is a good indication of the importance of cultural factors in defining what it is to be Indian, and of the growing importance of such a cultural definition to local Indian people during the last twenty years. Winter Dancing defines participants as Indian because Indians themselves say "This is what God gave us Indians." As an aboriginal tradition derived from the ancient past of their people, Indians see it as connecting them directly with their ancestors. Furthermore, it is an exclusive system because participation is limited to those who are Indian by birth, or who have committed themselves to life in an Indian community. The very few non-Indians who become spirit dancers are almost all married to Indians. One exception—a non-Indian dancer whose commitment did not involve taking an Indian spouse—is a young Catholic priest. During the debate which preceded the decision to make him a dancer, people worried that he "would not stick with it," in other words, that he was not really committed to the Indian community. At this writing, four years after his initiation, he still dances every winter and most of those who were skeptical are convinced he will persevere.[4] So, despite the fact that consanguinity and affinity are a big part of being Indian, at a very basic level—the level of spiritual meaning—participation is open to those who will adopt Indian culture.

Even the Indian rhetoric—which defends the maintenance and restoration of tribal land bases, and which supports the controversial Boldt decision assigning half of the harvestable anadromous fish runs in Washington State to Indians from the treaty tribes—has emphasized cultural factors. The spiritual aspects of fishing and attachment to the land are stressed, despite the fact that there is obviously a powerful economic incentive for Indians to support tribal land and fishing rights. It is surely significant that the First Salmon Ceremony has been revived since Judge Boldt made his landmark ruling. Lest it be argued, however, that economic motivations are really central to the need to establish and define Indian identity, it is well to remember that the revival of spirit dancing preceded the recent economic gains of Indians by a good ten years. What economic effects Winter Dancing has on Indian people is hard to assess, but it is clear that from the insider's perspective economic factors are not consciously important (Kew 1970; Amoss 1978). Indians themselves see the ceremonial circuit, both Winter Dancing and Shaker Church, as a way of bringing them spiritual fulfillment, help in sickness and sorrow, and contact with coast Salish people from other communities. They also explicitly recognize it as preserving their ancestral traditions. At a recent gathering one speaker said, "this is our Indian identity."[5]

When we argue that traditional rituals dominated by the elders have become the keystone for building Indian identity, one question is immediately raised: if Indian spirituality is so essential, why has Winter Dancing, a major component, only been revived and expanded in the last twenty or so years? It is true that the revival of participation in aboriginal style rituals has only become significant in the 1960s, but there are indications that a comparable shift had taken place within the Indian Shaker Church twenty years earlier. In retrospect, this shift seems to have been a logical antecedent to the resurgence of pre-white religious traditions. Furthermore, there are reasons why the conditions in the 1960s were particularly auspicious for the revival of spirit dancing. This question has been address-ed elsewhere (Amoss 1978a) and the conclusions reached are particularly germane to why it is the elders—rather than politically active young militants—who have become the central figures in re-establishing the cultural base of Indian identity. During the last half of the nineteenth cen-tury, with the dislocations of white contact, the old people lost their central place because of their connection with the discredited old culture. During this period of disillusionment some Indians tried, usually without notable success, to assimilate to white society and culture. More found in the revelations of the Shaker Prophet a new cultural identity drawn from em-bracing the Shaker faith, which replaced the old sacred symbols with the new ones taken from Christianity (Amoss 1978b). The new religion allow-ed the people to remain Indian but to draw on the power of the dominant system's sacred symbols. By the middle of the 20th century, a massive shift in attitude was already under way. In the 1940s a protracted schismatic debate within the Shaker church dramatized a change in the meaning of these sacred symbols. Initially powerful because they drew on spiritual sources outside of old Indian culture, they had now become part of a specifically and self-consciously defined Indian tradition. Originally con-cerned to set themselves apart from the pagans, in the 1940s Shakers were at pains to distinguish themselves from charismatic white Christians. The Bible became the key symbol in the dispute. Using the Bible in a Shaker service had become the mark of heterodoxy (Richen 1974:30). In the 1970s, people say that real Shakers do not need the Bible because God has given them inspiration which comes "from the heart" rather than from a written scripture. With the cultural unrest that shook the United States and Canada during the 1960s, the confidence of the dominant society in its own basic cultural assumptions was being challenged from within (Eister 1972). As part of the change in attitudes, a number of American ethnic groups began actively to promote the virtues of their identity. What direct effect these currents may have had on American Indians in general and Coast Salish people in particular is difficult to say, but there is no doubt that there has been a resurgence of interest in Indianness (Williams 1980). The Coast Salish young people who are affected by the change in the domi-nant society must turn to their elders to learn the important cultural prac-tices that mark Indian identity. This need, generated by rapidly changing conditions outside Indian Society, has opened up an opportunity to the current cohort of Indian elders to assume once more the central position their predecessors enjoyed as transmitters of cultural tradition. As long as these traditions are seen as essential to being Indian, young Indians, and middle-aged ones, too, will reward the old people with prestige.

The association between death and old age, which I identified as a universal cultural theme, and which is at the root of much of the denigration of old age in the dominant white culture, figures in the cultural evaluation of the current cohort of Indian elders, too. However, rather than promoting a rejection of the old, it, too, is working to enhance the prestige of the old people. Younger people fear that when the last of these old people die, as they soon must, there will be no way of recovering the treasures of the past. The general threat of death associated with old age has been translated into a very specific fear of losing a resource that cannot be renewed. The shadow of death over the aged has made them more precious, in both the ceremonial arena and the tribal education programs. People worry over the illness of an old shaman: "Old X is the last one around here. I don't know what we'll do when he's gone." Education directors fret about the possibility that the old people who know the stories will die before the tribal council has arranged to have them recorded on video tape.

10. Perspectives for Future Cohorts of Elders

This cohort of elders, now that they have taken their place as leaders in the cultural revival, will not easily be displaced. The central role Winter Dancing and Shaker ceremonies play in community life and individual needs will continue to define what it is to be Indian. Old people—whose supremacy in these ritual spheres is unchallenged—will maintain their authority. Whether the people who are now middle-aged will inherit the mantle is less certain. A number are now active in the ceremonial domain, and are gradually sharpening their skills as speakers and fostering their reputations for ritual knowledge and spiritual power. But in the future, economic issues promise to become a more important part of Indian identity. For the first time since white dominion was established in the mid-19th century, the treaty tribes of Western Washington have been given control over a very valuable resource—one-half the commercial fish harvest. In addition, the Indians are prosecuting their land claims more vigorously than they have in the past, and although the outcome of some of the more audacious are in doubt, they will undoubtedly receive some of what they are claiming or compensation for it. In the meantime, a few tribes are buying or otherwise acquiring some lands that were part of their original treaty holdings, or originally homesteaded by Indians. For the first time in a long time being Indian will come to be—for some people at least—an economic advantage instead of a disadvantage. I would expect that the cultural system will begin to adjust to support the economic and political system more closely. Qualifications for leadership in the ritual sphere may shift, though I would hestitate to predict the form they will take. But because of the necessity of logical and stylistic integration, the cultural changes that come about as the two systems move together will be constrained and oriented by the innovative and creative re-interpretations developed by this generation of elders.

Notes

[1] They also include a "residual" component to explain high rank assigned to old people who formerly controlled, contributed or advised.

[2] Although he does not distinguish between culture and society in the same way that Geertz does, I believe Wallace's discussion can be interpreted in those terms without doing violence to it.

[3] There are limits on innovation, even for elders. One well-known contemporary elder is currently out of favor with many of his peers because they believe he is stretching the limits. There are even rumors that last year a number of ritually prominent old people met to consider how he should be censured. This kind of attempt to define community standards is most unusual in the very individualistic and decentralized Coast Salish milieu.

[4] The equally interesting question of how his religious superiors accepted his decision to become a spirit dancer is outside the scope of this paper.

[5] This is the first indication I have encountered that the more self-conscious search for identity apparent in the context of tribal education programs has surfaced in the rhetoric of the traditional gatherings.

4
The Conquest of Solitude: Singlehood and Old Age In Traditional Chinese Society

Andrea Sankar

1. Introduction

Until quite recently one entered into adult life in most cultures through the door of marriage. Great signficance was attached to this passage, in part because it had momentous results: on the other side of the gate of marriage lay the family—which among social scientists holds undisputed place as the molecule out of which societies grow, and as such has received all the attention it no doubt deserves. Still, not everyone married. Many servants, prostitutes, migrant laborers, and countless others who were too poor to have children, in a great range of different cultures, stayed single. How did they live out their lives? How did they fend for themselves in old age, when reduced physical capacity inhibited their ability to be financially self-sufficient? What kinds of arrangements did they make for themselves? How were these arrangements bounded by the culture in which single adults lived? Were there any cultural proscriptions against singlehood and if so, how were these handled? Finally, how did the awareness of self-sufficiency and independence affect life plans and self-perceptions?

To answer some of these questions, I will examine pre-revolutionary China—a society dominated by the family—in order to see how provision was made for adults without family in their most vulnerable time, old age. The focus will be on single adults in old age because problems a single person faces through adulthood are exaggerated by the increased dependency of old age. Lacking children, who are the means of support for the elderly in traditional societies,[1] these elderly have had to create new relationships and arrangements to sustain themselves. How these relationships were formed and the shape they have taken should shed light on the general condition of the elderly in that society.

In traditional Chinese society, the family was the most important form of social organization. It provided the individual with a social identity, and with material and emotional security. Cultural values centered around the family, and it was to the family that the individual owed his allegiance. These values, such as interdependence and obedience, were further reflected in social and political organizations. Non-kin based organizations—such as religious cults, secret societies, and artisans—often took on the terminology of kinship to tie the members together. In addition to the social, political and economic structures which supported the family,[2] traditional Chinese folk religion placed sanctions on family creation. Unmarried adults without descendents to care for their souls faced the danger of becoming Hungry Ghosts wandering alone in the Underworld.

To confront old age and death without natural or adopted descendents was a grim prospect for those who had been denied families through poverty, disfigurement, "ill-fate," or personal choice. Yet the thousands who found themselves in this position coped with their dilemma through a variety of cultural solutions.[3] This chapter examines some of those solutions—particularly those of single women, whose lives were culturally and economically extremely marginal. One of the culturally most radical and anthropologically intriguing solutions to the problem of singlehood is provided by a group of spinsters from Kwantung province.[4] Much of the ethnographic discussion to follow tells part of their story.

2. The Burden of Singlehood In Traditional China

If it did not occur for religious reasons, remaining single was regarded in Western cultures primarily as the individual's presonal loss and secondarily as a possible burden on his or her natal family. Until the last century, children usually provided the main support for an elderly person. It was ultimately to one's material advantage to procreate, and few religious or moral principles were needed to detail the necessity of doing so. This was not the case in traditional China, where failure to produce heirs was regarded as an affront to one's ancestors, as unfilial behavior toward one's parents, and as a serious spiritual and supernatural threat to one's own soul, as well as one's family's future prosperity. A man was seen as a link in an unending chain of kinship stretching back in time through his ancestors and forward by means of his descendents. To break the chain was a failure to honor his obligations to his own parents and ancestors, and to place their souls in jeopardy by providing for no future worshippers. The individual himself was in the greatest peril of suffering from a lack of material security in old age, as well as having his spirit become a Hungry Ghost. Confucian works which constituted the orthodox political and social ideology of traditional Chinese society held that a man's failure to produce descendents was one of the most serious crimes a son could commit against his parents.

In actual practice, however, ancestor worship did not consistently make harsh judgments against the childless. Men were considered to be full members of the family in which they were born, and as such could sometimes receive ancestor worship even if they died childless and unmarried.[5] Men who died in early manhood without producing heirs could still be honored as ancestors on the basis of their potential contribution to the family heritage, depending on the local custom and the strength and internal cohesion of the individual's lineage. Men who died as bachelors later in life, however, were often consigned to the anonymous status of Hungry Ghost because of their failure to contribute to the lineage's progeny. In some parts of Kwangtung the situation was less bleak, for there the elderly bachelors were cared for by the lineage. Southern Kwangtung came closer to approximating the Chinese cultural ideal of the extended family than any other area of China. Some lineages were so large as to constitute single sur-name villages. In some of these large and powerful lineages, elderly bachelors were allowed to live in the lineage hall at lineage expense. It was even possible for such a bachelor to posthumously adopt a nephew who would then carry out his ancestor rights (Spencer 1948:464).

For women the situation was grim. They did not belong to the family of their birth; they were destined to leave to become a wife and mother for another family. In this strictly patrilineal society, women had little right to draw on the kinship ties of their natal families. Should they die before marriage they could not legitimately be worshipped by the family, having never been a member in the first place. A woman only gained her social and often personal identity through becoming a man's wife, and finally another man's mother. No daughter, married or unmarried, was supposed to die in her natal home;[6] however, should a married daughter visiting her natal home choose this inauspicious occasion to expire, her spirit could be led back to her husband's home, where it would then be properly cared for. In the case of an unmarried woman, there was no place for the spirit to go; it remained in the home, causing trouble for the inhabitants. The seriousness of this problem increased with the age of the single woman at death. Very young children—boys or girls—often were not worshipped, nor did they necessarily become Hungry Ghosts. According to some, these infants had been specifically sent to punish the parents by their early death and thus did not possess real souls (Ahern 1973:125), but the spirit of a woman near or past marriageable age could legitimately seek retribution from her family for not discharging their duty to find a husband for her. The Ghost of such a daughter could haunt the family no matter where the woman died, but its power was greatest if she died in her natal home.

The soul of a socially mature unmarried woman was believed to become a Hungry Ghost because it could have no permanent resting place nor receive ritual attention in either a woman's natal home or the lineage ancestor hall. The woman had not contributed to the prosperity of either her family or the lineage, and thus was not entitled to recognition in death. The soul tablet could be kept in her family home in some out of the way place, but this arrangement was considered to be an impermanent one.

Having been denied a permanent resting place and proper care, the soul of such a woman could cause misfortune and sickness for her remaining family members until they satisfied her demands for attention. Several cultural solutions existed to placate the ghost, and thus ensure the security of the family as well as the well-being of the woman's soul. The most effective and common measure was to arrange a ghost marriage for the deceased woman. There were many varieties of ghost marriages, some involving the spirits of unmarried dead men, others involving married men (Jordan 1972:140; McGough 1976:114). In the ghost marriage, a woman's soul was appeased by finding for it a place to rest in her "husband's" family. This solution stopped her from making trouble for her natal family. Although her soul would probably not receive specific ancestor worship, it would be included in the family's general observances of all ancestor rites. Some areas established maiden's temples, where the soul tablets of unmarried women could be placed. This was not a frequent practice and seems to have been confined largely to the south of China and Taiwan (Yang 1959:89; Ahern 1973:127; Sankar 1978:82). These solutions primarily ensured the safety of living relatives and secondarily gave relief to the individual woman's soul. They did not address the needs of the living woman. Few legitimate cultural roles existed for single women; nevertheless; these woman had to find a means to support themselves, and they tended to do so in standard ways.

3.   Practical Solutions

Childless, single women were denied the security and assurance concerning their old age which the existence of offspring helped to provide. From early adulthood, single women began making plans for old age. The ways in which they chose to support themselves usually reflected their awareness of the need for care in old age, thus many of the occupations chosen, such as maid and nun, entailed family-like relationships.

Of the possible employment opportunities open to women, domestic service tended to provide many of the benefits which would have accrued from natural family membership. Traditionally, free servants—as distinguished from bond servants or *mui tsai*[7]—were considered members of the master's family, albeit distant relatives. Servants were included in family activities and were expected to devote their life completely to the family. Not all servants were unwed, but those who were found this inclusion into the master's family a secure arrangement. An unwritten code of behavior kept masters and mistresses from the abuses of rape and harsh physical punishment sometimes resulting in death which were suffered by many bond servants. In return for long years of service with little financial remuneration, a free servant could expect to be cared for when she was too old to work. This obligation on the part of the employers was reflected in traditional law. According to these codes, a wet-nurse was entitled to an ancestor tablet and three months mourning by the children whom she had nursed. In a more recent Hong Kong statute, any servant who had served more than twenty years with a family was entitled to care from the estate of the family head after his death.

The legal codes reflected what was in many cases a strong and compassionate attachment to servants. Long-time servants were taken on family vacations and were included in festivities and in the family's leisure activities. Servants often had a particularly close and intimate relationship with the children for whom they cared, especially with the sons of the family. Some servants managed to ritually adopt the child they cared for. This adoption, called a *kai* relationship, was roughly similar to our god-parent, god-child relationship. It could range from a polite formality to a deep, lasting relationship.

One informant related how the eldest son of the family for whom she worked had his new American bride serve tea to her before the bride served tea to his mother. Serving tea was the new bride's traditional way of showing respect and submission to her mother-in-law, and this man felt emotionally much closer to his former nurse than to his mother, a mahjong-playing society lady. In such cases, the obligation to care for a servant in old age arose from natural strong affections.

Although domestic service traditionally served as a safeguard against destitution and isolation in old age, this strategy has not survived the strains and stresses of the rapid social transitions which occurred in post-war Hong Kong. Inflation and a severe housing shortage have made it difficult to honor traditional obligations. Masters, however, continue to expect the devotion and unpaid labor of their servants, but are more and more unable to care for them in old age. The story of Ah Meih can illustrate this conflictual situation.

Ah Meih had worked for the family of a high government official since long before the official was born. Originally, Ah Meih had come into the family to care for the official's mother when she was a young girl. Upon his mother's marriage, Ah Meih accompanied her to her husband's home. Ah Meih was completely devoted to her mistress and her family and had few friends. As Ah Meih approached old age, she developed trouble with her legs. Finally she had to have an operation and had to remain in the hospital for several months. Her mistress paid for this and helped care for Ah Meih once she returned to the family. Ah Meih tried to resume her servant's duties, but it soon became apparent she would have to retire. The family hired a new servant to replace her and Ah Meih remained in the servants' quarters. But the new servant complained that it was too much to care for both the mistress and Ah Meih, so the family decided to find an old age home for Ah Meih. Not wanting to cause any trouble, Ah Meih consented to this arrangement. Since she had no savings, the family placed her in a government-run home for the indigent elderly. The official was puzzled that Ah Meih was very depressed, even though she was well provided for and did not have to work anymore.

Unfortunately, Ah Meih's case is by no means atypical. A large portion of the inhabitants of the few nursing homes in Hong Kong are former servants who are unable to support themselves with their savings. Domestic service is no longer a form of old age insurance.

Prostitution was another avenue open to single women. The fate of such women was not as bleak as one in the West might think. A career in prostitution could be considered a filial act if the woman in question was doing it to support her parents. Sometimes the prostitute saved enough money to marry an uxorilocal husband. (No man who could afford a wife would pay a bride price for a former prostitute [McGough 1976:64]). Often the prostitute would bear her own children, which her parents raised while she plied her trade in distant cities. More often the prostitute had enough savings to purchase a slave girl, whom she raised to care for her in old age.

The religious life was an option, especially for women living away from cities; but women, living in the orthodox recognized nunneries, either Buddhist or Taoist, were few in number and represented the elite who could afford the membership fee. Most women who chose the religious life lived in informal nunneries. These women simply shaved their heads, made their own religious gowns and joined the nearest "nunnery." Often abandoned infant girls were brought there. These village "nunneries" had no official training or supervision. They usually consisted of six to eight women who worshipped the Buddha or Taoist gods, but whose time was mostly spent on communal agricultural labor in order to support themselves. The children raised in the "nunnery" became nuns and cared for the elderly women who had provided for them as children.

Those monks and nuns who lived in the orthodox monasteries and nunneries were well cared for in old age. The ones who had obtained a minimum religious rank were given separate living quarters; they were also exempted form physical labor and the rigors of the mediation hall.

4. Childless Couples

Many problems faced by single individuals were also confronted by childless couples. In spiritual concerns their plight was less serious. Membership in a lineage organization often guaranteed the couple at least minimal ancestor rites. In some areas a nephew could be adopted by "spirit adoption" to care for the ancestor rites of the deceased (McGough 1976:167). This practice varied from region to region and depended on the lineage to which the couple belonged. More important were the problems of physical maintenance in old age. Very few extended families had enough surplus income to support elderly childless relatives. If a wife failed to bear children, families who could afford it purchased a concubine. When the fault was thought to lie with the husband peasant mothers-in-law were known to encourage discreet affairs which ended in their daughters-in-law's pregnancies.

In some cases, contracts were arranged between an invalid husband and a poor man by which a husband could "rent" out his wife for periods of up to ten years. The first son born from such a liaison went to the renter and the rest of the children went to the original husband (McGough 1976:85).

Because sons were the only culturally legitimate heirs in a family responsible for the parents' care and ancestor worship, couples who bore only daughters often considered themselves to be childless. Theirs, however, was far from a desperate situation, for many different forms of uxorilocal marriage existed.

Uxorilocal marriage meant that a daughter remained at home and the husband, usually for lack of money, agreed to reside with her. Agreements of this type varied from area to area and according to the needs of the specific situation, but the details of such arrangements were usually explicitly stated in contracts drawn up at the time. Uxorilocal marriage took roughly three forms. The most common form was for a son-in-law to agree to care for the wife's parents until their deaths, after which he could take his children and wife and return to his own lineage. In this form the husband retained his surname and the right to his wife's property (McGough 1976:56-7). Other forms involved arrangements where some children took the mother's surname and some the father's. In these forms, the husband had to change his surname to that of the wife's and become an adopted son as well as son-in-law; but this created a problem of technical incest (McGough 1976:56).

Truly childless couples could adopt a niece and invite in an uxorilocal husband for her (McGough 1976:171), or purchase a slave girl and marry in a husband for her. In these cases, the same variety of arrangements with the husband as discussed above applies.

For married couples a variety of forms of adoption and uxorilocal marriage for daughters, multiple marriages for either husband or wife existed to help cope with childlessness. All of these forms lay within the boundaries of the kinship system. The alternatives required forethought and planning, but they did not dictate a distinctly different lifestyle for those who chose to follow them. Although the family structure was the dominant form of social organization, it was flexible enough to encompass a great variety of deviant forms and still admit the individuals involved to the categorical rights and responsibilities of family membership.

With rare exceptions, families were unable to care for their permanently single, elderly adults; and the single elderly could not rely on manipulating the family structure to solve their problems. At the same time, there were very few social alternatives to the family; therefore, the success of the single individual in solving the problems of aging and death without children depended on his or her ability to form fictive kin relationships, which provided the emotional and material support found in family membership.

The fictive kin relationships established by single women were usually hierarchical. The servant could become a fictive mother, aunt, or elder sister. Nuns became fictive brothers[8] to each other and fathers to their followers. Few strategies worked out by single women were based on peer support, although this form of relationship was popular among single men, especially those in secret societies. The sisterhoods formed among non-marrying spinsters in Kwangtung were an interesting and important exception. These sisterhoods embodied both the necessity of adequately replicating the family structure in order to insure the single individual's emotional, spiritual and economic security as well as the remarkable—and in many respects modern—strength of peer associations in meeting the full range of demands of the elderly.

5.   A Case Study: The Spinsters of Kwangtung

The spinsters of southern Kwangtung Province are part of a loose group called the *sou-hei* or "self-combers," referring to their practice of dressing their hair in the adult fashion themselves, rather than having it done for them in a wedding ceremony. This phenomenon, called "marriage resistance" by Marjorie Topley (1975), lasted from about 1831 to 1935. It arose out of a combination of several key factors: a breakdown in social controls in the area;[9] the institution of the girls' house, which allowed adolescent girls greater personal freedom than was generally true for traditional Chinese society; introduction of wage labor, with the mechanization of the silk industry, in which many of the region's women were employed; and the unique cultural configuration of the area. The movement went through several changes before the choice of spinsterhood became popular and well-accepted. At each stage, a primary concern was the provisioning for old age and ancestor worship.

The movement passed roughly through three stages. The earliest stage involved a strong commitment among adolescent girls who formed sisterhoods, usually arising out of the girls' houses to which they belonged. The members took vows of celibacy and would not consummate their marriages until all of the sisters had been married. The abstinence sometimes lasted up to six years. Eventually the sisterhoods disbanded and the women went to live with their husbands and to bear children. Had they remained separated from their husbands, these women would have had no means to support themselves in old age, unless they were gentry daughters.

After the mechanization of the silk industry in 1867 and the introduction of wages, the sisterhoods entered into a brief second phase of celibate marriage. Members married but never consummated their marriages. Instead, they jointly saved money to purchase concubines to replace themselves as wives and mothers. The celibate wife continued to send money to her husband and his family. When it was time to retire, the sisterhood disbanded, and the wife returned home, expecting to take her place as first wife and technical mother of the concubine's children and to be supported by them in her old age.

Needless to say, this arrangement caused many problems. Not a few concubines were unwilling to relinquish their position to a woman they barely knew. This insecure form of old age insurance was soon abandoned as women's wages continued to rise. More and more women began to choose a life of spinsterhood in a sisterhood. This choice was facilitated by a local ceremony, similar to marriage, in which a woman attained adult status in return for a vow of permanent celibacy. In so doing she renounced her claims on her parents to provide her with a husband and freed them from retribution from her ghost after her death, as long as she did not die within her natal home. This vow did not entitle her to ancestor worship or care in old age from any specific group or person; these she had to provide for herself.

The spinster had a number of options for dealing with old age. She could adopt a fraternal niece and raise her. This niece in turn became a spinster, caring for her aunt in old age and maintaining her soul tablet. Sometimes the spinster chose to contribute to the welfare of a brother's family. This family then cared for the aunt in old age and worshipped her soul after death. Through her contribution to the family, she earned for herself a place in the lineage; thus, her tablet could remain in the family home and could be worshipped. The willingness of the brother's family to perform ancestor rites for the aunt and her renunciation of the family obligation to find a husband for her guaranteed a calm, secure spirit, and the aunt was permitted to die in her natal home.[10]

The most common solution for old age for a spinster was to build a spinster house with her sisterhood. There the sisterhood retired and took care of each other until they had all died. Often young members were recruited into the sisterhood. These younger members performed the ancestor rites for the sisters who had died. They also inherited property from them.

The spinsters began leaving southern Kwangtung for Canton, and later the cities of Southeast Asia, because of periodic depressions in the silk industry in the early twentieth century. Separated from the local culture, which had supported their unusual life styles, the spinsters were forced to make different plans for old age. This latter problem was especially serious after the 1949 Revolution, which discouraged most spinsters from returning to China.[11] Some sisterhoods proved versatile and adaptive in meeting these new situations, others encountered serious problems. The great majority of former silk laborers chose domestic service as a form of employment. However, unlike the typical servant who accepted low wages in return for paternalistic care and the promise of a secure old age, the spinsters demanded wages and chose to rely on their sisterhoods in old age. The sisterhoods were often used as a primitive trade union, and the spinsters were able to secure the jobs and wages they desired. The spinsters had an advantge over other female immigrants seeking domestic service positions, because the sisterhoods both trained their members in servants' skills—such as Western cooking and hairdressing, and even in the English language—and also provided an extensive job-locating network. The decision to insist on wages rather than to depend on the employer to provide old age care proved extremely wise.

6. The Conquest of Solitude

The sisterhoods from Kwangtung survived in their new homes in Hong Kong, Kuala Lumpur, and other Southeast Asian cities, and their members for the most part thrived. Their success provides us with an example of a cultural solution to old age adapted to a new social environment. Hong Kong is predominantly a Chinese society; however, the difference between its largely immigrant population—affected by strong Westernizing influences—and the highly restricted local culture—from which marriage resistance and the spinsters emerged—is great. The rapidly changing society of Hong Kong has put serious strains on all traditional institutions, and the elderly have suffered from changes in the family structure and notions of filial responsibility (cf. Ikels 1980).

Several factors have contributed to the survival of the sisterhoods and have affected the way in which they continued to aid their members during their working lives and in retirement. The strongly committed nature of the sisterhood bond itself accounts for much of the success. In addition, the sisterhoods were often able to take advantage of the social and economic conditions prevailing in Hong Kong from the 1920s through the 1960s to purchase property and invest in the stock market. Many spinsters did remit some of their wages to relatives in China, but, unlike sons, they felt their greatest obligation was to themselves and their sisters, and they acted accordingly.

The movement of spinsters into Hong Kong coincided with the establishment there of a Taoist religious sect called the Great Way (Topley 1963:381). Great Way was organized around residential vegetarian halls called *jaai tohng*.[12] The sect was eager to recruit people after its persecution in China during the latter half of the nineteenth century. The residential halls were very attractive to the homeless spinsters. In addition, the spinsters' celibate lifestyle already qualified them for a high status in the religion. Although religious conviction had not been an important factor in the women's initial decision to remain single, the security and social contact offered by vegetarian hall membership encouraged many spinsters to join.[13] Following the popular example set by Great Way vegetarian halls, Buddhists began establishing their vegetarian halls in the mid-1920s. These halls have proven a crucial element in the successful solutions to the spinsters' problems concerning aging and death in a foreign environment.

Most of the data are from field work done among the residents of Buddhist vegetarian halls. These halls meet many of the needs of the aged as well as the specific concerns of the spinsters. The vegetarian halls are communally run and operated, which means the members keep busy at important day-to-day tasks well into old age. There are very few people suffering from senile dementia, but those who do are cared for by other members. The religious organization of the halls offers financial as well as social advantages. Being a religious institution, a vegetarian hall is tax-free. Although the halls are not open for public worship, members of the lay community of Buddhism and Great Way often donate money or services to the vegetarian halls. In addition, members of the halls engage in the production of religious paraphernalia for a small subsidiary income.

Belonging to a vegetarian hall gives the spinsters a place in the larger religious community. In the valley where the field work was conducted there is a sizable monastery and seven vegetarian halls ranging from two to fifty members. This arrangement can also be found in several adjoining valleys and other rural areas of Hong Kong. Vegetarian hall members participate in festivals and rituals of the religious community, which provides them with an on-going social life.

The translation of *jaai tohng* as vegetarian hall is a loose one, for the Chinese concept of *jaai* also includes notions of self-purification and self-realization. These notions are closely associated with diet, as well as with religious rituals and meditation. Thus meals are part of the religious ritual. The communal meals, which are well-balanced and nourishing, have religious significance while they also provide social contact and sustenance. Communal meals serve to reaffirm the group's identity and purpose.

From the special perspective of the spinster, one of the most important advantages offered by a vegetarian hall membership is inclusion in a religious family. Both Buddhist and Taoist vegetarian halls are organized around religious families. Once a woman joins a hall and the family represented there, she becomes part of their kinship system and as such is entitled to ancestor worship. This last feature is especially important to the informants. Lastly, the religious purpose of the halls allows for the re-cruitment of new members who join out of religious conviction, not social and financial need. These different recruits ensure that the spinsters are cared for even after they are too old to care for each other, and that after all the spinsters have died, their soul tablets will be maintained.

7.   Secular Sisterhoods

Not all sisterhoods in Hong Kong choose to form vegetarian halls. Among those secular sisterhoods which choose not to join, we can identify two types. One is composed of two to three members and is called a sworn sisterhood. These sworn sisterhoods are usually tied together by a vow of permanent faithfulness, and are often lesbian in nature. The other kind of secular sisterhood has five to ten members. Sometimes these sisterhoods—called seven sisters associations, despite the actual number of members—take vows of friendship before the Goddess of Mercy, Kuan Yin. Usually the secular sisterhoods have been together for a long time and have possibly come from the same girls' house in the Canton Delta. Although not necessarily lesbian, members of these sisterhoods are deeply committed to each other. The secular nature of these sisterhoods is in keeping with the original formation of marriage-resisting sisterhoods in the Canton Delta.

The sworn sisterhood has had the least success of all the sisterhoods in confronting the problems spinsters face in aging in the foreign environment of Hong Kong. The sworn sisterhood suffers from many of the problems of a marriage, but lacks some important advantages of it, such as children and extended kinship networks. It is difficult to discuss the sworn sisterhoods with any precision, because they tended to lead reclusive lives. But of the six couples or *menage à trois* interviewed, four were unhappy, some bitterly.

The stories of King Jye and Ah Saam may serve as examples of the problems and possible solutions created by this arrangement.

King Jye shared a *gung-si fong* (a small cubicle in a flat which had only one bed) with two sworn sisters. There they each spent days on which they did not have to work and stored their personal belongings. Trouble began when King Jye became sick with a foot infection and had to have an operation. She needed to remain in bed for several weeks. Her "sisters" became furious at her continual occupation of the room. At night they would kick at her in bed and finally pushed her out of bed. They said the bed was too small, but she knew they loved each other more than they loved her and did not want her in the sisterhood anymore. She was able to stay with some distant relatives while recuperating, but she felt she could not impose and so returned early to work. Her foot did not completely heal, and it was difficult for her to work, especially because she had no place to go on her day off. She remained with her employers, getting little rest. King Jye was over sixty-five and in poor health, but without her sisters—with whom she had planned to retire—she did not know what would happen to her.

Ah Saam's story is happier, but only because she had more foresight. Ah Saam and her two sworn sisters moved to Hong Kong to retire, after having worked in Singapore for thirty years as servants. Ah Saam had been able to save the most money, since she had had the best job and the most generous master. She bought three flats, one for her and her "sisters" to live in and two for the rent money. When she purchased the flats, she put her *kai di* (godson)'s name on the deed. Like many spinsters, Ah Saam invested much emotional energy and time in her *kai* relationships. She had always been very fond of this boy, who was the grandson of an old friend of hers, and had planned to make him her heir.

The retirement of the three sworn sisters was not as calm nor as happy as they had planned. Ah Saam and one of her "sisters" began fighting, and eventually this led to a very bitter fight. The "sister" said she would move out, and the third sister took sides against Ah Saam and moved out too. Ah Saam was quite despondent and isolated. She turned to her *kai di* for assistance and began to spend more and more on him. At one point, Ah Saam introduced the boy to her niece. To her satisfaction, they eventually married and now live with her. They care for her and eventually will inherit all her property.

Sworn sisterhoods were formerly an accepted, stable relationship among the spinsters of the Canton Delta. In many villages such arrangements were recognized as marriages, and the members were considered part of the village, but this is not the case in Hong Kong where, among other things, sworn sisterhoods are stigmatized by their supposed lesbianism. This stigma is a relatively superficial difficulty compared to the loss of a supporting social environment. Isolated from the village and presence of relatives who acted to maintain the stability of the relationship, the bonds tying the women together become fragile and easily broken in jealous disputes.

Even for those who manage to maintain a strong close relationship there are serious problems. In Hong Kong, such women have few other significant relationships, fewer than a married couple. Thus, if one of the sisters dies, the survivor faces a lonely and isolated life with no kin support, unless the survivor has developed strong *kai* relationships.

The extended sisterhoods of five to ten members have proven to be more flexible in meeting the demands of life and old age in Hong Kong. These sisterhoods tend to have been together for long periods of time, usually thirty to forty years. Unlike many sisterhoods found in vegetarian halls, they are rarely new creations, brought together for purposes of retirement.

Secular sisterhoods establish spinster houses, as was the custom in the Canton Delta. Traditionally, a woman, together with her "sisters," began building a spinster house soon after her spinster ceremony. These houses were specifically places where the spinsters were to die, but customarily they moved there within a few years of the spinster ceremony, and it was to the spinster house that the women planned to retire.

Most informants who had taken the spinster vow while still living in the Delta had built spinster houses there, to which they had planned to retire. The Revolution of 1949 delayed this move, and subsequent fears made it impossible for many women to ever return. During their stay in Hong Kong, some spinsters who had chosen to take up temporary residence in vegetarian halls eventually decided to make this a permanent arrangement. Others, seeing the advantages of vegetarian halls, built new ones. However, many spinsters eschewed the religious life, despite the practical advantages it offered, and preferred to establish the traditional secular spinster house.

The spinster houses established in Hong Kong are either flats in town or farms in the New Territories. One group of five sisters, who all work as maids in the same dormitory of the University of Hong Kong, has purchased a large flat where they all live. They own several other flats from which they derive income. The eldest member of the sisterhood has retired and takes care of the flat. Another sisterhood of twelve members bought a farm in the New Territories. They go there regularly on their days off, to work and to see each other. There too, the eldest member retired and runs the farm.

Although most secular sisterhoods are characterized by a deep, long-lasting commitment among the members, they seem to have been unsuccessful in meeting their needs in old age. There are many specific reasons to which one could point to explain this problem, but the general underlying cause is the loss of community. Let us examine some of the problems to which this loss has given rise.

The sisterhoods which formed among adolescent girls in the Canton Delta were an integral part of the culture of that area. The sisterhoods figured in myths and popular songs. They were tied together by recognized rituals, such as the celibacy vow, and were based on the girls' house, a well-accepted institution which still exists in the People's Republic. The presence of the supportive sisterhood, along with the spinster vow freeing women from marriage, played an important role in enabling women to make a significant economic contribution to the community. Even though they were unmarried women, the spinsters were considered to be lineage members. In some communities, the lineage constructed special spinster temples to house their tablets. Other lineages contributed to the building of the spinster houses. As long as the spinsters remained within the Canton Delta, they received support and security within the group and also from the community in which they lived.

In Hong Kong, the sisterhoods have encountered other immigrants and refugees from the Delta, but the community of their youth has never been re-established. The society of Hong Kong does not support or recognize the sisterhood. Sisterhoods withdrew into themselves, sometimes living near each other, and in that way have maintained observances of their rituals and life style. Unlike other distinct groups in Hong Kong society, however, the sisterhoods are clearly hampered in their attempt to maintain their autonomy and way of life by a lack of new recruits.

Although most secular sisterhoods have attained financial security—and the members have each other for social and emotional support as they grow older—they suffer more and more from the lack of a community. As the members age and begin to die, those that are left have become increasingly anxious about their isolation and growing weakness. Marriage resistance is over, and the secular sisterhoods of Hong Kong have no way to attract new members to care for them, as was the practice in the Canton Delta. Unless they have established strong *kai* relationships, members are cut off from contact with younger people, contact which would give them a sense of continued participation in the outside world as well as providing access to needed assistance. In addition, there is no community pressure to help maintain the responsibilities and rights of the members vis-a-vis each other, and no one to mediate disputes. Few outsiders can share the responsibility for the increasingly grim decisions which have to be made, such as to hospitalize a member or allow her to die at home. Despite all their careful planning, most secular sisterhoods have failed to meet many of the important needs of their older members.

In order to make a successful adaptation to the demands of Hong Kong and other Southeast Asian cities, the religious sisterhoods have had to undergo some significant changes. Often they have had to join with other sisterhoods[13] in order to establish a vegetarian hall. Although these new joint sisterhoods are comprised of spinsters who all share a similar cultural background, this move signified a serious departure from the traditional notion that a sisterhood was a bond among a fixed number of peers. This flexibility has allowed the religious sisterhoods to incorporate non-spinster members into their religious families. But this ability to recruit non-spinsters is not the most important benefit of the religious structure, for even those religious sisterhoods which chose not to recruit new members have generally fared better than their secular counterparts.

In large part, the success of religious sisterhoods had to do with the nature of vegetarian hall organization, and the religious community of which the halls are a part. The ritual of joining a vegetarian hall (one which established kinship ties) reinforces and strengthens the sisterhood bond. As one informant said, "We are twice as strong now because we are brothers as well as sisters." Vegetarian hall membership has given the sisterhoods a new role and definition within the religious community of Buddhism and Taoism. As members of vegetarian halls, the sisterhoods interact with the wider society, as well as with members of different halls. Within the religious community itself there is great concern for and commitment to the members of the various halls. Excesses in behavior are condemned, and responsibility is shared for serious decisions and problems.

8.   Conclusion

Singlehood has been a marginal way of life until most recently in most societies, in large part because it made provisions for old age very difficult. As we have seen, this was especially true in China. Not only was the elderly single individual often in physical and financial straits, but he or she also faced grim spiritual dilemmas. Yet even Chinese society made allowances for the single and childless elderly. Their solutions were not random, *ad hoc* arrangements, but tended to follow standard, regular—albeit deviant—patterns. The success of the various strategies adopted by the single elderly depended in large part on the extent to which they could emulate the traditional family structure.

The spinsters of the Canton Delta were possibly unique in being a widespread secular movement for singlehood. This movement was able to flourish in large part because the sisterhood organization and the local culture made provisions for old age possible. Unlike other areas of China—where women made significant economic contributions—the spinsters were able to take advantage of their economic freedom to resist marriage because a secure and stable alternative way of life was available to them. The girls' houses of the Delta encouraged the formation of deep, affectionate bonds among young girls; the spinster ceremony freed them and their families from possible supernatural retribution for failure to marry; the sisterhoods provided them with an on-going stable social and emotional life, and their valued economic contribution to the family and lineage ensured their care and acceptance by the community. In short, the choice of spinsterhood became popular in the Canton Delta in large part because the community accepted it, and community support could be relied upon in the women's old age.

The social networks and relationships that go into making up a community are crucially important for an individual's psychological, emotional and even physical well-being (cf. Berkman and Syme 1979). As one ages and becomes increasingly dependent on others, the community grows in importance. For the spinsters, the sisterhood provided such community support. This support was crucial in assisting the spinsters to resist marriage and later to make the transition from silk workers in the Canton Delta to servants in Hong Kong. But the demands of the aged are greater on the community, and the sisterhoods which did not adapt and expand their community base have been frustrated in achieving the kind of retirement for which they had planned and hoped. The bond which tied the sisters together often has proven insufficient to meet the demands and needs of the aging and weakening members. Without new members or community support, the sisterhood is doomed: not just to pass out of existence as all the members die, but more tragically, to fail those same members when they need it most—in their old age.

Although the sisterhood is locked in time to a particular cultural setting and cannot persist, it offers a lesson concerning aging. Elderly single people need not be lonely, isolated and deserving of others' pity. They may in fact have developed strengths from dealing with the demands of singlehood which can serve them well in old age. Possibly, as in the case of the spinsters, these strengths lie in the area of developing strong, enduring non-kin bonds, which, as one informant said, are built on compassion, decades of mutual knowledge and shared experience. Others simply have learned to be alone, having done so successfully most of their lives.

Notes

[1] I use the term "traditional" to refer to pre-1949 mainland China and the Chinese societies found in Taiwan and Hong Kong. Although the social and cultural provisions for elderly people in the People's Republic of China are not radically different from those exisiting in pre-liberation China, the applicability of the strategies for the single and childless elderly discussed in this chapter must nevertheless be restricted to pre-liberation China and to Chinese society as it now exists in Taiwan and Hong Kong, since the revolution has changed society in the People's Republic of China drastically. For a detailed discussion of single and childless elderly in the People's Republic of China, see Davis-Freedman, 1979.

[2] Here I am thinking of such things as the lineage and the *bao jia* system of collective responsibility.

[3] Irene Taeuber lists 2.5 per cent of all families as single-person households in her analysis of population statistics for the period of 1929-31 (Taeuber, in Freedman 1970:71).

[4] I use the term "spinster" because the women who chose to eschew marriage were spinners of silk.

[5] Uxorilocal husbands were sometimes brought in by the husband's family as a second husband for a childless widow (or a widow with small children). One or more children of this second marriage could be posthumously adopted by the first husband (McGough 1976:80).

[6] Exceptions to this rule will be discussed later in the chapter.

[7] *Mui tsai* were young girls purchased to be servants. The girls were supposed to work off the money given to their parents. When they reached marriageable age, the employer had a duty to arrange a marriage for them and to set them free. This "marriage" often turned out to be a form of prostitution.

[8] All members of the Buddhist Sangha adopt male kinship terminology.

[9] The breakdown in social controls from the early nineteenth century through the early twentieth century was caused by such things as decrease in moral authority and control of the lineage elders, due to consolidation of lineage lands in the hands of a wealthy few and the cessation of social welfare projects run by the lineage. This breakdown in authority helped women's associations—such as the girls' houses and sisterhoods—to gain power and autonomy.

[10] This is a rare exception to the rule prohibiting women to die in their natal home. Other notable exceptions are when a family had only one daughter who took the spinster vow, supported her parents in their old age, and performed their ancestor rites and could thus die at home, and an uxorilocally married woman who gave some of her children the lineage surname and was therefore also permitted to die in her natal home and have her tablet placed in the lineage ancestor hall (Ahern 1973:28).

[11] The spinsters were frightened by widespread rumors, which I was unable to confirm or deny, that local cadres were making the elderly spinsters marry widowers to care for them.

[12] Although similar to the unorthodox nunneries of rural China in some respects,

the *jaai tohngs* of Hong Kong are different in their nature and basic structure. Both Buddhist and Taoist *jaai tohngs* are formally associated with larger, publicly recognized religious associations, such as a major temple. Both kinds of halls have formally ordained members of the religion as well as lay residents. Both are aware of, and to differing degrees follow, formal religious teachings and monastic discipline.

[13]See Topley 1975 for a different interpretation of this decision, and Sankar 1978 for a detailed discussion of the contrasting interpretations.

[14]For a detailed discussion of different types of sisterhoods, see Sankar 1978.

5
Adaptive Strategies Of the Elderly In England and Ohio

Doris Francis

1. Introduction

Recently sociological research has focused on the status and role of the aged as retired people and on their modes of participation in contemporary industrial society. In one representative study of elderly socialization, Rosow argues that "unlike earlier status changes in American life, people are not effectively socialized to old age" (Rosow 1974:xii). One possible strategy to improve this situation is to concentrate older persons of similar background in local residential settings. Here cohesive groups and new norms would be generated, protecting the aged from the negative definitions imposed upon them by the larger society and facilitating socialization to new aged roles.

Evidence supporting suggestions for age-segregated housing comes from recent anthropological studies of emerging relationships among peers in age-segregated residences (Ross 1977; Hochschild 1973; Johnson 1971; Keith 1979, 1980). Ross observes, for example, that "More friendships, more social activity, more help in emergency and higher morale are consistently observed in settings where old people are available as potential friends and neighbors" (Ross 1977:2).

My research shows, by contrast, that this grouping of peers in age-segregated housing will not necessarily result in the type of peer community envisioned. This chapter hopes to add to the discussion by asking under what circumstances and through what processes age provides, or fails to provide, a basis for community formation. Two sets of factors are hypothesized as affecting the socialization and participation of aged residents: (1) the pre-existing patterns of kinship and friendship of the tenants; and (2) the history of peer relations within/and the management of the housing estate.

The initial focus of this chapter is on how the elderly adjust to an aged role, not just in terms of formal status, prestige, or responsibility, but on the difficulties of learning to become old and on the necessity of renegotiating roles within the family unit. As this chapter suggests, the number of close friendships people are able to sustain throughout their lives is one crucial factor in their adjustment to new roles in old age. Kinship and friendship are analyzed together as part of a set of ongoing social exchanges which concomitantly affect (1) the formation of attitudes by the elderly toward interaction with children, and (2) the participation and adjustment of residents to relations with peers. Questions are also asked on how patterns of mobility have influenced neighbor and friend relations, and how they, in turn, affect kinship relations and role adjustments.

The orientation of the initial section derives from anthropological research on kinship (Bott 1971; Schneider and Smith 1973; Needham 1971). These anthropologists argue that in industrial society, kinship organization cannot be isolated if we are to understand kinship role relations. The social context of interaction is what is important, and not a formal set of rights and duties. Kinship, according to Needham, is the analysis of a particular problem in different social contexts—it is not possible to make prior determination of what kinship is from what it is not, nor to presume arbitrary boundaries or neat categories. In emphasizing the importance of the social context, Bott has been even more specific and has shown how the friendship network of a couple define the husband and wife role. Here the friendship network is seen as the effective social environment of the family and the factor influencing the role relationships and reciprocal expectations of the husband and wife. Kinship provides a field for personal choice and selectivity; and as a result, wide variation in kinship norms and behavior is a characteristic of western, urban settings. Schneider, furthermore, suggests that the relevance of kinship may be only as a cultural idiom, and it is to non-kinship considerations—such as occupation, age differentiation, and the sex-role system—that he looks to explain the differences in family structure and kinship behavior. This research provides the theoretical basis for my initial arguments, which can be summed up with the following points:

(1) Roles are defined on the basis of class, ethnicity, occupation, age and sex differences, not just on the basis of kinship. But these defining factors vary in their relevance throughout the developmental cycle. Kinship responsibilities, for example, are heightened for the parents of young children, but later on other social factors, such as occupation and class,

may take precedence. Yet when men and women enter the period of retirement, a retreat to a reliance on kinship ties to again define their position seems inevitable.

(2) But unfortunately, the kinship obligations of the retired father and mother are less clearly specified than other kinship roles, which in industrial societies are generally loosely defined. There is no clear legal, economic, or religious framework that helps delimit kinship roles for aged parents.

(3) Instead, elderly parents have to think out, negotiate, and operationalize their new roles, mostly on the basis of kinship rights, obligations, and responsibilities.

(4) This process of self-definition cannot be done in the abstract. It is achieved through the exchanges the elder father and mother make with other older parents who are their friends and kinsmen, as well as in the course of exchanges with their children and grandchildren. Socialization in old age depends heavily on the characteristics of others with whom the older person must negotiate. The social context of interaction is what is important, and not a formal set of rights and duties. As Bott suggests, the social relations with friends are a necessary part of the analysis of kinship relations in industrial society. To understand the attitudes and adjustments of informants to an aged role, it is necessary to look at their pre-existing patterns of social interaction.

There are other reasons why people differ in their adjustment to old age. It is necessary to examine the history of peer relationships in different residential settings to determine under what conditions, and through what processes age provides, or fails to provide, a basis for community formation. In a later section of this chapter, I assess the contribution of the social milieu to successful role adjustment of the elderly and concentrate on the issue of how the social environment may further, or hinder, role definition. The histories of peer relationships in two different residential settings are contrasted: an all-Jewish working class estate in Leeds, England, with a high-rise, low-income building for the elderly in Cleveland, Ohio. The Leeds housing has engendered a community of interdependent elderly with a sense of self-identity. The contrary is the case in Cleveland. Community life failed to develop here, and many of the residents remain uncertain and isolated and are outsiders to organized activities. The purpose is not to furnish psychological explanations of why various individuals do or do not participate in either residence. Rather I examine the factors leading to the greater success of the Leeds community and attempt to determine whether life in a successful community does add to the sense of well-being and self-esteem of the residents.

2.1   Field Sites and Methodology: Cleveland

The data on which this paper is based derives from three years of comparative anthropological field-work among similar groups of elderly Jewish residents in Cleveland, Ohio, and Leeds, England. The first sample of informants is selected from among the Cleveland Jewish elderly, who live in an integrated suburb in a neighborhood called Cornell.[1] These people are in their mid-70s and early 80s. They came to the neighborhood when they were over 60 years of age, after having moved many other times during their lives.

In the 1960's, elderly Jews found Cornell a desirable place to live. This area provided a refuge from older, deteriorating neighborhoods. Rents were comparatively low, and there was a variety of housing in the large three-story apartment buildings on the side streets, or above the shops along the avenue. Public transportation, a synagogue, and Kosher meat and poultry markets were within walking distance. Cornell was a "Jewish neighborhood," with Jewish people and Jewish shops.

Over the past ten years, however, residents witnessed many changes in Cornell. In the mid-1960s, conditions began to deteriorate. Few neighborhood residents had extra cash, and local businesses had difficulty surviving. Many of the merchants were old and decided not to relocate in new neighborhoods. The small markets closed. The bakery shops, fresh produce, and fish shops were gone, and only two Kosher butchers remained.

At the same time, university students began to move into this "gray, shabby" neighborhood. Many found the large suites with low rents suitable for a communal life-style. Landlords discovered that they could ask higher rent without making repairs from these new tenants than they could from older residents. "Head shops"—which catered to a young clientele and sold leather goods, candles, incense, etc.—opened to replace the older Jewish stores.

When low-income housing for the elderly was built in other parts of Cleveland, many older Cornell residents seized the opportunity to escape.[2] As the reputation of the neighborhood as a place for hippies and drugs grew, the more affluent moved to better areas further east. The synagogue was sold. Many other old people passed away. Gradually the number of elderly residents in Cornell declined. By the early 1970s, only a few old people were left in each apartment building. The informants in this study chose to remain.

In 1974, the Cornell neighborhood was slated for urban renewal, and a low-income, high-rise apartment structure was built for the elderly. For many neighborhood residents, this new building offered a desirable solution. They could move into a clean, new apartment in the area they knew, and many were eligible for rent supplements. Fifty percent of the initial applicants to the high-rise were Cornell residents. Also elderly people living in other parts of Cleveland decided to move to Caroll Arms.[3] Presently 70 percent of the occupants of this new building are Jewish, helping to make Cornell a "Jewish area" again.

2.2 Leeds

In the autumn of 1974, a comparative study of a similar group of elderly Jewish people in Leeds, England, was conducted. In the late 1950s, many of the older members of the Leeds Jewish working-class community remained in the same neighborhoods where they had been living for the past 25-35 years. Gentiles had moved into these older neighborhoods of back-to-back houses as the younger and more upwardly mobile Jews moved further north. At this time, the Leeds City Corporation was beginning urban renewal programs and some of these older neighborhoods were slated to be torn down.

The Leeds Jewish Welfare Board was anxious to prevent the dispersal of aged Jews and to reunite families which had been separated geographically. They also wished to provide improved accommodations for people living in dilapidated housing where a number of families had to share outdoor toilet facilities. In 1956, with a grant from the Leeds Corporation, the Jewish Welfare Board built the Knightsdale Housing Estate[4] in a developing Jewish section of Leeds. Tenants saw it as a desirable place to retire where they could be near children and family. Thus many of the elderly, working-class Jews in Leeds had been living on the Knightsdale Estate for almost twenty years when this study was undertaken.

3. The History of the Impact Of Kin and Friends on Role Adjustment

Among elderly Jews living in Cleveland and Leeds, two different reactions to old age are found. The group from Cleveland is lonely and uncertain, afraid they are no longer needed. They are apprehensive about asking for favors from adult children, afraid they will be resented. Competition and caution characterize their social relationships, and friends are used to bolster a desired self-image. In contrast, the group from Leeds, England, is content and confident. They are accepting of family and old friends whose regular companionship they enjoy. Their lives closely mesh ideal values and actual behavior. Cleveland and Leeds children both provide a relatively similar set of services for their aged parents. They assist in illness, give financial help, telephone and visit regularly, and demonstrate concern. The crucial difference, however, lies in the perceptions of informants. Why?

In analyzing this data, four factors emerge which help the aged person to readjust to role changes throughout the life cycle. These variables are: (1) the quality of earlier relationships within their family of orientation; (2) the presence of life-long, intimate friends; (3) the shared life-styles of-aged parents and adult children; and (4) the quality of the residential environment where they settle in old age. First we examine the three background factors as they relate to old age adjustment, and then assess the contribution of the present residential milieu to successful role adjustment.

3.1. Cleveland

The Cornell elderly arrived in Cleveland as part of the influx of Eastern-European Jews and other immigrant people between 1905 and 1912. During this seven-year period, the total number of Jews in Cleveland increased from 25,000 to 75,000. Immigrants were young people in their teens and early twenties, many of whom—because of poverty or broken homes—had to leave behind parents or siblings. Informants settled near maternal relatives (primarily collateral) in overcrowded, impoverished, and ethnically mixed neighborhoods. But these aunts and uncles did not become true surrogate parents, so that the young immigrants were denied a possible role-model and the anticipatory socialization experience of learning from elderly parents as they aged. Memories remain frozen at the time informants left Europe. Undoubtedly, many mythologize about what their relations with their parents might have been, and they incorporate an idealized Eastern-European code of respect and reverence as part of what they wish from their children.

Informants found employment in clothing factories or neighborhood workshops and businesses, while their spouses worked as hucksters, painters, subway drivers, or milkmen. There were few opportunities for economic advancement available to these immigrants. The socio-economic composition of the older Jewish neighborhoods had changed and could no longer support marginal businesses. The more well-to-do Jews had abandoned these areas, and the newcomers were forced to rely on the reluctant patronage of other ethnic groups.

From its inception, an ecological pattern was established for Cleveland Jewish neighborhoods which has continued until the present. This pattern is marked by the rapid and frequent migration of people through neighborhoods, with the resulting dispersion of the Jewish community. Informants lived in heterogeneous neighborhoods, worked in different areas from where they resided, and moved often—usually every five years. Only during the brief, relatively stable residential period after their arrival in America, and during their first years of marriage, did a few informants make one or two close friends. Unfortunately, most of these relationships did not survive the next move. Denied a constant environment, they were never able to build up a stable repertoire of exchanges with neighbors and friends. Informants first relied on family members to whom they turned for moral support and economic assistance. As their own families grew up, these informants continued to focus on kin, but transferred their involvement with relatives to a concern with children and grandchildren. Their social relationships rarely extended beyond the family. Unhappily for the parents, their adult children—as they became more affluent—moved to the suburbs. These suburbs attracted the native-born, wealthier Jews, who had abandoned the Yiddish-speaking, Orthodox *shuls* for Conservative and Reform synagogues.

When informants moved to Cornell at age sixty, their own middle-aged children were moving to the suburbs. Furthermore, this move was accompanied by role uncertainties. Parents were no longer asked for advice or financial assistance, nor were they regularly informed of family affairs. Often they do not understand or accept these changes. Informants say that their children no longer treat them as they once did, yet they are not clear how things should be. Many are uncertain how these status changes affect their relationships with children and to what extent they, themselves, may have been instrumental in bringing about these changes. Most informants have abandoned the reciprocal exchanges which characterized their earlier relationships with children. They now have little left—such as offers of material assistance, counsel, or even moral support, etc.—with much to initiate new exchanges, or to continue transactions which allow them to negotiate role changes and to more easily define their roles.

Uncertain of their status, which they must redefine vis-a-vis their ever-changing social milieu, Cornell informants use the attributes and accomplishments of their offspring and the services children perform for them as criteria in establishing status relationships with new neighbors. They try to convey an idealized image of intergenerational relations to bolster their own uncertain position. Informants do not dare to share with peers the strains in their relations with children, nor to admit disappointment. Most of their peer relationships are with associates, whom they see in the local neighborhood or at the Jewish Center. These relationships are limited; contact is rarely continued at home and peers do not know each other's children. Informants are thus in an opportune position to present only the image of themselves which they wish to convey. Even when old friends discuss loneliness, they are never totally open. Parents publicly excuse their children's failing toward them and cover their own feelings of dissatisfaction. This concealment works to perpetuate the myth of ideal children and the belief that other people have better family relationships. Hence, contact with friends increases their feelings of dejection; furthermore, it also prevents them from gaining insight into the family relations of others and from defining realistically their own status position and their relations with adult children. They cannot adjust their expectations to what is possible and probable. Their negotiations with children are blocked by their unrealistic expectations. This competition and jealousy also inhibit the development of friendships among peers in the Cornell neighborhood. Here it might be suggested that the earlier kinship experience of Cornell informants in their own families of orientation—where relationships were characterized by ambivalence and tension, or by mythologizing what relations with their elderly parents in Europe may have been—probably influences their present-day relationships with their own adult children. These interactions with family, in turn, may inhibit their ability to develop further intimate transactions with friends.

3.2. Leeds

Leeds informants share in many ways a similar background with Cornell Jews, yet their experience was different in some significant ways which helped them avoid role confusion and feelings of rejection. The contrast illustrates the hypothesis that the number of close friendships people are able to sustain throughout their life is crucial in the adjustment to new roles in old age.

The Leeds Jewish community is almost exclusively a product of Russian and Polish immigration. The Jews arrived between 1880 and 1905, before the passage of the Alien Act, and sought employment in the clothing trade, the staple industry in Leeds for the past hundred years. The economic and social structure of the city produced a different pattern of mobility and social relationships than in Cleveland.

Leeds Jews were a homogeneous group with similar socio-economic and religious background. They lived closely together, bound by overlapping relationships and ties of mutual assistance. This common history has worked to minimize the uncertainty of an individual's relative social status in the community. The stable, kin-based nature of Leeds neighborhood life contrasts strongly with the more mobile, economically segregated, and dispersed Jewish community of Cleveland.

Unlike Cornell people, Leeds informants benefitted from being raised by their parents and from growing up within family units. They continued contact with their parents, and renegotiated relationships with them as they aged. Informants derived a sense of family indentification and assuredness in kinship relationships from these experiences, which they transferred to their children. The socio-economic position and life-style of elderly parents and adult children has also remained relatively similar, and children continue to follow an Orthodox way of life. Disparities in residence, wealth, and religion do not divide Jewish families in Leeds as they do in Cornell.

Neighborhood life in Leeds is relatively stable and homogeneous. Changing neighborhoods did not wrench family members apart. This constancy of environment allowed for the development of exchanges with kin, neighbors, and friends which served to define the status of informants. Many informants lived in the same district, and even in the same house, for 35 or 45 years before moving into their present location at the Knightsdale Housing Estate. Not only did informants live near parents, siblings, and *landsmen,* but long-standing relations with neighbors developed into intimate and enduring friendships. These friendships provided a source of comfort during difficult times, when women exchanged child care, groceries, and emotional support.

Today these long-standing reciprocal exchanges with neighbors and kin have been maintained, and informants still discuss family problems with old friends who know their children well. They are able to assess their own status and the behavior of their children in comparison with that of their friends. They learn what is reasonable to expect from adult children, and they can adjust their expectations to conform to reality, rather than to an unrealistic ideal. This adjustment of expectation helps them to adapt their own behavior and to accept their changed status in their relations with children.

With this certainty of status and acceptance of an aged role, Leeds informants can build additional companionship among peers, who supplement the assistance of old friends in making adjustments to role changes and in overcoming loneliness. In Leeds, the location of housing for the elderly in close proximity to the homes of family members, as well as the placement of the day center at the housing project, work to produce "multiplex relations," which further reduce the disparity between ideal expectations and actual relationships.

4. Community, Socialization, and Mental Health

Anthropological and sociological studies on aging support a policy encouraging age-segregated housing for the elderly. Such residences are designed to foster new social relationships which stimulate participation, morale, and self-esteem and counteract loneliness and isolation. For example, in Rosow's recent discussion of the weak processes of socialization and of the devalued position of the elderly, he suggests the concentration of socially similar older persons within local residential settings as an alternative to facilitate socialization to new aged roles and to raise the self-esteem of the elderly (Rosow 1974). For these proposals to be effective, old people must be anchored in peer groups which are homogeneous in age, social class, race, ethnicity, and marital status, and these concentrations must be large enough to insulate the elderly from conflicting external norms and definitions. Within these residential settings, cohesive peer groups develop which provide a positive reference point for the members.

In a later empirical study, Ross examines Rosow's proposals and specifies further conditions which encourage socialization and the development of a peer community of the elderly (Ross 1977). Her examination of the process of community creation provides a valuable framework for analyzing and evaluating the various conditions under which the elderly form, or fail to form, community. Like Rosow, Ross also sees homogeneity as an essential background factor, but expands the scope of age-sameness to include sex, previous residence, occupation, political affiliation, region of origin, and religious preferences, in addition to those attributes detailed above. Other prerequisites are the lack of alternatives perceived to living in the new residence and the investment in/and irreversibility of the decision. Also important are a minimization of material differences in life-style, the presence of individuals with leadership skills, and a size small enough for face-to-face relationships to develop. The physical setting should provide ease of mobility and public visibility, which promote social contact and an awareness of social homogeneity. The residents must also feel independence from staff. The present research suggests that the freedom of tenants to engage in decision-making, to organize their own activities, and to oppose staff policies, is crucial to the development of community. This point is developed later.

If these basic background factors are provided, the conditions are right for the development of new patterns of social relations and the emergence of a distinct social organization. For example, residents should begin to participate in community-wide events and decision-making. The more tenants share in these activities within the residence rather than with outsiders, the stronger their attachment and the greater their sense of interdependence with fellow tenants. An involvement in communal unpaid work also promotes this sense of group involvement. Over time, strong ties and interdependence should develop inside the emerging community, and the immediate social situation should become a major source of prestige, with new group symbols and internal sources of status.

Basic to the arguments of both Rosow and Ross is the idea that the development of a successful community aids the adjustment of the elderly, and that this new peer group facilitates socialization to new aged roles. In the following section, we explore the adjustment of the elderly to an aged role and concentrate specifically on the impact of the residential setting on furthering, or hindering, role adjustment. Two different residential settings are compared, and the history of each estate is described in order to investigate the reasons why one became an active community while the other did not. In discussing under what conditions and through what processes age provides, or fails to provide, a basis for community creation, we follow the comparative framework delineated by Ross (see above).

4.1. The Knightsdale Estate and The Caroll Arms: Contrast in Mood

The general feeling on the Leeds Knightsdale Estate is of active, involved people leading independent lives. In discussing their reasons for moving to the Estate, no informants ever spoke regretfully of their decision. Tenants proudly invite visitors to see their flats. On one occasion, I was present when a relatively new tenant was encouraging a single man, whose mother had just passed away, to move to the Estate. She explained that while she had privacy and freedom to lead her own life as a single woman, she was not alone when she needed neighborly assistance, and noted the concerned telephone calls and offers of grocery shopping when she was ill with the flu. She recommended it as a desirable place to live. Similarly, those with varied interests and leadership skills find a wide range of activities to be involved with. By living on the Knightsdale Estate, these individuals build their own independent sense of status and self-respect, and their leadership skills and involvements provide a structure enabling others to participate.

In contrast, many of Cleveland's Caroll Arms residents seem uncertain, isolated, and apprehensive. One woman is angry with her children for forcing her to move out of her spacious suite into the smaller Caroll Arms apartment. Another hoped that the clean, new building would be an inducement for children and grandchildren to visit more often, but this wish has not materialized. Some residents attend Sunday afternoon entertainment and town-meetings as much out of fear of the manager noting their presence or absence, as out of interest. Their own involvement continues to be mainly at the Jewish Center, or with other synagogue organizations where they were members before they moved to the Arms. They do not serve on committees or volunteer for activities which would help them to get to know their new neighbors better.

4.2. Leeds

In 1956 the members of the Leeds Jewish Welfare Board proposed a Jewish Housing Estate. Their aim was to provide accommodations for members of the Jewish community living in the older, deteriorating sections of the city, and to strengthen Jewish family life by bringing elderly parents to live near children and grandchildren. A comprehensive physical and social service plan underlay the construction and management of the Knightsdale Estate. A location was chosen in Medina,[5] a desirable Jewish section of Leeds. Here are located the synagogues, religious schools, social clubs, and Kosher butchers.

Social service personnel, who are employed by the Jewish Welfare Board, selected prospective tenants according to need and capabilities. All applicants were visited in their homes and were assisted in moving or in purchasing new furniture or household goods, if necessary. Today this system of social welfare remains an integral part of the management of the Estate. Applicants are still interviewed by social workers and are assisted in applying for supplementary benefits. Social service personnel are also available to handle emergencies or to recommend that an ill tenant receive meals-on-wheels. Informants who are beginning to fail physically express a feeling of security. They are confident that if they need assistance to remain independent and in their homes, that this help will be provided. Many tenants, for example, have a home-helper who comes once a fortnight to help them clean their flats. When necessary, this woman will accompany them to shop or to fetch a pension check.

The construction of the Estate also evidences planning and foresight. Flats were built in units of four, and two tenants share a common entrance. With their small gardens and closeness to neighbors, these homes have a similar feeling to the row-houses where informants used to live. There is also enough room to entertain children for meals, or even to accommodate weekend guests. Many new groups of flats, as well as a communal hall—where the synagogue and day center are now located—have been added since the original construction. When the Estate was built, a small parade of shops, including a green-grocer and a Kosher butcher, were included as part of the original scheme. There are also a variety of shops at Medina Corner, which is a ten-minute walk or a short bus ride away.

Over the years, the number of units on the Knightsdale Estate has grown. Today there are over two hundred flats, housing 310 residents. New units with special facilities for the frail elderly are being added. Rents have risen because the Estate is classified as a Housing Association and must meet government fair-rent standards. Many residents, however, are eligible for rent supplements and receive benefits to help pay rent and heating bills. While the initial aim of the Estate was to rehouse "people of necessitous means," who lived in deplorable conditions, this goal has been largely met. Applications are now being made by elderly people who live in areas isolated from other Jews, or from those who have sold homes but still lack adequate capital to purchase a new flat. There are long waiting lists. Originally there were a number of families with young children on the Estate, but these youngsters have grown up and moved away. The family home is still occupied by their aging parents, however. Many husbands have passed away. Thus the character of the Estate has gradually changed over the past twenty years and now houses many elderly widows who live alone. Recently, however, there has been an effort to diversify the residents, and a few young families are being encouraged to move in.

Informants moved to the Knightsdale when they were in their late 50s and early 60s. Many had an ill spouse who could no longer climb stairs, others had lost a husband and the family home was too large for them to manage alone, or their house was slated to be torn down by the Corporation. A number of the first residents were purposely selected for their leadership skills, and they were encouraged to form a tenants' association.

The tenants' organization set up social, religious, and welfare committees. A synagogue was established, voluntary visitors called on sick neighbors, and the social committee hosted bingo and card evenings, as well as day trips. Today these activities are still run and managed by the tenants' committee. Through these functions, tenants became acquainted with other new neighbors, and many residents developed a sense of involvement and commitment to the Estate. Today, fifteen years later, informants still serve on these committees and remain actively involved. Many say that now they would no longer join as they are too old, but they remain and serve because they are used to the work and enjoy the sociability.

One community-building activity on the Estate is the Knightsdale Synagogue. Services are held on all Jewish holidays and every Friday night and Sabbath morning. While two younger men from the Leeds community assist in leading the more difficult portions of the prayers, the organizational work is done by the synagogue committee. The Knightsdale Synagogue is managed differently from other Leeds synagogues which reward their wealthy, generous members with the honor of being called up to read from the Scriptures. On the Knightsdale, in contrast, an effort is made to promote a sense of equality and involvement among male congregants. The leaders try to honor every man present and to call them up to read by using their Jewish names. A particular attempt is made to involve new worshippers and to make them feel welcome.

In addition, a *kiddish* is held at the Knightsdale Synagogue every Saturday morning after the service. Here the worshippers have an opportunity to share a glass of wine and to wish one another a "good Sabbath." The women on the synagogue committee prepare the tables, and this shared work is a source of friendship. The wine is pledged by the tenants each year at the time of the Jewish New Year, and the cake is supplied by the person who volunteers to host the *kiddish* that week, usually to honor the memorial of a relative. Prayer books are donated in honor of a deceased husband or parent.

Not only do the synagogue services help to foster a feeling of community, involvement, and service among the tenants, but—like the card evenings, Friendship Club, Ladies' Aid Society, and the day-center activities, which are all held in the communal hall—they encourage the formation of new friendships and allow tenants to view one another in a variety of capacities. Not only do neighbors live next door, but residents also meet while shopping or collecting pension checks, and they go on vacation together, in addition to associating at social and religious activities. Many cross-cutting ties bind them together. The geographic lay-out of the Estate is such that housing patterns work to reinforce social homogeneity with physical intimacy. Fuller knowledge of fellow residents is fostered by the physical layout of the Estate.

As mentioned, there are a variety of housing styles on the Knightsdale. In each section, people are grouped closely together with neighbors. Tenants walk to the communal hall for religious services and social programs. Residents can observe or talk to neighbors through their kitchen or living room windows, or they can easily go out to talk with someone passing by. This ability to watch what is going on outside helps residents to feel socially involved. By carefully observing what their neighbors do, tenants gain a fuller knowledge of each other's social routines. They can see how often their children come to visit and how long they stay. The Estate is located in the heart of the Jewish community, and informants and children can call on one another easily. The move to the Knightsdale thus helped to foster a continuation of the close family interaction informants had known in their previous neighborhoods. Its location works to support already existing family ties and helps elderly parents to remain closely involved in family activities.

Although some residents on the Knightsdale were acquainted from the old Jewish neighborhoods where they had grown up or worked together, they had never lived together under the conditions of the Estate and new relationships had to be established. Tenants developed friendships with neighbors, who supplement the support they receive from old friends. These new neighbor-friends help one another to adjust to new situations, such as widowhood, and to overcome loneliness. Not only do these neighbor-friends offer companionship and emotional support, but they also do favors for each other. A strict code of reciprocity governs these exchanges, however. Many tenants realize that as they get older, they may have to rely more on neighbors and they recognize the need to forge new relationships as a type of social insurance. Utilizing this code of reciprocity, they initiate kindnesses in order to create good will, and even indebtedness. Thus there is a code of proper, expectable behavior on the Knightsdale, and peer pressure fosters conformity. Neighbors are concerned with what others think of them and are careful of their reputations.

Many tenants try to fight loneliness by keeping occupied, by making new friends on the Estate, and by serving others. They try not to depend on the social service activities offered at the day center, but instead assume a service role as voluntary helpers. With this code of service, involvement, and independence, they volunteer at the day center as well as in other charitable activities, such as the tenants' committees and the ladies' welfare society. Nonetheless, the day center activities and lunch program represent an unspoken source of security. They are there if residents need them.

Informants can also rely on government transport to take them to a hospital appointment or for physical therapy. Doctors will make house calls. Socialized medicine saves large bills for doctors' fees, medication, and eye glasses, as well as the difficulty and embarrassment of filling out Medicaid and Medicare forms. Also, some of the flats have a night-watch person on duty who can be called by pressing a bell near the bed.

Thus the socio-economic and ethnic homogeneity of the tenant population, their long-standing service on committees, the community-forming functions of the synagogue, the physical plan allowing for easy access to and observation of neighbors, the feeling of security from social service supports, all work to encourage multiplex social relationships, participation, and high morale, and to combat isolation and loneliness. The location of the Estate fosters contact with children and old friends, and thus assists continued self-definition and adjustment to an aged role, as well as the confidence to initiate reciprocal exchanges with neighbors and new friends. The Knightsdale Estate functions as a community itself, as well as a sub-community within the larger Leeds Jewish community.

4.3. Cornell

In contrast to the Leeds Estate, the Cornell high-rise was sponsored by a non-sectarian organization and given zoning-board approval as a desirable urban renewal project. No effort was made by the builders to devise a comprehensive physical and social service plan, nor to provide extra services needed by a large, elderly population. The Caroll Arms is a residence for the elderly, but it has not yet become an integral part of the neighborhood or the larger Jewish community, nor have the tenants coalesced to form a community.

In 1974, the Caroll Arms was constructed for a group of elderly persons different from that it now serves. The builders approached the Musicians' Union to sponsor a high-rise residence for the elderly. The Cornell site, where single family homes were located, was selected by the Union because of its accessibility to the Cleveland concert hall, its relatively low price, and because it was located in a "Jewish neighborhood" and many members of the Cleveland Musicians' Union are Jewish. Nonetheless, only a very small percentage of the present occupants are elderly musicians; the majority of residents are Jews over the age of 65. Because of accessible shopping and transportation, the neighborhood was a good choice for a residence for the elderly, but extra services, such as medical and religious facilities, were neither provided nor encouraged.

The Cornell high-rise building for the elderly is composed of a relatively homogeneous group of 250 residents. Between 75 and 80 percent of the tenants are widowed Jewish women. (The remainder are of Black or Eastern-European origin.) While there is not the additional identity of common social class, occupation, and region of origin that unifies the Knightsdale residents, most tenants do share a similarity of ethnicity, marital status, sex, religion, and the cultural tradition of having lived in the same older Cleveland Jewish neighborhoods. Although the social distinctions of the larger Jewish community, such as wealth, education level, or family connection stratify the residents, all tenants share the common condition of renting a one-bedroom apartment in a building where income is restricted to $6,500 a year.

Tenants moved to the Caroll Arms for a variety of reasons. Many wanted to maintain their independence, but were lonely and craved the company of peers their own age. There were no longer companions in their old buildings, and rents were being raised. Others had children who wanted them to live in a clean, new apartment and arranged for them to move. Many specifically chose to live in an integrated community in preference to a predominantly Black suburb. Residents are keenly aware that there are more expensive and prestigious buildings in newer Jewish neighborhoods. Many feel that their friends look down on the Caroll Arms as an undesirable place to live, because of its location and because it is a low income, senior-citizen building. Nonetheless, they are resigned that this is their home and that they will not move again.

Not only do status factors operative among Cleveland Jews continue to exert pressure on Caroll Arms residents, but previous social activities and relationships are also continued. Identity within the building is confined to a small group rather than to the tenant body. Traditional neighborhood patterns continue. Cornell residents were among the first to move into the Caroll Arms. Many are foreign-born and frail, and chose apartments on the first and second floors. In the evenings, they gather in each other's apartments to talk and gossip, just as they were accustomed to visit on the stoops in the summer. Although they assist with the shopping when someone is ill, there is competition and back-biting among these neighbors, and a member may be ostracized when hostilities develop.

Other former Cornell residents also continue their usual organizational activities and weekend luncheons outside of the building. Some were already acquainted with a few other tenants who also moved into the Arms from other areas. These acquaintances did not intensify with proximity, however. Instead, relationships are maintained at a distance. Neighbors prefer to talk on the telephone or to visit while getting their mail, rather than to chat in one another's apartments.

The physical environment, with its absence of easily accessible medical facilities, makes day-to-day living more difficult for Caroll residents than for Leeds informants. One of the most difficult tasks is getting to the doctor. Many of the physicians have moved their offices to the more prestigious medical buildings in the eastern suburbs. These centers are located at the confluence of major throughways, and are easily accessible only to people who drive cars. It might take a Cornell resident three changes of bus and a minimum of three hours just to get to a doctor's appointment! Some informants ask their children to drive them, but for the follow-up visit, they take a taxicab or put off going. Other residents also need assistance with shopping and cleaning, and again feel guilty about troubling children. Thus Cornell informants lack the assuredness that Leeds informants gain through socialized medicine and the program of home-help.

In other important ways the Caroll Arms is not linked with the surrounding neighborhood. Unlike Leeds—where the communal hall serves as a meeting place for the Leeds Friendship Club and day center, which bring other elderly to the Estate—the assembly room is reserved only for Caroll Arms events. When the building was first opened, for example, the Jewish social service agencies asked to sponsor a drop-in center for neighborhood elderly, but their request was denied. Although the Jewish Federation is permitted to conduct religious services at Caroll Arms on important Jewish holidays, the infrequency of these observations does not encourage continuous contact between Caroll Arms residents and neighborhood Jews to build a new community based on religious worship.

The Jewish Center remains the meeting place for many Cornell elderly and is where most informants spend their days. Because of its programming, the Center is a competitor with the Caroll Arms. On Sunday afternoon, when both institutions sponsor a special event, the rivalry is apparent. There is little cooperation between the Caroll Arms management and social service agencies to give assistance and support to needy tenants. Thus the kind of integration of residence, activities, and social services that help to make the Knightsdale Estate a community—by creating an atmosphere where residents get to know one another in a variety of capacities, and have a strong sense of security that they will be assisted to remain independently in their flats for as long as possible—is lacking at the Caroll Arms. The Cornell high-rise was not built as part of a strongly integrated neighborhood, but was constructed as an urban-renewal effort, thereby further destroying a potential community. The manager discourages indentification with the neighborhood, and has avoided affiliation with neighborhood, religious, and civic organizations.

In addition to the continuation of activities outside the residence, another possible factor inhibiting the development of community is the controlling hand of the manager. Although minor status differences also separate Leeds Jews, participation in decision-making and community-wide events has worked to override these distinctions and to allow the development of a new social organization unique to the Estate. Such is not the case in Cleveland.

Even before the official opening of the Caroll Arms, the manager[6] set a pattern of intimidation that frightened the elderly and stiffled initiative and self-reliance. The word passed in the neighborhood that he did not like old people who are ill. Many left their canes behind when they came to apply. Others were apprehensive about receiving necessary rent supplements, as a certain number were being reserved for retired musicians.

Also, other occasions existed during which the elderly were again intimidated. After the building was opened, new furniture was purchased for the lobby. At a town-meeting the manager asked the tenants, "How many of you think the Caroll Arms is an old home?" "How many of you want to live in an old home?" "Picture the lobby of an old home with everyone sitting in a straight line talking to one another, or themselves." He said he did not want the Arms to look this way, and had ordered the new furniture "to make a good impression or to sit on only while you're waiting to be picked up, not all day long." "If I had wanted people to sit in the lobby, I did not need this new furniture. I could have ordered benches, or better yet, rockers for everyone." In these statements, the manager emphasized the negative image of elderly people as sedentary and unproductive. The frightening comparison of the Caroll Arms to an old home reinstilled the fear that elderly, unwell people are not wanted. This perception was reinforced on numerous occasions when the manager ordered senile or chronically ill people to move out immediately, or when tenants were repeatedly told that there were no plans for a resident nurse or even for a railing in the elevator. People are also not allowed to congregate in the lobby;[7] office personnel ask groups who sit there to move.

The manager of the Caroll Arms seems to desire a smooth-running residence for well-elderly tenants, who continue their involvements in the larger society. He uses "town-meetings" and Sunday afternoon entertainment to set this policy, to calm tenant fears, and to minimize complaints. Unfortunately these events are often marked by an atmosphere of intimidation or impatience, which lowers the confidence of residents and plays upon their dependent position. Phrases such as "a few rotten apples" are used to characterize those who are dissatisfied. Individuals are singled out as complainers if they publicly raise embarrassing issues. There is no resident manager in the building, nor is there any intermediary body between the manager and the tenants who can negotiate about complaints or problems. Only a secretary is on duty from nine to five.

Tenants have not been able to organize in opposition to managerial policies, nor to participate in decision-making. Whenever a few residents discuss policy issues and security, or even question how money is being spent, management finds out about their conversations. Residents fear that building personnel, and even some fellow tenants, are a "direct line" to the manager and report gossip. On public occasions, energetic people with leadership potential are personally praised by the manager and are thus publicly bound to his camp. Here the manager effectively thwarts the natural evolution of a status hierarchy based on responsibility and leadership within the building by choosing and rewarding his own leaders. His administrative secretary organized all committees, and the manager selected or confirmed people to head many of these activities. There are no elections. Leadership energy is thus siphoned off and channelled as the manager desires.

The effectiveness of these techniques at discouraging tenant opposition was proven when two administrative personnel were fired without the residents' knowledge. A petition-campaign was proposed to retain the assistant manager, to improve building security, and to form a tenants' union. One spokesperson—who offered potential leadership because he is a relatively young man and a retired musician—eventually backed off from leading the petition drive. He feared reprisals from the manager, who might ask him to move, and worried that he did not have the support of his peers. Residents were reluctant to join his campaign, saying, "I'm only a greener," or remarking that their English was not good or their personalities not dynamic or forward enough. Almost everyone feared working too hard and becoming ill. "The lazy ones are smart, they live longer." (Other residents were unwilling to support the action, believing that it is the sole right of management to decide who should be employed in the building. Still others did not want to become involved with fellow tenants. They believe that to pay their rent is sufficient.) The petition was never circulated.

Ironically, on one occasion when the manager's position was at risk, the residents did take united action—but to support him! An uncomplimentary article appeared on the front page of the local paper specifically about the manager of Caroll Arms. The reporter said HUD officials were displeased with his "unacceptable performance" as the manager of another federally-subsidized building, and that his continued position as manager of Caroll Arms was uncertain. Among other things, he was criticized for spending insufficient time in the other building. Despite the fact that this complaint could be applied to his management of the Arms, three women circulated a petition praising the manager's compassion and fine job. One hundred and twenty-seven tenants signed the petition. Many residents later confided that they signed the petition because the manager is Jewish and they wanted to support a fellow Jew. Others felt that if the manager were fired, HUD might replace him with a Black manager. Still others were concerned that if the manager remained and did not see their name on the petition, then he might take punitive action against them.

Sunday afternoon entertainment works as a type of "bread and circuses" to keep the residents happy and involved. The programs are planned and directed by the manager, who acts as the master of ceremonies. He puts on a very impressive afternoon. On many occasions, a large band and singer perform and the manager leads the tenants in singing old-time favorites. But these events—like the bi-weekly bingo games and seasonal holiday parties—involve limited initiative or active participation on the part of the residents. They have little opportunity to mingle and to meet their neighbors in new capacities.

To summarize this comparison of the Leeds and Cleveland housing experiences, a number of factors emerge as contributing to the failure of community to develop among Cornell residents and in inhibiting further role adjustment among the tenants.

(1) First is the already-discussed failure of many residents to establish a workable self-definition. Competition and concealment continue to keep neighbors apart, and discourage the development of interdependent networks which would provide support and assuredness. Previous relations with kin and friends thus must be included among the background factors necessary for the emergence of community (Keith 1980a).

(2) Second is the authoritarian nature of the manager, who keeps decision-making in his own hands and discourages opposition to his policies.[8] In contrast to Leeds, where tenants were encouraged to form a tenants' association and to participate in the management of the Estate, public decisions are made and activities planned and coordinated solely by the Caroll Arms manager. The threat of eviction and the fear that conversations are reported keeps tenants in a frightened position and thwarts attempts to form a tenants' union. The few leaders who did step forward in opposition to management felt that their fellow residents would not stand with them, and they were unwilling to go it alone. Here earlier feelings of competitiveness, status distinctions, and a lack of trust and self-esteem blocked concerted action.

(3) Third is the fact that an internal status system based on unpaid work, responsibility, and decision-making has not evolved among the tenants. One reason is the manipulation by the manager, who singles out individuals for praise and then arbitrarily drops them from favor. Those with leadership skills are asked to head committees, instead of being

elected by their fellow tenants. The few women who voluntarily organize building parties or who serve food at special events are praised by their peers as "wonderful," but it is felt that these are thankless tasks, which they can do because they are still young and strong. These creative people have devised ways to serve others within the authoritarian structure of Caroll Arms. But unlike the Leeds Estate, where the efforts of the leaders have created an organizational structure which involves the administrative talents and decison-making skills of other residents, most of the efforts of Arms volunteers serve only themselves, and cannot build a permanent edifice where others can develop their own status and self-esteem.[9] There are virtually no heroes, leaders, couples, or workers who have evolved as symbols of a Caroll Arms way of life and who act as role-models for desirable conduct in old age.

The second reason why a new status hierarchy and alternative reward system based on voluntary, unpaid work has not developed within the Caroll Arms is the fact that residents continue to participate in activities and organizations outside of the building. Residence, programming, and social service support are not part of one estate, as in Leeds. Tenants volunteer their time and skills elsewhere. External sources of status—such as wealth, appearance, and health, etc.—remain relevant. Residents feel that their friends look down on Caroll Arms as an inferior place to live, like a nursing-home or an orphanage, where people of one age group live together. Although there is some interdependence and shared help, a distinct social organization and a "we-feeling" have not developed among Caroll Arms residents.

(4) Fourth, the physical plan and social programming do not promote contact and an awareness of social homogeneity. The Caroll Arms is a thirteen-story high-rise building, but there is no communal dining-room or day center. Nor are there balconies, porches, or common rooms on each floor, where neighbors can visit regularly. Although there are communal rooms behind the lobby, few tenants walk the distance to watch TV or play cards. Because of the sedentary nature of the group activities and the limited call on individual initiative and participation, neighbors rarely get to know each other in new roles. Children rarely attend these events. Even at the Jewish religious services held at Caroll Arms, there is limited opportunity for personal participation. Both the High-Holiday and Passover services are led by someone from outside the elderly community. Here it might be desirable to have this religious leader work with the residents to develop a service in which they could actively participate, and thereby increase their sense of leadership and involvement, as in the Leeds Knightsdale Synagogue.

5. Conclusion

In this chapter, the adjustment to old age by two groups of elderly people in different residential settings has been examined. The contrast in adjustment to an aged role between informants in Leeds and Cleveland points out that patterns of aging cannot be summarized in terms of a simple set of variables, such as sex or ethnic background, but rather involve the complex interrelation of many variables.

Four factors were isolated as helping the aged person to readjust to role changes throughout the life cycle. These factors are: (1) the quality of earlier relationships within the family of orientation; (2) the shared life-styles of aged parents and adult children; (3) the presence of life-long, intimate friends; and (4) the quality of the residential environment where they settle in old age. In Leeds, long-term relationships with friends—who lived together in the same neighborhoods when children were growing up—helped the older person to accept and adjust to an aged role. The fact that informants were able to continue to live near kin and friends on the Knightsdale Estate encouraged further adjustment. In Cleveland, because of frequent residential mobility, informants never developed life-long friendships and consequently did not easily adjust to old age. Unlike Leeds, their present housing was built as an urban renewal project aimed at destroying a blighted area, rather than integrating the elderly into a developing community. Involvement with social service agencies and programs was blocked by the management; and residence, programming, and social-service support are not part of one estate, as in the Knightsdale. The paternalistic nature of the manager, who keeps decision-making in his own hands and discourages any opposition to his policies, has also worked to hinder the development of an internal status hierarchy and sense of community within the Caroll Arms.

Community has been defined as a possession of a common territory, "we-feeling," and a social organization unique to a body of individuals (Ross 1977). In Leeds, such a community developed, while in Cornell it failed to evolve. In Leeds, the different skills and capabilities of the residents were encouraged, and role differentiation, interdependence, and a strong sense of self-identity have emerged among the tenants. Leeds informants moved to the Knightsdale having begun a successful adjustment to old age, and the Estate and the development of a successful community further encouraged this process. In Cleveland, informants had difficulty adjusting to their increasing years, and residence at Caroll Arms stunted a possible better adjustment.

Notes

[1]Pseudonym for an inner-core Cleveland suburb where this anthropological research was conducted.

[2]The informants in this study, however, chose purposely to remain in Cornell because of the inexpensive rents, Kosher meat markets, and accessibility to transportation and shopping. They also believed that the new, low-income housing for the elderly was being built in neighborhoods which were deteriorating even more rapidly than Cornell. They felt that they would have more options and better control of their environment if they remained in Cornell.

[3]Pseudonym for a low-income, high-rise apartment building for the elderly located in the Cornell area.

[4]Pseudonym for the Jewish Housing Estate in Leeds.

[5]Pseudonym for a Jewish section of Leeds.

[6]It is useful to compare the manager of Caroll Arms with the manager of the Aliyah Senior Citizens' Center described by Myerhoff (Myerhoff 1978), and to analyze the contrasting environments each has helped to create and their impact on the further adjustment of these two groups of elderly, Eastern-European Jews.

[7]The Caroll Arms has a large lobby with a mail-room in the corridor leading to the elevators. Off of this lobby is a glass-walled office which tenants must pass to go to the communal rooms where bingo, entertainment, and town-meetings are held. The building is thirteen stories high and was constructed in two wings. There are no balconies, porches, or common rooms on each floor where neighbors can visit. Residents do move lawn-chairs outside in the summer, however, and sit together in a large group on the patio.

[8]My findings support the hypothesis—advanced by Kleemeier and also by Fry—that the degree to which social settings for older people are institutions with social control over the residents has a negative relationship to social activity (Kleemeier 1954; Fry 1979).

[9]For a discussion of this point, see the excellent article by Fry (Fry 1979).

6
Women's Age-Set Systems in Africa: The Latuka Of Southern Sudan[1]

David I.Kertzer
and
Oker B. B. Madison

1. Introduction

Age is rivalled only by sex as a universal principle of social differentiation. And just as analysis of sex roles must consider the impact of aging, analysis of the nature of the aging process must consider differences by sex. Males and females age differently, and the social mechanisms each society has to allocate and reallocate roles and statuses to individuals through their life course differ for males and females. In this life course perspective, old age cannot be understood in social isolation, for it represents but one portion of a life-long aging process. The ways in which different societies deal with the elderly is conceptualized as an integral and inseparable part of how the society handles the entire aging process, from birth to death (Riley,Johnson and Foner 1972; Riley 1979).

In looking at the question of sex differences in the aging process, seen cross-culturally, an intriguing riddle is presented by the case of African age-set societies. These societies provide a particularly rich field for the comparative study of aging, for in them age is a formalized principle of social groupings and explicitly regulates the allocation of social roles (Foner and Kertzer 1978, 1979). People join a named group of their coevals during a specific point in their life course, generally by the time of puberty, and ther pass the rest of their life as a member of the group, formally making transi tions through a series of age-graded roles together with their fellow age group members. Note here the distinction made between an *age set* and an *age grade* (Kertzer 1978). An *age set* is an actual group of people who recognize common membership in a named grouping based on common age. Members of an age set generally remain in that same age set throughout their life course. *Age grades*, on the other hand, constitute the strata (e.g., childhood, adolescence, adulthood, old age), each associated with a bundle of social roles. While relatively few societies have age sets, all have age grades, though these latter are more sharply defined in some societies than in others.

Returning to the question of the intersection of age and sex, African age-set societies present us with a particular problem whose solution may shed light on more universal processes of aging. Whereas age-set systems have been described for many African societies, the great majority of these are said to pertain directly only to males. Indeed, in many ethnographic reports, women are totally ignored, with references to "everyone" or "all the youths" signifying only males.[2] In other accounts, while passing mention has been made of female age sets, these have been briefly dismissed as transient and underdeveloped, a mere shadow of male age-set systems.

In this chapter we will try to address the question of how age sets differ for females and why age-set principles have been found so much more commonly to operate among men than among women. While our focus is on a limited number of African societies, as we shall see this question has more universal implications for the asymmetry between the processes of aging among men and women.

2. The Latuka[3]

In order to examine these issues and to contribute to an understanding of the relationship of sex roles to age-set organization, we begin by analyzing the case of women's age sets among the Latuka, an East African society which has not previously been studied in depth.[4] By comparing the operation of women's age sets to that of men's in Latuka society, some points relevant to the larger theoretical issues will be raised. Following this, available data on women's age-set organization in Africa will be analyzed, and an attempt will be made to frame the major theoretical issues and their implications for a theory of aging.

2.1. Social Setting

Numbering over 150,000, the Latuka are the main inhabitants of Torit District, eastern Equatoria, in the Southern Sudan. A majority live in the plain, with a variety of other Latuka-speaking peoples living in the surrounding mountains. Speaking a Nilo-Hamitic language, the Latuka are related to the nearby Bari and Iteso. A sedentary people practicing subsistence agriculture (based on the cultivation of sorghum, millet, groundnuts and maize), they also keep some cattle, goats and sheep. Twenty-four permanent Latuka villages are found in the plain, with each—except the smallest—divided into wards. Both men and women participate in cultivation, with the men responsible for the heaviest tasks, such as clearing virgin fields. Women are responsible for cooking and housekeeping.

The Latuka are outside a money ecomomy and disparities in wealth among the people are minimal. Ritual leadership is provided by the office of Chief (there being two rival chieftaincies, each composed of a number of villages among the plains Latuka) and by the offices of village and ward headman. The villages are largely autonomous politically and economically, and local-level political decision-making resides in the hands of the ruling male age grade, the *Monyemiji* (literally: village-owners).

Tracing descent partrilineally, the people are divided into several exogamous clans, but corporate descent groups are lacking. Marriage is polygynous and largely village endogamous.

2.2. Men's Age Grades and Age Sets

There are four primary men's age grades—*ADURI* (Children), *ADURI-HORWONG* (youths), *MONYEMIJI* (village-owners) and *AMARWAK* (elders). The first, *Aduri,* has no corporate existence. Boys from birth until induction into *Aduri-horwong* (at the age of 15-17) are categorized as *Aduri,* but while charged with various errands by their parents, they are not organized for any collective activity. *Aduri-horwong* consists of youths aged approximately 15-20 years old who are tapped for membership by the ward's *Aduri-horwong.* They perform various tasks as a group on behalf of the ward or village, under the supervision of *Monyemiji.* They also have their own public meeting ground in the ward where they regularly gather.

Monyemiji are the central political and social force of the village, responsible for ensuring the safety and welfare of the ward and the village. Matters of public concern are regularly discussed by *Monyemiji* of the ward in their own central meeting ground (*Amangat*),where decisions are reached and ensuing action coordinated. An individual enters *Monyemiji* at the time of his induction into an age set. Each age set is open approximately seven years, during which time people are individually initiated into it in a ceremony presided over by the ward headman and held in the *Amangat.* These age sets are futher organized into generation sets. To see how this is done it is necessary to explain the custom of *Efira,* a ceremony held every 22 years at the level of the chieftaincy, at which men from many villages

TABLE 6.1

MEN'S AGE-SETS AND AGE GRADES IN LABALWA, 1975

AGE GRADE	AGE SET	WARDS			TOTAL
		IMIRA	FWARA	ANGAUR	
Aduri-horwong (Youths)		(1958-1960) 16,	(1958-1960) 12,	(1958-1960) 5	33
Monyemiji (Ogugu) (Village Owners - Junior Generation)	3rd	(1951-1957) 8,	(1952-1958) 12,	(1952-1957) 4	24
	2nd	(1946-1950) 5,	(1946-1952) 3,	(1948-1951) 4	12
	1st	(1938-1945) 7,	(1936-1945) 10,	(1946-1949) 3	20
Monyemiji (Choho) (Village Owners - Senior Generation)	4th	(1938-1940) 1,	(1938-1939) 4,	(1937-1940) 3	8
	3rd	(1927-1937) 23,	(1927-1937) 3,	(1935-1936) 2	28
	2nd	(1916-1930) 20,	(1918-1925) 6,	(1919-1926) 5	33
	1st		(1913-1919) 2		
Amarwak (Nyong) (Elders)	4th	(1908-1915) 5,	(1912-) 1,	(1910-1915) 3	9
	3rd	(1900-1907) 6			6
TOTAL		91	53	29	173

SOURCE: Census conducted in the village in 1975. Dates in parentheses refer to years of birth of age-set members.

TABLE 6.2

WOMEN'S AGE SETS

WOMEN BORN AND RESIDING IN LABALWA, 1975

IMIRA

Year of Birth	Age Set	#
1898	Ngungusia	1
1900	Tatadang	1
1909-20	Musuru	5
1915-25	Somok	5
1916	Haririk	1
1918-19	Molongo	2
1916-24	Tilu	2
1921-31	Hawanga	7
1922-29	Gala	6
1932-40	Ngadupe	17
1934-39	Ohoyo	2
1938-42	Obeng Hiteng	3
1940-45	Ohiri	14
1946-51	Ibwoyo	27
1951-56	Seniya	21
1959-62	Balu	16
TOTAL IMIRA		127

FWARA

Year of Birth	Age Set	#
1912	Musuru	1
1914-16	Somok	2
1925-35	Tilu	3
1924-32	Hawanga	6
1920-21	Gala	2
1935-40	Ngadupe	3
1937-39	Ohoyo	2
1939-40	Obeng Hiteng	2
1943-45	Ohiri	5
1948-53	Isiak Omina	4
1954-55	Kamsana	8
1956-58	Twuluhuny	4
TOTAL FWARA		43

ANGAUR

Year of Birth	Age Set	#	Age Grade*
1898	Ngungusia	1	
1915	Musuru	1	Amarwak
1920-27	Tilu	3	
1923-28	Tome	2	
1937-38	Hawanga	3	
1915-16	Gala	2	
1937-39	Ngadupe	2	
	Monyemiji		Angoro
1949	Isiak Omina	1	
1951	Ikoto	1	
1952-54	Nyalaba	4	
1958	Kamsana	1	
1960	Hayu	1	Odwo
TOTAL ANGAUR		24	
TOTAL LABALWA		194	

*As transition from one age grade to the next is an individual affair, this indication of age grade division by age set is approximate.

come together. At the time of *Efira,* men who had been members of *Monyemiji* (the "ruling" grade) during the last *Efira* ceremony are retired to *Amarwak* (elder) status. The younger men who had been inducted into *Monyemiji* over the course of the previous 22 years remain in *Monyemiji* and constitute its new senior generation. Over the next 22 years, as new age sets are formed, a junior generation of *Monyemiji* is created (see Table 6:1) Thus—except in the period immediately following *Efira*—there are two generations of age sets in *Monyemiji:* those inducted before the *Efira* rites and those inducted after them. All *Monyemiji* are considered among the rulers of the village, but in fact members of the age sets of the senior generation are the most influential, for it is felt that the junior generation members will one day have their opportunity to rule the village.

Individuals in *Amarwak* (the elders) lack any formal political leadership role; they do not act as a corporate unit. However, they do command respect from their juniors and they are entitled to certain allocations of food (as after a community hunt). Younger members of *Amarwak* continue to be economically active as long as their strength permits. *Amarwak* are also involved in dispute arbitration in the ward, along with members of *Monyemiji.* Disputants bring their case to the central common-ground (*Amangat*), where it is discussed with individuals from *Amarwak* and from the senior age sets of *Monyemiji* who happen to be present.

Men's age sets are based in the ward. However, the village headman designates the name of one of the concurrent age sets to serve as a common age-set name for all of the contemporaneous age sets in the village. Similarly, some neighboring villages, particularly those which trace a common origin, acquire common names for concurrent age sets.

2.3. Women's Age Sets and Age Grades

A close parallel exists between men's and women's age grades among the Latuka. Four female age grades are discerned: *ADURI, ODWO, ANGOR-WO MONYEMIJI,* and *AMARWAK.* The first and last of these carry the same name as their male counterparts. *Odwo* corresponds to the men's age grade of *Aduri-horwong,* consisting of adolescent girls; *Angorwo Monyemiji* consists of married women in their childbearing years.

As in the case of the boys, the girls of *Aduri* perform no collective activities. However, girls do begin to form age sets earlier than the boys, some age sets forming among the older girls of *Aduri.* Girls' age sets are formed informally around cliques of girls who are about the same age living in the same ward. Thus, particularly in larger wards, there may exist two or more contemporaneous female age sets, composed of socially distinct groupings of playmates.

As in the case of male age sets, female age sets facilitate the allocation of certain social activities, those activities varying by age grade. Women's age sets are most active and most socially salient during the *Odwo* grade, at which time—like their male counterpart *Aduri-horwong*—the girls are subservient to the commands of *Monyemiji*. It is noteworthy here that *Monyemiji* themselves do the recruitment of young girls to the *Odwo* age grade, rather than delegating the responsibility either to the members of *Odwo* (which would parallel the male system) or to *Aduri-horwong*.

Just as girls make the transition into *Odwo* as individuals and not *en masse* by age set, they pass from *Odwo* to *Angorwo Monyemiji* individually, at the time of their marriage. Both the marriage itself and the transition to *Angorwo Monyemiji* are devoid of ritual markings. Marriage is considered performed when the bride-wealth is paid and *ipso facto* the girl becomes part of *Angorwo Monyemiji*. For a time, then, members of the same age set are separated into two age grades.

Finally, the transition from *Angorwo Monyemiji* to *Amarwak* is also an individual affair and, again, lacks any ritual marking. When a woman is considered to have passed childbearing age, she is considered part of *Amarwak*. By this time age-set membership, while remembered, is of little social import.

The distribution of women into age sets is illustrated in Table 6:2 with data from one village, Labalwa. A few observations are in order here. First, there are more women's age sets than men's and, since age sets are formed at an earlier age for girls than boys, they cover a longer time span. Unlike the men's system, there is no thoroughgoing comparability between age sets in the different wards of the village, let alone among different villages. It often happens, however, as is demonstrated in Labalwa, that girls of different wards in a village assume the same name for their age set. This comes either as a result of direct interaction among the girls of the different wards, or by imitation by the girls of one ward of their age-similars in other wards.

It is generally during the *Odwo* stage that girls have the greatest social contact with girls from other wards. A girl may have a good friend of her age in another ward, and through this friendship an informal bond may be created between the two age sets. However, this interaction between females of different wards gradually atrophies as the individuals marry and age. The older women become, the more remote their contacts with women of their age in other wards.

Collective activity among females based on age groupings thus occurs in two age grades: *Odwo* and *Angorwo Monyemiji*. *Odwo*'s activities are, as indicated above, directed by *Monyemiji*, yet most of the activity of *Angorwo Monyemiji* is organized by the women themselves and not under the direction of the men. *Odwo* and *Angorwo Monyemiji* never join together for any collective activity. This contrasts with the men, where certain activities (such as *ekuboi*, cultivation of the chief's garden) are jointly undertaken by *Aduri-horwong* and younger *Monyemiji*.

Of special interest is the fact that *Angorwo Monyemiji* members are themselves undifferentiated by age in their joint activities. When, for example, the women cultivate a garden collectively, all *Angorwo Monyemiji* are called on to participate, not simply specified age sets. This contrasts with the activities of the men, where certain activities are organized by age set, and there is a differentiation of authority and power between the older and the younger age sets. Women's age sets are utilized, however, in enforcing group norms. For example, should a woman not contribute to the collective labor done by *Angorwo Monyemiji*, she may have some of her property confiscated. This is normally done by members of her age set.

Various responsibilities may be placed on the girls of *Odwo* by the ward's *Monyemiji*, some involving the benefit of the men of *Monyemiji*, others involving duties performed for the chief. In activities which also involve *Aduri-horwong*, the boys normally assume responsibility for overseeing and organizing the work of the girls. Otherwise, it is up to the girls themselves to carry out the assignments of *Monyemiji* without outside supervision.

The same procedure is used by *Monyemiji* in directing the labors of both *Odwo* and *Aduri-horwong*. The men of the ward's *Monyemiji*, gathered in *Amangat*, discuss the types of activities to be done by the youths. In the late evening, after such a discussion, one of the men bangs a piece of wood against a log, attracting the attention of the residents of the ward. He announces what *Monyemiji* want *Odwo* (or *Aduri-horwong*) to do, specifying the time when the activity must be completed. Common activities include providing provisions for the harvest-season thanksgiving ceremonies (*ebworo*), providing firewood for *Amangat*, and collective agricultural labor (*elulung*).

The activities of *Angorwo Monyemiji* are organized by the women themselves. Lacking any common meeting ground comparable to *Amangat*, initiation of collective activities is generally left to the initiative of a few women (different women serving to initiate action at different times). Once decided upon a project, these women go around the ward (or more rarely around the whole village) ringing gongs or bells, telling other women what it is that should be done and when. It is assumed that once the time, place, and nature of the activity is made known, all the women will participate. Those who deliberately absent themselves from such collective labor are subject to the sequestration of their property (*abiala*).

Various activities may be organized in this way. Some are performed on behalf of the Chief, such as weeding or harvesting his garden and fetching ebony wood from the forest for his fence. The women may also work on behalf of an individual in the ward, either after being solicited by the individual or as repayment for a collective debt. Such a debt may be incurred by the women of the age grade when they undertake ritual activity for which some key resource is lacking. For example, when the rains do not come the misfortune may be attributed to some offense the villages had committed against the Chief, who is credited with the power to withhold the rains. The women may seek to mollify the Chief through payment of goats, sacks of grain, or other valuables. When such items are borrowed, the women work off their debt to the creditor through their collective labor. Solicitation of the labor of the women may also occur when a person approaches a few women with a request for the labor of *Angorwo Monyemiji* in return for payment. Should those women thus approached accept the offer, the contract becomes binding on the entire age grade.

As in the case of the men, collective activities of female *Amarwak* cease with their transition into this age grade. Although there is some identification of the point of retirement of women to *Amarwak* with the retirement of their husbands to *Amarwak* through *Efira* ceremonies, the recognized point of transition is the time when the woman ceases bearing children. *Amarwak* status does entail certain social duties, however, most notably those associated with funeral rites. The benefits which *Amarwak* men enjoy are not directly shared by the women of *Amarwak*. Thus, after a community hunt *Amarwak* men are owed choice parts of the meat, these being formally distributed to them. A similar distribution occurs during thanksgiving ceremonies. Although women are excluded from these offerings, they generally receive portions indirectly from the men, who bring their portions home.

Before concluding this description of the women's age-set system, it is necessary to consider the effects of population movement, for thus far we have been assuming lack of geographical mobility—i.e., that a girl goes through her life course in the same locality. In fact, most women live their lives in the same village and generally in the same ward. Seventy-one percent of the adult women in Labalwa were born there, compared to ninety-six percent of the adult men; moreover, a slender majority of all women were born in the same ward as that in which they reside. Here we find reflected the norms of patrilocality and village endogamy.

When a woman moves into Labalwa or into a different ward it is almost always because of marriage to a man of that ward. In making this move, she becomes assimilated into the kin grouping of her husband and at the same time becomes a part of the local *Angorwo Monyemiji* and its relevant age set. She participates on an equal footing in the activities of *Angorwo Monyemiji* with the other women of the ward, and she is subject to all the rules governing participation in communal activities.

2.4. Comparison of Men's and Women's Age Sets

It is appropriate here to distinguish the similarities and differences between the age-set system of men and women among the Latuka. The *similarities* include the following:

(1) Universalistic membership. Past a certain age, virtually all men and all women belong to an age set, the exception being people having severe mental handicaps. Groupings are not based on kinship, nor on wealth, nor any other personal attributes linked to other stratification systems.

(2) Comparability of age grade structure. A four-grade system pertains to both men and women, and these grades are roughly parallel. The first and the last grades, significantly, are given the same name for men and women; hence only during the most sexually active years are men and women given different age grade names.

(3) Lack of formal stratification within age sets. In neither men's nor women's age sets are there any formal leadership roles. To the extent that one person is more influential than another, this is based on personal qualities of persuasiveness.

(4) The age system is utilized to organize collective labor, both on behalf of individuals and on behalf of the Chief. Such collective labor involves men and women in the middle two age grades.

Differences between the age system of men and women include the following element:

(1) Formality and ritualization of life course transitions. None of the women's transitions from one age grade to the next is marked by elaborate ritual. In contrast, men's transition to *Monyemiji* and to *Amarwak* status is marked by well developed public ritual activity and is thus sharply defined. Whereas the transition to elder status among the men is marked by the most spectacular ceremony in Latuka culture (*Efira*), no ceremony at all marks the ill-defined transition of women to elder status.

(2) Collectivity of life course transitions. Entrance to both the age grade of youths and of adults is an individual affair for both men and women. However, assumption of senior generation status in *Monyemiji*—and thus the taking on of valued social roles—is a collective transition occurring through *Efira*. Likewise, transition to elder status is a collective experience for men but an individual experience for women.

(3) The responsibility for recruiting young people into their first formalized age grouping differs between males and females. Among the former, it is the youths themselves who are primarily responsible for selecting and inducting youngsters to the age group. Among girls, however,

responsibility is not vested in the girls themselves, but rather is assumed by the adult men (*Monyemiji*). However, formation of age sets and induction of people into an age set is under the control of adult men for the males, but is largely in the hands of the girls themselves for females.

(4) Stage of life cycle at which age set entered. An age set is a grouping of individuals on the basis of similarity in age (however defined), membership in which lasts throughout the rest of the life course. Females enter such groupings at an earlier age than males; this is related to the fact that boys participate in an age group (*Aduri-horwong*) before they are inducted to age-set membership. Girls belong to age sets by the time they are in the age grade of youths (*Odwo*).

(5) Localism of age sets. In neither the case of men nor women are age sets organized on a societal basis. However, the geographical range of men's age sets is greater than that of women's. A direct equivalency structure exists in the village for men's age sets, a structure which more loosely ties together men of all plains Latuka villages. For women such comparability does not exist. Not only do age sets have different names in different wards and cover different age spans, but there are different numbers of age sets in different wards. However, in both the case of men and women it is expected that a migrant to another ward or village will become identified with an appropriate age set, roughly corresponding to the one the person left behind.

(6) Number of age sets. There are more women's age sets than men's age sets extant at any point in time. This is due not only to the earlier formation of women's age sets in the life cycle, but also to the often shorter span of women's age sets compared to men's age sets and the phenomenon, not found in men's age sets, of more than one age set being open for recruitment at a single time.

(7) Division of the life course into age grades. The first two age grades divide both males and females into groupings of approximately comparable ages. However, the workings of the age system yield a different division of the rest of the life course. The age range of the women's age grades *Angorwo Monyemiji* and *Amarwak* remains constant over time, for the dividing line between them is that which separates the childbearing woman from the woman past childbearing. Among men, however, the comparable dividing line between *Monyemiji* and *Amarwak* depends not on any individual attributes of the men in these grades, but rather on the *Efira* ceremony, held every 22 years. The result is that the age separating adult from elder among the men varies considerably depending on the point in the *Efira* cycle. In the village of Labalwa two years before *Efira* was to be held, *Monyemiji* ranged from 18 to 62 years old, thus including men 17 years older than the oldest *Angorwo Monyemiji* woman; the youngest male elder at the time was 60

years old, and the age span of the elders covered just 15 years (60-75). Yet projecting ahead two years past this census to 1977, immediately following *Efira, Amarwak* would include men aged 37 and older, the age span of *Monyemiji* being reduced from 18-62 as it was in 1975, to roughly 18-41. Hence while the stratification of women into age grades leads to a stable division of the female population into the adult and elder age strata, the comparable division of men varies dramatically through time, in predictable oscillations pivoting around the *Efira* ceremonies (see Table 6:3).

TABLE 6.3

AGE GRADE STRATIFICATION (POST-CHILDHOOD)
BY SEX, LABALWA, 1975

	Men		Women		Total	
	N	%	N	%	N	%
YOUTH Male: Aduri-horwong Female: Odow	33	19.1	30	15.5	63	17.2
ADULT Male: Monyemiji Female: Angoro Monyemiji	125	72.3	118	60.8	243	66.2
ELDER Male/female: Amarwak	15	8.7	46	23.7	61	16.6
Total	173	100.1	194	100.0	367	100.0

(8) Age set as basis of social identity. Although both men and women are organized into age sets, among women age sets appear to be less important in organizing social activity. The more important age grouping among women is provided by the age grade; those in the *Odwo* and *Angorwo Monyemiji* grades organize for various activities as groupings largely undifferentiated by age set. Age-set membership is of considerable social importance among adult men, who make distinctions in social and political status and appropriate role within the *Monyemiji* age grade based on age-set affiliation. Among both men and women, age-set membership is of little social significance in the elder (*Amarwak*) age grade.

(9) Power of older age sets over younger age sets. Among the men, adults have the power and authority to order youths (both male and female) to do their bidding. Thus, the age grades of youth (*Aduri-horwong* and *Odwo*) are perceived as under the authority and at the beck and call of the men of *Monyemiji*. Among women, no comparable hierarchy exists. The women of *Angorwo Monyemiji* are not seen as having the girls of *Odwo* under their command or at their disposal.

(10) Roles. The men's age system is important in allocating political and judicial roles, as well as organizing collective economic and ritual activities. The women's age system entails these latter two spheres, but is not involved in the allocation of political or judicial roles.

3. Women's Age Sets In Comparative Perspective

Whereas men's age-set systems ae quite common in East Africa, comprehensive systems of women's age sets are rare. If we take as our sample 20 East African societies selected by Foner and Kertzer (1978) as having adequate documentation of male age-set or generation-set systems (see Table 6:4), only three have documented women's age-set systems, and one of these is the Latuka. In addition, three societies have systems in which women become in some sense assimilated to the age-set system of the men, generally by acquiring the age-set membership of their husband. In other cases, such as the Rendille (Spencer 1973:35), young unmarried women are grouped together but these age-groupings do not survive marriage. It might also be added that even where women have no age sets, they may take on important social identification on the basis of men's age sets, such as in rules governing marriage (e.g., the Kuria, described in Ruel 1958).

If we examine the two instances other than the Latuka in which women's age sets are reported in East Africa, there is little evidence of much social importance of the age-set system. For the Kikuyu, Kenyatta (1938:4) reports the existence of a system of women's age sets paralleling the men's, but has little else to say about it. Lambert is noncommittal on the subject of the existence of Kikuyu women's age sets, but maintains that however the women are organized, their activities are limited to domestic affairs, agricultural matters, and "the discipline, and the regulation of the social life, of girls and women" (1956:100).

The other society represented as having formal women's age groupings—the Konso—has similarly been the subject of little analysis in this regard. Here, women as well as men belong to generation sets, based on the generation-set membership of their father, but for women this identification is apparently of little significance. As it is claimed that the centerpiece of the generational system is the articulation of the relationship between elders and warriors, and as women can neither be warriors nor, in the political sense, elders, women's generation-set affiliation only relates to women's "maternal role" (Hallpike 1972:204).

To find a well-documented and socially significant system of women's age sets, we must turn to West Africa, where apparently women's age sets

TABLE 6.4

WOMEN'S AGE-SET SYSTEMS IN EAST AFRICA

	Present	Assimilated to Men's	Not mentioned or Absent
Arusha			X
Galla			X
Jie			X
Karimojong			X
Kıkuyu	X		
Kipsigis		X	
Konso	X		
Kuria			X
Latuka	X		
Masai			X
Meru		X	
Nandi			X
Nuer			X
Nyakyusa			X
Pokot			X
Rendille			X
Samburu			X
So			X
Turkana			X
Zanaki		X	

SOURCES: Arusha (Gulliver 1963); Galla (Legesse 1973, Prins 1970); Jie (Gulliver 1953); Karimojong (Dyson-Hudson 1963, 1966); Kikuyu (Kenyatta 1938; Lambert 1956; Middleton 1953; Prins 1970); Kipsigis (Peristiany 1939; Prins 1970); Konso (Hallpike 1972); Kuria (Ruel 1958); Latuka (Seligman and Seligman 1925, 1932; Kertzer and Madison 1980); Masai (Jacobs 1958; Bernardi 1955; Fosbrooke 1958); Meru (Holding 1942); Lambert 1947); Nandi (Huntingford 1953); Nuer (Evans-Pritchard 1936, 1940), Nyakyusa (Wilson 1960, 1963); Rendille (Spencer 1973); Samburu (Spencer, 1965, 1973); So (Laughlin and Laughlin 1974); Tiriki (Sangree 1965, 1966), Turkana (Gulliver 1958); and Zanaki (Bischofberger 1972).

are more common. Here the two most complete analyses are provided for the Afikpo Ibo (Ottenberg 1971) of Nigeria and the Bassari of Senegal (Gessain 1971). Both societies also have comprehensive male age-set systems. In fact, in both cases the female system of age groupings parallels that of the men's.

Afikpo women organize into localized age sets soon after marriage. As marriage is patrilocal and often village exogamous, women often find themselves at marriage moving into a strange village. Organization into an age set occurs informally, at the instigation of a young married woman who calls together the young married women who have not yet entered an age set. The membership of this nascent age set shifts continually in the ensuing years due to marital instability, as some women are divorced and leave the village, while other women marry into the village. Like the men's age sets, a new women's age set is formed approximately every three years. However, women join age sets at an earlier age than men, who wait until their 30s. It is said that membership in an age set is of special signficance for a woman who marries into the village, for it provides a mechanism of rapid integration into village life.

Collective activities on the basis of age groupings begin even before age sets are formed, for unmarried girls living in a compound form a named organization charged with certain cleaning duties, and they may also be called upon by the elder men's age sets to do communal labor. Women in age sets assist their fellow members throughout their lives by performing various rituals on their behalf. Women in the same age set living in the same compound are particularly involved in collective activity, ranging from domestic and agricultural labor to moral support. Collective labor organized by age set at the ward and village level is rare. However, women of the executive age grade (generally in their 40s and 50s) may call on the unmarried girls to perform communal labor. They may also make rules pertaining to the women of the village (e.g., regarding littering, fighting, neglecting communal labor).

Like the men, women also have a grade of elders, which however has less internal differentiation than the men. The female elders have much less power than the men, and their power is largely confined to the regulation of women's trade.

Of the importance of women's age sets compared to men's, Ottenberg (1971:102) writes:

> The fact that [the women's system] is not so actively or effectively organized as the male system reflects the females' lesser role in directing political and ritual affairs. It is also a result of their greater mobility. . . . Nevertheless, the same forms of authority relationships are found between the elder and the not-so-old females as in the case of males. But for females there is the everpresent possibility of male intrusion in their affairs; the reverse rarely occurs.

Interestingly, Ottenberg (1971:106) speculates that in precolonial times women's age-set organization was less developed, that recent social change providing women with more independent positions may have sparked the flowering of the women's age-set system.

Unlike the double unilineal reckoning of descent among the Afikpo Ibo, the Bassari are a matrilineal people numbering about 8,000. Gessain

(1971) describes Bassari society, with its sedentary horticulture, as having very strong age-set organization for both males and females, a system which the Bassari enter as youngsters and continue in until old age. Male and female age sets form a parallel and linked hierarchy, moving from one age grade to the next every six years. The age system provides for societal integration cross-cutting kinship allegiances:

> Accéder aux classes d'âge masculines ou féminines, c'est quitter ou au moins s'éloigner de sa famille, groupe vertical autant qu'horizontal, et entrer dans le monde horizontal de la camaraderies de promotion (1971:159). Si le système de classes contribue ainsi—à côté d'autres institutions—à assurer la cohésion du village, gros généralment de 100 a 500 habitants et où les lignages ne contitutent pas le système de clivage le plus important, il paraît jouer un rôle primordial pour assurer la cohésion au niveau des groupes de villages (1971:183).

The duties of Bassari women's age sets are primarily ritual in nature, but include collective labor organized by age set or groups of adjacent age sets. In particular, the senior adjacent age set is viewed as "mother" to the junior, and the latter must make offerings through feasting their elders. It is noteworthy, however, that once old age is attained, no distinction between age sets is made and the women are seen to have passed out of the age-set system.

Analysis of the three women's age-set systems reviewed here reveals certain structural commonalities as well as differences. These include the following:

(1) In all three cases the women's age-set system parallels that of the men's. This is most pronounced in the case of the Bassari, where men and women alike undergo transition every six years. It is least pronounced in the case of the Latuka, where age grade rather than age set tends to be more important as the badge of female social identity and as a means of allocating social roles. In the case of both the Bassari and the Afikpo Ibo, a ceremonial link is formed between paired men's and women's age sets; this is lacking in the case of the Latuka.

(2) In all three societies women's age sets are formed at an earlier point in the woman's life course than is the case for men. Latuka and Bassari females enter an age set while they are still unmarried; Afikpo Ibo females enter an age set soon after marriage.

(3) The frequency of formation of the age set, and the span of ages represented in an age set, are similar for both men's and women's age-set systems in these three societies. Among the Bassari there is an identity between men's and women's age sets in this regard; among the Ibo there is a close approximation; while among the Latuka we find the most variation.

However, even among the Latuka, the mean age-span covered by a women's age set is not far from that of the men.

(4) Both Afikpo Ibo and Bassari have ritualized transition points in their women's age-set system. These are largely lacking among the Latuka. But even among the Afikpo Ibo there is relatively little ritualization of transition points.

(5) In both Latuka and Afikpo Ibo society, women's age sets provide a means of integration of women entering a new village or ward upon marriage. Gessain does not report on this phenomenon for the Bassari.

(6) In all three societies, women's age-set formation is a localized affair. In the case of Bassari and Afikpo Ibo society, in fact, there appears to be considerable differences in customs regarding women's age sets in different localities. Only in the case of Afikpo Ibo is there any activity connected with women's age sets reported which brings together women from different villages. This may be tied to the greater organization of women in Ibo society for trade purposes.

(7) In all three societies, women's age-set activities involve ritual roles and economic cooperation. Political and judicial power is formally vested in the men. However, in all three cases women's age-set organization entails a degree of women's self-governance (i.e., the making and enforcing of various rules applicable to women only).

4. Explaining the Differences Between Men's and Women's Age-Set Systems

Women's age-set organization is less common than men's, and where women's age sets do occur, they are less well developed and less socially significant than men's age sets. A note of caution is in order, however, for little systematic data have been published on women's age sets. This has generally been assumed to reflect the absence of such organization, but this void in the literature may be partially attributable to the sex bias of ethnographers. It is interesting, in this context, that the two hitherto published analyses of women's age sets have both been products of fieldwork involving female anthropologists (Monique Gessain for the Bassari and Pheobe Ottenberg for the Afikpo Ibo). In the ethnographic literature, intriguing references to women's participation in some sort of age-set system are occasionally found, only to be buried beneath descriptions focusing exclusively on men.

Gulliver has suggested that age sets involve men and not women because the female roles embodied in marriage and motherhood "effectively curtail relationships by age" (1968:161), a point with which Baxter and

Almagor (1978:11) are in sympathy. Conversely, the assumption is made that the roles of spouse and parent for men need not militate against age homogeneous groupings. Hamond and Jablow have argued along similar lines that

> Age homogeneity. . . is far more characteristic of men's associations. Women tend to bond vertically, ignoring age differences to join forces on issues of common concern. Peer relationships that crosscut kin lines do not figure as prominently in women's lives as do links with related women of all ages on the basis of shared responsibilities, joys, and sorrows (1976:114).

In this perspective, the vertical bias in women's age relations is particularly pronounced in patrilocal societies, where all women, coming to the village as outsiders, "may combine to form a united front in the face of male kin solidarity" (1976:115).

But do women of different ages have the same interests? Do not older women generally have more prestige and more power than younger women, in a way which parallels age-related statuses of men? Is it not in the interest of older women to band together to protect their interests in the same way it is claimed that men's age-set systems work (e.g., among the Samburu, as described by Spencer 1965:134)? If kin lines need not act as a barrier to the formation of men's groupings, why must they bar the formation of groupings of women?

Perhaps we may come closer to an answer by turning the question around a bit and looking at some of the more common explanations for the existence of men's age-set systems and then inquiring into their applicability to women. Four general explanations have been proposed:

(1) Age sets serve to preserve and strengthen the power of the old at the expense of the young. Through such practices as forbidding marriage until a man has, with his age-mates, passed into a certain age grade, age-set systems allow for widespread polygyny among older men, with concomitant concentration of economic and political power. Such a system would not apply in this way to women; in fact, age-set organization for women would be precluded, at least insofar as the age sets would serve to delay the age of women at marriage.

(2) Age-set systems have sometimes been explained as mechanisms for military organization, establishing a grouping of warriors (e.g., for the Nandi, Huntingford 1953:70). This would account for why men and not women have age-set organization, but in fact not all age-set societies organize warfare by age-sets and—in a number of societies in which age-sets *were* utilized in warfare—age-set systems have survived long after warfare has been eliminated.

(3) Age-set organization serves to wean the boy away from the confines of his natal family, bringing him into closer contact with the outside world (Legesse 1973:110). Such a system is seen as aiding the boy in developing the personal autonomy he will need in later life. This explanation implicitly contrasts the wide social horizons of the male with the limited social horizons of the female, who is presumably not involved in the process of meeting and getting along with strangers (excepting her affines).

(4) In what is perhaps the most parsimonious explanation of age-set organization (Dyson-Hudson 1963:398-399, 1966:174; Gulliver 1958:13-14), age-set structure is portrayed as providing a basis for social interaction and social control among temporary and fortuitous groupings of otherwise unrelated men. Hence Dyson-Hudson (1963:398) analyzes the age-set system of the pastoral Karimojong:

> By creating society-wide units based on the neutral criterion of the time span, the age system breaks down this tendency toward separatism. And by establishing an order of precedence among such units in terms of their priority of formation, it counteracts the otherwise general assumptions of social equivalence. It then becomes possible for individuals and whole groups, between whom there are otherwise no clear links and thus no grounds for establishing relative authority, to engage in joint activity in their general interest.

In pastoral societies such as the Karimojong and the Turkana, this account seems reasonable and would also indicate—given that men are generally the herders—why an age-set system would exist for men and not for women. However, many age-set societies are sedentary and horticultural, and this explanation is not applicable here. It is noteworthy that the Latuka, Afikpo Ibo and Bassari are all sedentary, horticultural societies. Among the Latuka, there is relatively little inter-village contact among either men or women. Among the Afikpo Ibo, there is considerable inter-village contact, but it involves both men and women.

Aging has different implications for males and females, and the nature, sequence, and timing of the allocation of social roles to males and females through their life course differ. This sexual duality has led to a lack of structural parallel between the intitutionalization of aging for men through age-set systems and the weakness of age as an organizing principle for women in those same societies. In this light, the seeming monopoly by men of age-set systems is simply the dramatic expression in societies which employ age as an explicit principle of social groupings of the universal principle that social processes of aging are sex-specific.

This can be illustrated with an example from the elderly end of the life course, for the societal and personal implications of growing old often differ markedly between men and women. Insofar as older men are occupying positions of economic and political power, they are preventing younger men from taking on these valued roles. To enable the younger men to replace the older in a communally sanctioned fashion, and to ease the personal effects of such role change on the elders, a formalized age-set system with specified points of collective transition has much to recommend it. In most of these societies, though, the valued roles that adult women occupy are of a different order. While the son's economic status and ability to wield influence is often linked to his father's relinquishing of these prerogatives, the daughter's economic status and ability to influence others is rarely inversely linked to her mother's status. There is thus no individually- nor societally-generated pressure to have a ritualized and clearly agreed upon transition to old age for women, nor is there the gap between pre- and post-transition status that would make collective sharing of such transition for women personally and socially beneficial.

5.   Theoretical Implications

Aging can be conceived of as a stratification system, in which both people and societally defined roles are differentiated by age (Riley, Johnson and Foner 1972; Foner 1979). Insofar as roles are assigned on the basis of age, the individual's passage through the life course represents a series of transitions, the repeated sloughing off of old roles and the taking up of new ones. People of similar age, by virtue of that similarity, have certain interests in common vis-à-vis occupants of other age strata. Yet, at the same time as age similarity can be the basis of common interest, it may also be the basis of conflict, insofar as individuals are competing for the same scarce resources (whether material or symbolic). Hence, in some circumstances individuals may make common cause with their age dissimilars in order to further their own self-interest as this is perceived.

Seen from this perspective, the subject of male and female age-set systems in Africa has universal theoretical implications. At issue here is the extent to which age acts as a principle of social solidarity and social grouping in a society, and the societal variables which determine the significance of age in this respect. The male/female contrast can be viewed—if somewhat unorthodoxly—as a controlled comparison. We may inquire into the differences in the processes and effects of aging among men and women in a society as a means not only of better understanding sexual stratification, but also of sharpening our conceptions of age and age relations. We can, indeed, address some of the classic questions of age stratification through such a sexual comparison: the significance of both productive and reproductive roles in determining the nature and effects of aging on the individual in a given society. The contribution of men and women to the productive sphere, for example, may be differentially affected by aging in a society. In such cases, the ways in which societies deal with aging and the kinds of role transitions which occur and their timing may be compared for men and women. In this fashion, two societies having similar reproductive roles (by sex) through the life course, but having different productive role careers through the life course, may be compared to control for the reproductive role variable. Seen in these terms, African age-set societies provide simply another realm for the universal comparison which must be made if we are to satisfactorily understand the process and determinants of aging in any society, including our own.

The study of age-set societies is perhaps most important in providing us with a view of the range of human solutions to the problems of life course transition and of relations between age strata in a society. In particular, what is most striking about strict age-set systems is that transitions from one age stratum to the next are not made—as is generally the case in our society—as individuals, but in groups. Yet, as we have seen, it is just this feature which seems to be lacking in women's age-set systems. Thus, any understanding of the social advantages and disadvantages of collective life course transitions—occasionally suggested as an antidote to the atomizing and personally disorganizing effects of individual transitions in our own society—must consider why men and not women have constituted such collective transition systems.

Pending further, and urgently needed, field research in the progressively diminishing number of societies having age-set systems, generalizations about women's age-set systems must remain tentative, for the ethnographic record is scanty at best. Clearly, though, the case of African age-set societies illustrates the fact that societal mechanisms for dealing with aging are closely linked to other elements of social organization, particularly sex, kinship, and economic relations. The cross-cultural study of just how these elements interrelate to produce characteristic patterns of aging remains in its infancy.

Notes

[1]The research on which this article is based was made possible through the sponsorship of the Russell Sage Foundation Program on Age and Aging. Thanks are also due to the Surdna Foundation and Bowdoin College for support provided to the junior author.

[2]This is true not only of ethnographic studies, but theoretical works on age-set systems as well. Noteworthy in this regard is Stewart's (1977) recent book-length study of age-set systems, in which women are wholly excluded from consideration.

[3]The Latuka have never been the subject of sustained, systematic anthropological research, and there is no published account of the organization of Latuka women's age organization. The literature on the Latuka consists of missionary reports (Molinaro 1940-41; Muratori 1949, 1950, 1954), some early colonial reports (Somerset 1918, 1921-23), and the ethnographic survey research done by the Seligmans (Seligman 1925; Seligman and Seligman 1926, 1932). This last, the most complete account of Latuka society, is based on a winter's fieldwork in 1921-22 done through the aid of interpreters.

[4]Analysis of the Latuka case is based on fieldwork carried out in May through August of 1975 by the junior author, who is himself a Latuka. Several local research assistants, working through December, 1975, aided in conducting a census. Two villages, Labalwa and Torit, were the focus of fieldwork. Methods included participant observation and interviewing.

7
Friendship and Kinship In Older Women's Organizations: Curlew Point, 1973

Valerie Fennell

1. Introduction

An awareness that age defines a status in the structures of societies, and that age ought to be studied within a larger framework which includes all age groups, is a tenet of the social sciences (Linton 1942; Neugarten 1968). Anthropologists call taking this larger framework into consideration a "holistic" perspective. The holistic approach marks the anthropological tradition, requiring all practitioners to study social and cultural settings as completely as possible, always including two genders and three generations.

For anthropologists in large-scale societies, the holistic approach is not an easy tradition to keep. Most gerontological research by anthropologists has focused on aged subgroups in particular settings. Careful attention to other age groups is sacrificed in a methodological compromise for research in large-scale societies. Faced with the whole of San Francisco, Clark and Anderson (1967) focused on the aged, providing naturalistic descriptions of a few settings but giving scant attention to other age groups. Other anthropologists (Angrosino 1976; Jacobs 1974; and Ross 19974b and 1977) have solved the methodological dilemma by choosing *small* self-contained communities made up entirely of aged persons. Thus they kept the value placed upon holism in carrying out anthropological research, but were still left without perspective on generational and age group interactions.

Studies which have focused attention upon intergenerational relations usually do so only within the familial context (Shanas and Streib 1965; Townsend 1957). The collective and synthesizing work, *A Sociology of*

Age Stratification (Riley, Johnson and Foner 1972), examines age-group interactions and intergenerational relations bringing together an extensive but
fragmented sociological literature on age strata in Western societies. But
studying the broader context of age relations, for the most part, is not
methodologically emphasized in sociological research. Nor does *familial* intergenerational relations fully explain *community* age group and intergenerational interactions.

Traditional anthropological "holism" in the community studies has only
begun to offer its valuable perspective to gerontological inquiries. Until it
does, understanding of the vast majority of the aged, those living in age-
heterogeneous communities, will be deficient. The very dynamics which
define the status of the aged will continue to be obscured. Old people
always exist within larger communities, in cooperation and conflict with
those of other age categories, all being differentially esteemed, assigned
tasks, and allowed privilege partly on the basis of age. Studying the aged
will ultimately involve researchers with this broader context as knowledge
grows.

2. Studying a Multi-generational Community

In this study of Curlew Point,[1] attention to the whole community gave
strength to the research, as did other anthropological strategies of data
gathering. Anthropological methodology requires the fieldworker to live
among the people, to participate in their activities, to observe and record it
all with excruciating carefulness. This was done. While this chapter examines only a small portion of the whole data, these social-structural
descriptions of older women's voluntary associations are based upon insights derived from analysis of diverse situations which would have been
unavailable to researchers using more restricted methods.

The comprehensiveness of the anthropological perspective is seen in
this chapter's analysis in two ways: (1) the data are based upon the investigation of an *entire* multigenerational community, utiliizing the
guidelines for anthropological community studies suggested by Arensberg
(1954); and (2) *all* age groups are considered in the analysis, in order to better understand the status of aged persons in the community.

A primary goal sought throughout this research was to examine the
lives of independently-living aged persons in an unobtrusive manner. As a
retirement town, Curlew Point offered that opportunity, as well as a population representing all age strata. These characteristics, added to the town's
small size and charm, encouraged its selection for a year of research.

Contact with townspeople grew out of attendance at local public
events such as religious services, town meetings, celebrations of historical

and religious events (the Fourth of July Festival or Christmas), and out of the consumer role (simply living in the community and needing services) and the role of volunteer worker (through school and church activities). Key informants emerged gradually to take a personal and sustained interest in the work and daily life of the anthropologist. As a result the researcher eventually enjoyed a measure of community acceptance.

Another methodological device by which the fieldworker achieved a familiar identity to local persons proved to be mapping. No existing maps of the town showed houses and buildings. This knowledge of the area was important for establishing guidelines for sampling. Thus the mapping of streets, houses and buildings was undertaken. Natives often encountered the researcher during this early mapping phase of her data collection. There was no better way to become known and learn about territoriality and neighborhoods. The map itself became more significant later in the field year, when the local custom of assigning house numbers only after two years became apparent (some informants reported this). For a number of households, then, identification was efficient in record keeping only because of this map—and the researcher's own unique household numbering system based upon it.

The research plan included in-depth interviews to follow several months of opportunities to explore age relations with the key informants. The biases of early ethnographic mapping were offset in later research phases by systematic procedures. A survey of households on east-west streets in the town afforded an opportunity to (1) discover household composition, (2) select a population from which to choose a sample of informants to interview in-depth, and (3) discuss age relations with those cooperating in the survey of their households. A survey of businesses, offices, and organizations in the community also brought similar opportunities. By the time in-depth interviews were begun, the researcher had a sense of the patterning in many Curlew Pointers' perceptions of age relations, past and present, in their community. Supplementing the verbal reports were extensive records of observed daily interactions in community life.

The in-depth interview schedule was designed with an awareness of the native's perceptions, the "emic perspective" of age relations, as well as the researcher's rather academic ("etic") inquiries. Many of the questions were also deliberately open-ended, making later quantification difficult, but allowing informants to deluge the research with rich details of their experiences.

Throughout all the various data-gathering activities (participant-observation, surveying households, mapping, photographing, casual interviewing and in-depth interviewing) there was the constant, daily, laborious record-keeping which accompanies any event observed that might be relevant. Anthropological field work which strives after "holism" is a creative and judicious balancing of known biases through methodological diversity. Out of this emerges a naturalistic description of a human community that is remarkable for its thoroughness and objectivity. Upon such a background, then, this paper describes patterns of age relations among older women in voluntary organizations in Curlew Point in 1972-1973.

3.   Curlew Point: The Town

Curlew Point (a fictional name) is a community located on an estuary of a river in the Southern part of the United States. In 1973, there were 2,492 persons living inside the city's limits and an additional 1,400 persons in the immediately surrounding areas. The community enjoys a relatively long history; its oldest cemetery dates from before the Revolution. This history, and the town's pride in it, acts to attract retirees and tourists. Curlew Point is a fishing community, a county seat radically changed in the early 1970s by the construction of a nuclear plant (Fennell 1977).

More important for older women's organizations was the influx, since the 1950s, of increasing numbers of retired persons looking for a propitious environment within which to grow old. Many discovered the town as middle-aged tourists and decided to return annually, finally to retire there. They came to Curlew Point in increasing numbers during the 1960s and early 1970s, attracted by the natural beauty of the riverine environment, where great live oak trees provide shade and foliage the year round.

Local people called these retirees "new," expressing the attitude that birth in the community has local importance enough to require a special label for later arrivals. "New " persons tease about the long probationary period they must endure before acceptance, but the label discomforts them, too. When the researcher explained to a man in his seventies that she was "new" in town, he grinned and quietly commented that he had resided in Curlew Point for seven years and he was still called "new" by natives. This boundary-maintaining categorization of recently-arrived retirees suggests that retirees faced some difficulties in achieving integration into the community.

The year of research affirmed that older persons did have problems becoming integrated into community life. Among those who were successful, integration depended upon either existing kin or friendship ties, or their ability to establish friendships. This was as true for aged women as for others (Fennell 1977). Realizing this, then, the structural features of friendship relationships are vital background for understanding elder women's organizations in Curlew Point.

4. Structural Requirements for Friendship

Age statuses form a hierarchy which, in some situations, allows privileges to a senior person in an interaction (Fennell 1974). This hierarchical aspect of age relation has implications for intergenerational friendships (Suttles 1970). The norms of friendship encourage people of similar hierarchical status to seek sociability with one another so as to prevent the possibility of exploitation (Kurth 1970:145). In the case of the age hierarchy, then, persons who are age homogeneous may seek one another as friends, but persons of markedly different ages may not. The Curlew Point research suggests 5-8 years junior or senior are the boundaries which most persons observe (though scarcity of age-appropriate persons may encourage one to extend these boundaries). However, persons of markedly different ages may become friendly if a relative of one of them makes the introduction and initiates their being together in the early part of the friendship. Such a person will be called a *familial peer-link* in this chapter. A person who is seven years junior to one person and seven years senior to another may bring together two people with as much as fifteen years difference in their ages. Such a person is here called a *peer-link* because both persons brought together feel this person is a peer and thus tend to act as if they are peers of one another, otherwise fifteen years is usually seen as too great an age difference for friendship to develop.

People generally view intergenerational friendships as suspect; friends should be of the same generation. Curlew Pointers preferred persons relatively close in age as friends, saying "we would have more in common." Further, as Hess notes,

> "age similarity tends also to be a normative component of the friendship role, implicit when not explicit. This normative emphasis becomes apparent as one realizes that age similarity is seldom seen as a fact to be accounted for, whereas dissimilarity in age between friends may arouse suspicion, require explanation from the participants, or evoke societal control reactions ranging from ridicule to attempts to enforce segregation" (1972:374-375).

The way in which Curlew Pointers explained age dissimilarity in friends first became apparent when persons of the researcher's parents' generation repeatedly wanted to include their adult children when she was included in social affairs. If their adult children could not be included, future arrangements were made to be sure she could meet their children. In one instance, the researcher, too, suggested that a friend of her mother's generation meet her during a visit.[2] Here the *familial peer-link* operated to fulfill an unspoken social requirement that one interact with members of other generations only if a peer of one of the persons is also involved, in these cases also a relative.

The concept of the familial peer-link does not specify which person in the relationship involves her/his peer. If *ego's* parent played the familial link in the relationship, then *alter* would be a close-peer of *ego's* parent, as in bringing together the researcher's mother and her friends of her mother's generation. If *ego's* child played the familial peer-link, then *alter* in the relationship would be a close peer of *ego's* child, as on the occasions when the researcher was introduced to the children of her older friends. These two examples might be drawn as in Figure 7:1.

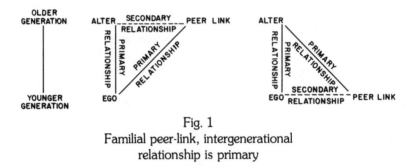

Fig. 1
Familial peer-link, intergenerational
relationship is primary

While the introduction of a familial peer-link made the intergenerational relationship acceptable, it also created tension between the generational peers, suggesting that some social requirements were not being met in the situation. Peers are not only those with whom one is most likely to be friendly, they are potentially one's rival, since the age hierarchy encourages direct competition with peers and diffuses it between generations. Peers who have not chosen one another as friends but are brought together may interact uncomfortably. The unfulfilled social requirement in these situations is this: the peer relationship should be the first to be established, then the intergenerational relationship may follow. In other words, the establishment of intergenerational relationships of sociability depends upon peer relationships. The above situations *reversed* the appropriate sequence for establishing intergenerational ties. The intergenerational bond existed before the peer bond. Yet the participants attempted to explain the atypical bond in one of the most accepted ways available, even though the rule that peer bonds should come first was *not* kept. Somehow the participants in the situation felt that the involvement of the familial peer-link eased a covert feeling that the intergenerational relationship might be suspect to themselves and others.

Such intergenerational relationships where the familial peer-link is introduced *later* are unusual; exceptional circumstances call them into being. That is, the researcher had the added incentive of professional research and informants had the added incentive of curiosity about her work. Probably, others find different added incentives to establishing intergenerational bonds in this misordered fashion, but the pervasiveness of age-grading in the U.S. suggests that the norms separating such persons are strong. Figure 7:2 illustrates the normative pattern for establishing intergenerational relationships.

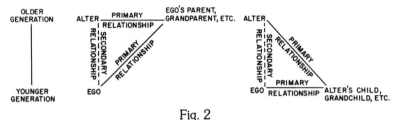

Fig. 2

Familial peer-link, normative pattern in
establishing intergenerational relationships

Because kinship is involved in the familial peer-link's function in establishing intergenerational ties, grandparents and grandchildren may serve, as do parents and children as well as any relative. This enables nonadjacent intergenerational relationships to arise when several generations of one kin group reside near one another. It is also likely that the intergenerational relationships thus established via familial peer-links can then serve to break down the barriers of age hierarchy for still others.

The *peer-link*, too, can facilitate the establishment of relationships between persons of adjacent generations. With the involvement of the peer-link in intergenerational sociability, the explanation offered for the relationship is "being a friend of a friend." The peer bond remains crucial, and the sequencing still requires the peer relationship to precede the establishment of the cross-generational one. But, here the peer-link introduces two other persons who are peers to her/him but not to one another. Rather they are members of adjacent generations with 15 years difference in their ages. Obvious generational differences become obscured when one recalls that people's ages are in fact a continuum without clear distinctions between generations. The peer-link concept takes an individual's perspective, defining one's generation as all persons seven years older and seven years younger than oneself. A diagram of the peer-link intergenerational relationship may be found in Figure 7:3.

The familial peer-link and the peer-link serve to satisfy the structural requirements for intergenerational relationships. They give permission that allows people to seek one another, though age hierarchical norms ordinarily separate them. The analysis of seven Curlew Point women's organizations shows the operations of the age hierarchy, the familial peer-link, and the peer-link in both inhibiting and facilitating community age integration.

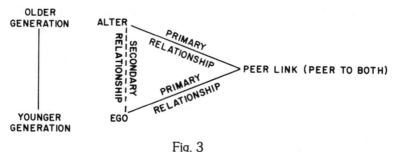

Fig. 3
Peer-link's operation in an intergenerational relationship

5. Older Women's Organizations

The seven women's organizations here discussed had many diverse purposes (See Table 7:1). Four organizations were religious groups; one promoted community service generally; one was a homemakers' club; and one

TABLE 7.1

CURLEW POINT OLDER WOMEN'S ORGANIZATIONS

Organization's Name	Stated Purpose	Member's Age Range
1. Carrie James Circle	Common interest in a local church	52-90
2. Curlew Point Garden Club	Common interest in plants	55 +
3. Curlew Point Extension Homemakers	Common interest in Household Crafts	56-85
4. Curlew Point Woman's Club	General Community Service	36-90 +
5. King's Daughters and Sons*	Common interest in Christianity	54-85
6. Suzanne Georgia Circle	Common interest in a local church	55-85
7. Woman's Society of Caring Service	Common interest in a local church	33-90 +

*Internationally this organization includes both sexes and may be variously age-graded. Locally only women currently over 53 years of age were members.

was a garden club. Besides these special purposes the elder women's organizations all gave attention to improvements in the local hospital and nursing home, whose residents were mostly aged. They arranged holiday celebrations and helped with things such as acquiring pillows and blankets. They also assisted the county home-care service in acquiring some equipment. They contributed to a variety of charities. County organizations which utilized volunteer help and charitable contributions occasionally solicited the help of these elder women's organizations. Two of the church groups had annual bazaars and seasonal take-out dinners to raise a substantial portion of their churches' budgets. The women worked all year to produce items to sell at the bazaar. The take-out dinners required a large team of women to work long hours.

6. Recruitment and Age-grading

In older women's organizations in Curlew Point, new members attended meetings only when invited by (1) a friend close in age, (2) a kinswoman, often of a different generation, or (3) a friend not so close in age, but one introduced to the new person by a peer-link. When a kinswoman of another generation brought a new member, the kinswoman acted as a familial *peer-link* between the new member and the established members who were older.

These patterns of informal recruitment resulted in women's organizations which tended to be age graded, though no rules required this. In fact, the older (60-80 years old) native women reported that their clubs were *not* age homogeneous when they were young adults. When the long-time leader of one woman's church group (Women's Society of Caring Service) resigned, saying the group should have "younger-blood" take over (she was in her mid-seventies), no younger woman could be found to accept the presidency. At another meeting (Suzanne George Circle) a woman in her late sixties tried to understand why no younger women participated. She mused that younger women were busy with their families, but then added that young women had always had families and they used to participate in the church women's organizations. It required several months of pressuring the younger church women to get officers. The woman who finally yielded to pressure was the daughter of a woman in her sixties who had been part of the leadership for many years. The younger woman, then, had a familial peer-link in the organization. In another organization (the Extension Homemakers), one elder woman (73 years old) recalled that she and several of her peers had joined the club together as young women. She didn't know why younger women had not continued to join. The membership had grown old together, and currently their new members were fifty years old and older, except for the county extension agent in her mid-thirties, whose job it was to meet with them. New members were informally recruited in the ways mentioned above, which may offer some synchronic explanation for the age grading. The familial peer-links and peer-links were too few, given the in-roads of change and geographical mobility upon community, kin, and friendship ties.

The Curlew Point Woman's Club was the most prestigious organization to which a woman could belong locally. It was also the only one which

prescribed age grading in cooperation with a younger women's organization. Membership included only women who were 36 years old or more. In
1962, a local Junior Woman's Club formed with the approval of the
Woman's Club. When a woman became 36 years old she was given an "aging out" ceremony. A representative of the Woman's Club attended and
presented any "aging out" person with a year's paid membership in the
Woman's Club as an invitation to join the elder women's group. Leaders of
the Woman's Club were asked to many ceremonial functions of the Junior
Women and had considerable informal influence in their activities. At the
tenth anniversary celebration of the Junior Woman's Club, a sixty-year-old
leader from the Woman's Club carefully suggested goals for the organization to seek during the coming year. She even suggested informal strategies
to be followed. These did become that year's goals for the Junior Women,
though they formally voted on all goals at later meetings.

The Woman's Club was probably most influential among older
women's organizations because they had formalized procedures for involving middle-aged women in their organization. As a result, they had more
than one or two middle-aged women in their membership. More women
combined physical vigor with middle-aged ambitions to make the Women's
Club more dynamic in community affairs than other older women's
organizations. Town officials seeking women's representation in events
were most likely to seek out the Women's Club.

7. Integration of "New" Women

As Curlew Point has experienced change and some growth, strangers have
arrived. Many persons retired to Curlew Point having lived their entire lives
elsewhere. As noted above, local people call them "new," and they never
really get to know younger generations. They are classified as retirement
aged and are approached by natives close to their own age. The hierarchical barriers to age-heterogeneous relationships make this inevitable. The
women are then invited by peers to attend meetings of the local women's
organizations. However, many of the newly retired women are in their late
fifties and do not always enjoy the local clubs whose membership is
predominantly in their 60s, 70s, and 80s. They are classified locally as "aged" because they are retired; they revealed some uneasiness with this
classification. For instance, one "new" older woman in her late fifties or
early sixties attended a club meeting (Carrie James Circle) of elder women,
many of whom were in their 70s and 80s, though two or three were
younger. She quietly explained to me that she would not belong to the club
if it were not for her ninety-year-old mother. Her mother enjoyed the
sociability with the older women who were *her* peers. By implication, the

younger woman did not prefer participating but brought her mother, who, by the way, then acted as a familial peer-link to involve her daughter with an older generation of women with whom she did not want to be identified. This example suggests that some covert attitudes of disesteem encourage the age-graded segregation of elder women; at the same time it illustrates the strength of the familial peer-link in overcoming such segregation.

The Carrie James Circle organization of women also had another mother-daughter pair in a similar situation. The daughter and her husband had retired to Curlew Point and her mother came later. The daughter attended the meetings with her mother, but became active herself as well. Another younger retired woman was married to a man in his seventies and was active with women of his age group (her husband is a peer-link). She explained this only to younger women like the researcher whom she encountered at the meetings of older women. Still another younger retired woman in another organization (King's Daughters) simply accepted the kindly sociability of the elder women, saying she had always worked and needed to be socially active, and they offered her ways to be.

These four "new" younger retired women were each active in the leadership of at least three of these seven elder women's organizations in Curlew Point (though not the same groups). Three reported that earlier in their lives they had not been active in women's formal organizations. Three also said that because of family experience with the plight of aged people they felt obligated to contribute to the preservation of the local aged women's organizations. It was good for the older women to get out of the house, to socialize and do things which contributed to the community. One frankly admitted that taking the officer's post gave her a feeling of belongingness and importance in her first year of residence. These women organized workshops, bought materials for them, taught skills, kept records, and presided at club meetings. These leaders acted as liaison's with the broader community for the organizations, often involving the other women in ways they would not have sought given their more restricted social experiences. These younger retired women, so recently involved in the more public working world, bridged the spheres of private agedness and public working adulthood.

The elder women's organizations were revitalized by the leadership of younger retired women. All the clubs seem to have problems recruiting officers. I observed many subtle struggles between native elder women as a leader—seeking to turn her office over to another—approached each member in turn. Several women had held office five and sometimes ten years, and they expressed feelings of weariness at the prospect of continuing in the responsibilities. Native women did not seem to want the responsibilities, yet they faithfully attended meetings and expressed great pleasure in the sociability they enjoyed at the meetings. When "new," younger, retired women attended, they were usually asked to accept an office or some other responsibility immediately.

Taking leadership responsibilities offered new women the opportunity to work directly with a larger number of organization members than they would have gotten to know otherwise. These club members then knew and approved of the "new" person, spoke well of her to friends and family. On future occasions the "new" person was introduced to friends and family. In this gradual way the "new" person became integrated into the community life. This process occurred for persons who were simply "new members," too, but not as quickly or as warmly as for those who accepted leadership. The younger generations of local people waited until familial elders approved of these "new" older natives before they extended friendliness. In effect, the younger generations waited for their kin elders to act as familial peer-links, and in doing so the structural requirements for intergenerational sociability were met for the younger natives and the older retirees. Without the approval of age category peers, integration into the community was inhibited. The women's organizations were structures which formalized and facilitated this community integration of "new" people.

8. Conclusion

Elder women's organizations in Curlew Point were informally age-graded, because recruitment depended upon the personal relationships of existing members. The relationship that was most important was that of friend, which is normatively restricted to persons close in age. However, relatives can serve to bring persons of diverse ages together. These *familial peer-links* help to integrate the interactions of people in different generations. The *peer-link*—a person senior and junior to two others whom she brings together—can function similarly. These recruitment mechanisms accounted for the occasionally dissimilar ages of members in women's organizations and for the predominating tendency toward age-grade similarity in memberships. By recruiting "new" older women recently retired, elder women's organizations facilitated their integration into the community.

Ironically, the only older woman's organization with prescribed ages included a much broader range of ages among its membership. This suggests that informally observed age-grading customs—as seen in women's groups with *no* prescribed ages for members—are even more stringent when no age limits are stated. The disesteem attached to older age-group status may be even more significant in creating social segregation for the aged when *no formal* structures are laid down at all. As long as friendship is the only structural device for recruiting organizational membership, the demands of age hierarchy will create age segregation in older people's organizations.

An understanding of the function of friendship and peerage in community integration of generations is possible only by studying age relations in a community context by taking a holistic perspective on the life course of individuals and upon their age-integrated communities. It is impossible to understand the social condition of the aged without this broader context. It is this overview which anthropology is especially equipped to offer, and it can do more to enlighten gerontological research than many perspectives currently being explored.

Notes

[1]Funding for the research was provided by the Center for Studies of Metropolitan Problems, National Institute for Mental Health -1 RO1 MH21550-01. I wish to thank Virginia Finne, for her articulate dialogue during the development of these ideas, and John Honigmann, for his academic supportiveness and egalitarianism. All *names* of places, persons, and organizations have been changed to protect the privacy of those who worked with me in the research.

[2]I am, in this case, using myself as an informant. Along with Schneider (1968:13), I recognize my own personal experience as a source of information. Since I share the same United States culture and regional subculture as Curlew Pointers, this did not seem inappropriate.

8
Labor and Domestic Life Cycles In a German Community

J.M. Weatherford

1. Introduction

Since introduction into the anthropological literature, the concept of life cycle has been used to compare aging in a number of non-Western societies (Fortes 1949). In the field of demography, the concept has been used even more extensively than in anthropology, but it has been confined primarily to intra-societal changes over time or to variations between socio-economic groups within the same society (Glick 1947; Glick and Parke 1965). Only a few efforts have been made to compare life cycles among industrialized nations (Shanas et.al. 1968; Giraldo & Weatherford 1978). Too often there seems to be a tacit assumption that variation among industrial nations represents a minor difference in life style or is only a temporary holdover from the pre-industrial era. Yet, there is in fact no more reason for assuming basic homogeneity of life cycle among industrial peoples than there is reason for assuming basic homogeneity among all horticultural peoples or all pastoral peoples.

Part of the variation among industrial societies is examined here in reference to the life cycles of men and women in an industrial but non-urban community in West Germany. Emphasis is given to three particular aspects of the aging sequence: (1) the labor or working-life cycle; (2) the domestic family-life cycle; and (3) the transitions within these life cycles. It is shown that even though there are a few differences between the labor-force cycle in this community and other industrial communities, there are substantial differences in the domestic arrangements, in the manner of handling role transitions in the life course, and thereby in the social and cultural patterns of aging. This variation is accounted for by: (l) particular values which are pronounced in German society; (2) ensuing laws and government policies which support these values; and (3) the rural environment in which the community is located.

2. The Community

The town of Kahl lies on the Main river at the edge of West Germany's highly industrialized Rhein-Main region.[1] Even though it is relatively small— only 8,000 inhabitants—it is neither a suburb of a larger city nor is it still a village. But it does contain elements of both. The majority of people in the town work in either industry or commerce; even though there are numerous large gardens, no one is employed full-time in agriculture. Several small factories are located in the community; these supply employment for residents as well as for commuters from smaller villages. Many residents of Kahl also commute to work in one of several larger urban centers within forty-five minutes of Kahl (Sheuring 1972).

Despite the small size of Kahl, it has a long industrial history. Because of the poor quality of the soil, it was never a profitable agricultural community. Instead, the residents took advantage of the river to mill agricultural products for surrounding communities. The mills were transformed to small manufacturing plants early in the 19th century (Sheuring 1972; Bergman 1974; Weatherford 1980). At first this was for low technology production of barrels, cigars, and textiles. By the end of the nineteenth century, however, the technological base of the community had shifted from textiles to the manufacture of textile machines, and to the new technology of manufacturing electrical equipment. This high technology base has continued to the present, with the addition of nuclear power facility and extensive manufacture of electrical equipment (Bergman 1974).

Even though a small community, Kahl is very much a part of the modern, industrial world. Kahl was one of the early industrial communities in continental Europe, and it persists in maintaining a high degree of technological sophistication. It has managed to stay small by design, and through local ordinances which fostered moderate-but-steady growth in population. Even so the population has grown from just over a thousand residents in 1900 to its present size of 8,000. Until the labor shortage in West Germany in the 1970s, the community usually supplied more jobs than it had residents. Today, however, the ratio of jobs to workers has stabilized (Weatherford 1980).

Industrial growth reached a peak in the 1970s and there are signs that it may decrease in the 1980s. Commuter access to the higher-paying jobs of urban areas removes the need for more factories in the community, and there is a general backlash against the nuclear facilities of the community. The small size of the community and its location (with rivers and forests) make it a desirable place to live, and the residents are now more interested in protecting that quality of life as long as they are able to find employment elsewhere. Under present conditions, it seems unlikely that the town council will allow further expansion of the nuclear or the manufacturing facilities. The community is small and is likely to remain so.

For the people of Kahl, the two major arenas in which they live out their lives are the home and work place. Social identity and status are derived from these two arenas. As the individual moves through the life cycle, transitions and status changes in the two arenas are intertwined, but do not necessarily occur at the same times or speed. Attention is now turned toward the separate examination of these two arenas, and to the differential impacts which these have on the life cycles of males and of females. Despite the differences in the two arenas and the differences in male and female development, it is shown that there are social and cultural factors which influence how transitions are enacted. Certain common features underlie all of the changes, whether it is a boy entering school, a girl being apprenticed, a man retiring, or a woman dying.

3. Labor Life Cycle

For both males and females, entry into the labor force can come at any time after age 14, but for the few who may have advanced education, it can be as late as the mid-twenties. Among working-class families the entry of young people begins earlier than for middle-class and professional families; the working-class child is usually apprenticed by age 16. According to German law, the parents are financially obligated to support their children not just to a particular age such as 18, but until the child has a viable occupation. Having an occupation means that the child officially completed an apprenticeship, obtained a certificate of advanced training, or graduated from a university. Because of this law, parents begin planning early for the occupation of their child, and the law insures that every female as well as every male will be specifically trained in an occupation.

Planning for a child's profession usually must begin prior to the child's entry into school. With the three levels of schools corresponding roughly to the three major socio-economic classes, the type of school which the child attends severely limits his or her occupational choices (Warren 1967). In Kahl, there was only the basic elementary school (Grundschule), which ended with the ninth grade and prepared children only for the lowest apprenticeships. Some parents did manage to send their children to other schools in nearby towns, but this type of planning and finance took a great deal of extra effort on the parents' part. The vast majority of children were simply tracked into the elementary system for preparation to be workers. As shown in Table 8:1, over three-quarters of the adult population have on-

TABLE 8.1

POPULATION BY EDUCATION AND SEX: 1970

	Adults			Current Students		
	Female	Male	Total	Female	Male	Total
Elementary	2316	1972	4288	415	479	894
	.42	.36	.78	.36	.41	.78
Middle	337	240	577	81	75	156
School or	06	.04	.10	.07	.07	.14
Gymnasium						
Technical	172	368	540	20	43	63
School	.03	.07	.10	.02	.04	.05
University	35	81	116	11	22	33
	.01	.02		.01	.02	.03
Total	2860	2661	5521	527	619	1145
			1.00			1.00

ly an elementary school education. Females have a slight educational advantage in that they are more likely to receive middle-level education in preparation for clerical jobs, but they are severely under-represented in the upper school categories. The 78 percent of the population with only elementary education is indicative of the strong working-class orientation of the town.

With the legal requirement that women be trained for an occupation, and with the working-class orientation of the town, it is not surprising that over half of the female population above age 15 is a part of the labor force (Table 8.2). Fifty-one percent of the women in this age category are active wage earners, but 84 percent of the men in these ages are wage earners. Men comprise 63 percent of the total labor force of the town, even though they represent only 48 percent of the total adult population. Lower female participation can be accounted for by the fact that a minority of German women do not work; these tend to be the wives of middle-and upper-income professionals (Solomon 1977). The bulk of the non-working women, however, are older females who have left the labor force in their 50s but who do not begin drawing their retirement until their 60s. Despite the fact that male labor force participation is higher than that for females, the participation of women still accounts for 38 percent of the total labor force and for a majority of adult women, and most women do work for substantial parts of their adult lives.

Unlike the guild system, from which the current apprenticeship system is derived, modern youths are more likely to be apprenticed into factories than to individual craftsmen. Some professions—such as bakers, grocers, plumbers, and barbers—are still conducted on a "small shop" basis, in which one or two Apprentices work directly under the Master, but the majority of youths would more likely be apprenticed to textile mills, a chemical factory, or perhaps a retail department store. There the young men and women begin by learning how to clean up and do general maintenance; gradually, they become more active in the production process. In principle, all apprenticeships are open to members of both sexes, but in practice there is a clear differentiation between male and female occupations. A young man may be apprenticed as a butcher, but a young woman would be apprenticed as a helper to the butcher's wife to specialize as a meat server. Similarly, a young man might be apprenticed to a chemical or electronics factory, while a young woman would be apprenticed to a textile mill or a shoe store. Obviously these differences in the original apprenticeships will have life-long repercussions on the labor force participation and earning power of the individuals; this is particularly so in light of the difficulty in changing occupations. The two or three years invested in an apprenticeship—combined with another three to five years in a journeymanship—make the educational process long, and once completed it is difficult for the individual to begin again as an Apprentice in another occupation.

TABLE 8.2

LABOR FORCE PARTICIPATION BY SEX
OF POPULATION ABOVE AGE 15: 1970

	Out	In	Total
Female	1438	1508	2946
	.25	.26	.52
Male	179	2579	2758
	.03	.45	.43
Total	1617	4087	5704
			1.00

When a child completes the apprenticeship and passes the examination into Journeyman status, the legal obligations of the parents to support the child are finished. In the eyes of the law, the parents have completed their requirement to educate the child to self-sufficiency, and at this point in life the child begins to earn minimum adult wages. The next step is to complete the journeymanship and take an examination for the Master status. For the majority of men this is a normal progression; if they are to advance in their careers they must become Masters. For females, however, there are fewer pressures and expectations about becoming Masters in their fields. For most female occupations there is the shared assumption that the woman needs no more than to complete her apprenticeship to perform successfully the duties of that profession. Even if she did become a Master in the field, most of the female professions have no established routes of advancement. For example, a seamstess in modern Kahl is usually a woman who works on the looms or in the sewing room of a textile mill. For her the two-year apprenticeship teaches her most of what she needs to know to operate the assembly-line machines, and there is no advancement incentive for her to become a Master. Only if the woman were to set up an independent shop to make clothes or do alterations would she need to become a Master. Within the factories the supervisory positions are mostly closed to her, because those jobs do not fall into the seamstress profession; the supervisors are a different occupational group.

In terms of salary women are substantially below men, both because they hold lower occupations, and because they are less likely to be advanced in these occupations. In terms of benefits such as sick pay, vacations, and holidays, however, there is general parity for male and female workers. These areas are strictly controlled by government policy which, for example, specifies that all workers must be part of the basic health insurance plan of the nation, or that all workers be guaranteed a minimum of four weeks paid vacation. The primary distinction, then, between male and female life cycle in the labor force is in terms of occupation, and consequent pay and advancement with the accompanying distinctions in prestige. These differences begin with the process whereby parents select their child's occupation and apprenticeship, and the differences are reinforced by the fact that women are less likely than are men to ever become Masters in any given profession.

4. Domestic Life Cycle

Despite the industrial base of Kahl and the modernity of the community, domestic life seems to be a blend of traditional kin organization and more modern forms.[2] Three-generation households are common, and nuclear family households tend to be grouped together on the basis of kinship (Weatherford 1980). This organization of households within the same building results in a functioning unit of domestic life which resembles stem family households, even though the residences are technically separate (Weatherford 1977). Domestic activities such as child care, housekeeping, yard work, and cooking is organized across household lines, with three or more generations of the same family operating in many respects as a single domestic organization.

Despite some early disclaimers by Parsons (1943), the importance of kinship and family for working-class people is well-established in the anthropological literature (Firth 1964; Adams 1968; Komorovsky 1964;

Stack 1974). Most of this research, however, has focused on urban residents. The correlation between urban and industrial life is so taken for granted that the terms are often used synonymously. Rural industrialization is hardly considered anything more than a temporary anomaly. There seems to be a tacit assumption that either rural industrial areas will grow into urban areas, as has often happened, or that the rural residents will take on the characteristics of urban residents in due time. Rural industrialization, however, is a process which has been underway for well over a century (Weatherford 1980), and gradually there is an awareness that perhaps the social forms accompanying it are neither urban nor peasant (Fischer 1973; Braun 1970; Scott and Tilly 1975). Rural industrial workers may organize their lives in a unique way, combining characteristics of both traditional peasant life and modern urban life (Friedman 1978). This combination appears in the social organization of a community such as Kahl, but there is no reason to assume that it is only temporary or only a partial modernization.

Four important factors underlie the present form of domestic, and familial, organization in Kahl. First, there is the historical importance of stem-families in the area. Peter Laslett (1972) cites parts of German-speaking Europe as the only areas in Europe where stem-families were commonly found. Even in contemporary urban areas which are organized into nuclear households, Germans tend to be very family-oriented (Rainwater 1962; Devereaux et. al. 1962; Spindler 1973; Warren 1967; Solomon 1977). Secondly, Germany has one of the lowest birth rates in the world; this removes some of the internal family pressure to split into smaller households. If a family has only one or two children, it is easy for one child to bring a spouse home to live, or to take an adjoining apartment to the parents; in families with three or four children this would be more difficult.

Thirdly, the spatial conditions of a rural or village community are more flexible than those of an urban environment.[3] It is easier for family members in Kahl to live close to one another, or to adapt the family house for three generations. This would be more difficult to arrange in an urban area which is more densely constructed. Fourthly, German law details the responsibilities of adult children to care for their parents. This, combined with inheritance practices and related government policies, makes it more practical for several generations to live together or nearby.

Almost all adults in Kahl marry, and stay married for life. As shown in Table 8:3, 78 percent of the population above the age 18 was married in 1970. The 11 percent who were single were mostly the young people in their late teens or early twenties. Ten percent of the population was widowed, but only slightly over two percent of the adult population had ever been divorced.

At the time of marriage, the wife has few economic resources available to her; she cannot even support herself. Her only experience outside of the home has been in the public school and as an Apprentice in a local factory or shop, and she has always lived at home in the household of her parents. The man enters marriage with considerable economic resources; he has a higher income, and usually a substantial savings account. He has experience in several institutions outside of the home—school, the military, and employment in separate places as both Apprentice, and as Journeyman. And he has lived at least the term of his military service away from the home of his parents. The husband is then experienced in interaction with a larger social network, is financially independent, and functions in the world with minimum assistance. The wife is financially dependent, has little experience beyond kinship and employment network, and is not capable of living on her own. Thus at the onset of marriage, the wife is dependent—financially, socially, as well as often emotionally—on her husband. These conditions result not just from social and economic factors, but they are reinforced through the cultural understandings of what it means to be male or female, and to be a husband or a wife.

TABLE 8.3

SEX AND MARITAL STATUS
OF POPULATION ABOVE AGE 18: 1970

	Female	Male	Total
Single	253	341	594
	.04	.06	.11
Married	2017	2049	4066
	.38	.37	.78
Divorced	60	36	96
	.01	.01	.02
Widowed	462	83	545
	.09	.02	.10
Total	2792	2509	5301
	.53	.47	1.00

As in most Western societies, the status of the husband is tied with a core set of expectations about his job, and his functioning as financial provider. The status of the wife is similarly tied to a set of expectations associated with running the home, and becoming a mother. At the very start of marriage, the man is in a position to meet his expectations; he is the breadwinner by virtue of his economic position. The woman, however, is not in a position to run the house, since that is already being done by the senior woman (her mother or her mother-in-law). With the passage of the family cycle, the younger woman gradually learns, and acquires the tasks which are performed by the senior woman. Included in this are not only cleaning and cooking, but the management of the budget as well. The senior woman pays the bills and taxes, and allocates money for food, clothing, recreation, and other expenses. In time this expertise in handling money leads to the wife's exerting control over that money. Accomplishing this the woman obtains experience and competence in interactions with agencies outside the home. It is she who deals with the bank, the tax office, the electric company, the school system, and the government bureaucracy, as well as with shopkeepers.

In the meantime, the man's social relations outside of the home are centered around his work and a male friendship clique. Even though it was the husband who began with greater experience in finances and with outside agencies, he does not continue to develop such activities. Instead, the wife performs these acts and represents the family in these various social contexts (Lamouse 1969). Even though the wife herself may also be employed, she gradually learns to take over the management of the home (Lupri 1969).

At the age of retirement, the man ceases to enact those expectations which had been the major focus of his status as husband; he is no longer employed. In his own eyes and in the opinion of others, the primary functions of his role have ceased. By this time, he is the old man living in the house with one of his married children. The home is under the management of his wife, who is now the senior female. Although the wife usually retires at an even earlier age, the understandings about what it is to be a wife, a woman, and a mother, keep her from losing the primary activity associated with these statuses. Even if she is no longer employed, there are a host of culturally supplied expectations of what she is to do and what her importance is. In addition to the cultural supports, she is still pushed by the practical concerns of her being the only one in the family who knows how to manage the household. She knows how to pay the taxes, how much potatoes to buy for the winter, whether or not they can afford a color television, and how to handle the insurance policies. Rather than decreasing through the years, the importance of these activities has increased since the family has grown to include grandchildren. Because of the inexperience of her daughter or daughter-in-law, it is the senior woman who has the major responsibility for managing the household.

By the time of retirement, a certain amount of role reversal in the husband-wife relationship has been achieved. Whereas the husband is financially strong and socially independent at the time of marriage, during old age he is quite dependent on his wife to manage the finances, take care of primary social relations with outside agencies, and provide for his material comforts. Whereas at the start of marriage, the husband was already performing his primary life-activity as a working man, the woman had not yet begun her performance of her primary activity as the resident manager of the home and family. At retirement the man ceases to perform his activities as the principle breadwinner, but the woman is at the height of her efficiency in managing a household.

As long as the elderly woman is healthy and strong enough to continue as resident manager, she plays the pivotal part in family relations. The man, despite what vigor and strength he may still have at retirement, becomes somewhat tangential to the main functioning of the family. He does do minor repairs around the house and assumes management of the garden, but overall he is dependent on his wife for the running of the household.

5.   Life Cycle Transitions

The process of aging is also the process of moving through the socially prescribed role sequence of life (Riley et. al. 1972; Riley 1976), but every society must develop a mechanism or a way to move people through this sequence. Unlike biological aging, the process of social aging does not just happen, it must be pushed along. Time tables and key age norms are used to judge this process and help to pull or push the individual through the sequence (Riley et. al. 1972). In some tribal societies, relatively standardized age-grades are used as markers and mechanisms for moving people through the sequence (Van Gennep 1909). In most industrial societies, however, the individual is in a number of different age tracts or sequences at once (Riley et. al. 1972; Riley 1976). Movement through the work or occupational life does not exactly correspond with movement through the family sequence. Still, in societies like the United States, there is a tendency to cluster role transitions together; changes in role relationships in one field, such as the family, often occur at roughly the same time as changes in another field, such as work. Thus, a young person may leave school, marry, start a career, and set up an independent household all within a very short span of time (Glaser & Strauss 1971; Brim & Wheeler 1966).

This American pattern of clustering large numbers of major transitions is analagous to the age-grade transitions among some tribal societies, but it is not necessarily a characteristic of industrial societies in general. To the contrary, in the Kahl example, the people move through the sequence at quite different rates and on a much slower timetable. The common pattern for transitions in the two areas examined (domestic life and work life) is that major transitions are separate from one another. Additionally, transitions in both areas are broken down into numerous small transitions each of which is vital to the change, but each step alone appears almost insignificant (Weatherford 1978).

After birth, two of the most important changes in a child's life are entering school and leaving school to enter the labor force (Warren 1967). Unlike the United States, where these two changes have precise temporal and behavioral markers (Glaser & Strauss 1971; Brim & Wheeler 1966), the changes in Germany are spread out into a number of small occurences (Weatherford 1978). Even though the German child may have attended kindergarten as a type of pre-school, the first day of the first year of formal education is a precise one. On this day, the child comes to school for a few hours with one of his parents or grandparents. After the first day, the child will attend school for only a few hours each morning during the first year. During the first few months of school, one of the child's family members will probably walk the child to and from school each day. In this way school is not something which suddenly begins; rather it is slowly phased in, with the child's being taken to school after breakfast and brought home before lunch. As the school years continue, the number of daily school hours will expand. The transition is then slow and methodical rather than abrupt.

This transition into school life is hardly complete before the transitions to the work force begin. Beginning with the fifth grade, the child's training is oriented toward one of three types of occupations—manual, clerical, or professional. The children begin taking occupational courses such as shop, woodwork, sewing, with continued emphasis on basic skills of language and math. By the end of the ninth grade, this has shifted away from the basic instruction to extensive occuaptional classes. With the beginning of the apprenticeship, the youth is still in school a few days a week, while working the other days. Gradually the school time is reduced further until the pupil is a full-time worker.

In addition to these gradual changes by degree from at-home child to pupil to full-time worker, other changes through childhood and adulthood are also occurring. These include baptism, first communion or confirmation, cutting of long hair (around age 14 for girls), and being addressed in formal terms (as *Sie* rather than as *du* at age 16). These small changes in various spheres (economic, religious and linguistic) occur at different times. The cumulative effect, however, is to provide a distinctly undramatic change from childhood to adulthood.

The transition from being single to married is also divided into a number of small steps. One of the first steps after courtship is that a serious couple will establish a savings account. Once this account is large enough, they may begin buying things, such as a car or some new furniture for their future home. Slowly the couple begins spending more time at the residence of the parents, with whom they will eventually live. During this time they become formally engaged and they begin preparing an apartment in their new residence. Sexual intimacy is usually initiated well before engagement, and often the couple will spend nights together in their new residence. As a final step, the couple will be married legally, and on a separate occasion they will probably also be married religiously. But the two ceremonies are never done on the same day. In this way the wedding and the celebration accompanying it are symbolic statements of something which has already occurred. Throughout this process the economic, sexual, legal, religious, and familial aspects of getting married are parcelled out over a long period of time. An individual's change in status from a single person to a married person is not something which occurs overnight. This makes the separate parts of the transition less emotionally laden since the components are not clustered together.

These transitions from courtship through marriage also overlap the economic transitions from pupil to apprentice to worker. In combination then, there are a series of gradual transformations being enacted at the same time, but by spreading them out and making each one a relatively minor event, the movement from one life status or role set into another is almost imperceptible.

The series of labor force and familial transitions into old age are also as small and imperceptible as those from childhood to adulthood. Retirement itself is a slow process rather than an abrupt adjustment. Senior workers are apt to have considerable time free from their work. This extra free time comes about through very liberal vacation policies which grant extended leave (often around two months a year) to older workers. In addition, sick leave is much more liberally interpreted and granted than in the United States. This refers not just to times of illness but also to extended periods of preventive rest and recuperation, often combined with long visits at health spas. These month-long visits to the spa are reputed to forestall heart disease and numerous ailments which are likely to strike the older worker. While the medical benefits are uncertain for any specific disease, such rests improve worker morale and help to lessen the work burden of the older workers.

What is of primary interest here, however, is the fact that these various types of extended leaves provide a gradual transition from full-time worker to retiree. This is further slowed down by the extensive use of part-time and piece-work employment. After formal retirement many workers (especially women) continue to work part-time. This varies greatly with the type of oc-cupation, but it may be temporary during peak seasons, relief work during vacations, or half-day work. A variation on this is the piece work which the elderly do at home. In Kahl, this is usually the assembly of small electrical parts, which are delivered to the home and picked up after assembly. Through both piece work and part-time work, the change from full-time employment to retiree is spread out over a number of years. A worker as young as 45 may be working only nine or ten months a year, and yet a worker of 75 still may be working the equivalent of two or three months a year.

In the domestic cycle, the transitions are equally as gradual, with older women helping in the care of children, the running of the house and management of the garden. As noted, this is easier in the case of women than men, but men can take over gardens and assist their wives. Generally, though, there is not enough work around the house to fill up the time of two adults full-time, and it is usually the man who ends up with free time on his hands if he does not have part-time employment.

Eventually, however, the senior members of the family become ill or feeble and die. This is—of biological necessity—an abrupt transition for the family unit. Nevertheless the social and psychological processes accompanying this are structured much like the other transitions. The transition is broken down into as many component parts as possible and spread out over time.

The first such transition is often the financial one of transferring ownership of the house. This inheritance is not handled as an after-death event as in many societies: rather, it is usually made at the time when the senior person ceases to be the primary wage earner in the family. Here again, depending on the family, this may come as early as age 50 or as late as age 70, but it is generally made well in advance of death. This transfer of property is well established in law, as well as tradition. The senior person who gives over the residence to the younger generation will still retain in law the right to live in the house until death. The older couple need not fear that the children might sell the house, or ask the senior couple to leave. Even in the rare event that the younger couple may divorce or die before the parents, the legal right of the parents to live in the house until death will not be altered.

In less defined ways, the transfer of other properties is likely to parallel that of the house. In this way death is not lumped together with major property changes. Usually, by the time the older person dies, the only property changes will be that of a few personal belongings, such as a television set, family heirlooms, a small amount of furniture, and a small bank account.

The social transitions are further eased and extended by the natural reduction in domestic work which the old person performs. As the senior man or woman enters the final years of life, he or she will be able to perform fewer and fewer of the duries around the house. This facilitates a gradual change of tasks from one generation to the next, as well as a gradual transition in domestic roles. For the most part, however, the senior person is not bed-ridden or incapacitated until just before death.

Psychological adjustment of the family to the death of one of the senior members is anticipated by open discussion of a pending death. Whenever an older person is ill, chances are that it will be referred to as dying. Thus a 65-year-old woman may be bed-ridden for a few weeks with the flu, and she as well as other members are likely to say, "Grandmother is dying." Even though the woman recovers and lives to be 75, by the time she actually dies, the family would have had time to adjust to this inevitable occurrence. By the time the final episode occurs, the family would have in a sense rehearsed it enough to make it less painful and debilitating to other family members.

The elderly are also allowed special privileges in their final years as part of the long process of dying. They may be allowed to smoke more, consume more alcohol, stay up late at night watching television, or eat only what they please. This is viewed as only natural, since it is too late for the dying person to worry about high cholesterol in the blood, too much alcohol, or the possibility of lung cancer from smoking. If the person is dying, then a few days one way or the other is not worth giving up salt, fat, sugar, tobacco, alcohol, or so many of the substances which doctors say are unhealthy. This practice indirectly rewards a dying person for the proper acceptance of the death role. By admitting that they are dying or talking about it, they can justify some activities which are otherwise not approved. This extra license also makes the older person less burdensome for the other family members. If Grandfather can watch television, drink a bottle of wine, or eat a box of candy, he is less likely to need as much attention or care. It also relieves the family from providing special meals or special forms of cooking for the elderly.

Most people in Kahl die at home. Even though they may be hospitalized several times in their final years, once it is decided that the person is actually dying, it is unlikely that they will return to the hospital. Medical care is continued through frequent house calls by the doctor or through visits from a nurse or paramedic, but no herculean efforts are made to keep the person alive through intravenous feeding, oxygen tents, or other elaborate devices which are so common in the United States (Riley et. al. 1972; Riley 1976).

Once the person is dead, the body is usually kept at home for the first night and day after death. During this time friends, neighbors, and relatives will visit the family and view the body. Final leave is taken from the deceased and some people may use this occasion to talk privately to the body. Even the burial is not the end of the long process, since the deceased is allowed to use the grave for only twenty years. Then the body is removed and the grave is prepared for the next generation.

In this way the death of an individual is spread out over a long period of time. The psychological, social, and economic components are separated into various steps which occur through several years and are separated as much as possible from the biological act of death. The transition of death is handled as a process analogous to other processes such as leaving school, entering the labor force, or retiring.

6. Conclusion

The transitions through the labor life cycle and the domestic life cycle as described here represent just one possible sequence for workers in an industrial community. Even though the economic system and the industrial environment in which these people work is basically similar to those in most industrialized areas, particular social and cultural variables influence the sequence through which the individual passes. The structuring of roles within this organization and the transition between roles is conducted in a particularly German fashion.

The life cycle of the individual in the Kahl family varies significantly from that which one encounters in more urban areas. Even though the inhabitants of Kahl may have a labor life resembling that of workers in the Ruhr or in Berlin, the physical and social environment of Kahl is essentially that of a rural town. Consequently, the domestic arrangement of family life is much more traditional or peasant-oriented, despite the fact that the townspeople abandoned agriculture more than a century ago.

The frequent equating of urbanization with industrialization by social scientists and by policy makers creates difficulty in distinguishing these two variables. Consequently, the pattern of family life and aging in urban areas is often assumed to be an inherent part of industrial or capitalist society. As shown in this analysis of Kahl, however, industrialization does not always coincide with urbanization, and the social process of aging for rural workers can vary significantly from their urban counterparts. These distinctions could become increasingly important in the latter part of the twentieth century, as rural areas become more industrial and the work lives of residents in small towns become similar to work lives in urban areas. The recent industrialization of the United States' Sunbelt is obviously a much different process from the industrialization of the North. The degree to which this changes the life cycle and domestic arrangements of people in these rural areas is still an open empirical question; it is by no means predetermined by what occurred in urban areas.

Many of the social difficulties associated with the life cycle process in countries such as the United States could be more an artifact of urban than industrial conditions. The turbulence of adolescence, as well as the neglect and isolation of the elderly, seem part and parcel of the abrupt changes clustered at decisive points in the life cycle of urban Americans. The cluster of transitions from youth to adulthood, like the cluster of transitions from work to retirement, seems patterned to maximize difficulty for the individual and the family. Patterns like those in Kahl, however, make the process more gradual and the transitions far less problematic. The gradualness of this process in Kahl is attributable to traditional family values, which are recognized and supported in German law and in the policies of the government.

German social policy toward the family and toward the labor force tends to be both extensive and complex; yet it retains a decisive flexibility. In the sphere of family law and policy, there is less reliance on specific age norms, such as age 18 for the end of parental responsibility, or age 65 for retirement. German family policy keeps a focus on the basic need of children to be educated for a career and for the elderly to be cared for within the community. These concerns are also in the inheritance laws which distinguish between house ownership and dwelling rights—a distinction which allows parents to pass home ownership to their children without fearing that they themselves may become homeless or destitute. An entirely separate but schematically similar set of labor laws allows for greater individual flexibility in the work cycle. Adolescents are phased into the labor force in a way which would be contrary to United States laws; yet at the same time older workers are allowed to remain at least minimally productive for longer periods of time.

In more subtle ways, government policies allow for family diversity and individual variation according to circumstances. Programs such as social security, housing assistance, health insurance, children's allowances, student tuition support, workers disability pensions, and general welfare allow more family and individual diversity than in the United States. German policies are less tied to rigid specifications of age, narrow definitions of family relationships, or predetermined concepts of what constitutes a family or household. Thus, the programs can be more accommodating to individual family variation.

A prime example of the rigidity of American policy versus the more flexible German policies is evident in their respective housing policies. The United States has had a succession of very specific and narrowly focused housing polices which were geared to specific subpopulations. The Federal Housing Authority and the Veterans Administration supported housing loans to middle-class nuclear families. The poor were accommodated in small urban apartments under a third set of programs. Because the elderly were essentially excluded from these solutions, yet another set of programs had to be constituted to provide separate housing for the elderly (Hirschorn 1977). Other programs could then be established for the handicapped, or whatever population happened to be in policy consideration at the moment. The result is an unfocused and often unsatisfactory housing policy. In contrast, German housing policies have been integrated for all segments of the populations. Rather than just building units for the poor or specifying only small houses for government-supported loans, German policies provide subsidies to those in need and loan supports for others. This is done with little consideration of whether or not the family includes grandparents or meets a specific bureaucratic definition of a family. One basic approach is modified to account for special needs (such as poverty, handicap, old age, etc.), rather than having a variety of separate programs. These policies are not only more adept at meeting the housing problems of families (in even as densely a populated nation as Germany), but they do not worsen the isolation of the elderly, as do so many American policies. American policies tend to push older adolescents as well as the elderly out of the family, thus contributing to the clustering of transitions and its ensuing problems (Giraldo & Weatherford 1978).

American labor policies are hardly more accommodating to the individual. Despite modifications in mandatory retirement laws and the benefit scale of social security payments for the working elderly, distinct biases against the elderly persist. Similar inflexibility is noted in labor and wage laws as well as training programs for teenagers.

Despite the research of numerous social scientists concerned with aging, family, life cycle, urbanization, and public policy, social programs in the United States have remained persistently blind to the diversity in life-cycle structuring and to the process of aging. From tax policy to housing policy and from child care programs to social security programs, government practices in the United States largely reinforce a life cycle studded with abrupt and far-reaching transitions. The points of severe stress in the life cycle, such as adolescence or old age, may have been worsened in recent decades by well-intentioned policies which fail to account for the potential and actual diversity in individual and family life.

Notes

[1]The data for this study were gathered during fieldwork in Kahl, West Germany from 1974-1976. Various parts were financed by the following sources: The German Marshall Fund, National Institutes of Mental Health (MHO5209), The German Academic Exchange (DAAD), The National Science Foundation (Soc75-18044), and the Council for European Studies.

[2]The research on family life was part of a study under the direction of Marc Swartz. A more detailed analysis is to be published in *Family Goals and Culture in Five Societies* by Marc Swartz, Joshua Akong'a, Michael Murphy, George Saunders, and J.M. Weatherford (manuscript in process).

[3]A detailed examination of the differences between urban and rural social networks in this part of Europe may be found in Crowe (1978). The contrast between family and friendship ties in an urban German community is also analyzed in Solomon (1977).

9
Being Old In the Inner City: Support Systems Of the SRO Aged[1]

Jay Sokolovsky
and
Carl Cohen

1. Introduction

Recent research on America's aged population has centered on the extent and nature of support provided by their interpersonal relationships. This concern has flowed from two interrelated social science perspectives dealing with the lives of older adults. The first—a theoretical persepctive generated mostly from sociology and psychology—has long sought to understand the impact of growing old on social interaction, the performance of roles and the impact on psychological states. A second perspective—emanating from social work—has tried to understand the practical implications of informal social support for delivery of services to the aged living in non-institutionalized environments.

In both sets of research, the issue of social isolation has been a central point of discussion. This is apparent in research describing the poor urban elderly, especially residents of inner-city single room occupancy (SRO) hotels. Much of the literature has generated an axiomatic perception of such elderly as being almost total isolates, lacking personal networks of any significance and possessing a "nominal culture" (Hertz and Hutheesing 1975). It will be the contention of this chapter that certain aspects of these assertions are a convenient myth, fostered by both (1) a failure to examine the totality of interaction of the aged and (2) the lack of concern for the cultural significance of their social linkages. To demonstrate this, we have

163

used an anthropologically based network analysis to examine quantitative and qualitative aspects of social interaction for a particular aged center-city population.

We will also briefly suggest how the knowledge gained from such analysis can assist community agencies and other professionals in maximizing their assistance to the elderly.

2.   Social Isolation, Networks and Growing Old

The coming of old age presents some universal problems for maintaining interpersonal relations. As death removes coevals and older persons from the various linkages in which a person was active, some shifts are expected in the interactional relation between and within age groups. Naturally occurring decrements in health and mobility also potentially limit the physical activity necessary for many forms of human contact. Social isolation in the latter stages of life may thus be considered a logical possibility for many entering the last stages of the life course.

Most studies of isolation in old age have centered on the extent of interpersonal isolation from family, work and friends. The largely discredited disengagement theory (Cumming and Henry 1961) argued that a universal, progressive, interpersonal isolation of the aged occurred, and was functionally linked to the needs of both the aging individual and the ever-changing society. While at first glance the process of growing old may seem to necessitate a great decrease in the size and complexity of personal linkages, this is not necessarily the case. Anthropological studies of certain non-Western societies show that the elderly can often retain and even intensify their cultural linkages into familial, socio-political and sacred spheres of activity by: (1) creating new younger-generation contacts through adoption; (2) marriage of a young spouse; (3) sponsorship of initiation rites (Guemple 1969; Hart and Pilling 1960); or (4) changing the content of behavior in pre-existing role relationships, such as from executor to mediator (see especially Guttman 1974, Turnbull 1965). In certain societies—such as the Kapauku Papuans (Pospisil 1971) of Melanesia, or the Abkhasians (Benet 1974) of the Caucasus—for women especially the onset of old age means the lifting of taboos on various types of social intercourse and a consequent increase in interaction beyond the household. Yet it is also clear that those aged, particularly in certain hunting and gathering and horticultural societies, have relatively small, weak, interpersonal support systems, are in tenuous social and economic positions, and may be the focus of intergenerational conflict via accusations of witchcraft. (Pospisil 1971; Holmberg 1969).

However, it is in industrialized, capitalistic societies like our own that the aging process is most often equated in the gerontological literature with irreparable disjunctures in networks, especially in familial and occupational role relationships. It is often presumed that our culture—with high levels of industrialization and an emphasis on youth and the isolated nuclear family—has deprived our aged of interaction and support available in more traditional societies. The overall impact of these social losses is summed up by Rosow, who asserts that "our current institutions do not offer a choice between marginality and integration of the aged but simply between alternative forms of alienation" (1974:168). Given such a statement, there is little surprise in noting that perhaps the most distinctive social characteristic atttributed to America's urban elderly is social "isolation." This appears to be most emphasized in studies of the inner-city elderly, who have been identified as a uniquely troubled category of our aging population. (Carp 1972; Clark 1971; Clark and Anderson 1967; Lawton and Kleban 1971; Lopata 1975; Stpehens 1976). In studies of poor Jewish aged in a Philadelphia slum area called "Strawberry Mansion," Lawton and Kleban (1971) describe them as having poorer health, lower morale, very limited mobility, and low levels of interaction with family and friends, in comparison with other groups of aged. Clark, an anthropological pioneer in studies of the inner-city aged, remarks that the social interaction of inner-city aged is "simple, seldom intimate and narrowly circumscribed" (1971:64). However, Clark is appropriately cautious, and notes that virtually nothing is known about these social networks, and that our culture's preoccupation with productivity "has trained us to dismiss such people from our range of perception" (p.64).

By far the strongest statements about isolation in the later years stem from the growing number of studies of dilapidated center-city hotels, to which the elderly poor have flocked. Starting with the early studies of Zorbough (1929) and Hayner (1936) center-city hotels have been depicted as representing the ultimate negative effects of urbanism on social life. These studies report pervasive levels of extreme anonymity and isolation from personal contacts and general social activity. Some recent studies centering more specifically on the elderly have come to similar conclusions. The most emphatically stated is the work of Stephens, based on a research sample of 100 tenants in a downtown Detroit SRO, the Guinevere. She views the elderly as living in a "society of the alone," dominated by social "atomism" and norms of freedom, privacy and utilitarianism. She describes virtually the entire aged population (90 percent male) as strongly alienated life-long "loners," who "have broken all ties to family, friends and for the most part do not attempt to replenish what was already an impoverished repertoire of social relations" (1976:91). The few ties that do develop are claimed to be non-intimate and utilitarian, based on either economic exchange or leisure-time activities in public places. It is also maintained that those few aged women who live in the Guinevere have a particularly hard time in generating even the few utilitarian ties which the men maintain. Another recent study echoes Stephens' analysis, particularly with regard to female SRO residents. Lally et. al. (1979), studying a number of Seattle hotels, focused on a small sample (16) of older women who had higher than average education for their age cohort, and a majority of whom had worked in traditionally male occupations. Based on interviews, the authors depict these women as having only limited functional ties with hotel staff, and nearby business proprietors as respondents "consistently claimed to neither be friends with or even know other women in their hotels" (p.70).

Despite the emphatic denials of much personal contact occurring for the urban aged, when studies have been designed to measure the extent of social interaction, the results have been surprising. Starting with the studies of intergenerational family relations by researchers such as Sussman and Burchinal (1962), Rosenmayer (1977) and especially Shanas et. al. (1968, Shanas 1979) it has been found that despite the high levels of mobility, diversity of interests and preponderance of separate dwelling patterns for urban families that "family help, particularly in time of illness, exchange of services, and regular visits are common among old people and their children and relatives whether or not these live under a single roof" (Shanas 1979, Shanas et. al. 1968). What has essentially been found is that the structure of the family network, rather than having disintegrated, has adapted to high levels of change and diversity by maintaining generational "intimacy" at a distance through the maintenance of frequent contact and the exchange of mutual services.

In similar fashion, a limited number of large-scale studies concerning the social linkages of the inner-city aged have indicated low levels of extreme isolation. Marjorie Cantor's study (1975) of a cross-section of New York's poorest residents (sample of 1552 persons) provides data to strongly indicate the "importance of friends and neighbors in the life of urban elderly" (p.25). More than 60 percent know at least one neighbor well, and, importantly, "live alones" are significantly *more* likely to report knowing at least one neightbor well. In strong contrast to previously discussed studies, 50 percent of the sample maintained intimate contacts and two thirds saw their children monthly (p.25-26). The study also notes that only eight percent appear to have no significant personal support system, although some of these "true" isolates have contact with community organizations or religious institutions.

Other studies of center-city aged—by Tissue in Sacramento (1971), Lawton, Kleban and Singer (1971) in Philadelphia, Bild and Havighurst (1976) in Chicago and Ehrlich's (1976) St. Louis hotel research—while not indicating the high interaction rates found by Cantor, show that many elderly maintain at least a few close personal ties. Anthropologically oriented studies of hotels in San Diego (Erickson and Eckert, 1977), New York's Upper West side (Siegel, 1977) and the Mid-town area (Sokolovsky et. al., 1978; Sokolovsky and Cohen, 1978), provide cultural and empirical data disputing the claims of total isolation for the SRO aged.

What is emerging from a growing body of data on the inner-city aged is a confounding picture bearing on the question of the extent of their social isolation. It is the contention here that the glaring contradictions are not simple matters of variations in sampled populations. Rather, the inconsistencies stem more from a failure to both secure reliable data on *total* social networks and to place this data in its proper cultural context.

3. Social Interaction and Gerontology

The methodological issue of empirically defining social networks is of great importance in gerontological studies. Measures of social interaction have been utilized in studies of the elderly in testing various theories relating levles of sociability with: (1) the aging process itself (Cumming and Henry 1961); (2) community creation (Johnson 1971; Hochschild 1973; Ross 1977; Keith 1979, 1980a); (3) loneliness (Townsend 1957, 1968); (4) life satisfaction (Rosow 1967; Lemon, Bengtson and Peterson 1972); (5) adaptations to total institutions (Granick and Nahemow 1961); and (6) measures of mental health (Lowenthal 1964, Clark and Anderson 1967). While researchers in social gerontology strongly advocate the need to understand the social networks of the elderly (see especially Lowenthal and Robinson 1976) virtually no research has investigated the total extent of personal ties maintained by the aged.[2]

Moreover, in the limited number of attempts to research the entire scope of elderly social interaction, little concern has been taken to delineate the relative importance of given relations. For example Townsend (1957), followed by Tunstall (1968) has taken a behavioral approach in measuring the societal integration of his British elderly sample by a scale based on the number of social contacts per week (social contact score). Although these excellent studies are some of the few attempts to measure the total extent of elderly interaction, the significance of each social link is essentially determined by the frequency of contact.

Granick and Nahemow (1961), trying to measure the isolation of Jewish Home elderly populations during adulthood and just prior to entering the home, devised a more complex scale. This is based on a restricted measure of contacts in a person's prior job career, marital status, kinship connections, friendships and organizational activity. They considered anyone under the mean figure for each scale to be relatively isolated. However, such a scale can underrepresent the social interaction of those not having a large family. This is particularly problematic for many inner-city elderly, who have life histories showing early disjunctures from much of their kinship networks. By their scale, for example, a person, all of whose close kin members were dead, but who maintainted 20 intense non-kin friendships, would be considered isolated.

A more ambitious approach was taken by Clark and Anderson in a study of elderly persons in San Francisco. They sought to establish a measure called "social interaction level" which intended to determine "to what extent does the subject extend himself into the social world around him?" (1967:49-50). This scale combines levels of personal, economic and cultural activity. Yet, as the authors note "no effort was made to distinguish these levels on the basis of the duration, content or frequency of the social interaction" (1967:151). Still, it was clearly shown that for the community elderly gross measures of social interaction, rather than social roles, were most important in explaining variations in mental health.

Other approaches have used simple enumerative sociometric techniques, eliciting data by questions such as, "How many good friends do you have?" or, "How many relatives have you seen in the last week?" However, as we have argued in greater detail elsewhere, (Sokolovsky and Cohen, In Press) such methods not only fail to illuminate the complexities of social interaction but tend to inaccurately portray actual behavior.

This observation is replicated by the work of Killworth and Bernard (1976), which casts serious doubt on simple enumerative methods. In an intriguing study of teletype communication among the deaf elite of Washington, D.C., persons were asked to rank others they "talked" to (via teletype) on a "most to least" scale. In comparing the cognitive perception (who do you talk to, most-least?) with behavioral action (recorded frequency and length of communication), it is shown that neither the amount of communication nor the number of alters chosen relates to the ability to rank communicants accurately (p.226). The authors' conclusions confirm what we discovered impressionistically, "group structure based on one-choice socio-grams are unlikely ever to yield significant results" (p.281).

4. Social Networks and the Network Profile

As a solution to this problem, anthropologists building on the earlier work of Barnes (1954), Bott (1957), Epstein (1969) and Mitchell (1969) have begun to see networks analysis as a useful tool, especially in urban settings in which the informal ties of friendship, kinship, and neighborliness are not easily subsumed by formally bounded institutionalized groups or categories, (see especially Boissevain and Mitchell 1973, Boissevain 1974, Sanjek 1978, Sokolovsky and Cohen, In Press). Network analysis has also become a major research strategy in allied social sciences, with the work of Pattison (1977) and Caplan (1974) in psychology, Fisher (1977) in sociology, and Collins and Pancoast (1976) in social work.

In our work studying elderly hotel dwellers in mid-Manhattan, we attempted to avoid the pitfalls of simple sociometrics by using a hybrid form of network analysis based on an anthropological approach to social linkages. Such an approach focuses on behaviorally analyzing egocentric social networks—"persons with whom a given person is in actual contact, and their interconnections" (Boissevain 1974:25)—within an ethnographically described cultural context.

In doing our analysis, we combined: (1) participant observation; (2) a 100-item questionnaire, consisting of standard biographical/demographic items and several health/psychosocial inventories; and (3) a revised "network analysis profile" which had been developed in previous research (Sokolovsky et. al. 1978). The "network profile" is an interview schedule which consecutively structures questions around separate networks sectors (hotel resident, kin); characteristics of each contact (sex, age); and the specific behavioral (recruitment, frequency, type and directional flow of transaction), environmental (in hotel lobby, park) and emotionally salient (intimacy, overall importance) features of interaction. The profile distinguished five network sectors involving social ties; ego-hotel tenant; ego-outside non-kin; ego-kin; ego-hotel staff; ego-agency staff. Only those links behaviorally active (including mail and telephone contact) within the prior year are included as a part of the networks.

It is important to realize that we developed the network profile only after four months of field work and casual discussion of interaction with SRO dwellers. Only after such ethnographic work began to reveal the settings and contexts in which social behavior was likely were we able to ask culturally meaningful questions that revealed information corresponding to our observations.

In total, the resultant methodology provides what anthropologists have called the "first order zone" (Barnes 1972) network, and what others define as the "support system" involving "an enduring pattern of continuous or intermittent ties that play a significant part in maintaining the psychological and physical integrity of the individual over time" (Caplan 1974:7). The network profile enables us to distinguish further the "informal support system" (also referred to here as the "personal network") from the "formal support system." In the former support system—measured by the first three network profile sectors—personal ties are selected by the elderly from among residential neighbors, outside acquaintances and relatives. This leaves for the latter support system the last two network sectors developed within the context of a formal or bureaucratic relationship, such as tenant-management, client-social worker or patient-psychiatrist.

The data collected on the total support system allows us to compare the interactional and morphological variation in our respondents' networks. Links to a given network member can be either single-stranded (uniplex)—involving only one transactional content (e.g., casual conversation)—or multistranded (multiplex)—having multiple contents. They may also vary in terms of the frequency of activation, directionality (the direction in which aid in a relationship flows), and cognitive importance. Variation can also be noted in the interconnectedness of an ego's social relations represented by density (ratio of actual to potential links) or by overall structural design. In this way support systems may be understood in their quantitative and qualitative diversity, varying in size, intensity, intimacy and morphology. What then does this methodology show for a particular set of persons growing old in SRO hotels?

5.   The Sample—Its Setting and Characteristics

The elderly that we studied resided in 11 SRO hotels in the eastern section of midtown Manhattan. These hotels—as is the case of other cities where they are numerous—are found mostly down narrow, commercially-zoned side streets, surrounded by bars, office buildings, sandwich shops, and small retail and grocery stores. The hotels themselves range in size from six to 12 stories, and house between 90 and 400 persons of whom 15 to 25 percent are over 60 years of age.

Our sample consisted of 96 persons (47 males and 49 females) ranging in age from 60 to 93 years (mean: 72 years). In similar proportion to the elderly in general living in New York's SRO hotels, 90 percent of our sample are white, nine percent black and one percent hispanic. The educational level was surprisingly high, with just under a third having some years of college and just over a third having at least some high school education. However, this high educational attainment is also a characteristic noted in the studies by Lally et. al. (1979) and Bild and Havighurst (1976) for the hotel populations they studied.

Perhaps the most dramatic demographic characteristic of our sample is the fact that 39 percent have never been married. This compares with only ten percent for the rest of the country's aged 60 or over. Almost identical figures were found for the hotel and inner-city populations studied by Ehrlich (1976) and Tissue (1971). Thus much of our sample has had a long history of residing alone, with 97 percent now residing by themselves and the mean number of years living alone being 25. On the average, 17 years have been spent in SROs in general and 11 years have been lived in their present hotels.

5.1. Informal Support System

The total extent of personal contacts ranged from zero to 26 persons, with a mean network size of 7.5 individuals (see table 9:1). Males averaged only one person more than females in their total informal support systems (n.s.), and no correlations were found between support system size and age or education. While only one percent had 20 or more personal ties, 89 percent had at least three persons in their personal networks. Importantly, only two persons fit the myth of total isolation by having no personal ties, with the majority of residents maintaining viable and often complex networks which allows them to live independently in the urban community.

TABLE 9.1

TOTAL INFORMAL SUPPORT SYSTEM
OF A SRO HOTEL ELDERLY POPULATION (N = 96) †

Network Characteristics	Mean	Range	Percent 3 or More	Percent None
Total Contacts	7.5	0-26	2	89
Total Multistrand Contacts	4.5	0-18	6	71
Total Contacts Involving Three or More Transactions	2.6	0-16	25	36
Total Contacts Rated "Very Important"	2.4	0-8	18	46
Total Contacts Considered "Intimate"	.9	0-3	41.0	5

†Table 9.1 is adapted from Sokolovsky and Cohen 1978:332.

While the average number of personal ties are not impressive, more than half of these links involved at least minimally multiplex relations. Only six percent of our sample lacked such relationships, with 71 percent of the networks having three or more multiplex ties. Moreover, more than a third of the sample had at least three very complex relationships consisting of three or more transactions, and on the average just over a quarter (28 percent) of a respondent's total informal support system contained such ties.

The gamut of human relations is seen in these complex network components involving casual conversing, advising, and providing emotional support; visiting or the passing of time in a local park or by the exchanging of food, cigarettes, drink, money and medicine; or helping in securing benefits from intricate welfare bureaucracies. When asked to rate contacts in terms of their importance, it turned out that about a third of all ties were

TABLE 9.2 A & B

INFORMAL AND FORMAL SUPPORT SYSTEMS: INDIVIDUAL NETWORK SECTORS

9.2A Informal Support System: Hotel, Outside Non-Kin, Kin †					
Network Sector	Network Characteristic	Mean	Range	Percent 3 or More	Percent None
Hotel	Total Contacts	2.7	0-15	44	26
	Total Contacts Three or More Transactions	.8	0-6	8	57
	Total Contacts Rated "Very Important"	.4	0-5	4	76
Outside Hotel: Non-Kin and Kin Combined	Total Contacts	4.8	0-23	68	6
	Total Contacts Three or More Transactions	1.8	0-16	—	—
	Total Contacts Rated "Very Important"	2.0	0-12	—	—
Outside Non-Kin	Total Contacts	2.7	0-17	40	24
	Total Contacts Three or More Transactions	1.1	0-16	12	61
	Total Contacts Rated "Very Important"	.8	0-4	9	51
Outside Kin	Total Contacts	2.1	1-12	28	29
	Total Contacts Three or More Transactions	.7	0-10	8	66
	Total Contacts Rated "Very Important"	1.2	0-10	14	48

Network Sector	Mean	Range	Percent 3 or More	Percent None
Hotel Staff	1.8	0-7	30	26
Institutional Ties	1.4	0-6	15	32

9.2B Formal Support System: Hotel Staff and Institutional Ties

†Table 9.2A is adapted from Sokolovsky and Cohen 1978:333.

considered "very important," and 45.8 percent had three or more such relationships. On the average, whole networks contained between two and three relationships which were either cognitively very important or functionally complex. A considerable smaller number of informal support systems contained intimate ties (mean .9) with only five percent having three or more persons to share personal thoughts with. No intimate links existed in 41 percent of the personal networks, about double the number which lacked any very complex or very important ties. A more optimistic way to view the extent of isolation from emotionally and instrumentally important support is to consider that while 59 percent of the residents maintained intimate ties, 82 percent had some "very important" ties and 75 percent had at least one very complex relationship.

One of the strongest contentions made about SRO dwellers, regardless of age, has been that contact beyond the hotel walls is virtually non-existent (Shapiro 1971, Stephens 1976, Hertz and Hutheesing 1975, Lally et. al. 1979). For the population under study, examining how personal ties are distributed throughout the components of the total networks gives a somewhat different picture.

While the number of personal ties (Table 9:2A) is fairly well distributed among the three sectors of informal support—hotel, outside non-kin, kin—almost two-thirds (64 percent) of all network links occur outside the hotel walls. In the hotel-network sector there was a mean of 2.7 contacts; less than a majority had three or more hotel ties. In terms of whole, informal support systems, on the average 40 percent of total networks were composed of hotel contacts.

Nonetheless, just over one-fourth were totally shut off from personal ties in their hotel, as compared to six percent who were shut off totally from the outside sectors. Importantly, although the frequency of interaction (see below) with residential neighbors is considerably higher than that for outside contacts far fewer of such ties are significant for our sample. Less than one-third (30 percent) of the very complex and fewer than one-fifth (17 percent) of the "very important" links generated were found among other hotel residents. Moreover, the vast majority (76 percent) did not consider any of their hotel contacts as very important to themselves.

In looking beyond the hotel, the mean number of ties is slightly higher for non-relatives (2.7) than that for kin (2.1), and a higher percent (29 percent versus 24 percent) were totally isolated from communicating with kin in the prior year. The highest level of functionally-complex ties occur among outside non-kin personnel, who include not only recently made acquaintances in nearby hotels, and workers and owners of the many small businesses in the neighborhood, but also long-term friends who have been known well before the responsdents had entered old age. This is reflected in the fact that these non-kin contacts outside of the hotel have remained part of the informal support system for an average of 19 years.

Turning to the statistics for ties to kin, it is seen that this network sector included the fewest number of contacts (28 percent of the total) and showed the highest levels of isolation from links providing instrumental support. Despite an extremely low frequency of interaction with kin and the lowest figures for three or more contacts in a total network, relatives are cognitively the *most* important part of the informal support system. This is seen in the fact that just about double the amount of "very important" relationships exist with relatives as is the case for either the hotel or outside non-kin sectors.

5.2. Formal Support Systems

Much attention in the literature on the SRO elderly has drawn attention to the importance of the "anonymous service fringe," those links generated by formal contact with various types of institutions or professional care givers. We have divided up such contacts between ties with hotel staff and representatives of service-giving agencies, such as doctors, nurses, social workers, or staff of senior centers, etc. (see table 9:2B). Lally (1979) even suggests that such links provide virtually the sum of all contacts her female sample of inner-city aged maintained. It should be clear by now that this is not the case here. However, considering the support system as a totality, 30 percent of all contacts are with these formally designated service givers. The most frequent formal source of contact is with hotel staff, usually the desk clerk or a maid, with an average of about two such contacts. Approximately the same amount of SRO aged (26 percent) have nothing to do with hotel staff, as was the case with regard to any one sector of the informal support system. For a small number of extremely isolated individuals with virtually no informal support, the hotel staff can be crucial for their survival. Despite the large signs at some hotel desks stating "Absolutely No Credit," and denials of such aid by the staff, many tenants rely at least partially on small monthly loans to maintain them through another cycle of woefully inadequate income. With rent as high as $200 a month, many elderly tenants have between $6 and $10 per day to spend on food, medicine and other essentials. As reported in other SRO studies (Shapiro 1971, Stephens 1976, Eckert 1979b), tenant-staff relationships—although potentially exploitative on the part of the staff—are often agreeably symbiotic. The aged tenants form the economic backbone of steady rental income for hotel owners, while the staff provides practical assistance with a minimum of emotional investment. In certain cases individuals told us that they would rather borrow money from a hotel desk cleark than endanger a close personal relationship by the potential conflict loaning can generate. Occasionally these formal ties may crystallize into informal personal ones, when exchange goes beyond the accepted norms of worker-tenant.

Among aged hotel residents there is generally manifested a great deal of distrust of certain service or care-giving institutions, especially hospitals. Many tenants perceive that if they are hospitalized for even a short period of time they will most likely lose their independence and end up in a nursing home or other long-term institution. Much of this fear is born out of ignorance, and the fact that with understaffed outreach services tenants often undertake costly travel only to confront large, impersonal bureaucracies. Nonetheless, with a mean of 1.4 institutional contacts, two-thirds of the tenants dealt with, on a person to person basis, some professional care giver over the last year.

6. Comparing Interaction

While this is the only study we know of attempting to quantify in detail the total support system of the aged, some of the data we have collected can be fruitfully compared to other studies. In terms of the size of the total informal support system, network sizes of 20-30 persons reported for a general urban population (Pattison 1977) and a younger group of SRO residents (Sokolovsky et. al. 1978) are several times higher than our findings for the SRO elderly. In the latter study of an SRO with an experimental program including an on-site recreational, lunch and social services program, such services appeared to stimulate considerably higher levels of sociability than is found in other hotels. In a study of San Diego SRO resident over age 50, Erickson and Eckert (1977) found residents (mostly male) have an average of 14 "acquaintances." Unfortunately, it is difficult to compare our figures with this study, as no indication is provided as to how the number of "acquaintances" was determined. However, it may be that the much lower rents in the San Diego hotels (almost half that in New York) and a benign climate may provide more spendable money and a more hospitable environment for interaction.

TABLE 9.3

COMPARISON OF SOCIAL CONTACT SCORES:
NEW YORK SROs AND TWO BRITISH SAMPLES

Social Contact Score	New York SROs	Bethnal Green † Sample	British Four Area Survey††	
			Total Sample	Living Alone
35 or More per week (not isolated)	28%	77%	54%	12%
0-34 per week (isolated/ rather isolated)	72%	23%	44%	87%

† These figures are taken from Townsend (1957)
††These figures are taken from Tunstall (1966)

Another way of comparing the degree of isolation is in terms of the frequency of interaction. In Table 9:3, we have applied the Townsend interaction scale to our sample in order to compare it to Townsend's)1957) working-class, urban Londoners (Bethnal Green) and the four-area survey study by Tunstall (1966) which includes both urban and rural areas of England. The results indicate relative isolation for the SRO population in terms of absolute numbers of contacts. Here 72 percent of the SRO elderly fell within Townsend's "rather isolated" and "isolated" categories, versus 23 percent and 44 percent for the other two British samples. Yet for that part of the Tunstall survey that live alone, as almost all of our sample did, relatively more were found to be at least "rather isolated" (87 percent) than in the Manhattan hotels. However, again we would note that the comparison must be viewed quite cautiously, as the scale has a strong bias in favor of those working, or those living in family households and being in close proximity to relatives; the scale gives substantial positive weighting to interaction in these settings.

This indeed becomes problematic in considering the variable frequency of interaction by the SRO elderly within the different sectors of their informal support system. In comparing (Table 9:4) the once-a-week or better interaction from two different hotel studies and two general surveys, one sees that the most dramatic delimiting of social interaction in the SROs occurs in the kin sector. While 49 percent in Exelrod's (1964) Detroit survey and 82 percent of the Shanas et. al. (1968) survey respondents communicated with relatives at least weekly, this occurred for 17 percent of the New York aged and for only three percent of the San Diego hotel population. Nevertheless a different picture emerges when considering the network sectors of residents/neighbors and friends. In both these segments of the informal support system, a reversal of sociability occurs and the SROs appear to equal or exceed the two general population surveys, although the pattern in

TABLE 9.4

COMPARISON OF ONCE A WEEK CONTACT:
TWO SRO POPULATIONS AND TWO GENERAL POPULATION SURVEYS

	Percent Once-a-Week Contacts		
	Kin	Residents/ Neighbors	Friends/ Aquaintances
New York SROs	17	72	45
San Diego SROs†	3 (8,33)	50 (38,92)	73 (73,96)
Detroit General Population††	49	29	28
National Survey†††	82	—	40

† The figures come from Erickson and Eckert (1977); the numbers not in parentheses are for the working class hotels which seem to be closest to those studied in New York. The numbers in parentheses are for "skid row" and middle class hotels, respectively.

†† These figures are taken from Axelrod 1964.

††† These figures are taken from Shanas et al. (1968).

the hotel samples vary in terms of which sector is most frequently interacted with. In the New York SROs, almost three-quarters (72 percent) interacted with at least one fellow resident, and under a majority (45 percent) had similar contact with non-kin outside the hotel, over a week's time. Of course this does not provide a relative notion of how many in a given network each ego communicates with weekly, but it shows that comparatively large segments of the SRO are *not* without any frequent contact both in and outside of their residences.

7. Network Structure, Function and Meaning

Although in this study we have stressed the sometimes drastic differences with other statements made about the SRO aged, our research concurs with others (see especially Stephens 1976, Eckert 1979a) who detail an exaggerated normative concern for self-reliance, privacy and instrumental social relations. A constant refrain one hears in speaking to SRO tenants are such statements as "I'm a loner, always have been, always will be, don't need no one, I don't bother no one, don't let anyone bother me, I just mind my own business." One hears such statements so often in such similar form that one soon realizes that this is a commonly accepted description of cultural and personal identity. It is a standard defense against further penetration by prying social scientists into the social world of the hotel tenant.

This proclamation of "loner" status represents a certain understanding of the cultural reality of being old in a SRO. Residing alone, these elderly must negotiate daily tasks of survival independently to prevent being sent to a nursing home. On very meager monetary resources—which are habitually depleted before the end of a given month—they must feed, clothe and medically provide for themselves. Group interaction and organization is typically discouraged by hotel managers, who are afraid of any resident groups emerging who could effectively protest the very poor living conditions in many hotels. The rooms themselves—by their very tiny size—barely provide private living space for the individual tenant. Indeed, for many of these poor elderly, who spend a good deal of time in their rooms, intrusions into one's quarters can take on the nature of a violation of one's physical being. Moreover, they have little control over who will be surrounding them in other rooms, and with the great human heterogeneity found in most hotels tenants often have little acutal basis for easy mutuality in social relation-

TABLE 9.5

PERCENT PREDOMINANT DIRECTIONAL FLOW
OF AID FOR EACH NETWORK SECTOR

Network Sector	Directional Flow of Aid		
	Ego to Other	Reciprocal	Dependent-Other to Ego
Hotel	10	67	23
Outside Non-Kin	6	70	25
Kin	8	63	29

ships. Nevertheless most of the SRO aged have developed informal support systems by erecting personal networks to help them negotiate survival within the constraints of their small urban world.

When one penetrates beyond the emic portrayal of social life by observing and participating in it, one finds that frequent socialization (at least in the hotels), room visiting, the exchange of food, money, practical services and emotional support occur at least within some of the social bonds which crystallize. The nature and structure of these bonds reflect the cultural ideals and environmental constraints of the population. One way of seeing this is by examining the degree of dependency manifested in the transactions that tie people together.

In analyzing (see Table 9:5) the number of network sectors in which relationships were predominantly manifested by either dependence, reciprocity, or instrumental transactions, it is seen that in all three areas of informal support about three-fourths of the networks studied lack a predominantly dependent nature. The data indicates that the provision of aid in all sectors is dominated by a reciprocal give-and-take, with no statistically significant variation existing for the population as a whole.

TABLE 9.6

PERCENT PREDOMINENT DIRECTIONAL FLOW OF AID
IN THE HOTEL SECTOR BY AGE AND ACTUAL HEALTH

	60 to 70 Years Old		70 Years or Older	
	Ego to Other or Reciprocal Aid	Dependent Aid	Ego to Other or Reciprocal Aid	Dependent Aid
Poor Health	91	9	50	50
Good Health	90	10	89	11
	N.S.		$P = .02$ $x^2 = 5.2$	

However, one does see (Table 9:6) an important relationship between flow of aid and the factors of age and health. Especially, within the hotel sector those who combine very old age (over 70) and relatively poor health are most likely to generate dependent support within their personal networks. Table 9:6 shows that those who are in the eldest and least healthy category are five times more likely to have a predominantly dependent flow of aid in the hotel segment of their informal support system than their younger, healthier counterparts. Similar trends occur in the other parts of networks, but they are not statistically significant for the combined effects of age and health. While this data cannot inform us about a causal relationship between networks, age, health and dependence, it does indicate that despite the ideal of "self-reliance," those entering very old age in poor health manifest considerable levels of support within their hotels.

Another important dimension of networks is their morphological structure, and here we distinguish four types of configurations among our sample. In Table 9:7 is shown the general distribution of these network configurations, which we have called: diffuse-cluster; cluster; diffuse; and kin-cluster. A majority of our respondents (51.6 percent) formed diffuse-cluster networks, in which there existed at least two other persons who formed a cluster of mutual interaction, while in the network as a whole less than 75 percent of the members were in contact with each other. Such networks tend to be the largest in total size, with the interconnected clusters typically containing two to four persons. These maximally dense parts of a network are most likely to be in the hotel, although they are also likely to occur among a set of outside friends who may meet frequently at a local bar, off-track betting parlor or inexpensive cafeteria. Yet, considered as a whole, diffuse-cluster networks are structurally dispersed, with linkages rarely(about ten percent of the time) transcending the boundaries of the three sectors we have distinguished previously.

TABLE 9.7
PERCENT OF EACH NETWORK CONFIGURATION

	Diffuse/ Cluster	Cluster	Kin-Cluster Diffuse	Diffuse	Totals
Total	51.6	20	14	13.7	100
Population	(49)	(19)	(14)	(13)	(95)

Besides being structurally dispersed, most such networks show a highly variable frequency in activating the ties that are maintained. Besides the general variation in interactive rates between network sectors noted above, there is an important diurnal cycle related mostly to a blighted and often dangerous urban zone. Although two-thirds of the residents had social contacts both day and night within the hotel, over three-fourths did not see anyone outside the hotel after dark. There is also an important monthly cycle, geared to the arrival of government or pension checks at the beginning of the month. It is during the prior week, when funds invariably run out or low, that the full extent of one's personal support system is activated.

Within such networks—especially in the hotel sector—there may be included "natural helpers" who serve as direct and indirect conduits of useful information or physical aid, and may serve as a point of contact between different informal support systems. One such man, 63 years old, known to tenants in one hotel as "Captain" (due to prior his seafaring occupation), had appeared to have mastered the intricacies of New York's social service bureaucracy. Although he tended to be reclusive, and directly helped only a few other persons in the hotel, through these other friends and even via a hotel maid several other tenants obliquely requested and received help from the Captain.

The next type of configuration, cluster network, encompasses one-fifth of the sample and involves an instance where at least 75 percent of all persons ego is in contact with interact with each other. The majority of such networks are focused exclusively in the hotels, with about 20 percent exclusively located among outside non-kin, and only one example of an exclusive, kin-focused cluster. As is the case with the other configurations, in very few instances (three) did the crossing of intra-network boundaries occur. In each such case, a hotel contact was linked with another sector of the informal support system. These cluster networks often have at least three members besides ego, and typically represent what Boissevain has called a quasi-group: "a coalition of persons, recruited according to structurally diverse principles by one or more existing members, between some of whom there is a degree of patterned interaction and organization" (1968:550). In some cases this may simply involve getting together at a regular time in a public place outside the hotel to eat, socialize or to play cards. However, especially for some elderly in poorer health and lacking mobility, cluster configurations can provide their means of survival in the hotel.

Such was the case of Ms. Austin, a 66-year-old black woman who, due to a bad back, retired from working as a housekeeper at the age of sixty. Ms. Austin finds it difficult to walk, spending most of the day in her small but neatly kept room. Once a day she goes to the hotel lobby for a short time, but returns to her room, where she waits for the daily visits from her three elderly friends or less frequently goes to visit in their rooms. The exchanges involved are quite varied and include visiting, food preparation and food borrowing, money loans, shopping, providing care during illness, and, in the case of one of Ms. Austin's friends, the exchange of personal thoughts. Her three hotel friends do not stay for long together in Ms. Austin's room, but rather float in and out during the day, gossiping, sharing meals cooked on a hot plate, or drinking some beer. Ms. Austin also maintains contact with a female cousin in Maryland who—she either phones or writes once a month, although she eagerly looks forward each year to a two-week summer visit down South. It is important to note that despite a great fluidity in hotel cluster formations, marked by the changing of personnel, in general ties are not especially transient, with the length of relationship averaging seven years with 90 percent being maintained three years or longer. In the case of Ms. Austin, all the members of her hotel network have been known to her for five or six years, and she has been drawn closer to them by the death of two other friends in the past two years.

The third type of configuration, kin-cluster, describes persons with at least 75 percent of their kin ties in contact with each other, but where non-kin segments of a network had no mutual interaction. Found in almost 15 percent of the sample, such networks typically display the highest levels of exchange and frequency of contact with relatives. Conversely, there is a tendency for kin-cluster support systems to maintain few or no hotel contacts, thereby enhancing even more the importance of relatives. Yet it must be recalled that kin ties in general—while having great "importance" compared to other parts of the network—are activated least frequently, with 80 percent of the respondents having no weekly contacts with kin. Moreover, with very few relatives either living in the respondents' neighborhood or in weekly contact with them, such configurations can provide very tenuous support in times of crisis.

Finally, we also have distinguished diffuse network configurations in which no interconnections link members of ego's network with each other. Such network structures occur in only 13.7 percent of the SRO elderly we studied, and represent in many cases the picture of severe isolation other researchers have noted. In a majority of such configurations, persons have three or fewer personal ties in their entire network, typically having no more than one contact in a given network sector. More than half of the persons with such networks have no social relatonship in their hotel, and of those that do only two have multiplex ties which go beyond the exchange of conversation. In fact, three-fourths of those with diffuse network configurations have no relationship which we have defined as "very complex." Many of these persons appear to be the "true" loners in etic, sociological sense, whose relationships are not only minimal in quantity but also lack the type of transactional complexity typical of strong human bonds.

8. Summary, Conclusions and Suggestions

This chapter has examined several aspects of social interaction for an elderly urban population whom many consider to epitomize the isolation of America's aged. In considering this we have used network analysis to determine the total extent of the "social support system" for our sample of SRO aged. The results do not provide an easy answer to whether or not and to what extent the SRO aged are really isolated.

It was found that a negligible number of persons were without any personal ties, and while the frequency of contact with kin was exceedingly low in the comparative sense, contact with residential neighbors and outside contacts occured at levels comparable with the general aged population. The total "support system" (informal and formal) averaged close to 11 members; however, there is virtually no data available to determine how this compares with other aged populations. In terms of the qualitative nature of ties, while persons averaged only two or three functionally or cognitively important links and about one person to share personal thoughts with, work by Lowenthal and Haven (1968) indicates that even a single intimate tie can be an important factor in deterring mental illness among the aged.

On the other hand, substantial portions of the SRO aged were devoid of instrumentally and emotionally important ties. This element of social isolation was particularly glaring with ties to residential neighbors and kin; in the former case, three-fourths did not consider any hotel contacts "very important" and in the latter instance two-thirds lacked even one kin tie involving several types of transactions. While this might appear to correspond very strongly to previous findings, a consideration of networks as a whole show that, far from the assertions of Stephens (1976) and Lally et al. (1979), personal ties *outside* the hotels are more likely to be considered of importance by the elderly tenants.

One must note, however, that the combination of the network profile and ethnographic research we employed appears far more sensitive to extant but weak ties than is the case in other studies. This points out the necessity of ethnographically examining social networks, especially among the most socially invisible elderly. Gubrium (1974), for example, in his study of a nursing home, notes that while the staff there perceived that many residents totally sever relationships with the outside world, he shows that the move from a private residence to "Murray Manor" does not necessarily eliminate social relationships as much as change their nature. While face-to-face interaction is sharply reduced, "hidden ties" (especially kin links) are maintained through knowledge about previously active network members facilitated by telephone calls and visits of friends who know the family and other friends (p. 104).

In understanding the lifestyle adaptation of the SRO aged, it was also necessary to explore the sometimes elusive features of network configurations that link them to their social environment. It was shown that network morphology varied considerably, from single, dense clusters to small, unconnected, dispersed sets of ties. But the prevalent pattern was one that combined both these characteristics. Such diffuse/cluster networks epitomize the cultural identity of these aged, generating a basis for support and self-sufficiency through the provision of a relatively complex support system which selectively maintains a few crucial ties structurally dispersed through the urban environment.

Finally, we may ask how such information can be of use in understanding and aiding the survival of the inner city elderly. It is relevant to note first that community care workers are becoming more sensitive to the need to recognize interpersonal systems developed autonomously by a client population. A recent book on social work notes that social workers are often trained to see the *lack* of pre-existing support systems and become absorbed in organizing and maintaining formal services; therefore they "may be blind to informal, positive, helping activities that go on outside the confines of formal services" (Collins and Pancoast 1976:25). In this light, we believe that the precise nature of the social support system can best be comprehended by the incorporation of a network analysis profile into clients' charts. This will add a new dimension to the provision of services for the urban elderly.

After mapping all personal linkages, where lack of support is noted, organizations can focus their activities. Where networks are strong, superfluous services can be avoided and resources directed where they are most needed. In times of stress, agencies will be able to utilize the strengths of the total support system to help the individual remain in the community.

Notes

[1] The authors wish to thank Alan Laskow, Lynne Stein, John Stern, Ann Avitobile, David Burns, Mary Beckor, Mike Braverman, and the Murray Hill SRO Project for their assistance. Special thanks to the residents of the SRO hotels we studied, who really made this research possible. The research was supported by grants from the Ittleson Foundation, the New York Foundation, the van Ameringin Foundation, Commonwealth Foundation, NIMH Center on Aging Grant No. 1-RO1-MH31745, and by computer time provided by the University of Maryland, Baltimore County.

[2] Possible exceptions to this statement are the work of Cantor (1976) and Babchuck (1978-9). However, both works focus on either very frequent ties or those considered emotionally very important.

[3] After interactional data concerning a given contact were elicited, the respondent was asked to rate the overall "importance" of the contact based on a four point scale: 1—"not important"; 2—"important"; 3—"very important"; 4—"the most important a person can be to you."

10
Food of Old People
In Center-City Hotels

Paul Bohannan[1]

1. Introduction

Residents of center-city hotels must be able to take care of their own food, clothing, drugs and medical needs, as well an any other requirements beyond the room and basic housekeeping services provided by the hotel. Thus they require an environment that provides a number of cheap restaurants, as well as cheap hotel rooms. It was possible, in 1974 and 1975, to eat a more or less balanced diet in the Horton Plaza Redevelopment Area of San Diego, for a little over $3 a day. Some aged residents did, and others did not. The difference was correlated not with income but rather with food histories and preferences, and with unwillingness of some who had struggled insecurely into the middle class to go into the cheap restaurants, and (in a few cases) with drinking patterns. Choice of where and what to eat is a highly valued area of decision that gives the residents a conviction of self-reliance.

Although it would probably be generally agreed that nutrition is as important for the elderly as it is for anyone else, it nevertheless seems that information about what elderly people eat is sparse. And for elderly people living in hotels, information seems to be non-existent.[2]

Food is the major need of hotel residents that is not supplied by the hotel. Hotels provide a room with furnishings and linens and more or less maid service; they of course provide basic utilities and heat, and more or less security. Because they provide so much as part of their contract, hotels create a fairly undemanding environment for residents. Besides food, the residents must see only to laundry, health needs and medicines, and special requirements such as tobacco, newspapers or sundries.

Anyone who lives in a hotel and who can provide all the needs not supplied by the hotel is said to be "independent," and independence is the highest moral value. An occasional "old-timer" (in the sense of long-term resident) is helped by clerks or management for a few weeks when he or she can no longer take care of these basic needs. A shallow network of people may help each other—someone either younger or a little more active may look after some of the needs of the disabled or the disadvantaged. But a hotel cannot care for the chronically ill or disabled, and it cannot closely oversee the food needs of residents.

This chapter is a report about the food habits of permanent residents of low-cost downtown hotels in San Diego in 1974-76. It does not put the practices of these people into a context of "adequate" or "good" nutrition—a specialized and (to the outsider) constantly changing subject. This chapter is about food habits and attitudes, not "nutrition" in any further sense.

2. Who Eats What?

Information was gathered during two-and-a-half years' consecutive fieldwork among the aging permanent residents of 32 cheap hotels in the area south of Broadway, the main axis of downtown San Diego. Our core area is the 16 blocks from Broadway to "G" Street and from Union Street to Fourth Avenue, officially designated the Horton Plaza Redevelopment area. For survey purposes, we extended the area for three blocks in every direction except north (an already redeveloped business area). The core area of the redevelopment project contains seven hotels (all but one scheduled to be destroyed to make way for a large retail center); the extended area contains 25 more.

We focused our ethnographic attention on two hotels within the redevelopment area, carried out intensive interviewing in eight of them, but surveyed residents of all 32. Most of the residents are blue collar people, except the largely middle-class residents of two retirement hotels, each less than two blocks from the core redevelopment area, and both within the survey area.

Besides ethnographic research, we collected life histories, carried out three interviews with a randomly selected panel of 100 aged residents of the 32 hotels, and collected diaries from 26 residents of the working-class hotels and 12 in the middle-class retirement hotels, all of them from persons in the interview sample. These 38 "diaries" contain information for one week about their food, sleep, and social interaction—but they are not diaries in the strict sense of the term. Our initial efforts to get residents to keep diaries was a complete failure—for $2 for the week (a more munificent sum "south of Broadway" than it sounds elsewhere, but not enough to influence people's actions much) they either could not or would not write down their food and their activities. In order to get the information, we created a diary "booklet" for each day of a week. An interviewer called on and assisted the diarists—in some instances calling every day.

Our diary-keeping subsample contained 11 women (nine of them in the middle-class hotels) and 27 men (only three of them in the middle-class hotels—the ratios represent the actual sex ratios in the two kinds of hotels). Ages vary from 50 (our minimum age for eligibility in the sample) to 91. The women are significantly older (51 and 65 in the working class hotels, but averaging 79.4 in the middle-class hotels) than the men (65.3 and 66.3 respectively). (See Tables 10.1 and 10.2).

TABLE 10.1

DESCRIPTION OF DOWNTOWN HOTEL RESIDENTS IN THE SAMPLE
SAN DIEGO, CALIFORNIA

	Cheap Residential Hotels		Retirement Hotels	
	Number	Age-Range & Average	Number	Age-Range & Average
Women	2	51-65 58	9	70-91 79.4
Men	24	50-91 65.3	3	52-81 66.3

TABLE 10.2

AGE AND SEX DISTRIBUTION OF SAMPLE HOTEL TYPE
BY DOWNTOWN HOTELS, SAN DIEGO, CALIFORNIA

	Men		Women	
Age	Subject Hotels	Control Hotels	Subject Hotels	Control Hotels
50 - 55	3	1	1	0
56 - 60	6	0	0	0
61 - 65	3	0	1	0
66 - 70	3	1	0	1
71 - 75	6	0	0	2
76 - 80	1	0	0	3
81 - 85	0	1	0	1
86 - 90	0	0	0	0
90+	1	0	0	2
Unknown	1	0	0	0
Total	24	3	2	9 = 38

3. Eating Patterns

Eating habits of hotel dwellers vary by whether a restaurant is maintained in the hotel. One informant in a working-class hotel with a grill told us:

> Like, the only place they have to go if they leave the hotel is to drink. They got their food here. Their checks come here. All their mail comes here. They get up. They go downstairs, look at some TV. They go into the restaurant, get something to eat. If they want to drink, they just have to go out and down one door and pop in. They never really leave the hotel.

We know several people whose preference for hotels with restaurants leads them to overlook some of the things they might not like in the hotels. Perhaps the social dimension is most important: there is a type of social interaction possible in a restaurant that gives the place value. Most of the people recognize one another. Some speak. Some even have discussions in restaurants. Thus, the regulars at a hotel restaurant lend a conviction of more multi-strand ties in the community.

One of our two middle-class retirement hotels, which we shall call The California, gives all residents breakfast and dinner. Breakfasts consist of eggs, cereals—the usual American breakfasts. Most dinners have a source of protein and vegetables, with an apparently inexhaustible supply of cottage cheese. Almost all residents say that they enjoy breakfast—although a few complained that they had to sit with uncongenial groups. Two seatings of breakfast are served, one at seven and the other at eight. The only complaint about the food at breakfast was a lack of fresh fruit—and that from only one person. Dinner is another matter. Many of the residents would prefer to sit at tables with their friends instead of at assigned tables. For some, dinner is an ordeal because of one or all of the other people at the table for four. Most say the food is adequate, although some noted that it was repetitive and boring. Some days, residents skip dinner—for example, one man of 81 often skipped dinner to drink a couple of beers at a local bar. One woman stayed in her room and ate fruit for three of the seven days for which she kept a diary—she was 74 and described herself as a very light eater, although she went out for a full meal about noon on each of those seven days. Many residents of these middle-class hotels have local kinsmen and friends who occasionally invite then for dinner.

At lunch, the residents of this middle-class hotel "go wild." With the exception of the woman mentioned above, most of them eat junk food for lunch—hamburgers, sundaes, waffles. Far more junk food was consumed by these middle-class people than was true of the residents of working-class hotels.

Two respondents occasionally ate something before going to bed: hot chocolate in one case, "cake and punch" in the other.

Here is a typical diet from The California: A woman, 79, ate seven breakfasts in the eight o'clock setting, usually "coffee, toast jelly, two eggs, and prunes." Then, for lunch each day she had: (1) a banana split; (2) milk and cheesecake in room; (3) turkey and dressing and an apple at the VA hospital cafeteria; (4) coffee, sandwich, bananas in room; (5) cold cereal, bananas, cheese in room; (6) hot roast beef sandwich and sundae at restaurant; (7) sandwich, coffee, cookies and bananas in room. She ate the hotel dinner six days, but the seventh went out for waffles and cocoa.

The second retirement hotel—the Balboa—has a restaurant on its ground floor, but residents need not eat there. The sample provided only two persons from this hotel, both male. One, aged 66, ate seven breakfasts between 8:00 and 9:30 a.m., but only two of them were in any one restaurant. He ate six meals at lunch time—in five different restaurants—and the seventh day had a Caesar salad in still another restaurant. He ate seven dinners, in five different restaurants. During the week he was in 13 restaurants.

The second resident of the Balboa (age 52) stuck closer to the hotel: five of his breakfasts were in the hotel dining room (the other two were cold cereal in his room); six lunches (between 3:00 and 6:00 in the afternoon) were in the hotel dining room, the seventh at the race track in Tijuana. All seven "dinners" were sandwiches in his room, between 7:00 and 10 p.m. Between meals he added ice cream, doughnuts, candy bars or beer on five days.

The residents of the working-class hotels eat much the same kind of breakfasts as those in the middle-class retirement hotels—breakfasts consist of eggs, toast and coffee (we came to call it the ETC breakfast), with perhaps some additions such as bacon, potatoes, doughnuts or sweet rolls.

Nine men of our sample come from the Wells Fargo Hotel. The biggest of the working-class hotels, it has a "grill" attached to it. Three of the nine ate most of their meals at that grill; three others ate there occasionally. The other three did not eat there at all—rather, they went to nearby cafes where the same breakfasts, as well as other meals, are a little cheaper. Six of the nine ate only meals at the restaurants—no junk food at all. Two ate breakfast and noon meal: one of these ate in his room at night, the other sometimes ate a meal and sometimes hamburgers and malteds.

The ninth man from this large hotel had the only bizarre diet we encountered. He was 72, and ate only one meal other than ETC breakfasts during the week that our interviewers helped him to keep a diary—and that was consumed when he bought dinner for his son. The rest of the time he ate eggs, vanilla ice cream and beer. Except for an occasional cup of coffee, there was nothing else. His expenditures ran from 82¢ a day to $6.00—depending not on the food, but on the beer.

One of the small hotels had a kitchen in which regular residents had cooking privileges. The sample produced two diarists from this hotel. One man, 75, drank coffee until about 11 a.m.—one day of the seven he fixed himself eggs and toast about 7 a.m. He ate both lunch and dinner "in his room," after having prepared them in the kitchen. Dinners were: (1) fish, rice and salad; (2) rice and fish; (3) meat, rice and salad; (4)meat and vegetable; three were not detailed. This man, thoroughly acquainted with American culture, nevertheless ate more in accordance with his original Asian culture. He walked the eleven blocks each way to the nearest supermarket six times during the week to buy his food.

The second man in the small hotel with the kitchen was 53 years old. He had nothing except coffee until evening on six of the seven days (on the seventh, he had two candy bars about 11 a.m.). Somewhere between 4 and 8 p.m. he either prepared a meal in the kitchen or ate cold food in his room: he mentioned cold cuts, cheese, fried chicken, pork chops. One day he ate nothing but a hamburger at about 10 p.m. He told our interviewer that he had a "vascular operation" that left him in constant diarrhea and pain.

One small hotel had a cafe attached, but only one person in this hotel fell into our sample—and she had the only room in the hotel that had cooking facilities. This woman, 51, spent a lot of time in the cafe talking and drinking beer, but she ate little there. This woman's diary refers to the middle of the month; by the end of the month, she had run out of both cash and food stamps—by then, she was putting food and beer on the "ticket" at the cafe. She claimed she prepared six dinners in her room, while on the seventh evening she had sandwich and coffee in a friend's room. We read her menu—roast beef, fried chicken, meat loaf—with doubt; on the basis of observation, her staples were bread and beer.

Residents in hotels without dining facilities tend to eat more randomly than those in which a cafe or grill is immediately available—but not more so than those who do their own cooking. A few of the residents of the non-dining room hotels were rigidly regular. One informant, an arthritic man of 54, ate eggs, toast and coffee every morning about 9 a.m., usually adding either bacon or hotcakes. Between 3 and 4 p.m. he had soup and sandwich, the same each of the seven days. Then, at 8 p.m., he had a hot meal at the Rescue Mission. His expenditure averaged $2.40 a day.

Some of the hotels cater to alcoholics, and several of our respondents have drinking problems—it is not possible to say exactly what percentage, for some do not admit they have drinking problems. And one man told us, when we asked, "I don't think I have a drinking problem, but some other people tell me I have."

Among the drinkers, we found one man of 58 who ate one or two meals a day and drank beer. He woke about 3 a.m. every day; he sometimes began to drink as early as six in the morning, although beer is the only thing he admitted drinking. His food expenditures for the week were $16.86. He spent $8.20 for beer in four days.

Here, on the other hand, is the diet and drink record of an alchoholic male of 50 (the precise number of vodkas on Friday is his guess).

> Tuesday: Eggs for breakfast, hamburger steak, grilled cheese, 4 small bottles of wine
>
> Wednesday: Bacon, eggs, toast and coffee; chef's salad, 1 small bottle of wine, ½ pint of Vodka
>
> Thursday: Eggs, toast, coffee; roast beef; grilled cheese (he mentions no drink)
>
> Friday: Eggs, toast, coffee; pork chop dinner; chef's salad, 24 vodkas at 50¢ each
>
> Saturday: Eggs, toast, coffee; sandwich in room, "Drank vodka 12 - 3 PM"
>
> Sunday: Hot dogs, potato salad, bread, candy 6-7 AM, vodka in room; wine and vodka in friend's room all day
>
> Monday: Ham and cheese sandwich at 1 PM, wine in own room, friend's room, lobby.

4. The Cost of Food

The amount of money spent on food varies. The residents at the middle-class California average $2.07 for lunch during the seven days. The lowest was 93¢.

The expenditure for food of the nine residents of the Wells Fargo Hotel (with grill) range from $2.32 a day to $5.42 a day. The average was $3.69 a day. The person who spent most was a professional gambler. He and his wife had lived in hotels most of their married life. They went out for lunch and for dinner every day, went to many different places and seemed to enjoy living in the hotel. They did not drink. The man who spent the least ate absolutely regularly—between 5 and 6 a.m. he ate eggs in one of the local Chinese-operated restaurants for 71¢. He returned to the same restaurant every day a little before noon and had a "dinner"—three days chicken, one ham, one short ribs, one hamburger steak (the seventh he recorded the cost, but not the menu). Between three and four in the afternoon, he ate something in his room: usually sandwiches and apples. He estimated the cost as 50¢ every day except one, when he ate "a lot of apples" and gave the cost as 75¢.

In the working-class hotels without dining rooms, eight people (omitting those who cooked in their rooms) averaged an expenditure of $4.23 a day for food—the range is from $2.39 to $7.90 a day. The man who spends $7.90 was the man who counted his wine and vodka in with his food, described above. Another—who had more income than most— spent $7.28 a day. Omitting these two high spenders, the average is $3.11 a day.

5.   Where Do We Eat?

The presence of several good cheap restaurants is as important to residents as the low-cost rooms. The "best" neighborhoods are also blessed with missions and church-sponsored lunches as a sort of back-up.

Restaurants. There are 58 eating establishments in the survey area; approximately two dozen are used by the older residents. Most are open from about six in the morning to six in the evening—although some are open earlier in the morning. Two are open all night, but are considered "expensive" and are not patronized by the elderly residents.

Three of the downtown restaurants are operated by Chinese, although little Chinese food is served in them. There are three restaurants for Mexican food, one for Filipino food. Just outside the area, there are several restaurants—one Chinese, MacDonald's, Jack-in-the-Box, Pancake House, one Greek "deli" and several "bar and grill" establishments—that are patronized primarily by daytime office workers. Working-class residents seldom use them; those in the California Hotel sometimes have lunch there, but just as often they go "north of Broadway" where middle-class restaurants—some of them expensive—are to be found.

The criteria for judging restaurants are simple: price is always first, followed by quality. Taste comes in a poor third, and occasionally cleanliness is mentioned. Here are two typical comments:

> At X, you pay $1.60 to $1.75 and that's the highest we've even seen down there, and that's sirloin tip with noodles. You get your belly full. You've got a salad and you've got vegetables, your potatoes and gravy, your main course. Like yesterday, they were serving sauerkraut and sausage. I didn't have the money for it and that's one of my favorite dishes. I didn't have the money for it, and they're serving the big platters and the damn things were piled six, seven inches high off the platter in the center, you know.

> I eat mostly at the Moon, you know. They're reasonable. They have reasonable rates . . . . I've tried the Sun Cafe and they're pretty reasonable too, you know you can get a meal for a dollar. The Moon is the best for the money. Like chicken, you know, he gives you three pieces, potatoes, rice and string beans, coffee, soup and that's not bad for $1.35.

The complaint most often heard is that the cheap restaurants should open earlier (most are open at 6 a.m.) and they should close later.

Missions. There are several missions within the area at which it is possible to get a meal. The largest fills its hall, locks the door, holds a religious service that lasts an hour and a half and only then provides food. This mission also has a dormitory with ten beds, but one can stay there for only five days. Old residents sometimes use this mission, and others similar, when they run short of money at the end of the month.

Several churches provide cheap lunches. One church-sponsored center sends buses around to pick up hotel residents and provides a nourishing lunch for 50¢. A few residents use this service regularly. Most do not; some complain (overlooking the bus) that the 50¢ lunch is too far away or (untrue in this case) that "they lay a trip on you before they feed you."

Several church groups and government welfare agencies also provide meal tickets for newly arrived residents:

> When I came here in October, I went to the first Baptist Church, and they gave me a ticket so that I could go and eat—a good restaurant up on Broadway. They put out a terrific breakfast and it looked clean up front. Of course, I didn't see the kitchen. But some of 'em—I could cook better than they do.

There is a sandwich line in the neighborhood, run by the local Catholic Church. About three in the afternoon, sandwiches—usually peanut butter and jelly—are handed out of a small window, one sandwich to each person in line. Anybody who wants more than one sandwich returns to the end of the line and gets it if there are enough sandwiches made up. Most residents do not take advantage of this line, but this kind of "iron rations" is available. On January 29, 1975, the sandwich line had almost 200 people in it. Usually, both before and after that time, it was much shorter—at that time, however, both the city and the country were in recession.

Several savings and loan associations and banks near the redevelopment area provide cookies and coffee for their customers. Some residents treat these services as if they were a food line—one savings and loan eventually had to stop putting out such refreshments in their "Investors' Lounge," because the traffic from local residents got so heavy. Most banks continue to do it, and one bank official (when asked) said it was the least they could do for the people who lived near their offices.

Eating in Rooms. The hotels all have regulations that forbid eating in the rooms—they are largely disregarded, as long as food in the rooms does not make an odor in the halls. The greatest difficulty is the ten to 12 blocks to the nearest store that sells groceries (other than over-priced picnic-type supplies). That is farther than many of the residents can walk—and farther than most of them carry their purchases. The local liquor stores sell milk—but the cost in 1976 was 29¢ per half pint.

Hotel residents are not eligible for food stamps because they have no place to prepare food. A few, however, have convinced the officials that their hot plates do entitle them to such assistance. Some residents of the hotel with a kitchen get food stamps; two women in other hotels have mentioned them to us. A man in his early 50s said:

> I think I'm the only one that's got food stamps. I lie to them down there. I know I can't make it on $120 but I'm making it up to $150 because I get them food stamps. See, they take $18 away from me but they give me $48 back in food stamps. I told 'em I had a hot plate, but I don't. I don't even have a percolator. When I get a can of spaghetti or a can of stew, I just throw the whole can in the sink and put the plug in and saturate it, cover it, with hot water. I keep changing the hot water and I let it soak in there, and when I open the can it's warm. A little above warm. I've got a plate and a salt shaker that I took from a restaurant. I've got a jar of hot peppers and I buy an onion once in a while; I keep a big jar of peanut butter in the room. If I know a guy in the hotel that's going up to the store to buy something to eat, like a quart of milk and a cupcake, I tell him, "Let me buy it with my food stamps and then you give me the value in money." That way I got cigarette money. I know it's illegal, but I'm not stealing or anything.

Vending Machines. Some residents eat what is provided by vending machines. When we began our work, a woman of almost 70 operated a stand in the lobby of the Wells Fargo Hotel. She sold tobacco, shaving and toilet needs, and a little food. Her prices were high because she could not buy in bulk—she bought at the supermarket and added a modest mark-up. When she became too ill to continue her operation, she was replaced by four vending machines—cigarettes, candy, coffee, and soft drinks.

The residents began to use the vending machines immediately. Each coffee cup had a poker hand printed on it. Coffee sales were high. Candy consumption, we think, went up. We are convinced that the machines (and the success of fast-food hamburgers and pancakes among the more affluent, especially those with middle-class tastes) indicate the workings of a sort of Gresham's Law of nutrition: convenience food drives out less expensive, more nourishing food.

6. Nutrition and Malnutrition

Most of the residents pronounce themselves satisfied with their diet. Some say they would like to have fancier food, but almost no one says he does not get enough to eat, except (a few added) late in the month just before their checks came in. Several people, however, told us of *others* who did not get enough to eat. When we checked these matters out, most claimed that they had no interest in food—that they ate to keep alive.

Outsiders' Views. It is the outsiders who say that residents do not have enough to eat. A former manager of a middle-class retirement hotel told us:

> This one man was receiving $155 a month. He had no other income.
> We were charging him $75 a month for his room and the rest of his
> money was going into a restaurant. I know many days that man had
> nothing to eat. Unless one of us on the staff would invite him down and
> take him into the restaurant and buy him something to eat.

A middle-class maintenance man who worked for a few months in the Wells Fargo had similar views:

> Most of these older guys don't eat that well. You gotta figure that most
> of them are well over 65. The amount of money they get in checks like
> social security, whatever it is, is not enough to cover. If they eat one
> good meal a day, they're doing good. Cause I've seen some of them the
> way they eat.

Both of these observers were in their 40s—probably a significant fact—younger people sometimes expressed surprise at how little the old people ate.

Money for Food. Some people also make overt choices to spend less money on food:

> I'd rather do other things with my money, like go the race track. There's
> a lot of people that want to spend all their money on wine. They don't
> want to spend it on food or rent.

Others say just the opposite: that if they had more money, they would spend it on food:

> I've let myself get run down. Maybe it's just not eating the right foods or
> something, but I find it pretty difficult to find good places to eat at a
> reasonable price.

Health and Food. People with special health problems often find it difficult to get the kind of food they need. One resident who had had a tracheotomy lived on soup and avocados. The former he bought in the restaurants; for the avocados, he had to make trips to the store.

Temperature of food is important to some people. One man told us:

> I have to watch coffee and anything too hot or too cold or it aggravates
> me, believe it or not.

One is reminded of the relation between dental care and malnutrition. Lack of teeth makes some residents poorly served by most restaurant foods. Other disabilities are found; when we first moved into the hotels, one field worker gave some oranges to an old man. A few days later, he heard that the old man had given them away. In a debriefing session in which he reported this, he was asked by another field worker: "Can he peel the oranges?" In response, the first field worker gave the old man tangerines, which he ate. It is doubtful if the old man ever told anybody that he could not peel an orange.

We have a number of references to malnutrition, but it is difficult to say just how much of it is referable to lack of funds and how much to eating habits or illness. One man told us:

> Many of them—including me—are suffering from malnutrition. Due in part to the inflated prices and the packaging of items such as cheese, which forces you to buy far more than you want. I like the old days when you could go in and say, "Cut me off a little slice."

It may be true that there is some undernourishment among residents, but more of it comes from poor nutrition habits that from lack of funds. Most of those who eat badly spend as much as those who eat well—but they spend it on pie and coffee and doughnuts rather than on protein and vegetables.

Indeed, we have cases of people who will not under any circumstances eat what the dieticians would call "well." One resident commented about an old man he had been helping:

> It's not going to be long, because he's getting weak. I try to get him down to the grill to eat, but he won't do that. I got him some milk. I've told him I'd bring up such things as canned fruit—it's food. But he doesn't want anything. The only thing he'll eat if I bring it is milk and cookies.

Individual "pap-food" tastes are undoubtedly difficult to cater for in restaurants.

Some illnesses cause loss of appetite. Some mental health problems—such as boredom and depression—can be both a result and a cause for loss of appetite. One waitress told us that one resident—a man who was well known to us—was "too plain tight to buy enough food." Several residents repeated the charge. There was a streak of resentment in these charges, we think, because this man claimed to have lost $2,000 cash in a robbery.

Following special diets is of unusual difficulty for hotel residents who eat in cheap restaurants. One such case—a man of a little over 50—is worth citing in detail:

> And this dietician. She give me a big chart of the meats and she tells me what not to eat—don't eat no pork, no bacon, only a little piece of butter. She's tellin' me what to eat and how much of each item: eat all the fresh fruits you can eat and if you eat any canned fruits she's tellin' me to throw the juice away, you know, 'cause there's sugar in the syrup, you know. You can eat a slice of toast, she says, or an orange for breakfast, black coffee, no sugar and no cream. She's against sugar. She says it turns to something in your body real quick. You don't utilize

it. It isn't that much food value, she says. It turns to something—energy or something, and that turns to fat real quick. But she tells me, eat peanut butter. It's high in protein. But she told me to stay off the bacon. Eat a little bit of cheese and one egg a day—but don't fry it. Boil it or poach it, you know, and don't eat no jelly or jam. I told her I drink skim milk—she liked that. She says eat lean meat. I went to her and told her, look, they give me $120 a month. I'm payin' rent and I'm livin' to where I can't cook nowhere 'cause I don't have enough money and I live in this hotel. And she says the doctors wants me to eat special foods. But you can't be that selective. I get vegetables—I got a can of spinach in my room.

This man told us his blood pressure was 180/130.

Hunger Season. What does not show up in our diaries is the fact that some people eat differently at different times of the month: more and better just after the checks arrive on the first of the month. The "hunger season" in the hotels follows a monthly cycle as surely as the "hunger season" in some peasant and horticultural societies follows the seasonal cycle.

Some residents buy meal tickets at a ten percent discount to avoid running out of money toward the end of the month. But others do run out. Some restaurant managers or owners run tabs for "regulars." At the lunch counter in one of the local cardrooms, for example, the Mexican woman who runs the place keeps a notebook where the men can reach it—they write their own amounts in it. She tells us that she loses very little this way, and that "the old guys" have to eat even when they don't have any money. Both hotel cafes run accounts for some of the residents—we think that the accounts at the cafe attached to the large hotel are kept accurately. The manager tells us that they are paid with good regularity, but he extends credit only to people he knows. However, we know several people who left owing him money. Residents are grateful to the restaurant owners who extend credit to them:

If it wasn't for the manager of the grill, a lot of us guys would really be starving. He gives us credit and then we pay him at the first of every month. We pay our bills. Maybe we don't pay it all in full, but we pay on it.

Residents help one another in two ways: they "do runs" for people too ill to get their own food, and they lend each other money. The amount of the loans seldom exceeds $10, and most of them say that these loans are "always" repaid.

The runs are more complicated than the loans of money. Although some residents are willing to help some others by doing errands for them, they give two reasons for not liking to do it. First, the beneficiary of their help may get used to it and not make an effort to get better. Any person who makes runs for another for more than a few days at a time is loudly and seriously criticized; he is said to be abetting the sick man in his illness. The other reason they give is that the people whom you help ultimately accuse you of cheating them.

> Now, I got two pints of milk and a package of cookies for $1.47, including tax. To me that's fantastic. Now, when you come and say, "Here's your two pints of milk and a package of cookies—it's $1.47, because the cookies were 98¢,"they don't believe you. They never remember the tax.

> They look in the paper and they'll find out that a special on this liver sausage is 37¢, then you buy it at the liquor store and he gets 59¢. Well, when they see it's 37 in the paper, they kinda wonder. They don't get out to check for themselves.

Food and Social Position. The only startling discovery that we made is that people in the cheap residential hotels south of Broadway eat better than the people who live in middle-class hotels north of Broadway—and spend less money in the process. The restaurants north of Broadway cater to office workers at noon and to theatergoers in the evening. The result is that the only places to get inexpensive food in their area are hamburger houses, pancake houses and their equivalent. When we asked residents of the hotels north of Broadway why they did not use the restaurants south of Broadway, they said, "I have spent my entire life trying to get out of a place like that." Thus, social pressure determines diet; the social situation was valued more highly than the cheap, good food.

7. Beyond Food

Restaurants provide far more than just food. We have already seen that they extend credit at the end of the month. They also provide predictability, and sometimes social relationships that amount almost to companionship. They are an important site of repeated social interaction, no matter how minimal it may be. Some waitresses also "look out for" residents:

> His usual breakfast was doughnuts and coffee until I started talking him into having mashed potatoes and gravy, and then I finally started talking him into eating eggs. He never used to. Just two doughnuts and coffee. What kind of food is that for an old man? He should take vitamins—but they don't want to spend their money for that. They spend their money for the horses, so there you are.

Waitresses and restaurant managers become important fixed social points, giving security and a semblance of friendship that some residents say is reassuring—"these are my friends." It provides one of the basic elements of a sense of community in situations in which intimacy, domesticity, or closer community are all avoided.

Most residents eat alone—even when they are in company of others whom they know. Several times our field workers were told that if they were going to live in the hotels, they would have to learn not to mind eating alone.

Perhaps most important of all, a large number of inexpensive restaurants gives residents a choice about where they will eat. Having such a choice is extremely important to people whose range of choices is necessarily rigidly curtailed by an area, and a life-style, in which choice is at a premium. The most denigrated characteristic of the retirement home (a dreaded spectre which hovers over the lives of many of the residents) is lack of choice—you have to eat what and when *they* tell you, go to bed when you are told, where you are told. These small elements of choice in their daily lives keep people going: they provide conversation and variety, and most important, a sense of controlling one's own destiny. One of the gravest aspects of urban redevelopment is that, in the interest of "economy," developers cut down on choice for residents.

In summary, then who eats well in the hotels? It seems that those who are on the edge of poverty, have a working-class background, and who drink little, eat best—they eat unimaginatively, but regularly, and have what seems to be an adequately balanced diet. Those who are slightly better off run into two problems: (1) the problem of the tasty quick-food houses, where they tend to eat pancakes, hamburgers and malted milks, which are not cheap; (2) they may be unwilling to "go back" to the kind of milieu that their self-respect insists they have escaped from.

Run-down urban neighborhoods supply a lot of choice about where to eat, and often supply nourishing food at very low prices. With urban renewal, these facilities are likely to be replaced first by fast-food chains who see the renewal coming, which cuts down on the nourishment, and then by planned eating places, which cuts down on choice and on sites for informal predictable social interaction. The choice is as important for some people to maintaining mental health as the nourishment to maintaining physical health.

The implications of these findings seem obvious: city planners should take care not to cut down on choice in the interests of economic efficiency—it is a fine line. Counselors of hotel-dwellers should be more aware of the difficult situations for special diets—but most residents would rather eat badly than to give up their independence.

Notes

[1]The research for this report was carried out under Grant 5-P01-MH-25996 from the Center for Metropolitan Studies of the National Institute of Mental Health to the Western Behavioral Sciences Institute, La Jolla, California. Mrs. Marian Ashton, of the WBSI staff, gathered the diaries from the residents. Four WBSI field workers—Anthony W. Gorman, J. Kevin Eckert, Lisa D'Arcy, and Wayne Rauschkolb—helped by making most of the observations. At "debriefing sessions," held every week or ten days, their oral reports were recorded. My notes derive from my own observations, these debriefing sessions, and (in the case of D'Arcy) their notes.

[2]Studies of the elderly living in single-room occupancy hotels are few. The major book-length studies are:

Shapiro, Joan Hatch. *Communities of the Alone: Working with Single Room Occupants in the City.* New York: Association Press,   1971.

Stephens, Joyce. *Loners, Losers and Lovers.* Seattle, University of Washington Press, 1976.

Siegal, Harvey Allen. *Outposts of the Forgotten: Welfare Hotels and Single Room Occupancy Tenements.* 1977.

Eckert, J. Kevin. *The Unseen Elderly.* San Diego: Campanile Press, 1980.

11
Drinking Patterns Of the Rural Aged

Barry R. Bainton

1. Introduction

Alcohol abuse and alcoholism are two of the nation's most costly health problems. According to the National Institute on Alcohol Abuse and Alcoholism (NIAAA):

> Treatment for alcohol-related conditions accounted for more than 12 percent of the $68.3 billion health bill for adult Americans in 1971. Approximately $8.29 billion was expended for alcohol-related health and medical problems, making this the second largest component of the economic costs of alcohol misuse, problem drinking and alcoholism (1974:51-53).

Health and social service workers are becoming increasingly aware that the use of alcohol can be a contributing factor to their patients' or clients' problems. Recently, service providers to the elderly have begun to express concern about possible alcohol abuse among the elderly. Anecdotal reports by service providers suggest that alcohol use and abuse may constitute a significant health problem among the elderly. For example, a recent Michigan survey reported that:

> ...One third of the aging service providers and nearly one-third of the nurses reported alcohol problems in a significant proportion (more than 20%) of their senior clientele, as did one-sixth of the physicians, Department of Social Service workers, and pharmacists (Michigan Office of Services to the Aging, 1979:23).

While such clinical reports can be useful, they are also biased sources of data. Only those who perceive—or are perceived by others to have—a problem seek out these services. The more important questions are: What is the extent of drinking by the elderly? And, how does this compare with the drinking pattern of the general population? To answer these questions, one must examine the drinking practices of the elderly.

Studies of American drinking practices began in the early 1940s (Jellinek 1942; Bacon 1943; Glad 1947; Riley and Marden 1948). In the 1950s and 1960s, a major effort was undertaken by a number of researchers to assess the extent of drinking n the general population (Maxwell 1952; Mulford and Miller 1960a, 1960b, 1960c; Mulford 1963; Knupfer and Room 1964; Cahalan, Cisin, Kirsch and Newcomb 1965; Cahalan Cisin and Crossley 1967, 1969; Cahalan and Cisin 1968a, 1968b; and Jessor, Graves, Hanson and Jessor 1968). These studies provide us with a general overview of the extent of drinking in the general population, and the principal correlates of drinking behavior. A general finding reported in these surveys is that as a group the elderly drink at a lower rate than the general population. However, despite these efforts, very little attention has been paid directly to the elderly and their drinking practices.

During the past decade, a number of studies have been directed specifically at the phenomenon of elderly drinking (Rosin and Glatt 1971; Carruth, Williams and Heyman 1973; Johnson and Goodrich 1974; Baker, Mishara, Kastenbaum and Patterson 1974; Rathborne-McCune, Lohn, Levenson and Hsu 1976). One of these is the study of the drinking patterns of the rural elderly in Arizona reported here. The study, sponsored by the National Institute on Alcohol Abuse and Alcoholism,[1] was carried out by the staff of the Office of Human Development and Family Research,[2] School of Home Economics at the University of Arizona. The goal of the project was to describe the drinking patterns of the rural elderly and the correlates of drinking behavior. It was not the purpose of the study to examine elderly alcohol abuse or alcoholism per se; but rather, to describe the context in which elderly alcohol abuse might be found. We have left the question of elderly alcohol abuse and alcoholism for future research.

2. Method

A statewide survey of 600 households in rural, non-standard-metropolitan-statistical-area counties in Arizona was conducted in the spring and early summer of 1977. Households were selected using an area probability sampling technique (Bainton, Christopherson and Escher 1977). Two separate data gathering techniques were employed. One-half of the sample was interviewed in a face-to-face situation while the other half was asked to fill out a questionnaire in private and return it the next day to the field worker. A total of 287 interviews were completed using the face-to-face technique and only 158 completed questionnaires were returned using the drop-off technique, producing a total sample of 445 usable questionnaires. Despite the low response from the drop-off households, there was no significant difference in the two sub-samples in terms of the major socio-demographic characteristics.

The low response rate produced by the drop-off technique may be attributed to two factors. First, persons who refused a face-to-face interview were frequently willing to accept a drop-off questionnaire. The initial reluctance to accept a face-to-face interview may have carried over to the drop-off questionnaire. That is, rather than telling the interviewer they didn't wish to participate, the individual was willing to accept the questionnaire but never intended to complete it. Second, those who accepted the face-to-face interview received the benefit of socializing with the interviewer. There was no such reinforcement for the drop-off respondents.

Drinking behavior was recorded using the standard set of quantity-frequency questions used in previous drinking surveys. The questions were asked in two forms—a short form based on the work of Straus and Bacon (1953) and a long form developed by Cahalan, Cisin and Crossley (1969) (Appendix 1). The different forms were randomly distributed throughout the sample. There were no significant differences between the responses of persons completing the short or long form. Respondents were asked to describe their current drinking patterns for beer, wine, and liquor. They were also asked to descirbe what their pattern was prior to reaching the age of 65.

3. Analysis

The data were analyzed in two ways. First, a modified version of the Quantity-Frequency Typology was used (Straus and Bacon 1953, and Mulford and Miller 1960c). This approach classified respondents in terms of their drinking pattern—i.e., abstainers, light, moderate and heavy drinkers. The classification is useful in distinguishing between different consumption patterns. The following definitions were used for these patterns:

1. An abstainer is a person who drank no alcohol during the past year—i.e., during the past 12 months prior to the interview.
2. A light drinker is a person who drinks no more frequently than once a month regardless of the quantity consumed per occasion.
3. A moderate drinker is a person who either only drinks several times a month regardless of the quantity per occasion, or who drinks as often as several times a day but never more than two drinks per occasion.
4. A heavy drinker is one who drinks at least once a week, but generally more frequently, and consumes at least three drinks per occasion.

The second analytical approach was to compute the average amount of absolute alcohol consumed per day. This approach was developed by Jessor et. al. (1968) and is hereafter referred to as the Jessor Score. The Jessor Score was computed by taking the modal quantity of beer, wine, and liquor consumed per occasion and weighting this amount by the absolute alcohol content of a standard drink for the beverage. These values were then multiplied by the frequency of drinking occasions for each beverage. The resulting products were summed and averaged. The Jessor Score has two advantages over the Quantity-Frequency (Q/F) Type. First, it produces a continuous variable which can be analyzed using parametric statistics; and second, it provides an estimate of the average amount of alcohol which the body is exposed to daily. Computer programs to generate both types of variables were written for analysis using SPSS (Nie, Hull, Jenkins, Steinbrenner, and Bent 1970).

4.   General Population Characteristics

The socio-demographic characteristics of the sample are shown in Table 11:1, "Socio-Demographic Characteristics of the Rural Elderly Sample By Number and Percentage."

The age distribution was skewed toward the younger-old as might be expected. Men slightly outnumbered the women, which may be attributed to two factors. The natural longevity of women may have been off-set by the high proportion of young-old in the sample. Second, the culturally accepted practice that the male represents the household to the outside world may have caused more husbands than wives to respond. In the rural counties of Arizona, whites were the dominant ethnic group, as the Table demonstrates. Further, there was a tendency for the other ethnic groups in the rural communities to live in enclaves. The sampling technique adopted for this study did not permit us to isolate ethnic groups before we entered the field. In the field, frequently ethnic enclaves were discovered to be outside the sampling unit.

The income distribution was skewed toward the lower median income levels. Almost 57 percent of the sample had a median household income under $7,500 a year. Protestants were the predominant religious group. This group includes a wide cross-section of denominations and sects, and ranged from liberal common denominators to very conservative fundamentalist sects. Mormons represented eight percent of the sample. Only two persons who were of the Jewish faith were found in the sample. They were included in the "Other" category. Over half of the sample were married and over another one-third were widowed.

Table 11:2, "Socio-Demographic Correlates," presents the correlation matrix of a set of selected socio-demographic variables. These variables are: Income, Age, Sex (Male, Female), Marital Status, Sex/Marital Status and Religion.

Age was positively correlated with widowed status for both men and women, and negatively correlated with income and marriage. Income was also negatively correlated with being widows, (especially being a widow), being a woman, and being Catholic. Income was positively correlated with being male, married and Protestant.

TABLE 11.1

SOCIO-DEMOGRAPHIC CHARACTERISTICS OF THE RURAL ELDERLY BY NUMBER AND PERCENTAGE

	Number	Percentage
Age:		
65-69	165	39.0
70-74	106	25.1
75-79	81	19.1
80-84	46	10.9
85 and over	25	5.9
Sex:		
Male	225	50.7
Female	219	49.3
Ethnicity:		
White	359	81.0
Black	14	3.2
Mexican American	52	11.7
Other	18	4.1
Median Income:		
$ 1,500	82	21.2
4,000	77	19.9
6,000	61	15.8
7,500	37	9.6
8,500	28	7.3
9,500	16	4.1
12,500	49	12.7
17,500	22	5.7
30,000	14	3.6
Religion:		
Protestant	263	59.5
Catholic	100	22.6
Mormon	35	7.9
None	27	6.1
Other	15	3.9
Marital Status:		
Married	247	55.9
Divorced/Separated	16	3.6
Widowed	160	36.2
Never Married	19	4.3

TABLE 11.2C

SOCIO-DEMOGRAPHIC CORRELATION MATRIX OF RURAL ELDERLY SAMPLE

	INCOME	AGE	MALE	FEMALE	MARRIED	DIVORCED/SEPARATED	WIDOWED	MARRIED MALE	DIVORCED MALE	WIDOWED MALE	MARRIED FEMALE	DIVORCED FEMALE	WIDOWED FEMALE	PROTESTANT	CATHOLIC	MORMON
AGE	-.22843															
MALE	.16583	.01584														
FEMALE	-.16082	-.01067	-.89997													
MARRIED	.32119	-.14473	.44142	-.32942												
DIVORCED/SEPARATED	-.04496	-.10494	.03068	-.03423	-.19842											
WIDOWED	-.29618	.21140	-.31781	.39529	-.76293	-.13551										
MALE/MARRIED	.20934	-.0283	.78578	-.70640	.71551	-.14197	-.54588									
MALE/DIVORCED	.01825	-.07982	.14518	-.13051	-.14768	.74428	-.10086	-.10567								
MALE/WIDOWED	-.04997	.12411	.32549	-.29261	-.33109	-.05881	.43398	-.23690	-.04377							
FEMALE/MARRIED	.15821	-.16416	-.42600	.47388	.41879	-.08310	-.31951	-.33474	-.06185	-.13866						
FEMALE/DIVORCED	-.07441	-.04922	-.10944	.12174	-.12019	.60574	-.08208	-.08600	-.01589	-.03562	-.05033					
FEMALE/WIDOWED	-.28711	.14672	-.56038	.62335	-.61542	-.10931	.80665	-.44033	-.08136	-.18240	-.25773	-.06621				
PROTESTANT	.14409	.07915	.06465	.05544	.11354	.00111	.03530	.06515	-.00113	.02250	.06847	.02453	.01758			
CATHOLIC	-.19573	-.09795	-.02170	.07716	-.00798	-.04026	-.03007	-.03656	-.03471	.01939	.03676	-.01281	.02010	-.58599		
MORMON	.05899	.03701	.00276	.02748	.02487	-.05325	.01726	.03817	-.03963	-.03204	-.01607	.03226	.03985	-.31973	-.14746	
NO RELIGIOUS PREFERENCE	-.04396	-.00590	.09181	-.08397	-.02284	.10492	-.00480	.04137	.09894	.01882	-.08457	-.02807	-.01758	-.27827	-.12835	-.07003

5. Drinking Patterns of the Elderly

Although previous national and regional surveys show that drinking in the 60-and-older age group is lower relative to the general population, these studies rarely provide finer age breakdowns of the elderly population. Gerontologists and others in the aging field, on the other hand, recognize the fact that those over 60, or 65, years of age, do not constitute a homogeneous group. Instead, there are clearly distinguishable differences between the "young-old," those 60 to 74 years of age, and the "old-old," those 75 years of age and older. The young-old who were recently retired and beginning to settle into a new life style, may be expected to be more active and physically better off than the old-old. It might be reasonably expected then, that the drinking patterns of the young-old would differ significantly from that of the old-old.

The rural elderly sample did show a significant difference in the distribution of respondents by Q/F Type for the young-old group and the old-old age groups (Table 11:3).

TABLE 11.3
CURRENT Q/F TYPE BY AGE

Age	Abstainer		Light		Moderate		Heavy		Total	
	#	%	#	%	#	%	#	%	#	%
65-69	69	41.6	18	10.8	30	18.1	49	29.5	166	100.0
		34.5		28.1		34.5		68.1		39.2
70-74	46	43.8	24	22.9	25	23.8	10	9.5	105	100.0
		23.0		37.5		28.7		13.9		24.8
75-79	43	53.1	13	16.0	19	23.5	6	7.4	81	100.0
		21.5		20.3		21.8		8.3		19.1
80-84	27	58-7	4	8.7	9	19.6	6	13.0	46	100.0
		13.5		6.2		10.3		8.3		10.9
85 and over	15	60.0	5	20.0	4	16.0	1	4.0	25	100.0
		7.5		7.8		4.6		1.4		5.9
TOTAL	200	47.3	64	15.1	87	20.6	72	17.0	423	100.0
		100.0		100.0		100.0		100.0		100.0

$X^2 = 39.6809$ df = 9   significance = .0000

Under 50 percent of the young-old were abstainers, while over 50 percent of the old-old were abstainers. Further, the rate of abstainers in the sample population increased with age. On the other hand, the percentage of heavy drinkers was highest in the 65 to 69 age group, almost twice that of the sample population as a whole, and was lowest in the older age group.

The overall pattern supported the earlier survey findings that the drinking rate decreases with age, but brings into question the practice of lumping the elderly into a single group such as "those 55 and older," or "60 and above." The young-old appeared to represent a transitional group. Between 65 and 74, persons may begin to change their behavioral patterns relative to the use of alcohol. The change may result from a natural decline in the use of alcohol after retirement which is not fully manifested in the population until sometime after retirement. Or the change may result from a natural attrition process, whereby heavy drinkers drop out of the population earlier[3] than non-drinkers or those who drink in moderation. Lumping all those over a minimal age into a single class has masked this change phenomenon in other surveys.

When the average age of each Q/F Type was computed for both the current Q/F Type and Past Q/F Type, the attrition hypothesis was partially supported. Heavy drinkers were younger than the other Q/F Types (Table 11:4).

TABLE 11.4
CURRENT AND PAST QUANTITY-FREQUENCY
BY AVERAGE AGE

Quantity-Frequency Type		Number	Mean	SD
Current				
(F = 4.3357)	Abstainer	196	74.05	6.38
(Significance = .0019)	Light	69	73.24	5.74
	Moderate	86	73.36	5.74
	Heavy	72	70.48	5.53
	TOTAL	417	73.16	6.34
Past				
(F = 4.1648)	Abstainer	145	74.15	6.42
(Significance = .0069)	Light	69	74.35	7.50
	Moderate	85	72.28	5.75
	Heavy	118	71.90	5.63
	TOTAL	417	73.16	6.34

Individuals who were heavy drinkers at the time of the survey were almost two years younger, on the average, than the other Q/F Types. Further, the average age of current heavy drinkers was a year and a half younger than those who reported being heavy drinkers in the past. On the other hand, the current moderate drinkers were about one year older, on the average, than those who reported being moderate drinkers prior to retirement. Therefore, one might hypothesize that some of the heavy drinkers who were in the younger age group at the time of the interview, may be expected to drop out of the population before they enter a higher age group. The data indicate that those former heavy drinkers who survived long enough to become part of the older age group, had reduced their level of alcohol consumption.

Some policy makers and advisory groups have suggested that the retirement life style and the decline in the elderly's standard of living create conditions which foster alcohol abuse. If this is the case, one might expect that the elderly would have an overall increase in the rate of their drinking. Using the past and current Q/F Types as the measurement for drinking rate, it was possible to show the direction and relative magnitude of change in drinking patterns (Table 11:5).

TABLE 11.5
PERCENTAGE OF CURRENT DRINKING TYPE
BY PAST DRINKING TYPE

| | | Past | | | | |
		Abstainer	Light	Moderate	Heavy	Total
	Abstainer	70%	10%	7%	13%	100%
Current	Light	7%	59%	20%	14%	100%
	Moderate	6%	9%	52%	34%	100%
	Heavy	1%	3%	17%	79%	100%

The table shows that in terms of Q/F Type the drinking pattern remained fairly stable. Better than half of the sample reported no change in their drinking pattern. Abstainers and heavy drinkers were the most stable types. Of those who reported a change, a fairly higher percentage reported a decline than an increase in their drinking. The current heavy drinker group was made up of 79 percent past heavy drinkers, 17 percent were former moderate drinkers and only four percent had been light drinkers or abstainers in the past. On the other hand, 34 percent of all current moderate drinkers were formerly heavy drinkers, and 13 percent of all current abstainers had formerly been heavy drinkers. Therefore, it appears that if persons do change their drinking behavior as they get older, they tend to do so in the direction of decreased rather than increased drinking.

6. Socio-Demographic Characteristics

Public concern about elderly drinking has resulted from certain perceptions about the relationship between such factors as poverty and bereavement and drinking. As shown earlier, income was negatively correlated with both age and widowhood. If these factors were to have a negative effect on the elderly, it would appear reasonable to assume that some people would turn to alcohol as a means of coping with the stress that these factors might produce. While the Q/F Type describes the pattern of alcohol consumption, it is not a very sensitive measurement to detect changes in consumption which may take place within a given Q/F Type. This is obvious from the definitions. The Jessor Score, which estimates the average daily intake of absolute alcohol, is a much more sensitive index for measuring differences in drinking rates. In this section, the socio-demographic factors presented in Table 11:2 are correlated with the Current Jessor Score, the Pre-65 Jessor Score, and the change in Jessor Score. These data are shown in Table 11:6, "Socio-Demographic Matrix by Jessor Score."

TABLE 11.6
SOCIO-DEMOGRAPHIC CORRELATION MATRIX
BY JESSOR SCORE

	Current Jessor Score	Pre-65 Jessor Score	Change In Jessor Score
Income	.08640	.02339	.00411
Age	-.13254	-.06699	.02374
Male	.16747	.27840	-.22468
Female	-.16741	-.27689	.22314
Married	.10597	.04378	-.00889
Divorced/Separated	.05627	.12494	-.10646
Widowed	-.13157	-.07576	.03411
Married Male	.12742	.13669	-.09515
Divorced Male	.10144	.19624	-.16341
Widowed Male	.02033	.14722	-.13889
Married Female	-.02433	-.11727	.11011
Divorced Female	-.03268	-.03134	.02105
Widowed Female	-.15646	-.17798	.12816
Protestant	-.05023	.09149	.07864
Catholic	.00718	-.01004	.01153
Mormon	-.10612	-.06603	.03165
No Preferred Religion	.21719	.30159	-.24760
Current Jessor Score		.21253	.13121
Pre-65 Jessor Score			-.94082

The current mean Jessor Score for the sample was .4664 ounces of absolute alcohol a day (s.d. = 1.1703, N = 436). This was equivalent to about one highball a day per respondent, assuming one ounce of 80 proof whiskey per drink. The factors displaying the strongest positive correlation with the Current Jessor Score were: "no religious preference" (r = .21719), male (r = .16747), married male (r = .12742), and divorced male (r = .10144). These data support earlier survey results (e.g., Cahalan, Cisin, and Crossley 1969) which have shown that men drink more than women, and men, as a group, are more likely to drink more than women. Many religions have proscriptions about the use of alcohol which tend to influence individuals to be moderate in their consumption patterns. Thus, for those who were without any religious preference, this moderating influence would not have been expected to be present. As expected, "no religious preference" had the highest positive correlation with the Current Jessor Score. The factors negatively correlated with the Current Jessor Score were, as expected, the opposite of those positively correlated factors. These negative correlates were: female (r = .16741), widowed female (r = .15646), age (r = .13254), widowed (r = .13157), and the Mormon religion (r = .10612). The negative influence of widowhood, both alone and in conjunction with "female," contradicts the view held by some that alcohol abuse may be a common problem among widows. The negative relationship between age and the Current Jessor Score confirms the results of the Q/F Type analysis reported in the last section and the findings of other researchers.

The Pre-65 Jessor Score revealed some interesting contrasts. Positive correlates of the Pre-65 Jessor Scores were: "no religious preference" (r = .30159), male (r = .27840), divorced male (r = .19624), widowed male (r = .14722), married male (r = .13669), and divorced/separated (r = .13669). The magnitude of correlation coefficients was greater in reference to the Pre-65 Jessor Score than for the Current Jessor Score. The overall decline in strength may be attributed to the overall decline in the magnitude of the Jessor Score. The Pre-65 mean Jessor Score was 1.1525 ounces of absoute alcohol a day (s.d. = 3.4190, N = 437). The absence of a religious preference was the strongest correlate both in the Pre-65 Jessor Score and the Current Jessor Score. The sexual dichotomy in drinking practices was the second strongest factor. Being male and having a high Pre-65 Jessor Score was positively correlated. Maleness carried over into all the marital classifications during the pre-65 period. Compared with the Current Jessor Score coefficients, it appears that maleness was the dominant factor. Currently divorced males had a higher positive "r" in relation to their pre-65 Jessor Score than their current scores. This suggests that their pre-retirement drinking may have contributed to their current divorced status.

Negative correlates of pre-65 Jessor Scores were: female (r = .27689), widowed female (r = .17798), and married female (r = .11727). Given the strong influence of male as a positive correlate, it is not surprising that female would be the dominant negative correlate. While age was still negatively correlated with the Jessor Score, it was not a very strong correlate. The Pre-65 Jessor Score was positively correlated with the Current Jessor Score (r = .21253). This relationship supports the previous analysis, which showed that over half of all respondents in each Q/F Type reported no change in their drinking pattern.

The analysis of the socio-demographic factors in reference to changes in the Jessor Score produced some interesting results. Increases in the Jessor Score are positively correlated with the following: female (r = .22314), current Jessor Score (r = .12816), and married female (r = .11011). On the other hand, it is negatively correlated with the following: Pre-65 Jessor score (r = .94082), "no religious preference" (r = .24760), male (r = .22468), divorced males (r = .16341), and widowed males (r = .13889). The data show that male drinking decreased relative to female drinking in the post-retirement period. There are two possible explanations for this change. First, the overall rate of male drinking after retirement may drop more sharply than that of females. This would seem reasonable, since men start at a higher average level than women. The second explanation is that while men decrease their consumption, women may actually increase their level. Table 11:7 compares the current Jessor Scores with the Pre-65 Jessor Score by sex.

TABLE 11.7
COMPARISON BETWEEN MEAN CURRENT
AND PRE-65 JESSOR SCORES BY SEX

	Number	Mean Jessor Score	SD	F	Sig.
Current Jessor Score:					
Male	221	.6595	1.4631	12.5192	.0004
Female	214	.2671	.7123		
Total	435	.4664	1.1716		
Pre-65 Jessor Score:					
Male	219	2.1010	4.6045	36.3478	.0000
Female	217	.2004	.6070		
Total	436	1.1551	3.4225		

From the Table, it can be seen that the men did show a significant drop in the average Jessor Score, while women showed only a slight decrease.

To summarize the socio-demographic factors, except for an overall decrease in the average amount of absolute alcohol consumed by the elderly sample as a whole, the differences in consumption attributed to socio-demographic factors did not vary from what one might expect in the general population of adults. Differences between the elderly attributed to aging must be sought elsewhere.

7. Aging Factors and Drinking Patterns

Four factors were examined which might be considered as factors associated with aging. These are leisure-time activity, health, religiosity and social adjustment. Since the elderly have more free time on their hands than the general adult population, some commentators have assumed that drinking may be used to fill the idle hours. An analysis of leisure-time activities and Jessor Scores was used to test this idea. Health is a commonly expressed concern of the elderly, therefore it may be hypothesized that the drinking rate would decline with declining health. Some respondents reported that religion played an important role in their current lives. An increase in religiosity might be expected to be negatively correlated with drinking. Finally, the problems associated with adjustment to old age and retirement might be expected to influence the drinking pattern. If these problems cause increased stress, it might be hypothesized that drinking would increase as a means for coping with the stress.

Four indices were used to measure these factors. The leisure index was constructed from responses to a list of 18 activities which people commonly engage in as leisure-time activities. The ratio of total activities and frequency of activity to the total possible score was computed. The index score ran from 0 to 1, where 0 equalled "no activity" and 1 equalled "very active." The mean score for the sample was .3817 (s.d. = .1831, N = 434). The health index was constructed from responses to a list of common health problems, and represents the ratio of health problems reported by the respondent realtive to the total number of problems. Problems were weighted according to relative severity or threat to life—e.g., "poor eye sight" having a weight of one and "cancer" a weight of three. The higher the score, the poorer the health status. The mean score for the sample was .1138 (s.d. = .1884, N = 467). The religious index was constructed from answers to two questions: the frequency of church attendance, and the degree of liberalism one had toward religious teachings. A high score reflected a high degree of religiosity while a low score reflected a low level of religiosity. The sample mean was .3737 (s.d. = .3363, N = 470). Social adjustment was computed on the basis of the Social Readjustment Scale developed by Holmes and Rahe (1967). The mean score was 154.1 (s.d. = 101.3, N = 373). The correlation matrix for these indices is presented in Table 11:8.

TABLE 11.8
AGING FACTORS CORRELATION COEFFICIENTS
BY JESSOR SCORES

	Current Jessor Score	Pre-65 Jessor Score	Change in Jessor Score
Leisure Index	-.09408	-.08903	.05468
Health Index	-.15633	-.02166	-.03753
Religious Index	-.18701	-.13274	.07274
Social Readjustment Scale	-.05464	.00849	-.01994

Health and religiosity were negatively correlated with the Jessor Score. As health declined—i.e., the health index score increased—drinking decreased. Religiosity in old age had a similar effect. Religiosity in the post-65 age period was not correlated with the Pre-65 Jessor Score, but was positively correlated with the Current Jessor Score. Neither leisure nor social adjustment demonstrated a significant relationship with either current or pre-65 Jessor scores. Leisure was negatively correlated with the health index score, showing that as health worsens, leisure activity also decreases. Religiosity was positively correlated with leisure activity and negatively with health status. This suggests that those who had a high score in religiosity were also active in leisure-time activities. It also suggests that as health declines, respondents were more concerned about their religion. Previous studies of social adjustment and health (Holmes and Rahe 1967, Rahe et. al. 1964) have shown that as the social adjustment score increases, the probability of poor health also increases. The data from this study supported these findings. The data also suggest that drinking behavior among the rural elderly had no relationship to coping with the stress produced by the items in the social adjustment index.

8.   Summary and Discussion

Public concern has recently focused on the question of alcohol usage by the elderly. A number of popular theories have been offered which suggest that the use of alcohol by the elderly may be dangerous, or at least undesirable. Underlying these popular theories is the public acceptance of the disengagement theory of aging (Cumming and Henry 1961). The concern, while well-intended, appears in light of our findings and those of other researchers to be misplaced.

Johnson and Goodrich (1974) reported finding a high rate of abstention among their sample of elderly residents of the upper-East side of Manhattan. Health was negatively correlated with drinking. Those who did drink, they report, derived some benefits from it. Baker, Mishara, Kastenbaum and Patterson 1974) reported similar benefits from an experiment involving moderate drinking by nursing home and minimum care residential clients. Carruth el. al. (1974) found that approximately 25 percent of those who had been treated for alcoholism 15 years before reported that they now abstain. Even among those who continued to drink, they had decreased the level of consumption. Rosin and Glatt (1971) reported that two-thirds of the elderly they observed with alcohol problems had these problems prior to old age; only one-third reported problems which arose as a result of events associated with aging.

Rathborne-McCune, Lohn, Levenson and Hsu (1976) have offered evidence to the contrary. In a community survey of aged alcoholics in Baltimore, they reported that the rate of problem drinking/alcoholism among the elderly was 12 per 100. These findings run counter to those of the other studies. An analysis of the methodology used to construct the Baltimore sample raises questions about biases in the study's results. The sample was not representative of the general elderly population of Baltimore. Instead four different sub-samples were used, and later in the analysis these data were pooled. As a result, the sample was skewed in favor of that segment of the population where alcoholism is known to be a major problem—the transient male.

Disregarding the Rathborne-McCune et. al. study, these studies of elderly drinking show that alcohol usage does not constitute a significant problem among the elderly. This is *not* to say that there are no elderly problem drinkers; but rather that, as a group, the elderly do not reflect unique patterns associated with aging that foster problem drinking.

The general conclusion one can draw from the study reported here is that the elderly tend to retain, in old age, drinking patterns that they established prior to retirement. The principle socio-demographic correlates of drinking did not differ from those found in general population and reported by others (e.g., Cahalan, Cisin and Crossley 1969; Mulford and Miller 1960a). Two factors associated with aging—increased religiosity and decreasing health—proved to be strong deterrents to drinking.

Where change did take place, the majority of elderly actually adopted a pattern, measured in terms of Q/F Type, which represented a decrease in drinking. A very low percentage of respondents reported an increase in their drinking. Despite the apparent stability in drinking patterns, the elderly as a group showed a significant drop in the average quantity of absolute alcohol consumed daily. One area that requires further study is the process of change that takes place in elderly drinking patterns. Do persons with patterns of heavy drinking prior to retirement undergo a change in life style at retirement that fosters more moderate drinking? Or, does heavy drinking in the post-retirement period lead to earlier death or institutionalization? Our data suggests that the latter may be the case. However, a longitudinal study following a panel of heavy drinkers through the ages 60 to 74 would shed light on the issue.

Several policy considerations are indicated from the data. First, except in areas of dense elderly concentration, alcoholism services fo the elderly should be tied to existing service agencies in the form of alcoholism counselors with special training in gerontology or aging counselors with special training in alcoholism treatment. In areas of high concentration, special geriatric alcoholism programs may be warranted. Second, prevention programs specifically designed for elderly and those entering retirement should be directed toward responsible drinking. Such a program might encourage more elderly persons to adopt moderate drinking patterns. One of the greatest dangers alcohol abuse or misuse poses for the elderly is an increase chance for a serious and costly accident, which may prevent them from enjoying their "golden years."

Notes

[1]The research reported in this chapter was conducted under grant #R01-AA-01914 from the National Institute on Alcohol Abuse and Alcoholism.

[2]Principal Investigators: Victor A. Christopherson, Barry R. Bainton, and Monika C. Escher.

[3]By "drop out" we mean that they may die earlier or become institutionalized. Institutionalized subjects were not included in the survey sample.

Appendix 1

Long Form

1. How often do you usually drink wine/beer/liquor?
    1. Three or more times a day
    2. Two times a day

3. About once a day
4. Three or four times a week
5. Once or twice a week
6. Two or three times a month
7. About once a month
8. Less than once a month, but at least once a year
9. Less than once a year
0. Never

2. When you drink wine/beer/liquor, how often do you have more than five glasses or five drinks?
    1. Nearly every time
    2. More than half the time
    3. Less than half the time
    4. Once in a while
    5. Never

3. When you drink wine/beer/liquor, how often do you have three or four glasses or drinks?
    1. Nearly every time
    2. More than half the time
    3. Less than half the time
    4. Once in a while
    5. Never

4. When you drink wine/beer/liquor, how often do you have about one or two glasses or drinks?
    1. Nearly every time
    2. More than half the time
    3. Less than half the time
    4. Once in a while
    5. Never

Short Form

1. How often do you usually drink wine/beer/liquor?
    1. Three or more times a day
    2. Two times a day
    3. About once a day
    4. Three or four times a week
    5. Once or twice a week
    6. Two or three times a month
    7. About once a month
    8. Less than once a month, but at least once a year
    9. Less than once a year
    0. Never

2. When you drink wine/beer/liquor, how much do you usually drink at one time?
    1. A bottle or more/seven or more bottles/seven or more drinks

2. Half bottle or five glasses/five or six bottles/five or six drinks
3. Three or four glasses/three or four bottles/three or four drinks
4. One or two glasses/one or two bottles/one or two drinks
5. Less than one glass/less than a bottle/less than one drink
6. Never drink wine/never drink beer/never drink liquor

12
Physician Influence
In the Selection
Of Institutionalization
Of the Elderly

Margaret Faulwell
and
Rhoda S. Pomerantz

1.   Introduction

This chapter is based upon two studies designed to identify characteristics
of physicians which are predictive of the selection of institutionalization as
the mode of care for the elderly after discharge from an acute-care hospital.
By "institutionalization" is meant confinement of the patient in a nursing
home or a home for the aged. Rehabilitation facilities and mental hospitals
are excluded from this definition. By "elderly" is meant an individual sixty-
five years and over.

1.1.   Demographic Trends in Aging

The United States is rapidly aging. Since 1900 the number of people who
reach age 65 has increased more than sevenfold. At the turn of the century
4.1 percent of the total population—or 3.1 million people—were in the age
group 65 and over. By mid-1976, 10.7 percent—or approximately 27
million people—were in this age category. It is currently estimated that the
number of elderly in the United States is increasing by 500,000 per year
(Brotman 1977a). Thus, at present death rates, the older population is ex-

pected to increase 40 percent to 31 million by the year 2000. If the present low birth rate continues, these 31 million will be 11.7 percent of a total population of approximately 262 million (USDHEW NCHS 1975a).

One of the principal factors in this rapid growth in the older population is the increase in life expectancy from birth. However, the life expectancy of those who attain age 65 has changed relatively little since the turn of the century. In 1900 a person could expect to live approximately 12 more years on reaching age 65 (USDHEW HCHS 1974b). In 1974 the figure was approximately 15 years—13 years for men and 17 years for women (USDHEW NCHS 1975a). In contrast, life expectancy from birth has increased by 25 years. In 1900 a person could expect to live approximately 47 years; a person born today can expect to live an average of 72 years. Assuming present death rates do not dramatically change, 80 percent of all female children and 65 percent of all male children born today will reach age 65 (USDHEW NCHS 1975a).

1.2. Institutionalization and the Elderly

The increasing numbers and proportion of individuals in the age category 65 and over have produced serious concerns about service delivery for this age group (Palmore 1972a&b; Petersdorf 1973). Since 1960 the number of elderly in nursing homes has increased by 245 percent (Brotman 1977a). At that time 3.8 percent of persons 65 years and over were in long-term care institutions; by 1974 this figure has risen to approximately five percent (USDHEW PHS 1975b). This represents over one million of the nation's elderly.

These data, based on cross-sectional studies, are not a true indication of the actual number of elderly who are affected by this increased use of institutionalization. Several studies based upon the examination of death certificates indicate that approximately one aged individual in four dies in a nursing home or home for the aged (Kastenbaum and Candy 1973; Wershow 1976). While such data provide more accurate indicators, here too the possibility of underestimation exists, since it can be assumed that some individuals are transferred to acute hospitals shortly before death. However, a recent longitudinal study on the chance of institutionalization before death among normal aged people living in the community is about one in four.

Factors associated with the risk of institutionalization are not fully understood. A review of the literature indicates that institutionalized elderly cannot necessarily be distinguished from non-institutionalized elderly on the basis of personal and health characteristics alone (U.S. Department of Commerce 1970a, 1970b, 1973; USDHEW BPA 1955; USDHEW

WCHS 1974a). Experts in aging feel that a substantial number of patients in long-term care facilities do not need institutional care, and would be better served by existing alternative care services. In a recent HEW report on skilled nursing facilities, 13.2 percent of the patients examined were fully ambulatory, able to leave the facility and walk outdoors at will (USDHEW PHS 1975b). In a study on the use and misuse of nursing homes in Buffalo, New York, it was found that 27 percent of the institutionalized population did not need nursing home care (Davis and Gibbin 1971). A Massachusetts Department of Health evaluation of nursing home patients reported that only 37 percent of the residents required full-time skilled nursing care, 26 percent required minimal supervised living, 23 percent needed limited or periodic nursing care and a full 14 percent needed no institutional care whatsoever (Levinson Gerontological Policy Institute 1971). Such data suggest that factors other than patient characteristics and availabiltiy of alternative health-care services are operational in the selection of the mode of care for the elderly.

1.3. Role of the Physician

Public policies such as Medicare and Medicaid have had a significant effect on the availability and utilization of long-term care institutions. It appears that they are also having an effect on where and by whom the decision to institutionalize is made. Until recently the majority of elderly individuals entered a long-term care institution directly from the community. At the present time most individuals are referred to a long-term care institution directly from an acute hospital. Among the factors which contribute to this trend are Medicare and Medicaid reimbursement requirements for long-term care, mandatory utilization review and other programs designed to monitor appropriateness of admission and length of stay for Medicare and Medicaid recipients. Thus, the physician and the organizational structure of the acute hospital in which he practices may be important factors in the decision to institutionalize.

The physician-patient relationship has been analyzed and debated in the literature of Medical Sociology since the early 1950s. Talcott Parsons, in his classic analysis of medical practice, argued that the physician was expected to be affectively neutral, to approach the patient in an objective and clinical fashion, and to place the welfare of the patient above his own personal interest. The patient for his part was expected to recognize his obligation to get well. Furthermore, both the patient and his family had an obligation to seek competent help and to cooperate with those who were attempting to help him get well (Parson 1951). In a later analysis Parsons defined the structure of the relationship between the physician and the patient as asymmetrical, and supported the notion that the expert (physician) should have a power advantage over the patient in order to ensure patient compliance (Parsons 1975).

The presence of the older individual in an acute-care setting places him in the "sick" role, and heightens his reliance upon the physician who is responsible for the coordination of the majority of his health services. Because of the dominant role of the physician, particularly in the hospital setting, his advice is highly significant. His recommendation to institutionalize must be seriously considered by the family, and indeed may overrule any objections which the family might otherwise have raised.

Although society tends to view the physician as "affectively neutral," the literature indicates that the cultural background of the physician influences his choice of treatment for the patient (e.g., National Committee on Maternal Health 1963; Sudnow 1967). It has also been suggested that the training of the physician, his general and sub-speciality orientation, and the nature and length of his relationships with his patients, have an effect on the way he evaluates the patient and manages his care (Mechanic 1978).

2. Study Methodology

In order to examine the association of personal and professional characteristics of physicians with their rates of institutionalization, studies were conducted at two hospitals located on the west side of Chicago—Rush Presbyterian-St. Luke's, an 865-bed acute-care teaching hospital, and Mt.Sinai, a 479-bed acute-care hospital with teaching affiliation. The study groups consisted of all physicians on the hospital staffs who were in solo practice and had discharged at least five elderly patients during the period of January 1, 1975 through December 31, 1975. One hundred twenty-nine physicians at Rush Presbyterian-St. Luke's and seventy-five physicians at Mt. Sinai met the study criteria (see Table 12:1).

For each physician in the study sample, the following personal and professional characteristics were obtained: (1) sex; (2) date of birth; (3) place of birth; (4) race; (5) marital status; (6) board certification and area in which certification was held; (7) year of graduation from medical school; (8) department appointment. At Rush Presbyterian-St. Luke's, sub-specialty appointments within the Department of Internal Medicine were obtained, where applicable. Mt. Sinai's organizational plan did not include subsection appointments. One additional variable, the number of years on the hospital staff, was also obtained for the physicians at Mt. Sinai (see Table 12:2).

In addition to the personal and professional characteristics of the physicians, their patient populations were defined by the following criteria:

TABLE 12.1
DEFINITION OF PHYSICIAN SAMPLE

Physician Sample	Number	Percentage
Total active attending		
Presbyterian-St. Luke's	634	100%
Mt. Sinai	280	100%
Approximate number eligible to		
admit patients ≥ 65 yr.		
Presbyterian-St. Luke's	501	79.0%
Mt. Sinai	227	81.1%
Total physicians with one or more		
admissions ≥ 65 yr.		
Presbyterian-St. Luke's	239	37.7%
Mt. Sinai	111	39.6%
Total physicians with five or		
more admissions ≥ 65 yr.		
Presbyterian-St. Luke's	193	30.4%
Mt. Sinai	75	26.8%
Total physicians in solo practice with		
five or more admissions ≥ 65 yr.		
study sample		
Presbyterian-St. Luke's	129	20.3%
Mt. Sinai	75	26.8%
Summary of Deletions for MD with One or		
More Admissions ≥ 65:		
Number of physicians with less than 5		
patients		
Presbyterian-St. Luke's	46	
Mt. Sinai	36	
Number of physicians in group practice		
Presbyterian-St. Luke's	64	
Mt. Sinai	0	
TOTAL PRESBYTERIAN-ST. LUKE'S SAMPLE	110	
TOTAL MT. SINAI SAMPLE	36	
Total Number of Patients Admitted by the		
Physicians in the Study Sample:		
Presbyterian-St. Luke's	2923	
Mt. Sinai	1778	

(1) proportion of patients in age category 65 and over; (2) median age of patients in this category; (3) male to female ratio; (4) racial composition; (5) proportion of patients who reside in nursing homes; (6) proportion of elderly discharged to a long-term care institutions.

The objective in the analysis was to determine whether each of the selected physician characteristics in the study was related to the rate of in-

TABLE 12.2
PHYSICIAN CHARACTERISTICS

	RPSL	Mt. Sinai
Sex		
Male	123	67
Female	6	8
Place of Birth		
United States	109	35
Other than United States	14	39
Missing data	6	1
Race		
White	123	63
Other than White	6	12
Board Certification		
Yes	93	41
No	35	34
Missing data	1	—
Marital Status		
Married	105	51
Single	11	7
Divorced	4	1
Separated	1	0
Widowed	1	3
Missing data	7	13
Department		
Ear, Nose, and Throat	1	2
Family Practice	—	6
General Surgery	13	13
Gynecology	3	1
Internal Medicine	75	30
Neurology	6	3
Ophthalmology	8	3
Orthopedic Surgery	7	2
Plastic Surgery	3	—
Preventive Medicine	2	—
Primary Health	—	8
Psychiatry	6	1
Therapeutic Radiology	—	1
Urology	5	5

stitutionalization. For discrete variables, a one-way analysis of variance was used to test for significant differences in the mean rate of institutionalization. The relationship between continuous variables and the rate of institutionalization was analyzed by means of zero-order correlations. For the Rush Presbyterian-St. Luke's data, a correlation coefficient of .173 was statistically significant at the .05 level; for the Mt. Sinai data the comparable figure was .224.

2.1 Results

For Rush Presbyterian-St. Luke's, the following results were obtained. By means of analysis of variance, three of the seven discrete variables used in the study were found to have a significant effect on the rate of institutionalization ($p < .01$); the institutionalization rate for sub-specialists in the Department of Internal Medicine was lower than the rate for those without sub-specialty appointments ($p < .0005$); the rate for white physicians was

TABLE 12.3
ASSOCIATION OF DISCRETE VARIABLES WITH RATE OF
INSTITUTIONALIZATION (RPSL)

Variable	Mean Rate of Institutionalization	Std. Dev.	P
Subspeciality section appointment in department of Internal Medicine			
Yes	.013	.026	
No	.051	.051	.0005
Board certification			
Yes	.030	.039	
No	.066	.090	.01
Physician race			
White	.034	.055	
Other-than-White	.135	.065	.001
Department appointment	(See Table 12.4)		.05 p .10
Marital status	—	—	NS
Sex	—	—	NS
Country of origin	—	—	NS

lower than that for other-than-white physicians (p<.001); the rate for board certified physicians was lower than that for non-boarded physicians (p<.01) (see Table 12:3).

Departmental appointment affected the rate of institutionalization at a lesser level of significance (.05<p<.1). Orthopedic surgeons, with an institutionalization rate of over 11 percent compared to the overall institutionalization rate of 3.9 percent, discharged the greatest proportion of patients to a long-term care facility (see Table 12:4).

TABLE 12.4

RATE OF INSTITUTIONALIZATION BY DEPARTMENT APPOINTMENT

Department	Mean		Standard Deviation	
	(RPSL)	(Mt. Sinai)	(RPSL)	(Mt. Sinai)
Ear, Nose and Throat	0	0	0	0
Family Practice	N/A	.051	N/A	.063
General Surgery	.017	.017	.032	.034
Gynecology	0	0	0	0
Internal Medicine	.038	.037	.048	.051
Neurology	.064	.033	.078	.058
Ophthalmology	.031	.083	.036	.144
Orthopedic Surgery	.113	.072	.099	.040
Plastic Surgery	.037	N/A	.064	N/A
Preventive Medicine	.018	N/A	.026	N/A
Primary Health	N/A	.083	N/A	.068
Psychiatry	.056	.143	.136	0
Therapeutic Radiology	N/A	.143	N/A	0
Urology	.018	0	.041	0

OVERALL INSTITUTIONAL RATE		
(RPSL)	.039	
(Mt. Sinai)	.041	

N/A - not applicable

Significant zero-order correlations with rates of institutionalization (p<.05) were obtained for three continuous variables: median age of patient population (r = .265), physician age (r = −.214), proportion of elderly patients who reside in nursing homes (r = .202). By controlling for median patient age, it was found that the proportion of elderly patients from nursing homes did not significantly correlate with the rate at which a physician discharged new patients to nursing homes. Therefore two continuous variables—median patient age and physician age— remained significant.

Analyses of co-variance were performed on the significant discrete variables, using median patient age and physician age as co-variants. As a result of these analyses it was found that the difference in the mean rate of institutionalization among sub-specialists in the Department of Internal Medicine was not significantly lower than that for those without sub-specialty appointment. Race, board certification, and department, however, remained significant.

At Mt. Sinai only two discrete variables were found to have an effect on the rate institutionalization—departmental appointment and physician country of origin—and this was at a slightly lower level of significance $(.05 < p < .1)$. The mean rate of institutionalization ranged from zero percent for the Departments of Urology, Otolaryngology, and Obstetrics/Gynecology to 15.3 percent for Psychiatry and Therapeutic Radiology (see Table 12:4). The rates for country of origin ranged from 1.1 percent for physicians born in India to 8.1 percent for physicians born in Europe (see Table 12:5). None of the continuous variables used in the Mt. Sinai study correlated significantly with rates of institutionalization. Furthermore the mean rate of institutionalization for nearly every category under investigation was characterized by a large variance. This demonstrated a lack of uniformity within the groups studies at Mt. Sinai.

TABLE 12.5
ASSOCIATION OF DISCRETE VARIABLES WITH RATE OF
INSTITUTIONALIZATION (MT. SINAI)

Country of Origin	Mean Rate of Institutionalization	Standard Deviation
United States	.033	.052
India	.011	.023
Mideast	.081	.061
Europe	.081	.070
Phillipines	.018	.031
South America	.033	.058
Orient	.040	.089
Race		
White	.044	.059
Black	.013	.015
Oriental	.032	.071

2.2 Discussion

An analysis of the results suggests three factors which appear to influence the decision to institutionalize an elderly patient upon discharge from an acute-care hospital—similar personal characteristics or cultural fit of physician and patient, the physician's length of association with his patient, and the method of patient referral to the physician. One of the most obvious examples of the apparent significance of cultural fit is seen in the negative correlation between physician age and rate of institutionalization found in the Rush Presbyterian-St. Luke's data—i.e., older physicians institutionalize the elderly at a lower rate. Older patients may feel more comfortable with a physician who approximates their own age, and thus closer rapport and cooperation may develop. Furthermore the older physician is likely to have a better understanding of the problems of the elderly and may himself share with the elderly the fears and anxieties surrounding old age and institutionalization. Older physicians, having been in practice for a long time, have also had the opportunity to form closer and longer-lasting relationships with patients and their family members and therefore are better able to muster the resources of significant others in maintaining the patient in the community.

The association of physician race and country of origin with rates of institutionalization is also suggestive of the significance of cultural fit between physician and patient. At Rush Presbyterian-St. Luke's, where the majority of elderly patients are white, other-than-white physicians institutionalize at a rate ten percent higher than white physicians. This difference in the mean rate of institutionalization remains significant, even when physician age and median patient age are controlled for. This situation is reversed at Mt. Sinai. Although the differences in the mean institutionalization rate by physician race in the Mt. Sinai data are not significant, this is primarily due to the small number of black and Oriental physicians and to the high variability of institutionalizing practice within the white and Oriental physician categories. However, the four black physicians on Mt. Sinai's staff have a strikingly low rate of institutionalization (1.3 percent), and the low standard deviation indicates that this practice is uniform for all four of these physicians. These black physicians serve a patient population which is 98.3 percent black. The data on the black physicians are also interesting, in that none of these physicians is new to the Mt. Sinai staff—they average 11 years in service at the hospital. Thus they have had the opportunity to be associated with their patients for a substantial period of time.

Country of origin of the physician was not associated with rates of institutionalization in the Rush Presbyterian-St. Luke's data. The majority of physicians were born in the United States, and the few who were born outside the country have lived in the United States for many years. On the other hand a large proportion (52.7 percent) of the physicians on the Mt. Sinai staff are foreign medical graduates (FMGs). Assuming the significance of cultural similarity between physician and patient, it was anticipated that these foreign born physicians would have higher rates of institutionalization. This is true for those physicians born in the Mideast and Europe. Physicians born in India, however, have the lowest rates of institutionalization. Old age is accorded more respect in India than in the United States, and these lower institutionalization rates may reflect this cultural orientation.

Mt. Sinai has two departments—Family Practice and Primary Health—which are not represented in Rush Presbyterian-St. Luke's organizational structure. The Department of Family Practice is characterized by physicians who have been on the Mt. Sinai staff for an average of 33 years. In contrast, the physicians in the Department of Primary Health have an average tenure at Mt. Sinai of only three years. The median age of elderly patients in both departments is older than that for the institution as a whole (72.5 years), with Family Practice having the older patient population (76 years vs. 73 years). The patient population in Family Practice is more than 80 percent white, whereas that in Primary Health is only 24 percent white. Of the six physicians in Family Practice, five are U.S.-born, whereas in Primary Health only three of the eight physicians are U.S.-born. By race all physicians in Family Practice are white, as compared with Primary Health in which three of the eight are Oriental. No black physicians are represented in either department (see Table 12:6).

TABLE 12.6
COMPARISON OF FAMILY PRACTICE WITH
PRIMARY HEALTH (MT. SINAI)

Variable	Family Practice	Primary Health
Mean rate of institutionalization	.051	.082
Standard deviation	.063	.068
Length of tenure (in years)	33.3	3.4
Standard deviation	13.1	1.4
Median patient age (in years)	75.8	73.4
Standard deviation	34.9	16.9
Proportion White	.804	.244
Standard deviation	.304	.235
Number of White physicians	6 (100%)	5 (62.5%)
Number of U.S. born physicians	5 (83.3%)	3 (37.5%)

These departments mirror the recent shifts in Mt. Sinai's patient population. In the second half of the twentieth century the predominantly white, Jewish, middle-class neighborhood surrounding Mt. Sinai changed to a predominantly poor, black neighborhood. The black patients coming into Mt. Sinai's neighborhood initially obtained care at hospital-based out-patient clinics. In 1972, all out-patient clinics at Mt. Sinai were reorganized into a single private group practice, and physicians were recruited to care for these patients. It is these new physicians that comprise the Primary Care Department. The reoganization was, in part, an attempt to establish continuity of care for the patient, with a single physician following his pa-tient both in and out of the hospital. This is a relatively new program, and it has been difficult to recruit physicians to practice in this type of setting.

The Family Practice physicians have had a long tenure at Mt. Sinai and are treating predominately white patients who lived in the vicinity of the hospital prior to the neighborhood change. These are patients with whom they have had the opportunity to establish a long relationship and with whom they share a similarity of background. Primary Health physicians are more recent members of the Mt. Sinai staff, and do not share similar backgrounds with their patients. The recent development of the depart-ment, the high turnover rate among the physicians, and the fact that the department serves the same patient population previously served by the clinics preclude the possibility of sustained association be-tween physician and patient. A comparison of the rates of institutionaliza-tion for the two departments reflects the significance of these differences. The mean rate of institutionalization for the Department of Family Practice is 5.1 percent, whereas that for the Department of Primary Health is 8.2 percent. Thus the Department of Family Practice has a lower mean rate of institutionalization, even though the patients which it treats are older and therefore at greater risk.

The relationship between board certification and the rate of institu-tionalization found in the Rush Presbyterian-St. Luke data may at least in part reflect the significance of the method of patient referral. Observers in the health field have recognized a trend toward increased numbers of board-certified physicians. Health planners have speculated that this specialization, with its emphasis on episodic and disease-oriented care, leads toward a fragmentation of patient services and ignores continuity and the total psycho-social health needs of the patient. Thus it was expected that board-certified physicians would be less sympathetic with the needs of elderly patients, and would therefore be more likely to have a higher rate of institutionalization. Contrary to this expectation, board-certified physicians at Rush Presbyterian-St. Luke's institutionalize their patients at a lower rate than non-boarded physicians. The difference between the rates remains significant even after the results are adjusted for differences in physician age and median patient age.

Boarded and non-boarded physicians receive their patients from dif-ferent sources. Patients are frequently referred to a board-certified physician by other physicians for management of specific and difficult problems. The very fact that an older patient is referred to a specialist, as measured by board certification, implies an interest in the patient and a belief that his problems can be treated. Furthermore the specialist, in order to sustain this referral system which is his principal patient source, is obliged to return the patient to the care of the referring physician after treatment of the specific problem. In addition he must maintain a high quality of service. Thus the patient may receive better care, and if the decision to institutionalize is ultimately made, it is the referring physician rather than the specialist who does so.

In contrast, the non-boarded physician at Rush Presbyterian-St. Luke's does not receive his patients by physician referral. While he may hospitalize patients from his own practice, he also accepts patients assigned to him from the hospital-based out-patient facility and emergency room. These patients are frequently black and/or poor. Both of these factors may subtlely affect the interest of the physician in and the quality of care he provides to these patients.

An additional organizational practice which appears to influence the decision to institutionalize is the existence of uniform discharge-planning procedures for all elderly patients. All elderly patients at Rush Prebyterian-St. Luke's are evaluated early in their hospital course by a department established to provide an assessment of needs for post-hospital care and information concerning alternative ways for meeting these needs. Mt. Sinai has no such uniform policy. Patients are seen by the Social Service Department at Mt. Sinai only if the physician makes the referral, and frequently this is done after the decision to institutionalize has been made. Thus, whereas the Department of Social Service at Rush Presbyterian-St. Luke's has a part in informing the family of the various care alternatives which exist for patients after discharge, the equivalent department at Mt. Sinai frequently has only a part in helping the family choose or gain entry to a nursing home.

A final factor associated with the rate of institutionalization is the departmental appointment of the physician. Institutionalization rates by department are for the most part similar at both hospitals. The Department of Orthopedic Surgery has the highest mean rate of institutionalization of any department at Rush Presbyterian-St. Luke's. The practice of orthopedics is characterized by a high percentage of patients with disorders of ambulation. When the onset of such a disorder is sudden, the patient is at particularly high risk for institutionalization. Orthopedic Surgery at Mt. Sinai has a somewhat lower mean rate of institutionalization than found at Rush Presbyterian-St. Luke's because fewer dramatic procedures are performed at that hospital. The two departments at Mt. Sinai with the highest rates of institutionalization—psychiatry and therapeutic radiology—cannot be adequately assessed in that only one physician is present in each group.

Finally, it should be noted that the physician sample for this study consisted of 20.3 percent of all physicians at Rush Presebyterian-St. Luke's and 26.8 percent of all physicians at Mt. Sinai. This is an interesting statistic. The principal criterion for inclusion in the study was the discharge of at least five patients 65 years and older from the hospital during the calendar year. Upon examination of the discharge records, it was found that only 37.7 percent of all physicians at Rush Presbyterian-St. Luke's had discharged even one elderly patient during the year in question. One possible interpretation of this data is that the majority of physicians at both hospitals do not treat elderly patients. Most of the training received by physicians in this country is oriented toward acute care, with little attention paid to restorative and/or long-term care. Most older patients may be characterized by the presence of at least one chronic disease. It may be that the older patient—with a host of interrelated chronic diseases and the need for care designed to maintain or restore minimal function—holds little fascination or challenge for the physician. It may also be that the physician, confronted with a patient whom he cannot "cure," experiences a sense of failure. Thus he seeks to avoid having to deal with the older patient, and prefers to delegate care to an institution.

Results of studies such as this have significant implications for physician training in the United States. Medical students rarely have the opportunity to meet and learn about elderly individuals. They receive an education oriented primarily to the treatment of acute rather than chronic illness. As such they are ill-prepared to meet the challenges presented by the elderly patient, who characteristically has several interrelated chronic conditions. Furthermore, the medical student is seldom exposed to elderly who are active and independent in the community. The majority of elderly patients seen by students are already the subject of medical intervention, and usually present severe problems. Therefore the experience of the education does not equip the student to deal with the realities of the majority of the elderly population. Medical education must recognize the significance of restorative care for the elderly, and begin to emphasize a more positive approach both to the medical and to the associated psycho-social problems of the elderly.

13
Quality of Care for the Institutionalized Aged: A Scottish-American Comparison[1]

Jeanie Schmit Kayser-Jones

1. Introduction

There are 20 million Americans over the age of 65, one million of whom live in long-term care institutions. Although there are some fine institutions for the aged, the prevailing image of institutional life in the United States is largely a negative one.

This chapter reports on an ethnographic cross-cultural comparative study of one long-term care institution in Scotland and one in the United States. Although these two institutions obviously are not typical of all such settings in the two countries, I believe they provide a representative illustration of institutionalized geriatric care in the two countries.

The comparison is based on observations made in one institution in Scotland; thus when discussing data from the Scottish institution, I am speaking of a single institution in Scotland. The current health care system in Scotland is basically the same as that in the rest of the United Kingdom including the financing and delivery of health care services. Although Scotland is only one part of the United Kingdom of Great Britain and Northern Ireland, the general statistics of the aged which I present, and the description of the structure of the geriatric service, apply to the entire United Kingdom. (Hereafter, instead of using "United Kingdom," I shall use the more common term "Britain" and "British" which refer to England, Scotland, Wales and Northern Ireland.)

The purpose of the research was to investigate criteria for quality care for the institutionalized aged, and to discover what institutional arrangements will encourage the maintenance of high standards of care.

2. Statement of the Problem

Since the beginning of this country, there has been a great increase in life expectancy; it has risen from 49 years in 1900-02, to 71.9 years in 1974 (Siegel 1978). This increases the number and proportion of people 65 years of age and over. Table 13:1 shows the increase in numbers and percentages from 1900 to 1975 in the United States and the projected increase by the year 2030.

TABLE 13.1

NUMBER AND PERCENTAGE OF PEOPLE IN THE UNITED STATES
65 YEARS OF AGE AND OVER FROM 1901 TO 1971
AND AS PROJECTED TO 2001

Year	Number (millions)	Percent of Total Population
1900	3.1	4.1
1940	9.0	6.8
1975	22.4	10.5
2000	31.8	11.7
2030	55.0	17.0

During the twentieth century, Britain has also seen a dramatic growth in the absolute as well as the relative numbers of older people. Table 13:2 illustrates the increase from 1901 to 1971, and the projected increase by the year 2001.

TABLE 13.2

NUMBER AND PERCENTAGE OF PEOPLE IN BRITAIN
65 YEARS OF AGE AND OVER FROM 1901 TO 1971
AND AS PROJECTED TO 2001

Year	Number (millions)	Percent of Total Population
1901	1.5	4.0
1971	7.1	13.3
2001	10.8	18.5

Advances in science, improved public health, health education, and the application of technology to the control of mortality and fertility are some of the factors responsible for the increasing numbers of aged people in our population. Although science has succeeded in extending the life expectancy of man, it has not been as successful with the medical, social, and cultural problems that accompany old age.

One such problem is institutionalization of chronically-ill elderly people in nursing homes. In recent years the number of elderly who are institutionalized has increased dramatically; the number of nursing home beds has increased from 331,000 in 1960 to 1,327,358 in 1976, an increase of 302 percent. (Moss and Halamandaris 1977:6). Moreover, with advances in cardiovascular and other medical research, the life expectancy of Americans will continue to rise, and in the future there will be even more older persons than today with multiple, chronic illnesses who will require institutionalization. In fact, it is estimated that 20 percent of the present elderly population will require at least some institutional care during the balance of their lives (Butler 1975).

As mentioned above, in the United States the prevailing quality of institutional life for the aged is largely negative. Several studies have reportd on the shocking conditions in nursing homes in the United States (e.g., Henry 1963; Townsend 1971; Mendelson 1974; Butler 1975; Moss and Halamandaris 1977). Some research studies have investigated the effects of institutionalization in general and speak to the depersonalizing effects of institutions (e.g., Bennett 1963; Coe 1965; Kahana 1973), while others have concentrated on mortality rates and the effects of relocation of the aged from the community to an institution and from one institution to another (e.g., Camargo and Preston 1945; Costello and Tanaka 1961; Aldrich and Mendkoff 1963; Killian 1970; Markson 1971; Boureston and Tars 1974; Tobin and Lieberman 1976; Pino, Rosica, and Carter 1978). Few studies, however, have focused on the quality of care in long-term care institutions for the elderly; Kosberg (1973), Kahana (1973), and Anderson (1974) all agree that there is a lack of knowledge as to what constitutes quality or effective care. Townsend (1962), in an extensive study of institutions for the aged in England and Wales, attempted to measure the quality of care and Henry (1963) describes, compares, and analyzes the conditions and poor quality of care in three institutions for the aged in the United States.

3. Rationale For a Comparative Study

The rationale for a comparative study to help find answers to American problems lies in the fact that, although needs appear to be similar, Britain and the United States have followed rather different paths in attempting to cope with the dilemma of the institutionalized aged. In both countries only about five percent of the elderly, at any given time, live in hospitals, residential homes, or nursing homes; the remainder live in their own home or with relatives. Yet attitudes toward and the approach to solving the problems of this five percent are quite different in the two countries.

Particularly since World War II there have been several important developments in Britain's approach to the care of the elderly. First, beginning in the late 1940's, British physicians established geriatrics as a specialty, and geriatic care—both acute and chronic—has become an integral part of the overall medical-care structure for the assessment, rehabilitation and provision for continuing care of the aged in Britain. By contrast, in the United States, geriatrics is not a specialty and although there is an American Geriatrics Society, the majority of the members are internists rather than geriatricians. Also, while the acute care of the geriatric patient is a part of the health care system, the care of the chronic, long-term, geriatric patient in nursing homes is not within the mainstream of medical care.

Secondly, in Britain, for philosophical and economic reasons, there has been a heavy emphasis on the development of supportive community services. This increased emphasis on community services is an attempt to keep the elderly person at home for as long as possible. By comparision, in the United States, supportive community services are poorly developed, there is no comprehensive range of services available to the elderly, and there is a lack of funding of community services both by the government and private insurance companies.

Lastly, much of the post-war legislation was motivated by a desire to treat all citizens equally, and gradually Britain has abandoned the nineteenth-century philosophy which centered on a belief in custodial care as a final answer (Townsend 1962:37).

A major difference to be taken into consideration when comparing the care of the elderly in Scotland and the United States is the financing, organization, and delivery of health care in each country. In Britain a welfare state has evolved, and within this the National Health Service (NHS) is the organ by which medical care is provided. The NHS—which came into being on 5 July 1948—pays for virtually the entire range of health and medical care without regard to age, income, need, or insurance qualification. Under the terms of the NHS: (1) health care is free to the patient at the time of service; (2) 97 percent of the population is registered with general practitioners, and most patients receive primary services through him; (3) when patients need the advice of a specialist or inpatient care, they are referred by their family doctor to a hospital consultant (specialist) who provides treatment in the hospital, clinic, or when necessary in the patient's home; (4) community care has been emphasized and is well developed, and all community care is paid for by the NHS or by the Department of Social Services.

By contrast, in the United States, the health care system fits into our national concept of free enterprise and free choice coupled with individual responsibility. The prototype for medical practice in the United States is the solo private entrepreneur charging a fee for services rendered. Public responsibility for financing of health care has been limited to groups such as members of the armed forces, veterans, American Indians, the medically indigent, and the elderly; health care in the United States remains largely a private, fee-for-service system (Knowles 1977). Although Medicare and Medicaid have provided considerable financial assistance for the elderly, those who require long-term institutional care are required by the system to deplete their personal financial resources before they are eligible for state aid. That is, to qualify for Medicaid the elderly must be indigent; they can have no more than $1,500 in cash.

4. Description Of The Geriatric Service

In Britain the NHS has made it possible to promote geriatrics as a specialty, and over the past 25 years, in an attempt to improve the care of the disabled elderly, a Geriatric Service has been developed. The aim of this service is to provide specialized medical care to the elderly and, as mentioned above, to keep them independent and in their home for as long as possible.

Scotland, for the purposes of health care delivery is divided into 15 regions. This research was conducted in a region on the northeast coast of Scotland in a city of about 250,000 people. The Geriatric Service in this region comprises about 650 beds. Of these, about 150 beds are set aside in a general hospital in the city. The remaining 500 beds are for continuing care (long-term) patients. Of these 500 beds, 250 are in or near the major city in the region, and the remaining 250 beds are in continuing-care units in small outlying community hospitals. It is important to note that the Geriatric Service is a part of the overall structure of medical services, just as obstetrics, pediatrics, or any other specialty.

To care for these 650 patients, there are three consultants (specialists in geriatric medicine). In addition to caring for the in-patients, the consultants receive about 1300 referrals a year from general practitioners and other hospital consultants. Upon receiving the referral, a geriatrician visits the elderly person in his home, at the acute-care hospital, in the residential home, or wherever the person happens to be. He does a social and medical assessment, and thus determines if the person can be treated at home, through the geriatric day hospital, or if he must be admitted to the assessment and rehabilitation unit of the general hospital. When patients are admitted, they undergo an extensive assessment and rehabilitation program, and if, after some weeks or months of care, it is determined that they cannot be rehabilitated and care for themselves in the community, they are admitted to a continuing-care hospital.

This progressive and innovative concept of British geriatric care provides an interesting model for comparison with long-term geriatric care in the United States. Strictly speaking, one cannot compare an institution in Scotland, a small, homogenous country of five million people, with one in a country as large and culturally complex as the United States. However, much can be learned from the study of a model institution in Scotland and such an institution may provide a standard of excellence from which we can learn, and subsequently improve the care of the institutionalized aged in the United States.

5.   Methodology

Using the anthropological field-work method, the data in this study are drawn from three months of field work (July-September, 1977) in a 96-bed, government-owned, continuing-care institution in Scotland and four months of field work (January-April, 1978) in a similar, 85-bed, proprietary nursing home in a Pacific Coast, metropolitan city in the United States. In Britain, with the development of the geriatric service, continuing-care units have become the predominant facility for long-term care of the disabled elderly. Thus, for the purpose of this research, a government-owned, continuing-care unit was selected for study. By comparison in the United States, approximately 80 percent of the institutions for the elderly and 96 percent of the nursing home beds are in a proprietary homes (Abdellah 1976, Butler 1975:263). Consequently, a commercially-owned institution (reputed to be one of the finest in the city) was selected for investigation.

Field work is the hallmark of cultural anthropology, and the fundamental task of anthropological field work is doing ethnography (Spradley 1979:3). An ethnography is an intensive, systematic description and analysis of a culture. The ethnographer, rather than collecting data about people, strives to learn from the people being studied and is concerned with the meaning of the actions, behavior and events to the people he seeks to understand (Spradley 1979:5). For example, in my research, I sought to learn from the aged what it is like to be old, disabled, and institutionalized, and what it is, from their perspective, that contributes to high-or-low-quality care.

Participant observation is a technique associated with anthropological field work. In fact, it is central to effective field work and is a major research tool utilized in anthropological research (Pelto 1970). As a scientific research tool, it is an active and intensive participation on the part of the investigator in the social or cultural context under study.

Ross and Ross (1974) have identified three distinct stages in the process of participant observation: Initial introduction, focused research, and systematization and measurement. These three stages provide a systematic approach to field work; thus, using them as an outline, I should like to describe the process of my field work in Scotland.

In stage one—initial introduction—the investigator is interested in gathering data on a broad range of community activities and begins to ask basic questions about the community being studied. In this stage, I attempted to get a broad overview of the geriatric service. For example, I learned what community and institutional services were available and how they operated to provide services for the elderly. During this period, I visited a range of geriatric facilities throughout the region, made hospital rounds daily on the wards, and attended patient care conferences. I visited the elderly in various residential settings, and made home visits with the geriatrician. These initial activities helped me to understand the purpose and function of the geriatric service, to identify key people (informants) in the institutions, and they were instrumental in giving me credibility and in establishing me in the research setting.

Stage two—focused research—begins when there is a shift in research activity from a general exploration to a more specific investigation of concepts. Hence, after spending several weeks gathering broad data on the geriatric service, I selected an institution for intensive study. The focus of the research at this time was to determine the quality of care at Scottsdale. In this stage, for example, data were gathered on the patients' physical and mental disability, patient-staff ratio, and the length of employment of staff. Observations were made daily at various hours and during the routine of patient care and at social functions. From these repeated observations, it began to appear that the quality of care was very good. Thus, it was necessary to validate my observations by doing in-depth interviews with patients.

During stage three—systematization and measurement—a method of data collection other than participant observation must be used (Ross and Ross 1974:74). Questionnaires and interviews were utilized to obtain both a quantitative and qualitative measure of the patients' self-evaluation of their care. To obtain some idea of the range of opinion, I asked 25 percent of the patients in each institution a set of structured questions. By asking patients direct questions such as: "How do you find the nurses?", "How do you find the doctors?", I began to get an insider's view of life in the institution. The interviews and questionnaires gave me a wealth of data, and they provided insight in the analysis of the research findings.

6. Research Findings

Findings disclosed that in Scotland the institutionalized aged have more choice, freedom, and independence, and their life more closely approximates life in the greater society. By contrast, the institutionalized aged in the United Staes have less choice, freedom, and independence. They live in a much more restricted environment and are more isolated from the culture and the normal life of the greater society. Also, in Scotland, the aged are cared for with dignity and respect, while in the American institution the patients are infantilized, depersonalized, dehumanized, and sometimes victimized by the staff. These findings evolved out of the data obtained from the ethnographic field work; thus, I should like to present data which will describe and compare the quality of life in the two institutions. Mealtime, social, recreational, and work activities, and the provision of medical and nursing care, make up the major part of the daily routine for the institutionalized aged. Hence, participant observation and the patient interviews focused largely on these activities.

7. Food

Food is an important aspect of care in institutional life. Beyond providing nutrients for life it has religious and symbolic significance and is a social and recreational activity (Whiteman 1966). For those who must spend the last days of their lives in an institution under restricted conditions, mealtime is an important event, and good food can contribute greatly to patient satisfaction and the quality of life.

Patients in each institution were asked: "How is the food here?" Their responses were ranked on a scale of one to five, one representing complete dissatisfaction with food and five representing complete satisfaction. Subsequently, a mean was computed. At Scottsdale the responses were overwhelmingly positive; 100 percent of those interviewed expressed complete or near complete satisfaction with the food: the mean response was 4.8. Patients commented on the quality and the quantity of the food; some said they would not eat so well were they living at home.

Although the quality and quantity was important, the outstanding feature of meal time at Scottsdale was the selective menu. Patients were given a choice of three entrees and three desserts for their midday and evening meal. This choice of food was highly valued by the elderly, and was often mentioned during any discussion of food. Despite the high quality and the choice of food, the patients at Scottsdale made frequent trips to a small shop within the hospital to purchase biscuits, cookies, and cakes for their morning and afternoon tea. Having personal money and a shop available within the hospital, provided them with yet another option and additional freedom in their choice of food.

By contrast, at Pacific Manor the food was often a source of displeasure. Forty percent of those interviewed said the food was very poor, 45 percent were moderately satisfied, while only 15 percent were very satisfied with the food; the mean response was 2.5. Although more than half the patients interviewed were moderately to very satisfied with the food, those who were unhappy with the food expressed very angry feelings. "The food is just terrible here," said one 80-year-old woman. "If I didn't have the cookies and graham crackers my sister brings me, I would starve." The patients who were dissatisfied with the food complained about the poor quality, the lack of choice, inadequate amounts, the absence of fresh fruits and vegetables, and added that often the meat was too tough to eat. A few of the elderly had relatives and friends who attempted to bring food to supplement their diet but, because of theft, they could not keep food in their rooms or in the kitchen refrigerators. To summarize, the experience of eating at Pacific Manor did not compare favorably with that of Scottsdale.

8.   Social, Recreational, and Work Activities

It is important to recognize that long-term facilities are "homes" for disabled, elderly people; thus, attention to social, recreational, and meaningful work activities is essential. In order for the institutionalized person to be socially integrated and have a meaningful life, it is desirable to create an environment within the institution that approximates life for an older person in the outside world.

At Scottsdale, patients are provided with regular, planned activities and they are also enabled and encouraged to pursue individual interests. There is a weekly Sunday morning church service; a full-length film, selected by a patient committee, every Thursday; and on Fridays patients gather in the recreational hall to hear an organist play their favorite songs.

Diversional therapy and reading are the favorite activities of patients at Scottsdale. On Tuesday and Friday, a diversional therapist is on duty to assist patients in making articles which can be sold or given as gifts to others. Patients make beautiful trays and toys for children; they knit, crochet, and do needlework. These activities are highly valued; 60 percent of the patients interviewed said making articles in therapy was their favorite activity. "I wouldn't want to live if I weren't useful," said one woman. Forty percent of the patients interviewed cited reading as a favorite activity. Fortunately the hospital has a voluminous library, with a wide selection of literary works, as well as books with large print for those with poor vision. Every two weeks volunteers visit each unit, and patients may select as many books as they wish from the library cart.

Visitors and outings were mentioned as highly valued social activities; relatives are encouraged to take the elderly out for an evening, a day, or the weekend. Eighty percent of the patients interviewed have relatives or friends who take them home or for an outing several times during the year.

A monthly social evening is planned for the elderly at Scottsdale. On these occasions the patients, dressed in their finest clothing, attend a program planned in keeping with seasonal and national holidays. For example, in December there is a Christmas party, in the summer a garden party, and in February—when all the people of Scotland celebrate the birthday of the Scottish bard, Robert Burns—there is a "Robbie Burns supper" with "haggis, tatties, and neeps" (a traditional meat dish, potatoes, and turnips), followed by a reading of Burns' poetry. The patients thoroughly enjoy these social evenings. It helps to keep them a part of the Scottish social and cultural life, and it gives them something to look forward to and to talk about with their family and friends.

By comparison, at Pacific Manor, although there is some activity planned daily, (the nursing home employs a full-time activity director), patients complain that there is nothing to do but sit in their rooms or walk idly about the hallway. Bingo is played twice a week, checkers and dominoes are played weekly, and although there are some regular musical programs, patients feel they are amateur entertainment of a low quality. There are a few books and magazines, no occupational therapy or meaningful work activity, church services are infrequent, and outdoor excursions are rare. Seventy-five percent of those interviewed said they never get out of the nursing home for short trips, 15 percent had been out on one occasion, and only ten percent have relatives who take them out on a regular basis. Because patients do not get out, they become isolated within the institution and lose contact with the real world.

Not only do the patients at Pacific Manor not get out of the nursing home for outings, the majority are never taken out of doors. Although a sunny outdoor patio is adjacent to the patients' dayroom, only a few of the elderly whose relatives visit them frequently are taken onto the patio. Staff feel they are overworked and underpaid and refuse to take the patients onto the courtyard. Some patients expressed a desire to go outside and recognized the importance of getting out. "I never go out," said one woman. "I think we get stupid when we stay in, but I can't ask the nurses to take me out."

Clearly, Pacific Manor activities are of a lower quality than those at Scottsdale. Despite the daily, planned activities, when patients were asked, "What do you like to do most of all?", fifty percent gave responses which indicated boredom such as, "I just lay here," or, "I don't do much of anything but walk around."

9. Medical Care

In both Scotland and the United States the doctor is seen by patients as the person most responsible for medical care. Thus, in order to assess satisfaction or dissatisfaction with their care, patients in each institution were asked, "How do you find your doctor?" If patients had difficulty interpreting this question, it was rephrased: "How do you feel about your medical care?" and the responses were ranked as described above. At Scottsdale, the mean was found to be 4.5.—i.e., a very high degree of satisfaction. Eighty percent of the respondents gave replies which indicated they are completely satisfied with their medical care, 16 percent gave an intermediate response which indicated satisfaction but not strong enthusiasm for their care, and only one patient out of 25 interviewed expressed some degree of dissatisfaction with medical care.

By contrast, at Pacific Manor the patients' responses to the same question indicate much dissatisfaction and concern about the lack of medical care—a mean of only 2.0 was obtained. Eighty percent of the patients indicated dissatisfaction with their medical care, 15 percent gave an intermediate response which suggested some satisfaction with their care, and only one patient reported complete satisfaction with her medical care.

At Scottsdale, three specialists in geriatric medicine (geriatricians) and one house physician provide medical care for all patients. Since the hospital consultant is a salaried employee, there is no cost for care to the patient.

The chief geriatrician is ultimately responsible for the care of all patients at Scottsdale; this responsibility is shared with two junior colleagues and other medical staff. Each of the three geriatricians provide medical care on a continuous basis for about one-third of the patients (i.e., about 32 each), and visits them weekly. This continuity of care is an outstanding feature of the medical care at Scottsdale. Since every patient is admitted from the geriatric assessment and rehabilitation unit, the geriatrician who has cared for the elderly during the period of assessment and rehabilitation continues to see them throughout their stay at Scottsdale.

In addition to the geriatrician's weekly visits, patients are seen daily by the house physician; a general practitioner is on duty from 8 a.m. to 12 p.m. Monday through Friday. Although she does not visit every patient individually, she makes rounds daily, consults with the nurse in charge, and personally visits any patient who needs medical attention. If a problem not within her expertise arises, she contacts the attending geriatrician. Even on weekends and holidays the hospital is not without medical coverage. Each weekend one of the geriatricians makes rounds; additionally, because Scottsdale is part of the geriatric service of a general hospital, the physician on call at the geriatric unit of the hospital is also on call for any medical emergency which may occur. At Scottsdale the patients were very satisfied with their medical care. They felt confidence in their physicians and knew that if they needed a doctor medical care was always available.

By comparison, at Pacific Manor each patient is cared for by a private physician, who charges a fee for service rendered. However, this does not mean that all patients are responsible for all of their medical expenses. Medical care for many is paid, at least in part, by Medicare Part B or Medicaid. Medicare Part B, a medical insurance program for which the aged pay a monthly fee of $8.20, does not provide comprehensive coverage for all medical services. It will pay 80 percent of reasonable charges for covered services provided by physicians. Doctors' services not covered by medical insurance—such as routine physical examinations, routine foot care, and eye or hearing examinations—must be paid by the patient.

There is a major difference in the amount of medical care patients receive at the two institutions; at Pacific Manor, physicians are required by law to make only one visit per month. Some doctors are conscientious and make the required monthly visits, while others visit infrequently; some of the elderly had not seen their physicians for several months. Many of the patients were very unhappy when their doctor failed to visit, and expressed much concern and dissatisfaction about the lack of medical care. One 89-year-old woman was literally abandoned by her physician when she was transferred from an acute-care hospital to the nursing home, and the doctor of an elderly woman with terminal cancer refused to make more than the required monthly visit even when death was imminent.

To summarize, there is a wide variation both in the quantity and quality of medical care in the two institutions. During the course of the research at Scottsdale, the adequacy of medical care was never a subject for discussion. Indeed, it was simply understood that patients would receive whatever medical care was necessary. Although the doctor's visit may be very brief, the patients are seen daily by a house physician and weekly by a geriatrician.

By contrast, at Pacific Manor the lack of medical care and concern for medical needs was frequently a subject for discussion both with patients and the nursing staff. In general there is no structure to ensure adequate medical care for the institutionalized aged. Inattention to patients' needs causes anxiety, stress, and fear among the elderly, who often feel neglected by their physicians.

10. Nursing Care

Although doctors are essential for the diagnosis and treatment of the institutionalized aged, it is the nursing staff which must provide care on a 24-hour basis. Hence, in some repsects the quality of care for the aged depends more upon the quality of nursing care than upon any other single factor. Many of the problems associated with the chronic illnesses and functional disabilities of old age can be dealt with successfully by a competent nursing staff. Thus, the importance of properly qualified nursing personnel cannot be overemphasized; it is a role that is essential to the care and general well-being of every institutionalized elderly person.

In both institutions, as with physicians, patients were asked: "How do you find the nurses?" At Scottsdale, the mean for the question was 4.5: eighty-eight percent of the respondents expressed complete satisfaction with their nursing care; 12 percent, partial satisfaction; and none complete dissatisfaction. By contrast, at Pacific Manor the mean response was 3.25: only 35 percent of the patients interviewed expressed complete satisfaction with their care, while 40 percent expressed partial satisfaction, and 25 percent complete dissatisfaction.

Clearly, there were significantly more patients at Scottsdale who were completely satisfied with their nursing care. Apparently, this is due to differences in staffing, length of employment and salaries of nurses at the two institutions.

11. Staffing

It is difficult to make exact comparisons in regard to staffing at the two institutions. Both facilities employ a large number of part-time employees—40 percent at Pacific Manor and 47 percent at Scottsdale—but there is wide variation as to how many hours a week the part-time employee may work.

However, at Scottsdale there is more professional staff on duty; typically, on a given day, there are four sisters (head nurses) plus the matron and assistant matron. At Pacific Manor there are only two nurses in addition to the director of nursing service. At Scottsdale there was a total of 81 on the nursing staff (43 full-time and 38 part-time) for 96 patients, compared to a 54-person nursing staff (32 full-time and 22 part-time) for 85 patients at Pacific Manor.

Staffing is a problem at both Scottsdale and Pacific Manor, and nurses in both institutions feel this is partly due to the fact that geriatrics is not a popular specialty. However, the staff shortage at Scottsdale appears to be related more to cuts in the budget for health care than to an inability to hire nursing staff. Britain has experienced a high rate of inflation in recent years, and, since 1974 shortage of staff in hospitals has become a chronic problem due to the financial squeeze.

By contrast, the staffing problems at Pacific Manor are caused by multiple factors. First and foremost is the poor image of nursing homes in the United States. To be associated with a nursing home is to suggest lack of competence on the part of a nurse, and to work in an institution for the aged is a low-status position. Secondly, working conditions are very poor in most nursing homes; salaries are low and fringe benefits are few. For example, a registered nurse at Pacific Manor earns a starting salary of about $960 per month, while her comtemporary in an acute-care hospital in the same city earns $1,270 per month. By comparison, in Scotland, all nurses who work in geriatric institutions are paid a salary equivalent to that of other nurses; additionally, they receive a "lead pay" (bonus) of about $300 a year.

The low salaries in American nursing homes add greatly to the problem of recruitment and retention of nursing staff; consequently, the professional nursing staff was unstable at Pacific Manor. The current director of nursing service had been there for less than one year, and in the past ten years there have been seven nurses in that position. There was one full-time head nurse who had been employed at Pacific Manor for five years; however there was a continual turnover of professional staff in other head-nurse positions. Again this compares unfavorably with the situation at Scottsdale, where there was little turnover among the professional nursing staff. The matron had been in her position for seven years, the assistant matron for 11 years, and the length of employment for the sisters (head nurses) ranged from two to eight years.

To summarize, at Scottsdale there were more professional nurses to care for the elderly, and the nursing staff was permanent and relatively well-

TABLE 13.3
SUMMARY OF PATIENT'S RESPONSES TO QUESTIONS
ON SATISFACTION OR DISSATISFACTION WITH
FOOD, MEDICAL CARE, AND NURSING CARE

	Completely Dissatisfied	Moderately Satisfied	Completely Satisfied	Mean
FOOD				
Scottsdale	0%	0%	100%	4.8
Pacific Manor	40%	45%	15%	2.5
MEDICAL CARE				
Scottsdale	4%	16%	80%	4.5
Pacific Manor	80%	15%	5%	2.0
NURSING CARE				
Scottsdale	0%	12%	88%	4.5
Pacific Manor	25%	40%	35%	3.25

paid; at Pacific Manor, there was a constant shortage, a rapid turnover of nursing staff, and the nurses were poorly paid. As a result the quality of nursing care was lower at Pacific Manor. The above-mentioned problems also contribute to the significant differences observed in the nature of patient-staff interaction and in staff attitudes toward the elderly at Pacific Manor.

12. Staff-Patient Interaction

At Pacific Manor employees are grossly underpaid compared to staff in acute-care institutions. Although some of them are poorly qualified and would have difficulty obtaining employment in other institutions, this substandard pay and lack of professional competence suggests that they have a poor self-image, and perhaps we cannot expect sympathetic and high-quality care from such personnel.

Caring for the disabled elderly is physically and emotionally demanding. Because the work is hard and the pay inadequate, staff morale is low and the desire to retaliate comes forth. These conditions may contribute to the significant difference in patient care which I observed in the American and Scottish institutions. At Scottsdale, on the whole, patients were treated kindly and with respect, while at Pacific Manor employees frequently were authoritarian and indifferent in their attitude towards patients and showed little concern for their dignity and individual rights. The principle problems which I encountered at Pacific Manor might be described as infantilization, depersonalization, dehumanization and victimization.

Infantilization. Infantilization is the act of treating older people like children. It includes such behavior as scolding incontinent patients, addressing them in casual or familiar terms, and dressing them in childish attire (Jaeger and Simmons 1970:38).

At Pacific Manor there were innumerable examples of childlike treatment of the aged. For example, staff often spoke to the elderly in a parental and scolding voice. They would give direct commands to them such as: "You shut up," "Stay in your chair," "Go to your place for lunch." All patients regardless of age or status were addressed either by their Christian name or in familiar terms such as "Mother," "Honey," or "Baby."

Depersonalization. Depersonalization has been defined as, "The process of depriving an individual of the factors that attach him to the social system" (Henry 1973:24). Thus, depersonalization is the loss of personality, individuality, and sense of identity; it is what follows when people are treated with indifference, as if they have no value and are of no significance. Addressing people improperly, ignoring them, or failing to communicate with them, all have depersonalizing effects (Henry 1973:28).

At Pacific Manor, the nursing staff do not always address patients by their proper names; rather they refer to them as, "the newly admitted patient, "the patient in 10A," or the "the woman with the colostomy." Frequently, staff ignore calls for help from the elderly. Patients put on their call light and when this signal is disregarded, they begin to call out for help. The staff pass by the door as if they do not hear the calls. On many occasions staff refuse to communicate with the patients. An elderly woman calls out "good morning" repeatedly to staff, who walk by as if she were not there.

Dehumanization. "Dehumanization is the loss of humanity" (Vail 1966:5); it is what follows when a person is treated insensitively, callously, and when he is subjected to experiences that are an affront to his dignity and sense of self-worth.

Many of the dehumanizing experiences at Pacific Manor centered around bathing and the toilet. For example, little attention was given to patients' modesty at bathtime. The patients' genitals were exposed, and men and women were bathed simultaneously in the same shower room. On one occasion an elderly man who was sitting in the hallway was incontinent. The nurse aide stood him up, instructed him to hold onto the wall railing, and changed his trousers in the public corridor without regard for his modesty.

Exposure of the genitals and urinating in public is a violation of a cultural taboo. When such actions are permitted and accepted as a matter of course, it is degrading and dehumanizing for those who violate the taboo as well as for those who must observe such behavior, for the person violating the taboo obviously is no longer considered a part of the social system. That is, he is no longer considered a significant member of the human race (Henry 1973:31). For the elderly who have been brought up under strict codes of modesty, violation of these norms is the ultimate indignity they must suffer in old age.

Victimization. Victimization is the act of being harmed or made to suffer through the actions of others. During the past several years, much attention has been focused on criminal victimization of the elderly, and in 1975 a National Conference on Crime Against the Elderly was held in Washington, D.C. (Goldsmith and Goldsmith 1976).

Although some attention is being given to the problem of the victimization of the elderly in the community at large, to the best of my knowledge the issue of victimization of the institutionalized aged has not been explored. Yet this sub-group of the elderly are the most vulnerable of all. They often are disabled, many are alone and have no one to whom they can turn for help, and they are dependent upon those who victimize them for their care.

Broadly speaking, infantilization, depersonalization, and dehumanization are forms of victimization; psychologically they are harmful to the aged. However, at Pacific Manor theft of personal possessions is a very blatant type of victimization; theft of patients' food, clothing, money, jewelry, and other personal belongings is a common occurrence. As mentioned earlier, many patients do not like the institutional diet and try to supplement it with food from friends and relatives. But due to theft, it is nearly impossible for them to keep food in their possession.

In addition to food, patients also talked about possessions they had lost. Mrs. O'Sullivan said that three coin purses, a billfold, flashlight, candy, and even her earplugs had been stolen. Mrs. Crawford's portable radio and a $40 robe, which her niece had sent her for Christmas, also were taken. Her vision is so poor she cannot read; thus, she depends upon the radio for entertainment and to keep her informed. "I don't mean to sound snobbish," she said, "but I like to know what is going on in the world and the radio keeps me in touch." The daughter of another patient said, "Everything goes here; that's par for the course. I can't keep my father in underclothes, and when I ask the staff about missing clothing, they say it has been lost in the laundry."

The prevalence of theft has a harmful effect upon the aged; they live in fear that their few possessions will be taken, and it is frightening for them to depend for care upon those who are stealing their belongings. Ninety-year-old Mrs. Snyder kept apples in her room. "If I eat an apple every day, it keeps my bowels regular," she said. "One day I walked into my room and an orderly was eating my only apple." "Did you say anything to him?" I asked. "Oh, no!" she replied, "He might have hit me!"

At first glance, it seems incredible that the institutionalized elderly, many of whom are unable to retaliate, should be victimized, but in fact their helplessness makes them ideal victims. Hentig (1948:438), a pioneer in the study of victims, classified them into categories such as minorities, immigrants, children, females, and the aged. Old people, especially if they are physically and mentally weak, are ideal victims of predatory attack. Reiman (1976) proposes that certain groups in our society have been labeled "legitimate victims"; they are defective human beings, and the message conveyed by society is that victimization of these groups is not as objectionable as the victimization of "normal folks." For example, public outrage is greater if a white student is shot than if a black student is the victim. Similarly, old people in America are viewed as substandard (Reiman 1976:79). In a youth-oriented culture, the aged are characterized as useless, dependent, physically and mentally weak, poor, and non-contributing; in short, they are a burden and a nuisance. Americans value independence and fear dependence; thus, it follows that if the aged do not "carry their own weight," they cannot be valued. This negative attitude toward the aged contributes to victimization of the elderly in the community, as well as in institutions. If one lives in a society which does not value the aged, it becomes easy to victimize that group, and the institutionalized aged, a weakened and dependent group, are "captive victims" for predators.

To summarize, at Pacific Manor the elderly are infantilized, depersonalized, dehumanized, and victimized by their caretakers. At Scottsdale, these phenomena were not seen. Thus, it is important to attempt to discover why this occurs in one institution and not the other. I propose that exchange theory might offer some insight into the situation, and prehaps explain the difference in the treatment of the elderly in the two institutions.

13. Exchange Theory

Exchange refers to the transaction of labor, resources, and services within a society, and plays a vital part in the social life of all societies. "Exchange is not limited to economic markets; social exchange is ubiquitous"(Blau 1964:453). Malinowski (1922), in his description of the kula, and Mauss (1925), in his analysis of gift exchange, were the first anthropologists to observe this phenomenon, and they have greatly influenced the development of exchange theory. In addition to Manlinowski's analysis of the Trobriand kula king, anthropologists have examined other social institutions, such as bridewealth in African societies and the potlatch of the North American Indians. These institutions illustrate reciprocity, which is the prevailing and characteristic mode of exchange, and they demonstrate the essentially social nature of reciprocal exchange of valued goods. Sociologists and social psychologists such as Homans (1961), Emerson (1962,1972), Blau (1964), and Ekeh (1974) have also made major contributions to exchange theory.

Dowd (1975), drawing upon the work of Emerson and Blau, has put forth a view of aging as a process of social exchange; he sees the problem of aging as one of decreasing control over power resources. As power resources decline, the aged, unable to engage in balanced exchange relations, are forced to exchange compliance for their continue sustenance.

Some of the major propositions of exchange theory as set forth by Emerson (1962, 1972) and Blau (1964) are as follows:

1. People enter into social relations because they expect them to be rewarding.

2. A person who derives benefits from another is under obligation to reciprocate by supplying some benefit in return.

3. When an individual fails to reciprocate, there is no incentive to continue to befriend him, and he is likely to be accused of ingratitude.

4. When the person does reciprocate, both parties benefit from the association, a social bond develops between them, and the interacton between the two will probably be continued.

5. In every interaction, inevitably, costs are incurred. Cost is defined as the resource one gives to the other party. If one perceives the cost to be equal to the reward, the exchange relationship is in balance.

6. If one participant values the rewards more than the other, an imbalance occurs and the latter person has power over the former—a unilateral dependence develops.

Power is the ability of persons or groups to impose their will recurrently upon others, despite resistance, through deterrence either in the form of withholding regularly supplied rewards or in the form of punishment (Blau 1964:117).

By supplying regularly needed services to others, who cannot reciprocate, a person establishes power over them, and they are forced to comply with his wishes. In power-dependent relations, individuals who need services have the following options: (1) they can supply a service in return; (2) they may obtain the service elsewhere; (3) they can use coercion to obtain the service; and (4) they may choose to do without the service. If they are unable to choose any of these alternatives, they must comply with the wishes of the one in power, as he can make the continuing supply of the needed service contingent upon compliance.

The propositions of exchange theory cited above are especially relevant to the care of the institutionalized aged. Due to chronic physical disability, mental impairment, and (for some) lack of friends and relatives, many are dependent upon staff for multiple services. They have few resources with which to reciprocate; hence, they are forced to comply with the wishes of the staff.

For example, Mrs. Lundgren is dependent upon the staff for bathing. She objects to being placed in the shower room with male patients. "I don't know how the men feel," she said, "but I find it disgusting! But what can I do?" None of the options mentioned above are open to her. She is too disabled to perform a return service for staff, she cannot obtain the service elsewhere, she has no power of coercion, and she cannot do without the service. Her only alternative is to comply with their wishes; if she complains, they can withhold the service.

In comparing the two institutions, I found that at Pacific Manor there are more examples of staff exercising power over patients than at Scottsdale. I propose that this occurs because these patients have fewer resources and are more dependent; thus, they are unable to engage in balanced social relationships.

Lack of resources create dependence and contribute to an imbalance in social-exchange relations. Resources are essentially anything which is perceived by the exchange partner as rewarding; it may be a skill, money, or food, anything that someone has and the other values or wants. Resources enable one to reciprocate in an exchange relationship; they serve as an inducement for staff to furnish service and protect patients from dependency and compliance (Blau 1964:119).

The patients at Scottsdale have more resources than patients at Pacific Manor. As mentioned above, they make items in diversional therapy that are valued by the staff and others which they can give in exchange for services. In addition to making products for exchange, the Scottish patients have money and access to a shop where they can purchase articles to give to others. Most have only a basic government pension as income, which must go toward the payment of their care. Nevertheless, patients are permitted by law to keep about $6.00 per week for personal use. By American standards, this may seem like a small amount, but because they are provided with virtually everything, it gives them considerable purchasing power. I frequently observed patients giving treats to a "special nurse": "I am good to those who are good to me," said one woman at Scottsdale.

By comparison, patients at Pacific Manor have few resources. They are not enabled to engage in any productive activity; consequently, they have no products which they can exchange for service. Additionally, many are without money; 50 percent of the Pacific Manor patients, who were formerly private patients, are now on Medicaid. They have become impoverished through their long-term illness. Several patients commented, "I feel just like a pauper." Although Medicaid stipulates they be permitted to keep $45 per month for personal use, due to theft, they are unable to keep money in their room. Although a few patients manage to hide small amounts of money, there is no shop in the facility where they can purchase food and sundry items.

It was intriguing to observe that despite the restrictive environment at Pacific Manor, some of the elderly, through their ingenuity, managed to develop balanced social relations with certain staff members. One 90-year-old woman, who has no living relatives, does sewing and mending for some of the nurse aides; in turn they shop for her. "Of course, I wouldn't charge them for it," she said. "When I can do a bit of a favor for them I do, and when they go to the store and I need something they shop for me."

However, patients who are devoid of resources do not establish social bonds; their care is custodial, of a lower quality, and staff have power over them. For example, Mrs. Arny's husband has died; her only son is mentally retarded, and lives with her brother in a city three hundred miles away. She sees them only once a year. Additionally, she is totally paralyzed from her waist down, she is poor (on Medicaid), and has no visitors. She virtually has no resources with which to reciprocate for the many services she needs. Consequently, the staff do only what they must do for her. They get her up in a chair and sit her beside a window—she cannot see out of the window because the chair is too low—and there she remains all day. "The nurse aides never bother to put her in the lounge," said one of the nurses, "because it is easier for them to put her in a chair beside the bed." When her urinary catheter leaks and her bed becomes wet, and they refuse to change her linens, she can do nothing. Obviously, she is not responsible for a leaking catheter, but the staff respond to this incident as if she were: "You just lay in it now," they have told her. "It is best not to get angry with the nurses," she said. "I just keep it inside."

There are many elderly persons at Pacific Manor with few resources who require long-term care. In our culture, they are seen by the productive members of society as useless, dependent, and non-productive; they are a burden and a nuisance. Clark (1972b:267) discusses how one who becomes a burden is seen as having nothing of value to exchange; he is in a non-reciprocal role. Further, if an individual is arbitrarily defined as having nothing of value to exchange, he is expecting something for nothing, and in our culture with its strong emphasis on self-reliance, negative sanctions are usually brought against such persons (Clark 1972b:270). The infantilization, depersonalization, dehumanization, and victimization described earlier illustrates the negative sanctions brought to bear against those who are in non-reciprocal roles.

Comparing the two institutions in summary, at Pacific Manor many patients have few resources and are unable to engage in balanced social relations. A unilateral dependence develops, and staff have power over them. At Scottsdale, patients have more resources, are able to engage in balanced social exchange, and are not as subject to the power of staff. Consequently, I propose that there is a direct relationship between power resources and the quality of care; the more resources one has, the higher the quality of care. Conversely, the fewer resources one has, the lower the quality of care.

The lower quality of care observed at Pacific Manor stems largely from three problems: (1) there is a lack of leadership and responsibility by professionals (doctors and registered nurses) for the care of the aged; (2) the proprietor of the institution needs to make a profit, and feels accountable to the State Department of Health rather than to health professionals; and (3) the financing and delivery of health care in our society forces the elderly into dependency.

American medicine has made tremendous progress in biomedical research in the past 30 years. However, we have made little progress in our approach to the delivery of long-term health care for the elderly, and our present system does not compare favorably with that of Scotland.

Although difficult to duplicate in the United States without national health insurance, the Scottish model of geriatric care provides us with an excellent example of quality long-term care. By comparing these two institutions, I have found that we cannot impoverish the aged, deprive them of virtually all their resources, place them in an institution which lacks professional leadership, and expect poorly paid professional and non-professional staff to give them quality care.

Notes

[1] A shorter version of this chapter was published in the *Western Journal of Nursing Research*, Vol. 1, No. 3, Summer 1979. A book-length report of the research contained in this chapter, *Old, Alone and Neglected: Care of the Aged in Scotland and the United States*, will be published by the University of California Press in 1981.

14
Illness and the Organization Of Health Care: A Sociocultural Perspective

Otto von Mering
and
Angela M. O'Rand

1. Introduction

The health-care system in the United States continues to rely on the cultural presupposition of "disease threat" more appropriate to an earlier era of disease patterns and care-giving. A major aspect of this dominant model is an underlying theory of health risk based on mortality expectations from "killer diseases" of heart, cancer, and stroke. The other major aspect stems from notions of "significant impairment" (Arling, 1972) and "limitation of activity" (U.S. Department of Health, Education and Welfare, 1978) that tend to exaggerate the impact of degenerative or crippling conditions like arthritis, atherosclerosis, brain failure (Caird and Judge, 1977) and metabolic disease among the elderly of 65-and-older population (Peterson, 1978). Both assumptions tend to restrict the health-care system to acting at the individual level in terms of disease definitions and curative strategies. Reductionist approaches to health-care delivery consistent with these views include the "regulatory" (Cronkhite, 1974), "manpower" (Edwards, 1974), "economic" (Saward, 1973a), "systems" (Fry, 1973), and "industry" and "spatial location" (Shannon and Dever, 1974) models of health-care delivery.

However, a growing body of research in the comparative anthropology and human ecology of aging (Barker, 1968; Clark, 1971, 1972b, 1973; Clark and Anderson, 1967; Estes, 1973; Byerts, 1974; Gubrium, 1974; Hammerman, 1974; Dovenmuehle, 1974; Kiefer, 1971, 1974a; Lawton,

1974; Maduro, 1974; Sparks, 1975) suggests that we can better understand and respond to the health problems facing post-industrial aging cultures, like the United States, by recognizing life-cycle variations in human health and disease patterns (Higginson, 1973; Knowles, 1974), and by assigning greater importance to health-care efforts that confront chronic, degenerative and regulatory afflictions. Such an "ethno-medical" (Fabrega, 1974) approach would delineate yardsticks of "ordinary" and "exceptional" morbidity among older persons, who range widely in age from the early fifties into the nineties, and better address actual aging-related patterns of ill-being, such as intermittent patienthood (von Mering and Schiff, 1968) and dying by degrees (von Mering and Weniger, 1959). An ethnomedical derivation of incremental illness risk and chronic disease precursors would stress age-specific and sex-linked life patterns in the learned capacity to care for specific and non-specific health problems within particular "behavior settings" (Barker, 1968).

A sociographic overview of the salient features of the aging U.S. culture underscores the importance of adopting an ethnomedical approach to health care. For the past one hundred years, the elderly or over-65 portion of American society has increased faster than the rest of the population. In 1870 only 2.9 percent of Americans were 65 and over; and in 1900 the average American could anticipate 47 years of life. Given an average life expectancy at birth of 71 years today, one American in ten is 65 or older. Moreover the number of those 65 and older will increase sharply after the year 2001, when the World War II "baby boom" becomes an "elder boom" (U.S. Department of Health, Education and Welfare, 1973).

Recent projection suggests that over one-fifth of all Americans may be 65 years or older by the year 2025 (Fowles, 1978). It is expected, moreover, that for these larger numbers of "older persons,"

> there will be no dramatic change in the length of the human life-span within the next few decades . . . Instead, there will be regular improvements with regard to medical knowledge and health care that will produce steady but slow reduction in mortality rates . . . .
> . . . However, a period of disability or failing health will continue to occur toward the end of life (Neugarten, 1975:6).

This will have important consequences for the delivery of health care.

A major feature of the aging population is that the large female majority among older Americans is increasing. In 1900, 102 men were 65-and-over for every 100 women. By 1970 there were only 72 men for every 100 women, and a ratio of 68 to 100 is expected by 1990. A related demographic development is that women 65-and-older continue to make up 10 percent of the work force, while the percentage of working men in the same category has dropped from 46 percent in 1950 to 25.5 percent in 1971 (U.S. Department of Health, Education and Welfare, 1973).

Concurrently, marked changes have taken place in the characteristics of women who work. In 1890, 13 percent who worked were married; by 1970, it was 58 percent. In 1940, one of ten female workers had children under 18; by 1970, it was one of three. Despite these work patterns more older women than men appear to struggle for economic survival. Three-fourths (77 percent) of non-white females living alone subsist on incomes below the poverty line, while 55 percent of all women over 56 find themselves in this predicament (U.S. Senate Special Committee on Aging, 1971). The rapidly increasing costs of medical and hospital expenses—Medicare and Medicaid programs notwithstanding—must be added to the ordinary economic burden of daily living for most aged. The synergistic effect of increased susceptibility to disease with increasing age, inadequate nutrition, and increased relative shelter and transportation costs due to subsistence-level income for people past the age of 65 is indisputable.

An interdependency model of cultural aging, ill-being and health care in the U.S. is proposed. It is intended to account for the reciprocal relationship between two overall components of contemporary living: (1) sex-specific life-cycle patterns of ill- and well-health, including an accounting of health aberrations during the procreative and productive family-and-work cycle as well as the later years; and (2) profiles of human services, health resources and utilization patterns across sociocultural subgroups at different stages of the life cycle.

2. Disease and Disability Patterns In Later Years

In essence, aging is "a decline in physiological competence that inevitably increases the incidence and intensifies the effects of accidents, disease, and other forms of environmental stress" (Timiras, 1972:465). Yet we "sicken and die differently than in the past" (Cooper, 1969), since more and more older people experience their bodies near the "limit of [their] compensatory processes" (Timiras, 1972). Beyond this limit, normal functioning can only be maintained at significant cost, or at a greater risk of system exhaustion and failure (Goldstein, 1971, 1974).

Indeed, life is increasingly and inextricably linked to diseases of regulation and so-called degenerative conditions. Self-regulating feedback mechanisms decrease in efficiency with age; hence different forms of health care come to be associated with different age groups. Recent advances in medicine have added to the complexity of this variation in need for service, by allowing people with "weaker health" but better resources to survive to old age (Riley *et al.*, 1968).

The prevalence of disease among people over 45 has been well documented. In general, people 45 years and above are less afflicted with acute disease (e.g. infections), more with chronic diseases, and more likely to suffer activity restrictions due to their health than young persons. Arthritis, rheumatism, heart conditions, and high blood pressure are prevalent among persons over age 45, and they increase with age. Other chronic conditions such as asthma, hay fever, and diabetes show little consistent increase after age 45 (Riley, *et al.,* 1968).

As might be expected, the risk of suffering intermittently and more frequently from a reduction in overall emotional responsiveness with advancing age has been well documented (Busse and Pfeiffer, 1969).

Specific, gender-linked diseases also add to the increasing risk of having to deal with statistically "ordinary" physical and mental conditions in the later years of life. For example, "cervical cancer—which affects up to 20 percent of all women; cancer of the endometrium or uterine lining—often associated with overweight and hypertension; overian cancer—most often found in women over 55; and breast cancer—leading cause of death in the 40-44 age group" (Institute of Gerontology, 1974) clearly fall into the category of gender-linked disease which are of special concern in the field of gerontologic medicine.

Recent findings on the relationship between aging, disease, and normal functioning beyond age 65 show clearly that many changes commonly ascribed to aging are more accurately seen as a result of disease process. Indeed, even in the absence of manifest disease, significant changes in physiological response occur with age, and, contrary to popular notions, there actually is far less impairment among the aged (65 +) than supposed (U.S. DHEW National Center for Health Statistics, 1966).

The classic study of 47 clinically healthy men between the ages of 65 and 91 in the early 1960's (Birren *et al.,* 1963), and an 11-year follow-up study (Granick and Patterson, 1971), clearly showed the interrelationships of various psychological, social, neurological, and medical factors in the aging process. The results documented a *slowing down* of reaction time, which is age-related *but* independent of mild disease, the sensory modality involved, and the muscles used in the response. The same studies also showed the influence of social and psychological factors: those subjects who *appeared* "physiologically older" did so in part because of identifiable social and psychological losses. Those men who were identified as asymptomatically or subclinically ill in the first study were less likely to survive to the follow-up study. Two behavioral variables—greater "organization of daily behavior" (including gratifying pursuits) and not smoking cigarettes—overwhelmingly "predicted" (80 percent) survival to the follow-up. The question of the nature of the relationship of these behavioral variables to disease raises the issue of how marked the psychosomatic factor is in mortality.

The multilayered impact of developmental, disease-related and situational forces on individual "willingness" or "reluctance" to retire, and on the capacity to adjust to later life, has been well-documented in several major studies. Two were conducted on retired populations approximately a decade apart (Reichard, Livson and Peterson, 1962; Streib and Schneider, 1971). Taken together, the findings make clear that people don't just consider themselves "old" when they stop working at their regular occupation, nor do they begin to worry in earnest "what will happen" to them at a reduced level of income (Riesman, 1954).

Evidently, the decision to retire and patterns of adjustment thereafter are determined by previous patterns of accommodation to change. Individual outcomes in the so-called retirement years are specifically determined by health status (e.g., the presence of palpable disease), socioeconomic status (reflected in levels of education, occupation and income) and, finally, coping strategies employed earlier at developmental turning points in the ordinary life-cycle. The answer to the American question, "what is retirement" is: "that time of life when more and more happens for the last time, and less and less for the first time" (Jeffers, 1970).

In a cultural and biological sense, it is fortunate that older Americans are not all sick and unable to care for themselves. While aging increases the likelihood of illness, only five percent of those 65 and over require hospital and nursing home care at any one time. A Harris poll of 1974 found that about "20 percent of people over 65 are doing some kind of volunteer service, and that another ten percent expressed interest in this kind of activity" (Havighurst, 1975). The possibility of debunking the common view of the progressive disutility of the old is, of course, implicit in Neugarten's (1974, 1975), and Havighurst's (1975) observations of the increasing number of "young-old" people (i.e., age 55-75) in the U.S. So long as they are in sufficient good health, they may continue to be included as members of the active generation because they can become "socially productive users" of leisure time by seeking what the *Carnegie Commission Report of 1973* calls "further education" and "doing some kind of volunteer service" (Havighurst, 1975).

3. Aging Into Perennial Health Care In the Middle Years

It is generally accepted that the dynamics of ordinary and exceptional care-giving/receiving contexts must be taken into account if the life-span development of an individual response system is to be interpretable. A cautionary scenario of behavioral overdependence on medical services is presented. It is derived from a variety of survey and longitudinal studies in the U.S. and Europe. It intends to dramatize what could become a present danger to effective health-care delivery in a rapidly aging post-industrial society. It also seeks to accent the urgency to rethink existing health-care policies, to take specific, remedial actions today, as well as to undertake more long-range and open-ended, or experimental health-care delivery alternatives on a regular basis.

Surveys of types of patient populations frequenting different ambulatory care settings in Europe and North America during the 60s and 70s document the existence of the "perennial out-patient" in general medical practice and psychiatry. The pertinent population parameters and medico-cultural realities of these middle-aged health-care consumers complement the socio-environmental findings on the "decremental turning points" observed in recent U.S. studies (Lowenthal, 1975). According to Lowenthal (1975) decremental transition cohorts—i.e., middle-aged parents and preretirees—exhibit more symptoms of stress than incremental transition cohorts—i.e., newlyweds and "high schoolers."

A study of consecutive admissions to a typical North American, urban poly-clinic over a nine-month period indicated that women generally present more persistent, vegetative complaints than men. The peak period for both sexes occurred between the ages of 40 and 60 (von Mering and Earley, 1966). In essence, these findings confirm earlier results from periodic USPHS household surveys between 1920 and 1940, as well as other regional U.S. studies (Collins *et al.*, 1955; von Mering, 1969).

A subsequent, retrospective case study of chronic multi-clinic patients explored the long-term (up to thirty years) relationship of persistent, health-seeking behavior with normative, medical-clinic practice. The results revealed that the customary care-giver/recipient relationship is fundamentally altered over time (von Mering and Earley, 1969). Despite many different working diagnoses, endless tests, few physical exams, and much medication, the patient does not, as a rule, contract a life-threatening disease (Earley and von Mering, 1969). Fortunately, most people past 60 years of age do not become involved in this form of dependency behavior.

The whole behavior pattern of "retirement from life into active ill health" (von Mering, 1969) seems to point to an apparent failure in "natural," familial support and individual self-help networks in the community. In part, this situation is exacerbated by the fact that the contemporary health-care system is geared to respond better to acute and specific, rather than chronic and non-specific conditions.

Another intensive study of 149 randomly selected cases from two specialty clinics (von Mering, 1972) with a record of a stable, primary, working diagnosis and high visit frequency, again showed that intractable, though non-fatal medical conditions tend to dominate the second half of the life cycle. The medical designation *Diffuse Health Aberration Syndrome*

(DHA) for these patients captures the following unique clinical and behavioral reality: the longer the affiliation with a clinic, the more numerous the individual visits. Eighty percent of the two-clinic population had a consistent clinical picture of primary medical conditions coupled with long-term moderate to severe psychological and social impairments. Detailed behavioral analysis confirmed that the habitual one-clinic care consumer "grows old the out-patient way" (Earley and von Mering, 1969). He or she is indeed suffering from the DHA, even if less resourceful than the multi-clinic visiting counterpart who is "sampling" a greater variety of available specialty treatments.

A recent re-investigation of salient bio-behavioral aspects of the DHA syndrome focused on the expressive significance of distance traveled to take a polyphasic screening test at a North Florida health center. A preponderance of female patients between the ages of 40 and 59 of modest economic means "traveled on the average twenty-one miles further to the test site than those for whom the DHA was not indicated" (von Mering, Shannon, Deal, and Fischer, 1976). Once again, there is extensive documentation of the clinical-social acutality of the intertwining of chronic, altered conditions of life, of regulative diseases with progressive, culturally-exacted alterations of selfhood, and their continuous interaction with a health-care system that is culturally primed to respond to acute rather than chronic disease. It would seem that the necessary and sufficient conditions exist for the rise of the phenomenon of the DHA patient in post-industrial U.S. clinic populations.

4. Medical-Cultural Patterns of Health Care Planning and Treatment

In contemporary nation-states, medical-cultural patterns of treatment find their quintessential expression in health-care policy for populations at risk at either end of the life-cycle. In the U.S., the planning, organization and delivery of health care grows out of an intricate aggregation of disconnected, categorical health-delivery programs insensitive to variations in the social environment of patients. The social environment in which we live clearly contributes to the likelihood of individual survival. For instance, fewer health workers practice in low-income, rural or ethnic areas than in the more affluent habitats. A decade ago, at least 5,000 communities were without physicians in the U.S. (Greenberg, 1971). In one of the worst slum districts of Boston, infant mortality has been nine times higher than the national average, and more than fifteen times higher than that of an affluent, nearby, suburban community (Greenberg, 1971). According to this Harvard Medical School Study, 90 percent of Boston's pediatricians, obstetricians, and other specialists care for the upper-income population segment which comprises only 40 percent of the city's population.

The same trend exists in all major cities; poverty areas have few doctors, dentists or public health nurses compared to wealthier communities (Greenberg, 1971). Most of the health care received by "ghetto" residents is only obtainable at large City-County hospital clinics. This bias in the provision of health-care services has been built into national health care by selecting physicians who themselves come from the higher socioeconomic layers, by training them to abide by attitudes, values and life styles which are *not* compatible with practice in the ghetto (Sidel, 1969), and by organizing all preventive and curative care around the physician (Lowy, 1970).

Despite massive federal Medicaid and Medicare programming, this problem of geographic maldistribution of health services has not changed substantially during the past decade (Brownlee, 1978; Rosen, 1976; Luft *et. al.*, 1976; Knowles, 1977). The most compelling issue in health planning for the middle and later years remains: *How can we prevent a premature decline in the ability to adapt to some chronic condition of impairment and regulatory disease?* (Shanas, Townsend, *et al.,* 1968; McMullen, 1979). Each geographically-designated planning area (i.e., state, city, district) requires health care tailored to its own unique distribution of ages, needs, resources, and utilization patterns. A variety of health-care plans adaptable to widely different circumstances must be available.

In spite of the need for regionally variable and local community-based as well as age- and life-style sensitive health-care programs, there continues to be an over-reliance on nation-wide, aggregate mortality statistics on health-care delivery and consumer patterns. Such data provide only a starting point for organizing health-care services. Yet, they are often treated as if they were capable of providing locally-specific answers for health-care planning.

The tendency to make macro-level needs assessment, rather than do micro-level planning for sub-regional and local variations in health-care needs is illustrated by representative statements such as these: "It can be anticipated (for the year 2000) that about one in five Americans aged 65 + will use a combination of intensive and extensive social and health services" (Tobin, 1975). Current survey data further indicate that about five percent of older Americans (65 +) currently reside in institutions at any one time, and that for *every* older person in an institution there are about two others who are homebound, one-fourth of whom are bed-ridden. These data are corroborated by planners of "protective service" programs for the elderly, who estimate that approximately one in six older Americans (65 +) who are *not* institutionalized are so impaired as to necessitate one or more types of direct social and health services (Hall *et al.* 1973).

In evaluating numerous psychiatric surveys in the U.S. and Europe,

Kramer *et. al.* (1975) reported that despite unanimous agreement on the magnitude and complexity of future general health and mental health care needs for the over age 60 population, no one has been more specific than that. The general medical assumption that the number of persons in need of services is identical to the number of persons with specified mental or physical disorders has encouraged health care planners to stay with a primary reliance on pre- and post-60 mortality statistics, which are insensitive to significant variations in psychiatric impairment or progressive biobehavioral disability. For example, the extent to which being unmarried increases the risk of being nursing home-bound is obscured by this assumption (Brody *et. al.*, 1978). Moreover, it is not surprising that the United States bio-med dollar investment form 1950 to 1972 shows persistent, increased funding for categorical research on high mortality, cardiovascular and neoplastic "killer" diseases. Federal support for the development of more complex technological aids for diagnosis and monitoring of named, acute medical conditions (Sprague, 1974) has continued to exceed funding for research on progressive and degenerative conditions associated with the entire life cycle.

It has become increasingly evident that the simple enumeration of gross changes in the volume of health services provided for the general population or selected age-cohorts is quite inadequate for making predictions of future service need. This has been well-documented in a recent study by Kahn (1975), whose conclusions about mental health care echo earlier observations on care program planning in the general medical sector of the health service delivery non-system. Between 1955 and 1968 "the number of [mental] patient care episodes for outpatient services quadrupled so that in 1968 these services accounted for 45 percent of all episodes as compared to ony 23 percent in 1955. The number of patient care episodes in *general hospital* in-patient psychiatric units more than doubled" during this period, while *all* in-patient services declined from "over three-fourths of the total episodes" to "only about one-fourth" (Kramer *et al.*, 1973:458).

In particular, "rather than helping older persons, the great mental health revolution [engendered by the CMHC Act of 1963] only led to their dropping out of the psychiatric system" (Kahn, 1975:25). It is indicated in a 45 percent reduction in the number of patient care episodes for the period 1966-1971. Concurrently, during the decade 1960-1970, a custodial redistribution of the institutionalized aged took place—out of state hospitals and into nursing homes. The number of nursing home residents rose from 554,000 in 1963 to 1,098,500 ten years later; and the bed capacity of these extended care facilities is currently over 1,200,000 (Kahn, 1975:26).

Contemporary advanced societies are characterized by the proliferation of formal service organizations designed to process, change and/or care for people. One of seven occupations in the American work force today is a human service occupation attached to a service organization. This trend reflects a notable shift of socialization, social control and care functions away from the primary group to third parties, i.e. professionals, the state. It is highlighted by the proliferation of complex clinical skills and changing techniques that cannot be carried out in traditional, non-specialized small social units, which are often accompanied by interorganizational competition and overlap of functions.

The organization of U.S. health care reflects this sociocultural phenomenon (Saward, 1973). Health consists of a set of disconnected, categorical health programs that include locally situated physical facilities and professional services, motivated and regulated by national programs like Medicaid and Elder care, VA services, Community Mental health catchment area care, USDA rural nutrition education programs, heart, cancer, and stroke programs, and HMO services. The functioning of any one program affects the actual workings of all other partial health delivery efforts. A change in type or manner of service made today by one of the larger United States health care components will affect the health care and well-being of every person in every geographical area. Moreover, the reverberating impact of specific changes may not be felt for five, ten, or more years (Knowles, 1977).

Managers of these coexisting categorical care components employ planning experts to help manage the normal risks of introducing a new care program. Final policy decisions are at least partially based on a planning specialist's judgment of available programs, options, and projections of probable consequences of alternative actions. Yet, most health care planners evaluate future consumer demand for a new service in artificial isolation from the effects of changes made by other categorical care units.

Miscalculations in health care planning can cause overinvestment of effort and funds in some well-publicized categorical programs, and a corresponding neglect of regional and local differences in pressing health needs in the general population, or among specific age groups. On the whole, the U.S. health delivery system has remained under-developed in providing the kind of direct, integrated and continuous form of care that about 85 percent of today's patients need (Glazier, 1973; U.S. DHEW, 1979). It is still too early to assess the extent of the beneficial impact on this of the post-1975 rise of federally mandated and supported, regional Health Systems Planning Agencies (U.S. DHEW, Health Resources Administration, 1979).

The lack of essential health care information for planning at both the macro- and micro-level of service delivery continues to plague national, state, and county-wide efforts to address the felt health needs of people. In a large measure, this is the result of an unintended, historical accretion of legislated and entrepreneurial ventures in non-complementary, special service programs. This spreading of competing rather than linked services is, in turn, traceable to an over-reliance on super-annuated concepts of the nature of key health hazards in a post-industrial culture.

The U.S. "tradition" of competitive co-existence of special health services for special classes of patients has delayed a thorough rethinking of the actual relation between aging and disease and well-being, apart from the socio-cultural onset of "old age" at 65 years. Hence, neither the health service administrator nor the planner are exclusively responsible for the evident tunnel vision in American health care decision-making. The lack of clear awareness of the cultural and time-bound nature of current perceptions of disease threat continues to endanger appropriate health care delivery to selected populations with high risk. They also underly the halting progress made in public health initiatives to prevent adolescent and young adult life-style precursors from experiencing chronic disability and disease in later years. A further evidence of culturally over-determined health care planning is the dramatic relocation during the last decade and a half of increasing numbers of impaired older persons into nursing homes and other total care centers.

The major medico-cultural features of the U.S. health care enterprise which make the delivery of integrative or "wholistic" services a special problem for the elderly population have been well-known for some time (von Mering and Earley, 1965). They include:

1. The increased relative importance of the hospital or "health center" as *the* place of diagnosis and treatment;

2. The growth of medicine as a science of tests and mechanical measurement, rather than as a "bio-cultural art" involving the five senses;

3. The proliferation of medical specialties and differentiation of paramedical skills;

4. The functional separation and distancing of personal care away from home and community;

5. The rapid spread and complexity of diverse private and public hospital and medical prepayment and reimbursement plans; and

6. The bureaucratization of hospital and clinical services, adding uncertainties to medical practice.

These patterns are in singular conflict with the needs of older persons, and lead to the devaluation of aging, reinforcing stereotypical conceptions of the aged patient.

American society adheres to a "formal" definition of old age rather than a "functional" one (Clark and Anderson, 1967). It is a definition which is linked to a cultural emphasis on segmenting the human life cycle in an oppositional or binary fashion. There is a first period of work and earned income, a kind of normative high road to social competence. It stops with the

onset of a second period—of uniform, post-retirement decline in performance among a presumably homogeneous group of older people—even
though they may span the sixth to the tenth decades of life (Bloom, 1972).
For most Americans, it would seem that "all people past the middle years"
represent a class of "persons-about-to-die," regardless of biological [and
mental] competence, and as such, "they are held to be without significant
social value" (Clark and Anderson, 1967). By this is variously meant that
with age there comes a diminution of individualism, future time orientation,
mastery over nature and "being a doer" (Barnouw, 1973). These negative
views, in particular, seem to account for the essential lifelessness of so
many contemporary nursing and convalescent facilities.

Such a perspective is usually rounded out by the cultural association of
aging with illness, as if "old age" were a specific disease entity, accompanied by essential non-productivity. The combined impact of medical
trends and stereotypical presuppositions about the aged lead a growing proportion of elderly to dread dying by degrees *more* than the inevitability of
death, which gives meaning to life (de Beauvoir, 1972; Kastenbaum and
Aisenberg, 1972).

There is a key health care corollary to the devaluation of aging as a
time of loss of health, income, status, youth, beauty, and activity (Gunter,
1971). Most direct care given to the elderly is done by non-professionals or
para-professionals, and to some extent by social workers, rather than by
physicians and nurses (Gillis, 1973). This is especially significant because
surveys show not only that from twenty-five to forty percent of patients in
general hospitals are over the age of 65 (Moses, 1967), but that a great
many of the more than 29,000 nursing homes in the U.S. have become the
"human dumping grounds" for the "unsalvageable" elderly, whose only
means of discharge is often the death certificate (Tivin, 1971). Indeed, it
has been estimated that less than half of these nursing homes offer skilled
nursing care under the direction of RNs or LPNs; and, while well over
300,000 personnel were employed in 1969 in work with the aged, only 25
percent had received any formal training for doing so (Schonfield, 1973;
U.S. DHEW HRA, 1979).

The popular health policy solutions of training more professionals,
especially physicians, nurses and hospital administrators, of building more
regional hospitals or health centers, of placing more stress on
"technological imperatives," and of monitoring "patient flow procedures"
(Fuchs, 1975), continue to hold sway into the 1980's. However, effective
care of the elderly is not likely to be the outcome of these solutions. The
prevailing negative cultural stereotyping of age in society as a whole is amp-
ly shared by the professions of nursing, social work, and medicine (Levin
and Roberts, 1976; Delora and Moses, 1969; Bloom, 1972; Spence,
1968). The reputed general U.S. nurse and physician "shortage" because of

choosing specialties and subspecialties (Fuchs, 1975) is said to be declining. However, it remains most unfavorably affected by the skewing of specialty choice preferences away from geriatric medicine and nursing to surgery, opthalmology, pediatrics, obstetrics, and even psychiatry (Spence, *et al.*, 1968; Delora and Moses, 1969). The culturally reinforced disinclination to keep or make older people more healthy through more direct personal caring is often even stronger among health personnel who work closely with older patients (Henry, 1973; Moss and Halamandaris, 1977). Moreover, other studies have shown that in many general hospitals the work to be performed by supervisory and higher ranking staff is so arranged to regularly avoid more than incidental exposure to the criticlly ill (Blauner, 1968; Glaser and Strauss, 1965) or the near-dead old and the dead (Sudnow, 1967).

5. A Behavioral-Medical Human Service Model of Health Care

This review of the state of gerontologic services in the U.S. indicates that the organization of health care must be brought into better alignment with actual disease patterns across the life cycle (Shanas and Maddox, 1976). The Diffuse Health Aberration (DHA) patient may serve as a cautionary paradigm for rethinking health care in the U.S. for the post-60 population, and other types of emerging elderly populations of the future. Current health services in the U.S. which are oriented to separate categories of acute mental or physical disorders cannot respond readily to palpable regional and local variations in the volume of services required by differences in population distribution. In particular, available services cannot provide continuous preventive and protective care either for the DHA patient or society's generation of elders.

In a manner of speaking, the DHA patient's dilemma and that of many of his aging contemporaries is that they are not ill without the diagnostician, and risk being not sick enough with him. Medicine views the language of diagnosis as an instrument of thought and reflection, rather than as a particular mode of human behavior. The purpose of symptom communication for most people, however, is not as much the transfer of objective information as it is the expression of a desire for an elementary agreement—a confirmation of an "obvious" condition of being.

Far too often, the older person-patient in today's society feels trapped into having to define the problem in terms of a general public standard of illness or of a medical finding of health. The aging patient, facing naturally altered body processes and changing status in the life cycle of reproduction, work, and play, is given the choice between being a vessel half empty or half full. Like the DHA patient, the elderly patient tends to make a self and health-problem presentation according to the dominant medico-cultural model of aging as disease and disability. Unfortunately for the patient, there is no specific care or cure for a cultural illness. He is left with what he knew before seeing the health professional, namely, that "health" as such is nothing, it only becomes something when we learn we have less than before.

A behavioral-medical model of human service must match health needs with flexible service programs for people of all ages. Such a model should include a focus on ordinary, transitional and protracted bio-behavioral morbidity and disability in the life course, as well as on exceptional or accidental afflictions, so as to arrive at developmentally and contextually rooted pathologies and service modalities. Such a model of health risk-service rate entails a major effort over time. The major elements of this model would include:

Multilevel Needs Assessment. Aggregate (national) morbidity/mortality estimates of service need must be augmented by ethnic-, class-, sex-, and locale-specific parameters of health risk based on actual population age distributions. As stated earlier, the base data requirements for this kind of planning cannot be satisfied by existing health information-gathering approaches. If available, levels of risk of acute, chronic, or accidental afflictions for different sex-age groups in given localities could then be estimated. Thus, the first two dimensions of the model would determine local service modalities. For example, relative levels (i.e., high vs. low) of risk of acute, chronic and accidental afflictions, respectively, could be determined for each local sex-age group.

FIGURE 14.1
LIFE CYCLE DISEASE PATTERNS AND SERVICE MODALITIES

Sex and social stratification-specific ⟶ life cycle stages	Levels of health risk by disease ⟶ pattern	Major treatment modalities
1. Childhood-Adolescence	1. Acute	1. Preventive
2. Adulthood-Middle Age	2. Chronic	2. Regulatory
3. Preretirement-Old Age	3. Accidental	3. Curative
	Major categories of service	
	1. Institutionalized	
	2. Community-based	

Risk tables following such a life cycle framework could proceed from estimates of the incidence of disease pattern by age-sex group to treatment-service categories.

Treatment Modalities. The prevailing treatment modality in current health care focuses on *curative* strategies that require physician-centered institutionalized (i.e., "hospitalized") modes of stress abatement. Two other modalities must be developed to the same level of sophistication and operation. The first, of course, focuses on *regulatory* strategies associated with chronic conditions that come to prevail toward the end of the life cycle, conditions which potentiate the onset of acute or accidental risk in old age. Such regulatory or maintenance and relaxation-oriented modalities lend themselves to both institutional and extra-institutional modes of service.

The third treatment modality emphasizes *preventive* health care in the forms of professional services and self-help knowledge. Acute, intensive and longterm institutional ("individual interventive") service modes do not suit preventive health strategies. Rather, lifelong, community-based educational and stress abating self-service programs are required. These would represent "social utilities" (Lowy, 1970) automatically available to all and accessible as public facilities. The health consumer in medically underserved areas—usually rural or central city—would benefit most form the acquisition of basic health care knowledge, beginning in early adolescence, to facilitate essential personal self-sufficiency in preventing common, contemporary precursors of chronic disease.

Categories of Service. Health care throughout the life cycle must combine institutionalized and extrainstitutional, community-based approaches to service. Human services fulfill three major functions: (1) the socialization of the member of a society, i.e., via schools, social and recreational centers, universities and colleges, and various youth and age serving agencies; (2) the social control and health maintenance of people, by identifying individuals who fail to meet standard, minimum prerequisites for continued full functioning in the existing social order, and by removing them, at least temporarily, from their current place in society (e.g., law enforcement, hospitals, correctional institutions, and social service agencies); and (3) the integration and redistribution of people within social networks—by providing the means and resources for the individual to become acclimated to various behavior settings on the basis of resocialization, therapy, material assistance and counseling (Hasenfeld and English, 1975).

Two requirements of an effective behavioral-medical care system include a manpower policy of training health service professionals in light of life cycle contingencies to health care delivery, and a plan of interagency linkage in the delivery of information, treatment and self-help support structures throughout the life cycle.

The foreseeable rising demand for better vocationally motivated and professionally qualified middle-level and advanced practitioners in the field of health services must be planned in light of the following manpower requirements:

(1) Training into a comparative socio-cultural perspective, to specify with greater precision what various human service specialty practitioners can and cannot deliver adequately to varied consumer populations, targeted for primary health care and well-being needs;

(2) Training with an emphasis on preventive health self-care, and especially on the prevention of precursors to chronic impairment and disease (McMullen, 1979);

(3) Training that includes content on the health care system itself, i.e. components of service, modalities of treatment, risk levels of target populations and resource levels affecting accessibility of care. This is all the more urgent because so many of these programs, separately conceived, funded, and managed, are in constant competition for similar or idential intellectual and motivational qualifications in their roster of human service employees.

Finally, and following from the above, an effective behavioral-medical care system depends on coordinated patterns of health delivery. At the local level a cooperative network of interagency communication can extend the impact of essential human services in a region, thus reducing the medically under-served pockets of human habitation in the city or county. Home health services of varying intensity following Trager's model of "concentrated," "intermediate" and "basic" home health care (U.S. Senate Special Committee on Aging, 1972) could draw upon different institutional arrangements and health practitioners to carry out programs of curative and regulatory clinical treatment (Shanas, 1971).

Educational programs utilizing academic, recreational and popular media could coordinate and disseminate much-needed preventive health self-help information. It is essential to devise cultural-transcending initiatives in the acquisition of age-appropriate health care knowledge; for, resistance to change has always been as much a matter of "information withheld" as of "facts not heard on time."

Such considerations are impossible without a coherent national policy of health care, which—in turn—would require a major realignment of cultural presuppositions regarding disease patterns and service responses. Current technological and economic imperatives related to energy conservation and stationary economic patterns may lead to major cultural changes long overdue in our aging society. In this case, it is well for society to confront the reality that youth, age, and disease have this in common: each is nothing but life under altered conditions!

It is equally important for us to note that throughout the cycle of life, human mal-practice on mind and body brings on more sickness and discomfort than can be attributed to natural causes. Finally, a national health care policy falls short of its goal so long as it seeks primarily to pacify or adjust categories of old and young people to the existing environment. Life circumstances are not altered without promoting the redistribution of vital resources and greater access to decision-making! Wellness is a matter of backtracking on disease features *before* they become actual.

15
Accidental Medicalization Of Old Age And Its Social Control Implications

Arnold Arluke
and
John Peterson

1. Introduction

The increasing medicalization of both normal and deviant behavior and the role of the profession of medicine as an institution of social control has received considerable attention in recent years (Carlson, 1975; Fox, 1977; Freidson, 1970; Illich, 1976; Kittrie 1971; Pitts, 1971; Zola, 1972). By "medicalization" we mean the process by which problems and behaviors become reinterpreted as illnesses, such that a mandate is given the medical profession to provide some type of treatment for them. Now classic examples of medicalization include alcoholism and drug addiction (Chalfant and Kurtz, 1971; Roman and Trice, 1968), mental health (Blackwell, 1967; Foucault, 1965; Szasz, 1970; Rosen, 1972), pregnancy (McKinlay, 1972; Merkin, 1976; Rosengren, 1962a; 1962b) and hyperkinesis (Conrad, 1976).

In the case of alcoholism and drug addiction, the profession of medicine is clearly replacing religion (morality) and law (criminality) as the major institution for controlling and understanding these problems. With hyperkinesis, the disruptive behavior of children at home and at school is made more socially acceptable by medically intervening—on behalf of family members, school teachers and administrators—with psychoactive drugs. Unlike alcoholism, drug addiction, and hyperkinesis, the medicalization of pregnancy represents the transformation of a normal and natural behavior, not defined by the public as disruptive behavior or deviance, into clinical and medical problem; its "proper" management is thereby taken out of the context of the family and put into the setting of the hospital.

In all of these case studies, however, analyses are more concerned with documenting that medicalization takes place than they are with isolating the basic parameters of the process. Furthermore, it is unclear from these studies whether there is only one medicalization process for all behaviors, or whether a unique set of parameters exists for each behavior that is medicalized. Clearly what is needed are more studies that examine the nature and character of medicalization and identify some of the basic dimensions of this process. As an exploratory effort in this direction, we will focus on one dimension of medicalization—the extent to which medicalization is either (1) an attempt by the medical community to create a "market" for services where none is recognized by lay people or (2) a response by the medical community to a set of social forces outside the profession. This latter condition we refer to as accidental medicalization.

Almost without exception, earlier studies of the process of professional growth have described such expansion in imperialistic terms. While sometimes described as an insidious process, medicalization is typically characterized as a process determined by professional decisions rather than by public definition (Stevens, 1971). The sociological literature on professional expansion has placed considerable emphasis on the impact of indigenous or narrow exogenous factors on professional change. Social change within professions, according to these studies, is influenced primarily by internal professional considerations rather than by external demands (Rothstein, 1973). Kuhn (1970), for example, argues that scientific professions develop paradigms for organizing the bodies of knowledge they use in their professional activities. Changes in such paradigms, Kuhn suggests, are caused by forces and conflicts within the profession, rather than by external social pressures. The model to be used in this chapter departs from the above tradition, and explores the role played by social forces external to the profession and beyond professional control in expanding the jurisdiction of medicine to include subgroups within society not previously included in the formal boundaries of medicine. Thus, certain subgroups of the population may be defined as needing medical intervention more as a consequence of the coalescence of these forces at a particular time than as a result of internally planned professional aggrandizement.

Our first concern in this chapter is with isolating the social and cultural forces that are leading to a formal inclusion of the aged as a subgroup requiring specialized professional attention. We cannot examine all the complex influences that are redefining *being old* as a sickness requiring medical attention and therapy, but we shall briefly examine two of the major influences in the larger society which have had a significant impact on encouraging and shaping medical jurisdiction at the end of the human life span. Once these influences are described, we can then consider the response of the medical profession to these influences and describe the professional treatment ideology toward old people that is emerging. And finally, we will appraise the implications of the medicalization of old age from a social control perspective.

2. Accidental Medicalization

The first influence on the medicalization of old age we shall discuss is change in the demographic composition and family structure of contemporary American society. While the age composition and change of populations that embed health service professions would seem to be a major factor influencing the nature and extent of medicalization within society, this factor has not received attention in the literature. Navarro's (1975) work, for example, examines the relationship between the social class composition of the population and health care services, but does not consider the impact of the age composition of society on the delivery of these services. One notable exception in the health services research literature is Krasner and Muller's (1974) study of the interaction between changes in fertility and the emergent charcter of obstetrics and gynecology. But, in general, there has been a void of studies examining the relationship between changes in the age composition of populations and services provided by the medical profession.

To begin with, the age and family structure of society is undergoing change, and evidence is already pointing toward adaptations in the knowledge base and structural design of the health professions. In a broad, comparative perspective, the age structure of the United States has a relatively large number of persons of mature years. Not only has the older segment of the population drastically increased in absolute numbers, but the proportion of older people in the total population has increased as well. Between 1900 and 1970 the proportion of persons 65 and over has more than doubled, from 4.1 percent to 9.9 percent. Current population projections estimate that by the beginning of the twenty-first century, 12.2 percent of the total population will be over 65. Further proportional changes are anticipated for the decade 2010 to 2020, based on the cohort of post-World War II babies. It is these people who visit doctors more often, experience more and longer hospitalization stays, and now require over 22,000 nursing homes with 1.3 million beds (Stroman, 1976).

Thus, with a decline in the general birth rate and an increase in the average life span, popular (Mayer, 1977), medical (Butler, 1975) and social scientific (Brotman, 1973) sources suggest that we are now facing an "elder boom." Indeed, the image fostered by these various sources, as well as by the mass media, is that of a major population reshuffling of near-crisis proportions. At the core of this boom imagery are discussions of the health and social problems of the aged (Cutler and Harootyan, 1975). It is not, however, that these problems are new. It is the extent and magnitude of the problems that has been recognized. In other words, the various commentaries and reports describing an elder boom are themselves raising public and professional consciousness of the quality of life faced by older people. And the quality of their life, according to these sources, is problematic. Demographic phenomenon thereby serve as the foundation for crystallizing the "needs" of a particular segment of the population and for increasing the visibility of its "problems."

As the proportion of older persons increases in the United States, so is the ratio of older persons who are dependent on individuals between the ages of 18 and 64. The ratio of older people who are dependent on those still active in the work force has changed from 0.097 in 1930 to 0.177 in 1970. This ratio is projected to increase to 0.213 in 2020, and, considering the trend toward early retirement, this estimate may be conservative. The changing size of the dependency ratio is occurring at the same time that changes in family composition are taking place. With the smaller family of the middle third of the twentieth century, and the longer lives of the population, there are fewer adult children to take care of more older parents (Goode, 1963). Moreover, Parsons and Fox (1952) suggest that the modern urban American family possesses certain structural and organizational weaknesses that mitigate against the performance of its traditional sick-care function, giving rise to its reliance on the services of extra-familial institutions of health care. The burden of old age has increased for the constricted kinship networks of postindustrial societies.

Although largely intuitive, Parsons and Fox's position has received partial empirical support. Litman (1971) reports that almost half of the families he studied, regardless of generation, claimed that they would find it fairly or very difficult to care for a sick member at home for a prolonged period of time. Almost 60 percent of the families surveyed indicated complete and ready willingness to relinquish responsibility for the care of the sick to the hospital, believing that the ill member would receive better care there. Approximately one-third of these families felt that convalescence could not be provided at home under any circumstances. Similarly, Peterson (1972) notes that the contemporary family is entirely willing to delegate responsibility for the cure and care of a sick member to the hospital.

Other studies of the modern family, however, point out that families have not entirely discarded their traditional function of taking care of those who are ill but who do not require hospitalization. Shanas (1963) observes that the elderly are not alienated from their families, and that those individuals who are disabled are usually cared for by a relative. Butler and Lewis (1973) also indicate that institutionalization takes place only after all other resources have been exhausted. Even if there is a willingness on the part of the family members to care for the aged, there is some question as to whether the aged would accept such care. Litman's findings, for example, point out that the elderly have misgivings about receiving care from family members. Furthermore, there is serious question whether families who wish to care for their elderly members, and who have senior members who are willing to accept this care, are equipped to perform this function.

In short, a growing and aging population is creating increased demand for more and different types of services, requiring additional medical facilities and personnel. Demographic changes are coupled with changes in the structure and functions of the American family that make it less capable of meeting the housing and health care needs of the elderly. Of course, as these changes have taken place, the "objective" health status of the older population has not varied. What has varied is the definition of the health needs of the older population and how they might best be met. Although insidious in character, these changes are straining the conventional medical paradigm and are leading to a reinterpretaton of old age as an inherently problematic stage of life from the perspective of health.

A second influence on medicalization which we will investigate is the extent to which there is a broadening cultural view of old people as sick-like in their behavior and a widening cultural perception of old age as synonymous with disease. Largely as a consequence of industrialization and accompanying institutional forces which have devalued the status of the elderly (Rosow, 1974), being old is now intolerable in the eyes of the young. Old age is seen as a stage of life that would be nice to avoid (if there were a way) and that certainly should be feared. It is to be avoided and feared because old people, even in the absence of medically diagnosed pathology, are now expected to adopt a social role which has all the characteristics of a sick role (Cassell, 1972). It is also to be avoided and feared because old age and the aging process itself have acquired all the symbolism of disease—as something "unnatural" about one's body that should be biologically studied and medically treated with cure in mind.

In advanced industrialized society, the *healthy* aged are expected to behave psychologically and socially as do the sick of any age. One way in which sick people are expected to behave is to separate themselves from the social world. They are disconnected form the world around them for physical (disability) and institutional (hospitalization) reasons. The aged are also separated from a world and reality previously familiar to them, although physical sickness may not be present. Rather, this separation is a consequence of the decline in status experienced by old people in mainstream society. Indeed, the attraction of elders to homogeneous old age communities is due, in part, to the irrelevance of age as a determinate of status (Ross, 1977). As the sick person retreats into a subculture of illness, so does the aged person establish new social ties with elders (Rose, 1965). Subcultures of the elderly, however, become communities composed largely of viable, healthy members (Keith, 1979).

A second way in which sick people are expected to behave is to reduce their normal social and occupational responsibilities. Sickness is seen as a legitimate excuse for deviating from everyday expectations of performance (Parsons, 1951). For those elderly persons who develop a chronic illness or face the recurrence of a latent chronic illness, the ability to continue activities which attach them to the social system is substantially reduced. Reduced activity and mobility are accompanied by a decrease in interaction with others. Similarly, the healthy old also undergo a redefinition of their normal role responsibilities if retirement or semiretirement are entered (Ellinson, 1968; Lipman and Sterne, 1968). Even old persons who continue full employment are likely to encounter changed performance expectations by others (Tuckman and Lorge, 1953).

In addition to being granted permission to reduce normal social and occupational responsibilities, the sick person is allowed to become dependent on others in a relationship of unequals. The sick person's social value is not equal to that of the healthy person upon whom the sick person depends. Certain cultural patterns in our society define the aged as dependent. They are seen as lacking anything of worth with which to establish reciprocal relationships with others. As Clark (1972:272) observes: "Dependency of all kinds apparently occurs in all cultures, and it seems to be an almost inevitable companion of advanced age."

Sickness, in most cases, is also believed to be a condition that is not willfully or voluntarily chosen by the sick. As the sick person is not held responsible for causing his illness, so the aged person is suspended from responsibility for becoming old. Indeed, from a cultural perspective, both the states of old age and illness should be (in the typical person) states that would be avoided if the person were able to exercise choice in the matter. To choose deliberately to enter these states would; (1) in the case of sickness, raise questions of malingering and exploitation of the role benefits of sickness (i.e., secondary gains); and (2) in the case of old age, raise questions of sanity or self-destructiveness.

Another characteristic of the sick is the loss of their sense of personal invulnerability. Sickness challenges our conception of the body as indestructible and provides an alternative—although perhaps temporary—view of human frailty. The elderly's sense of personal invulnerability is threatened by the aging process, as some elderly see evidence of their loss of physical capability. In many cases, such loss may be more due to a self-fulfilling prophecy than to actual physical change (Kahn, 1977), as recent studies have underscored the good health of many elders (Palmore, 1974; National Council on the Aging, 1977).

Sick people are also thought to lose the feeling that events and their causes can be understood and to some extent controlled. Sickness is beyond the person's understanding. Insufficient knowledge to comprehend the transformation of one's body results in magical and folk interpretations of events. Old people are frequently accused of not understanding the world around them and are portrayed as not "being at home" in today's world. There is, too, in the old, a loss of confidence in their ability to control external events, although this sense may be deeply rooted in the very real powerlessness of most elders.

Not only have the expected behaviors of the healthy aged become those of the sick, but the symbolism of aging and being old have been equated with disease and abnormality in contemporary society. The inevitability of physical decline, deterioriation and death of the human organism in old age are ideas that people have accepted over the centuries. As part of our view of the order of things, physical decline and death have been looked upon as beyond our control and as a natural part of life. In the twentieth century, this belief in the naturalness of aging and death has been questioned, due to the growing faith by the public in scientific conquest and biomedical technology. This faith attributes to modern medicine an increase in life expectancy (which actually stems from a higher standard of living) and assumes that medicine has the power to lengthen life still further, if not to abolish old age itself (Lasch, 1977). Aging and death are now coming to be seen as disorders in what is *normal* for the human body. As Kurtzman and Gordon (1976:14) comment: "Is it necessary to consider aging and death inevitable? Aging, after all, is the alteration or gradual cessation of normal processes, which brings about the increased likelihood of illness and death. *It is in effect a progressive disease*" (Italics added). Once aging and death are seen as abnormality and disease, they become medical problems which, according to one author, will be "something your doctor may some day hope to do something about" (Rosenfeld, 1976).

Clearly there is, at the cultural level, an equation of aging and old age with sickness and disease. Unlike the Parsonian model of the sick role, the ascription of sick-role attributes to the elderly does not depend on "official" legitimation of sickness by physicians. Instead, there are "taken-for granted" assumptions operating at the cultural level regarding what is appropriate and natural elderly behavior. Old people are the "living sick" (Gladue, 1975). It is precisely this sort of cultural conception of normal old age that invites and justifies the treatment and control of the elderly on medical grounds.

3.   Response of the Profession

While many social factors exist in Western industrialized societies that support an illness model for old age, legitimation of medical treatment and control of the elderly ultimately rest on the successful emergence of a professional treatment ideology toward old persons. Once old age is defined as pathological by the medical profession, it is likely that the same mechanisms and theories that underlie the prevention of and therapy for disease will be mobilized against the threat of aging—and thus against old people.

Paradigm change in professional bodies of knowledge is marked by dissensus within the profession as to the propriety of its work and the design of its jurisdiction. Medicine is now experiencing internal disagreement as to the necessity of geriatric medicine. Standard medical textbooks, for example, have traditionally avoided discussions that specifically focus on the problems of the elderly. Some physicians argue that this absence is acceptable; the general practices and knowledge of internal medicine are felt to be sufficient. Disagreement within the profession of medicine as to the need to create a board-certified specialty for diagnosing and treating the problems of old people is reflected in a number of statements. Comments by physicians and others question the need for and the existence of a unique body of knowledge for managing the elderly. At a recent Senate hearing on medicine and aging, for example, one medical school dean observed: "The diseases that are the causes of illness and death in the aged are the same as those that begin to appear in people in their thirties and forties. They have the same diseases as younger adults . . . I do not believe the interaction of aging and illness, which is so much a part of everyday medicine, is a matter that requires separate and specialized attention" (U.S. Senate Hearing, 1976).

Despite such dissent, medicine is now in the process of attaching the label of illness to being old by constructing special medical problems around the old and by advancing special treatment for these problems. The view that different age groups have unique medical problems and correspondingly unique medical therapy is described as early as 1888 by Dr. A. L. Loomis. He writes: "The life of man is naturally divided into four periods—infancy, youth, manhood, and old age; each period has its mental and physical characteristics, each its diseases, and each its therapeutics." It is only recently, however, that the profession of medicine has seriously considered using the life span or developmental approach as a device for organizing medicine along specialty lines. Those who have called for the creation of separate departments of geriatric medicine in medical schools and teaching hospitals suggest that the elderly have unique and specific medical problems that distinguish them as a group from other kinds of patients, but that have not been taken into consideration formerly. Rather than seeing pathology and disease process as a developmental phenomenon striking individuals of all age groups with essentially similar—although not necessarily identical—physiological dynamics, old people are portrayed as having special problems and disorders. By developing a medical specialty to serve the older population, it is argued that the short attention old people have gotten from medicine in the past can be remedied.

The uniqueness of geriatric pathology, according to some physicians, lies in the special patterns of signs and symptoms of disease. While the elderly are subject to the same acute disease processes as are persons in other age groups, they are thought to react to illness differently. The uniqueness of the elderly's reaction to disease, some physicians argue, makes for special diagnostic problems. A flurry of recent articles, for example, outline the special diagnostic problems of the "aging heart" (Burch, 1977; Mihalick and Fisch, 1977; Rodstein, 1977). In some instances, the elderly are believed to demonstrate no symptoms in the presence of disease, while younger patients produce a variety of symptoms to the same problem. Alternatively, aging people react to many diseases and pharmaceutical agents that produce few, if any, signs in younger people (Lawton, 1969).

The older person's problems are also believed to be less specific. Abnormal processes are no longer, in the elderly, separate difficulties of the bowels or of the kidneys. Rather than isolating distinct problems or complications in the older patient, physicians claim they encounter massive systemic deterioration of the "physical, behavioral and spiritual facets of life" in old people (Lawton, 1969). Thus, the elderly are portrayed by some physicians as presenting unique symptomatological reactions to multiple problems of a chronic, deteriorative clinical and social nature.

From this perspective, the role of the physician *vis a vis* the older patient is not only to assess his clinical status, but to appraise his social life. This comprehensive approach allows physicians to have a major role in decisions, such as institutionalization, that were formerly left entirely to families. One physician has recently argued that medical professionals must enter into family and patient decision-making, and "guide" them in meeting the psychosocial needs of the older person (Kleh, 1977). This social guidance by physicians is based on the determination as to whether the elderly person is having "good interactions" with family members, peers, professional caretakers and others. The body of knowledge required by the physician to make professional evaluations of this sort cannot be categorized by disease but is broad and diffuse in orientation, subsuming much of the special expertise normally reserved for social scientists and lay people.

Recent developments have furthered the physician's role in the process of institutionalizing older people in long-term care facilities and in formalizing a position for geriatric medicine within skilled nursing facilities. As of October, 1974, conditions of participation for Medicare and Medicaid require each skilled nursing facility to hire, "pursuant to a written agreement, a physician . . . to serve a medical director on a part-time or full-time basis as is appropriate for the needs of the patients and facility" (U.S. DHEW, 1974). In the same year, the American Medical Association established its own guidelines for the medical director role (American Medical Association, 1974). Discussions by Gladue (1973), Shaughnesy (1973) and Solon and Greenwalt (1974) indicate the potential significance of this role for the development of geriatric medicine.

Clearly, there is some reluctance within the profession of medicine to separate the problems of the elderly as medical entities distinct from the problems of younger patients. Those physicians that are resisting the development of a geriatric medicine do not deny that the elderly pose special diagnostic or treatment problems. They do feel, however, that the current medical paradigm for managing illness is adequate for coping with the problems of the elderly. The dominant thrust in medicine is running counter to this position and is rapidly developing a highly detailed and extensive body of knowledge that further substantiates the claim to a special geriatric expertise. The real issue that underlies the present realignment of medical practice around older people is not whether a new specialty should be carved out to service the special needs of the elderly and to generate and define the content of geriatric medical knowledge; rather, the underlying issue is: should a special mandate be granted to physicians to reinterpret and apply medical expertise to the physical as well as the social problems of people along age-stratified lines?

4. Some Implications

The fact that planning for the health needs of the elderly is a relatively recent concern underscores the diffusion and acceptance of the medical model of old age. Inherent in social policy and planning are implicit professional ideologies toward clients. In its simplest form, this ideology is expressed in the belief that the old need more medical care than they are now getting and that they need additional care in order to both maintain the "quantity" of their lives as well as to improve this quality.

That more care is somehow "better" for the elderly involves three major dimensions of professional expansion (Ehrenreich and Ehrenreich, 1974). Expansion in the *jurisdiction* of the medical system includes totally new types of services and functions not formerly seen as "medical." Long-term care of the aged, community mental health services, and home-care services are now believed to be necessary medical services if the elderly are to continue to lead active, worthwhile lives (Kovar, 1977). To say that many who provide these services are not medical professionals begs the issue. For the public is only taking their cues from professionals whose approach toward health has become an integral component of popular thinking.

Matching new medical services for the elderly are new technologies. On the whole, these are incomplete or halfway technologies representing a level of technology that tries to compensate for the incapacitating effects of the diseases common among the elderly. It is a technology designed to make up for disease or to postpone death (Thomas, 1972). In the public mind, this kind of technology is the equivalent of the high technologies of the physical sciences. Instead of considering the make-shift quality of this technology, the public has been led to believe that each new procedure is a therapeutic breakthrough. Not only is this technology an extremely complex and costly means of managing the chronic problems of the elderly, but it is also a dangerous and iatrongenic program.

There is also an expansion in the *number and kinds of services and technologies available* within the traditional jurisdiction of medicine that result in the use of large quantities of hospital and physician services. While the size of the aged population has been increasing in recent years, so has the rate of utilization of services. Since 1964, the average number of physician contacts has increased for the elderly. Utilization of short-stay hospitals by the elderly has also increased, from 3.4 days in 1965 to 4.1 days in 1974. Although the rates of utilization of health services by the elderly can be measured accurately, the effect of increased medical care on the health and quality of life of the elderly is far more difficult to ascertain. There is no available evidence, for instance, indicating that the longevity of the aged has been noticeably affected by expanded services and technologies. Indeed, some recent material suggests that halfway technologies may actually lower the quality of life for recipients (Abram, 1972; Wolstenholme and O'Connor, 1966).

And, thirdly, there is professional expansion in the *availability* of medical care along class and age lines. Though clearly not yet a right, medical care is far from being a luxury. A variety of programs such as Medicare, Medicaid, Blue Cross and others have put medical care within the financial reach of large numbers of poor, working-class, and old people who formerly stood completely outside the medical system. Total expenditure for the use of short-stay hospitals by the elderly has more than tripled in the past eight years. The acquisition of new equipment and the provision of more extensive patient care are responsible for about a third of this price increase. Approximately ninety percent of the payments for the hospital care of the elderly comes from public funds. Medicare benefits paid under hospital insurance in the fiscal year 1975 for the elderly amounted to $12.7 billion. Of this total, $9.7 billion was for hospital care. Almost the entire population of people over 65 are enrolled for hospital care under Medicare, and a substantial part of this hospital insurance money goes for halfway technologies described earlier.

What are the effects on the individual of a medical system that is expanding into areas of life previously considered outside the domain of professional expertise? From Illich's (1976) perspective, one can consider both the clinical, social and cultural toxicity of such expansion. That is, the very interventions made by physicians to improve and extend life too often result in repercussions at the individual, societal and cultural levels. Medications, for example, are commonly provided the elderly, and are believed to result in either better health or greater longevity. While making up only ten percent of the U.S. population, the elderly use 25 percent of the nation's prescription drugs (Basen, 1977), costing approximately $877.5 million (Food and Drug Administration, 1968). Hospitalized Medicare patients receive an average of ten prescription drugs (Nitham, et al. 1971); a significant proportion of these drugs fall into the psychotropic or mind-altering class of medications (Waldron, 1977). The chance for misuse of drugs—both by the elderly themselves, as well as by those who care for the elderly—is substantial.

A number of studies have shown that of all age groups, the elderly are most likely to have a drug-induced illness (Learoyd, 1972; Eisdorfer, 1975; Bender, 1974; Petrin, 1974; Hall, 1974; Hodkinson, 1974; Terri, and Franzini, 1972). Not only are many of these drug-induced illnesses fatal, but commonly prescribed psychotropics account for most of these deaths (Morton, 1969). The use of psychotropic drugs by older people is two-and-a-half to three times higher than would be expected from their proportion of the population (National Disease and Therapeutic Index, 1975). That many of these freely prescribed psychotropic agents have little to do with either the health or longevity of the aged seems apparent; in many instances, such prescriptions are for the "care and management of the geriatric patient."

The treatment by physicians of nonspecific emotional problems in the elderly is a leading source of drug abuse. The overprescribing of psychotropics is a common means of controlling patients' behavior in institutions housing the elderly, in addition to managing the behavior of old persons still living at home with younger family members. Both the nursing home and the family are concerned with the behavior of old people who may be very difficult at home and disruptive in the institution. The broad diagnosis of senility, which includes an ever-increasing number of specific senile designations, leads to prescribing psychotropic medications. The elderly person's behavior becomes more socially acceptable, reducing problems in institutions and homes.

By managing behavior in this manner, the cause of the problem is attributed to the older person; it is the individual that we seek to change. By focusing on the symptoms and defining them as senile psychosis, we ignore the possibility that their behavior is not an illness but an adaptation to a social situation. It is the "victim" who is being blamed (Ryan, 1970) and not the social system. Attention is thereby diverted away from the family or the institution; the notion that the problem could be a social-structural one is diffused. Thus, the medical perspective of diagnosing illness in individuals lends itself to the individualization of social problems.

While there is clinical and social toxicity in the expansion of medical practice, there are broader cultural implications of medicalization. The expansion of the medical system and the diffusion of medical thinking into all strata of society have been accompanied by a deepening public dependency on that system. Early forms of medicalization tended to replace religion and law as the major institutions of social control. Jurisdictional expansion of the profession of medicine according to the human life span now threatens to replace lay sources of control, such as the extended family. Although it is true that physicians themselves are encouraging this dependency by actively discrediting lay sources of advice and help, some physicians are uncomfortable with the continual generalization of expertise (Veatch, 1973). They feel inappropriately trained to manage many problems that have fallen under their jurisdiction. The body of knowledge and skills that are available to physicians seems hopelessly deficient in the face of problems that have no clear diagnosis or cure. Such professional anxiety may be particularly acute in the case of geriatric medicine, where clinical cures are rare and social and psychological problems are common.

5. Discussion

As an exploratory effort, this chapter has examined the extent to which the medicalization process is an accidental professional phenomenon, induced by social forces external to the medical profession. Our intent was not to review the entire array of exogenous factors that may play a role in shaping medical labels around natural behaviors. Rather, by carefully choosing two particular external conditions, we hoped to demonstrate that professional bodies of knowledge are in constant interaction with the surrounding social and cultural context. Such a position provided a preliminary critique of those studies that have focused on internal professional processes (e.g. Bucher, 1962; Coe, 1970) as the *primary source* of professional change. This analysis posited a model of professional change that is adaptive to the constraints faced by a profession at a particular point in time and space. From this perspective, the development of segments within a profession—each representing alternative ideologies toward practice—results from cues taken from its environment. Internal professional change may be a rather sudden response to a shifting context; it is not necessarily the result of the gradual, linear evolution of professional bodies of knowledge that some have suggested. Changes in bodies of knowledge may only be symptomatic of such external constraints.

To illustrate the accidental quality of medicaliztion, we have focused on how being old has become defined as a medical problem and how medicine is becoming a major agent for controlling the behavior of the elderly. Some of the immediate clinical, social and cultural ramifications of medicalizing old age were discussed, including the iatrogenic effects of expanding medical care, the individualization of social problems, and the generalization of medical expertise. The medicalization of old age, however, has more profound consequences for social control. Unlike other problems that have been medicalizied, old age is neither a specific behavior (as with hyperkinesis) nor is it a transitional state (as with pregnancy). It is the very ambiguity of viewing the aging process itself as a pathology that potentailly allows physicians to exercise their authority over a wide range of behavior in a variety of situations. In the past, defining behavior as a medical problem has permitted physicians to cut open bodies or to prescribe psychoactive medications. When medicalization is based on the problems of living and the determination of the "quality" of one's life, the limits of social control seem boundless.

16
The "Back to Anthropology" Movement in Gerontology

Jennie Keith

1. Introduction

Amoss' chapter proposes that cultural revivals lead to higher status for old people. In that spirit, this volume represents a "back to anthropology" revival for those of us who study aging; it should be beneficial for the status of both the subject and its students. This collection of papers represents a return to anthropology in the sense that ethnographers must return from their immersion in exotic data to integrate it into existing anthropological knowledge and theory. The ethnographic bounty that these papers bring home is a tremendous addition to the formerly very small store of first-hand information about old people outside the U.S. Although anthropological interest in old age is at least respectably middle-aged itself, data have been both narrowly focused and second-hand. Since Simmons' (1945) HRAF analysis of factors affecting the status of old people in various traditional societies, his questions as well as his method of secondary analysis have remained prominent in anthropological work on old age. This volume presents an anthropology of aging that has matured into first-hand studies on various aspects of old age, utilizing the full range of ethnographic methods.

The first step in a back to anthropology movement for research on old age is a review of what this ethnographic phase has produced. Next, that harvest of cases can be sifted for patterns suggesting variables and hypotheses for the next stage of more systematic comparison. Finally, the studies of old age must be integrated into the broadest anthropological theories in terms of which age *per se* must be examined as a principle of social organization, or the entire life course seen as raw material for cultural definition.

2. Ethnographic Findings

Like the ethnographic phase of anthropological work on other topics, the first rounds of fieldwork done on old age reveal three major themes: (1) an *emic* perspective that "vetoes" or refutes uninformed stereotypes; (2) *documentation of diversity* in the situations of old people and their responses to them; (3) a *holistic* view of cultural context as it affects the old.

Emic Perspectives. The well-fed SRO residents described by Bohannan are an instance of the "inside truth" that may be revealed by good ethnography. The outsiders' assumption that the hotel residents are malnourished is true only for those that the outsiders would probably except, the middle-class women in the retirement hotels. The San Diego studies, like Sokolovsky and Cohen's work in Manhattan, reveal the SRO and its surrounding cheap cafes as an adaptive niche for a specific category of old people: poor individuals who place a premium value on independence without intimacy. The ethnographic studies show how these settings make sense in their own terms, and consequently reveal the dangers of social action based on outsiders' interpretations. The residents of Horton Plaza may in fact be hungry in the future partly because misinformed outsiders think they are malnourished now.

Sokolovsky and Cohen also report that when the social world of the SRO elderly is seen from the inside, the old people do not have the problems they're supposed to. In this case, the elderly hotel residents are not isolated, but have social networks including individuals both inside and outside the hotels. The emic view of Manhattan has action implications as dramatic as that of San Diego. Social intervention based on the assumption that SRO residents have no networks ignores available and acceptable social supports that might be bolstered in crises, in favor of institutional assistance likely to promote dependence, or to be rejected entirely. The drinking patterns study directed by Bainton also demonstrate a non-problem: the alleged high incidence of alcoholism among the elderly.

Documentation of Diversity. Documentation of diversity in the situations of old people and the factors shaping these situations is available in these chapters both singly and in the aggregate. The class variation among residents of San Diego's hotels is a first example. The values acquired through previous lives shaped by middle- vs. working-class experiences have made atmosphere more important than food for some of the old people in Horton Plaza. The important point made by the ethnography is the diversity among old people, seen by outsiders to be the same. The point is all the more dramatic because, in this case, the diversity occurs within one small residential area.

The theme of this section on diversity might be: "It doesn't have to be that way." Poor people in SRO's don't have to be hungry. Or, as Kayser-Jones shows, old people in nursing homes don't have to be powerless, without dignity, and mistreated. There is profound diversity in the human situation of the old residents of the structually similar institutions in Scotland and the U.S. The influence of social change on the status of the old in the Coast Salish community, compared to that of the Asmat in New Guinea, documents another kind of diversity. Change itself may be of various types, e.g., revivalistic vs. technological; and various types may have different consequences for this position of old people. The confrontation of these two cases is a healthy challenge to assumptions of universaltiy for the negative relationship between status of the elderly and social change.

The gloomy residents of "Cornell" in Cleveland are a more negative example of "It doesn't have to be that way." Francis' comparison of these unhappy and alienated old people to the lively, contented, Jewish elderly of Leeds, England, shows that an age-homogeneous residence of old people—even if they share common ethnicity as well—doesn't necessarily become a community. In the scientific process, a negative case such as this is a particularly critical type of diversity. Since previous ethnographic studies of old people living together have consistently discovered communities, the no vote from Cleveland is a healthy nudge toward more complex explorations.

The very deliberate and quite active process of dying in the German town studied by Weatherford demonstrates, as he points out, the wide diversity in social circumstances of old people, even within what we sometimes think of as the uniform category of industrial society.

Holistic View of Context. Attention to the cultural contexts that produce diversity in any aspect of human social life is central to the holistic approach in ethnography. Several of these chapters demonstrate the powerful influence of cultural context on the lives of older people. The organization of health care in the U.S. appears in several chapters (Arluke and Peterson, von Mering, O'Rand, and Kayser-Jones) as a painfully constraining negative force in the lives of many American elderly. The medicalization of old age prescribes a sick role for old people, with consequent dependence and stigmatization. Financing of health care through Medicaid stigmatizes further through a welfare identity. Lack of a geriatric specialty lowers the status of care receivers as well as care givers. The focus of American medicine on acute care obscures the actual medical needs of old people for preventive and chronic care, and encourages institutionalization.

A more microscopic view of the interaction between old people and the medical system reveals the influence of the culture of physicians on the fate of their elderly patients. The close-up view of the hospital context provided by Faulwell and Pomerantz shows the factors promoting an identification of doctor and patient that may counteract the pressures for institutionalization implicit in the American focus on acute care.

The contrast between San Diego and China in terms of tacit tolerance of life styles perceived as deviant is another demonstration of the forceful influence of cultural context. The elderly spinsters described by Sankar have been allowed to use their "sisterhood" as an adaptation to the consequences of norm violation—i.e., not marrying. The similarly adaptive SRO niche of San Diego's "loners" is about to be urban-renewed out of existence.

The information brought home by these ethnographers of old age is precious in itself. Its emic perspectives, documentation of diversity, and contextual data, veto stereotypes and offer implications for more accurately guided action. In addition, these reports, especially viewed as an ensemble, define hypotheses to guide the next—more systematic—stage in an anthropology of age.

3. Variables and Hypotheses

The first source of hypotheses in this ethnographic phase are the findings of any one case study that must next be tested for generality through comparative research. Faulwell's interpretation of patient/physician identification as a brake on referral to institutions is an excellent example. In addition, some of these reports, seen in confrontation, offer alternative views that should be translated into alternative hypotheses, so that the factors conditioning one pattern or the other can be discovered in new research. Van Arsdale and Amoss, for instance, disagree thoroughly on the sources of status for the aged: economics, says Van Arsdale from New Guinea; culture, says Amoss from the Northwest Coast. Seen as opposing hypotheses, these points of view demand the refinement of possible conditioning factors, or combination of material and ritual sources. How important an ecomomic asset are the old people's pensions among the Salish, for instance? Is there any economic aspect to the ritual in which they are leaders? How significant is the type of cultural change involved, i.e., revival? What variation is there in the previous source of status for old people in these two settings, e.g., was status traditionally more materially and individually based among the Asmat than the Salish?

The significance of cultural roles for the old Salish also has intriguing connections with the papers by Glascock and Feinman about treatment of the aged, and by Kertzer and Madison on women's age sets. In their discussion of the Latuka, Kertzer and Madison refer to the venerable opposition of nature vs. culture. Is it possible that men need more culture (i.e, more ritualization of age-border transitions) because women's lives are more ordered by nature? Are old people well-treated when they are important culture-bearers, but rejected when nature takes over and they become physically frail?

The slowly and sociably dying German grandfathers, as well as the sad old people of Cornell, suggest further hypotheses, through confrontation outside this collection with existing wisdom in gerontology. Clear-cut transitions across age boundaries have long been thought to produce less anxiety and less inter-generational tension than gradual and less determined movements (cf. Foner and Kertzer, 1978). Since Weatherford argues that it is precisely the more gradual character of life-stage transitions in the German village that eases tensions and promotes adjustment, an important direction for further comparative research is clearly marked. The non-community in Cornell is a similar contrast to previous studies, which persistently report positive communities in age-homogeneous residences for old people (Keith, 1979, 1980; Ross, 1977). Francis suggests several factors that may be intervening between this group of old people and the development of community: their history of transience and lack of stable peer relations, their consequent lack of a clear role for old age, the obstructionist director. Especially the first two factors are important foci for future community studies.

4. Integration into Anthropological Theory

The final stage of the journey from the ethnographic field studies back home to anthropology is the integration of research on old age into anthropological theory. As researchers on old age, anthropologists have—like most gerontologists—resembled the integrationists who advocate moving minority group members into someone else's neighborhood. Although we talk a great deal about the need to integrate study of the old into anthropology, we have not moved them or our research about them into the mainstream of our own disciplines. It is time to integrate study of old age into anthropology, and, as Amoss has pointed out, such a revival movement should be beneficial on both sides.

Research on old age, first of all, needs to become part of research on *age*. Age—unlike other principles of social organization such as kinship or ethnicity—has never been given a thorough anthropological treatment. Perhaps (returning to the theme introduced by Kertzer) this is because age has been seen as too natural, and less desirable for anthropological attention than more culturally elaborated domains. The supposedly residual character of age, as a principle always superseded when others become available, may have contributed to this view (cf. Schurtz, 1902; Needham, 1974). Of course, as Glascock and Feinman vigorously demonstrate, age is culturally defined and used; age categories are no more "natural" than kinship groups are biological. Age appears residual—e.g., in Needham's analysis—only when the principle superseding it is the basis of corporate grouping while age is not. In that case, the competition is not between principles, but between types of grouping.

It is time for full anthropological treatment of age, and a major contribution of this early research on old age may be to stimulate that broader study. From a social structural point of view, for instance, under what conditions is age used to define social borders that are more or less sharply defined? What are the consequences of different types and degrees of border definition for contact across them? In cognitive terms, how is age used to categorize? With what consequences for action or for evaluation of persons? (Fry, 1976 and Kirk and Burton, 1977 are pioneering studies.) What are the views of age borders from inside and outside? What are the consequences of various alignments of age with other social borders? These are of course the most basic questions about the use of any principle in social organization, but we have not asked them thoroughly and systematically about age.

Anthropological theory certainly is available to guide this exploration, and, in return, data about age should lead to a more general theory of social boundaries. Theories of boundary definition and maintenance in anthropology rely heavily on ethnicity. Research on age differentiation could begin with Cohen's (1969, 1974) and Barth's (1969) hypotheses about conditions and consequences of various degrees of boundary definition. The resulting data about age borders will permit evaluation of their theories using boundaries based on a different characteristic. In addition, the phenomenon of border "passing" considered problematic in ethnic studies, should be illuminated by the study of age, where maintenance of boundaries while individuals "pass" across them is the normal state of affairs.

Another two-stage integration process must occur in research on the life course. Cultural definition of later stages of life, and attitudes toward them, must be considered in the perspective of cultural definition of the entire life course. In turn, what LeVine has called the "cultural phenomenology" of the life course, or the "subjective life course," must be integrated into our broader studies of world view and culture (1978). Theories and techniques are available in ethnoscience, symbolic anthroplogy, and psychological anthropology to guide this research. In turn, the comparative study of the life course as culturally defined will provide a stimulating new source of additional evidence about cultural inventiveness and its consequences for social life.

These chapters are, in short, reports from the first ethnographic stage of a back-to-anthropology movement by gerontologists. The journey will be complete and comparative research on old age matured as a subject when we transcend our own age boundaries to begin the anthropology not of old age, but of age.

17
Gerontology and Anthropology: Challenge and Opportunity

Corinne N. Nydegger

1. Introduction

Only a few anthropologists have participated in the development of the field of aging, but interest is accelerating. Anthropological gerontology is shaping itself into a distinct specialty. This is therefore an appropriate time to speak to interested anthropologists about some of the special challenges and opportunities awaiting them in the field of gerontology.

Dr. Keith and I have oriented our discussions according to our primary professional identities. Thus the opportunities afforded by the study of aging to the discipline of anthropology are dealt with by Dr. Keith, while my remarks are made from a specifically gerontological stance. I cannot, of course, presume to speak for the diverse aging field, but this is how I see it.

To a gerontologist, there are certain areas in the field which seem particularly opportune for anthropological research. But first I would point out some hazards. It must be emphasized that we are not talking about a leisurely academic liason. The involvement of a number of chronically underfunded disciplines in a problem-oriented field with mandated funding is highly competitive. The experience can be counter-productive if the anthropologist evades the challenges or ignores the opportunities the field presents.

2.   The Challenge of Gerontology

Multi-disciplinarity. The structure of gerontology as a field of inquiry exerts certain pressures on participating disciplines. For gerontology is not, itself, a discipline: it is a broad, multi-disciplinary focus on the last portion of the life span and the processes of aging. Aging, like the rest of living, respects no disciplinary boundary: biology, demography, psychology, political science, and so on—there are few disciplines that are not age-related to greater or lesser degree. The field of gerontology reflects this unusual breadth both in its membership and in the scope of the questions the field addresses, which inevitably lead from one specialty to another and onto still others.

Breadth of perspective provides an exciting intellectual milieu. Common interests and problems breach traditional disciplinary walls and facilitate truly interdisciplinary work and interchange. Gerontologists comfortably adopt or adapt research variables as needed from disciplines other than their own, and are conversant with the major work in aging across a spectrum of related fields and specialties. Disciplinary affiliations blur through repeated exchange of perspectives. To stretch an anthropological analogy, gerontology is a set of interlocking kindreds rather than a set of lineage-like disciplines.

But this aspect of the field, though rewarding, poses its own challenge. It places on all gerontologists the burden of keeping up with relevant work in a number of disciplines. Because gerontology is such a new field, for some time the literature was manageable. In the mid-1960s, for example, it was possible to have read every book or article in social gerontology, no matter how esoteric the journal sources. But since then the publication rate has soared and the scope of one's coverage has had to be reduced.

Nevertheless, the responsibility for serious study in other disciplines remains. Without it, we are all too likely to laboriously reinvent one another's wheels. Ignorance of basic work in the field, regardless of disciplinary provenance, is never excused by a multidisciplinary field such as gerontology.

Problem Orientation. Gerontology is primarily a problem-oriented field. I do not mean that it is atheoretical, for that is clearly not the case. But, in common with most such fields, the initial impetus for the creation of gerontology as an organized field of inquiry was a growing awareness of the many human problems consequent upon aging and the desire of various professionals, especially direct service providers, to understand and find solutions to these problems.

In the brief time since gerontology's inception and despite limited funding, the tiny band of researchers has made a good start at establishing the parameters of the most critical problems. Solutions are another matter, for almost all require major policy decisions and resource commitments at the societal level, for which gerontologists can act only as advocates through publication and persuasion. Meanwhile, more problems loom ahead, such as the escalating health delivery costs, poor services, and confused planning discussed in the second half of this volume.

Does a problem orientation pose more difficulties or more opportunities for traditionally trained social scientists? On balance, I think opportunities outweigh difficulties by a healthy margin. For example, interdisciplinary exchanges flourish when there are practical human problems to be solved, since no social problem can be encompassed by any one discipline. The realization that data or techniques from another field are essential in order for you to address *your* question is the one situation which reliably ensures interdisciplinary respect and fruitful collaboration. The permeability of disciplinary boundaries within gerontology is in large part a result of its problem orientation.

There is also an enormous personal satisfaction in working on social problems which are of vital concern to us all. Anyone who has ever visited a typical nursing home, such as Kayser-Jones describes in her paper, or has been admitted into an old woman's barricaded inner city apartment, knows how frightening and angering the experience is. But it is just this desire to do something about the problems threatening many older persons that poses a hazard for social scientists. Essentially it is a question of retaining one's professional identity. But the issue is not as irrelevant as it may appear; ultimately it bears on the value of the social sciences to gerontology and its human concerns.

There are strong pressures to direct one's research toward currently identified and narrowly defined problems. They stem from the researcher's own humane desire to rectify social wrongs, the immediate needs of practitioners in the field, and the encouraging interest of gerontologists, their journals, and the funding agencies in work that is directly applicable to these problems. The result is an implicit, pervasive pressure to focus research on narrow, pre-defined problems.

As I have suggested, one consequence is unusually good relations across disciplinary lines. But the problem-pressures can push this too far. Social scientists can easily lose their professional identities and, with them, their disciplinary intellectual base. Too often we stop thinking like anthropologists, sociologists, economists, or whatever we may be. Instead of examining aging itself within our disciplinary models, we have tried to adapt our concepts to narrow old-age problems. In so doing we minimize, rather than maximize, our long range contribution to gerontology. For example, until recently we focused exclusively on the already old and examined their situation, but we neglected the sociocultural examination of the broader question of how age functions as a basic factor in social structures.

Anthropologists in gerontology are particularly likely to be co-opted. All too often the anthropologist is expected to function merely as a translator of other disciplines' problems, concepts, and techniques in relation to ethnic minorities and, occasionally, other nations. This may be a worthwhile activity, but not if significant anthropological questions are neglected. Then it is simply bad social science. Anthropology as a discipline can only contribute something new if it deliberately brings its distinctive perspective to bear on gerontological questions.

Relevance to Aging. But here again, we must not go too far. The relevance of our disciplinary perspective must be clear to funding agencies, journal editors, and gerontology colleagues. In my experience, the difficulty of accomplishing this has been exaggerated; and I repeat, research need not be narrowly applied. Gerontology is receptive, and as committed to theory building as it is to applications.

What kind of work is considered relevant? Precisely because the age dimension pervades the behavioral and social sciences, standards of gerontological relevance are ambiguous. Broadly speaking, funding agencies whose monies are earmarked for gerontology legitimately expect aging to be a major concern of the research they support. Research in which aging is only of tangential interest is thereby not really relevant. Clearer guidelines cannot be established.

But the very ambiguity about what is and is not relevant has its bright side: it enables new issues and perspectives to enter into the field more easily. But do not forget that the burden of documenting claims to relevance rests on the investigator. And rightly so: we can at least hum for our suppers.

Nor is relevance solely a burden; it can be a challenge. When social scientists must take extra care in designing studies to satisfy both disciplinary and gerontological expectations, they often find that the extra care produces sounder research. Gerontology does need the challenging perspective of anthropology which demands re-examination of basic premises. But we can also profit by the challenge of gerontology to clarify our terms, detail our methods, and defend the formulation and significance of the problems we choose to study. If, during this process, we are forced to re-examine some of our own premises, we have nothing to lose and a great deal to gain as anthropologists.

3. Opportunities for Anthropology

Where are the clearest opportunities for anthropologists to contribute to gerontology? I cannot, of course, predict the development of either field, much less the direction collaborative efforts may take, nor can I predict the emergence of new problems to be addressed. Besides, the wide range of issues now being examined by anthropological gerontologists may soon render obsolete any suggestions I might make. Nevertheless, I would like to discuss a few general problem areas which I am convinced could most profit from the attention of anthropologists.

Age Articulations. First, gerontology is still struggling with the complex articulations of age with social age, with social roles, and with systems of stratification, both formal and informal. Age is a confusing variable, for it is confounded with virtually all social role changes. From some points of view age is critical, from others it appears artifactual; in life-span perspective, its importance forms a U-curve, high in the early years and again toward the end of life. Is this shape basic to the human condition? Or is it an artifact of the role structure of Western societies? Is age itself at issue or is it distance from death? Is age stratification general or a response to distinctive social patterns? How is it associated with patterning of social roles? How does age modify social roles? and so on. Endless inter-related questions arise, all of which involve major theoretical issues as well as aging problems.

The cross-cultural perspective of anthropology provides the essential base for investigations in this complex area. For example, previous work by anthropologists has shown that, in some societies, and more often for men than for women, becoming socially old means taking on new roles (as Amoss reports here), whereas loss is most typical in Western and acculturating societies (as in Van Arsdale's chapter). But we need to more tightly relate these data to systems of age stratification. Focused work on this question—using controlled comparisons and longitudinal data—should lead to a better understanding of the determinants of these varied patterns.

Social age attribution is another part of this complex begging for anthropological attention, such as Fry's detailed studies of age categorizations (Fry, 1976, 1980a). Cognitive studies in this area would enhance our understanding of the attitudinal data the aging field has generated. And Kertzer's work (partially) reported here in the paper by Kertzer and Madison) represents a major step toward the clarification of cohort succession in relation to age stratification. This work is a fine example of combining "exotic" anthropological data with sociological formulations to expand and reformulate basic theoretical issues.

Useful models of social aging cannot be constructed by simply stacking social problems documentations one on another like a house of cards. A firm theoretical framework is essential. Although we do need to know a great deal more about aging problems, it is not too early to attempt to integrate such materials as are available, try out models, and pursue the leads resulting from these efforts. One of the most heartening aspects of the research reported in this volume is the authors' commitment, not only to aging issues, but to the development of relevant anthropological theory. I hope other anthropologists are encouraged by these examples to attack the many thorny problems gerontology presents.

The Life Span. Second, gerontology developed in order to focus interest on issues specific to old age. Although we repeatedly have proven to ourselves that it is absurd to treat the topic as if all the years before 65 were irrelevant, we continue to do so. This is partly due to the old-age-problem concerns of the field, and partly due to a history of life-span partitioning among separate specialties. Infant, child, and adolescent studies have been distinct fields for a long time, but we now further distinguish between neonatal and infant studies and subdivide both childhood and adolescence.

Gerontology, then, studies the old. But even within gerontology, those who deal with the "old old" or the "frail elderly" over 75 are showing incipient signs of specialization. And the mid-life crisis notion has coalesced with a designated pre-retirement stage to produce a new field of middle age studies. I don't know how far this partitioning can go, but I am giving serious thought to specializing in the 33-year-old.

Of course dividing the life course into discrete age slices and proceeding as if they were unrelated increases fragmentation of knowledge and makes age-relevant theory building that much harder. But a life course field is developing. Still in its infancy, it is struggling with tough methodological and theoretical problems, not to mention a precocious disciplinary identity crisis.

I would like to see anthropologists in the forefront of this nascent life course field. Anthropologists are trained to take a life course perspective; they are holistic in outlook; and they traditionally have been interested in the processes of change and maturation-in-social-context (under the various rubrics of enculturation, acculturation, socialization, etc.). Here is a challenging opportunity to pull some of the fragments together, and contribute both to the field of aging and anthropology.

Aging Variation. Third, another consequence of the focus on "the old" is that we design studies of older people as if they were a homogeneous group. We know this is not true. We know that age *qua* age (even taking ethnicity into account) is a useful predictor only for gross social characteristics (income, housing, marital and occupational status, and so on) but that it is useless as a predictor of personal characteristics. As many have pointed out, we become more ourselves, hence more distinct one from another, as we grow old.

Nevertheless, we have treated individual variation as error from some putative mean. Here again, anthropologists are well equipped to challenge the field by directly focusing on these variations to establish ranges, patterns, and search out underlying causes. My hunch is that a good place to start would be with pattern analysis of life course materials from a number of societal and cultural types. Questions such as the following could then be examined: What are the empirical limits to variation in the shaping of lives? What aspects of social sytems are the major shapers? Socially speaking, is there a time to sow and a time to reap? Or is this true only of certain human conditions?

Cohort Ethnography. Fourth, another way of grouping lives together is by cohort membership which, because cohorts are defined by years of birth, highlights the impact of historic events lives have shared. To the degree to which cohorts are not mere devices for analytic designs but do reflect distinctive shared experiences, cohort members form a kind of subculture. This is recognized by social scientists and the media, which has popularized the notion in the imprecise term generation (as in Beat Generation, Depression Generation). Despite its ubiquity, numerous difficulties in the concept of cohort, and especially in the meaning of cohort experiences, have elicited serious attention only during the last few years.

Along with life course studies, anthropologists could well undertake ethnographies of these subcultures-cohorts. Who is better equipped with the necessary skills and experience? And in fact, the chapters by Van Arsdale, Amoss, Sankar, Francis, and especially Weatherford point in this direction, as does Eckert's work on cohort boundaries (Eckert, 1979).

Certainly there would be methodological obstacles, but I would like to see anthropologists systematically try out on cohorts the techniques already established in studies of subgroups defined by ethnicity, cult and self-help group memberships, occupation, and so forth. Cohort ethnographies would flesh out our meager understanding of history's impact and contribute materially to theory in anthropology and aging in the new era of cohort exploration.

Cross Cultural Research. Fifth, gerontology is keenly interested in research and programs world-wide and maintains close ties with international gerontology organizations. Its social scientists are among the most internationally minded in the problem fields. Therefore anthropologists can be assured of genuine interest in comparative studies.

However, gerontology has focused its own research on cross-national comparisons. These are studies of high-technology societies like our own, which have gone through the demographic transition and are now "aging societies," that is, ten percent or more of their populations are elderly. This limitation does not result from ethnocentric myopia, nor from naivete. It arises from the recognition that all aging societies do have many basic problems in common, and that these are not the same problems faced by young societies. Thus gerontologists are not likely to see a study of the old in an

Asian mountain tribe as directly relevant to their concerns, though they may be intrigued by it.

Despite the apparent reasonableness of this focus on societies like our own, the restricted cross-national approach poses severe limitations on analytic research. In all these studies the same variables reappear, at essentially the same levels, and equally confounded: level of technology (including public health and medicine), urbanization, aging population, low birth rate, nuclear family predominance, women in the labor force, geographic and social mobility, and so on. There are some differences, to be sure, but the similarities are overwhelming at the societal level: it may be Sweden or Japan but, when translated into figures, the data look like Kansas City.

Thus clear comparisons cannot be made. We have no analytic levers to pry apart confounded factors in order to assess the importance of each and understand the processes involved. What is needed is a broader, more varied set of societies for controlled comparisons.

However, any attempt to broaden the base and include societies not yet approaching the demographic transition runs into the same problem, for the confounded factors just discussed are usually present in their obverse and equally confounded: low level of technology, rurality, young population, high birth rate, and so forth. Therefore gross comparisons of pre- and post-aging societies can provide no new insights.

Further, we then meet the classic methodological obstacles to preliterate gerontology: inadequate chronological age determination, differing social criteria for old age (documented even among the chapters in this volume), confusion of normative prescriptions with acutal behavior, and the problem of referents (which I feel warrants attention, since it is a problem all field workers face). We most often observe, or are told about, behavior toward immediate kin, which varies due to life-long and unknown precursors. These data are then somehow merged and used as a direct index of behavior toward a different referent—"the aged" as a social category. But how many studies do we have which present data on cross-age interactions by degree of kinship? Without such documentation, I must question the validity of these inferential referents. And, based on my own field experiences, I question how many groups really do prescribe normative behaviors (beyond a term of address) to be accorded to a category of "aged" as distinct from their own kin.

Thus we most often have, on the one hand, behavior to old kin in preliterate societies and, on the other hand, normative attitudes toward (or social status of) the aged in industrialized societies. No legitimate comparisons can be made. We must have more data from industrialized societies which are comparable to data in the ethnographic record, and data from pre-literate societies comparable to data now available in the gerontological record.

These problems present tremendous opportunities and tough challenges, which I think anthropologists are uniquely trained to meet. No discipline is better qualified to provide the necessary comparable data from both pre-literate and industrialized societies. Indeed, some of the chapters in this volume have done just that.

As one example, Glascock and Feinman's holocultural analysis uses variables which are comparable across non-industrialized societies and with gerontological studies in our own society. Despite coding problems inherent in such analyses, this study replicates the recent distinction made by gerontologists between the "old old" and the "young old." It also supports the contention of social gerontologists that age is—first and foremost—socially defined. Replication across this range of societal types is convincing evidence indeed that our conclusions are sound and general.

Broadening the base for cross-national studies is not going to be easy. One suggestion is to find societies wherein it is possible to exert control over at least some of the confounded factors, and then systematically examine the correlates of variation in the others—in short, hunt for certain combinations of factors occurring naturally and design research around them. Sankar, for example, made good use of the natural occurrence of a very unusual combination of factors.

I suspect the Third World societies could provide many of these unusual combinations. Even if they prove to be short-term transitional patterns, with careful designs and sufficient replication, they may give us the analytic levers we need. And they certainly will tell us a lot about the processes of change in relation to age. Such systematic research will be more valuable to the field of aging than merely adding to the number of studies of the elderly in socieities which have been chosen, from the gerontological point of view, at random.

Network Interaction. Sixth, gerontology is heavily invested in studies of support systems, especially those involving intergeneration relations. This is an area in which gerontology as a field can have direct impact on program plans and governmental policy decisions. Yet gerontology is poor in studies of interactions between support groups or family members. And it is downright poverty-stricken in conceptual tools to organize such data.

Happily, a few anthropological network analyses are beginning to appear in the gerontology journals. And I trust that the studies of support systems in this volume by Fennell and by Sokolovsky and Cohen are an indication of things to come. For we need all the fine-grained analyses of structure and behavior in various natural networks that we can get. We must know how support systems function; the alternative is to base public policy on myth.

4. Conclusion

I find my few suggestions have grown into many and could easily be doubled, which is a good index of the tremendous opportunities open to anthropology in gerontology. I am confident that anthropologists will, in the years to come, find many more and better ways to contribute substantively and theoretically to the field of aging.

Bibliography

Abdellah, Faye G. Conference on Public Policy. National Association of Jewish Homes for the Aged. Mimeographed. Washington, D.C., 1976.

Abram, H.S. "Psychological Dilemmas of Medical Progress." *Psychiatric Medicine* 3 (1972):51-59.

Adams, Bert N. *Kinship in an Urban Setting.* Chicago: Markham, 1968.

Adams, Frances. "The Role of Old People in Santa Lemas Mazaltrepec." *Aging and Modernization,* edited by D.O. Cowgill and L.D. Holmes. New York: Appleton-Century-Crofts, 1972.

Ahern, Emily. *The Cult of the Dead in a Chinese Village.* California: Stanford University Press, 1973.

Aldrich, C.K. and Mendkoff, Ethel. Relocation of the Aged and Disabled: A Mortality Study. *Journal of the American Geriatric Society* 11 (1963):185-194.

American Medical Association: *Guidelines for a Medical Director in a Long-Term Care Facility.* Chicago: American Medical Association, 1974.

Amoss, Pamela T. *Coast Salish Spirit Dancing: the Survival of an Ancestral Religion.* Seattle and London: University of Washington Press, 1978.

———. "Coast Salish Elders." In *Other Ways of Growing Old,* edited by Pamela Amoss and Steven Harrell. Stanford: Stanford University Press, 1981.

———. "Symbolic Substitution in the Indian Shaker Church." *Ethnohistory,* in press.

———. "Hair of the Dog: Unravelling Precontact Coast Salish Social Stratification." Unpublished paper.

Amoss, Pamela T. and Steven Harrell, eds. *Other Ways of Growing Old.* Stanford: Stanford University Press, 1981.

Anderson, Barbara G. "The Process of Deculturation—Its Dynamics among United States Aged." *Anthropological Quarterly* 45:4(1972):209-216.

Anderson, N. et al. Policy Issues Regarding Nursing Homes: Findings from Minnesota Survey. Minneapolis, 1964.

Angrosino, Michael V. "Anthropology and the Aged: A Preliminary Community Study." *Gerontologist* 16 (1976):174-180.

Arensberg, Conrad. *The Irish Countrymen.* Blouchester: Peter Smith, 1937.

———. "The Community Study Method." *American Journal of Sociology* 60 (1954):109-124.

Arensberg, Conrad and Kimball, Solon. *Family and Community in Ireland.* Cambridge: Harvard University Press, 1940.

Arling, C.D. "On Aging, Senescence and Senility." *Annals of Internal Medicine* 77 (1972):132.

Arnhoff, Franklyn; Henry Leon and Irving Lorge. "Cross-cultural Acceptance of Stereotypes towards Aging." *Journal of Social Psychology* 63 (1964):41-58.

Arth, M. "An Interdisciplinary View of the Aged in Ibo Culture." *Journal of Geriatric Psychology* 2 (1968a):33-39.

Axelrod, Morris. "Urban Social Structure and Social Participation." In *Cities and Society,* edited by Paul Hatt and Albert Reiss, Jr., 1964, pp. 722-729.

Babchuk, Nicholas. "Aging and Primary Relations." *International Journal of Aging and Human Development* 9 (1978):137-151.

Bacon, Stanley. "Sociology and the Problems of Alcohol: Foundations for a Sociological Study of Drinking Behavior." *Quarterly Journal of Studies on Alcohol,* 23 (1943):19-40.

Bainton, Barry R.; Christopherson, Victor A.; and Escher, Monika C. "Sampling Procedures for the Study of the Drinking Habits of the Rural Elderly." Paper presented at the Annual Meeting of the Alcohol and Drug Problems Association of North America, Detroit, Michigan, September, 1977.

Baker, F.; Mishara, B.L.; Kastenbaum, R.; and Patterson, R. *A Study of the Alcohol Effects in Old Age (Phase II)*. Report to the National Institute on Alcohol Abuse and Alcoholism, February, 1974, #NO1-AA-0103.

Barker, Roger G. *Ecological Psychology*. Palto Alto, Calif.: Stanford University Press, 1968.

Barnes, John. "Class and Committees in a Norwegian Island Parish." *Human Relations* 7 (1954):39-58.

——. *Social Networks*. (Addison-Wesley Module in Anthropology, No. 26), Reading: Addison-Wesley, 1972.

Barnett, Homer. *The Coast Salish of British Columbia*. Eugene, Oregon: University of Oregon, 1955.

Barnouw, Victor. *Culture and Personality*. Homewood, Ill.: Dorsey Press, 1973.

Barth, Fredrik. *Ethnic Groups and Boundaries*. Boston: Little, Brown, 1969.

Basen, M. "The Elderly and Drugs—Problem Overview and Program Strategy." *Public Health Reports* 92 (1977):43-48.

Baxter, Paul T.W., and Almagor, Uri. Introduction to *Age, Generation and Time*, edited by Paul T.W. Baxter and Uri Almagor, New York: St. Martins, 1978. pp. 1-35.

Beaubier, Jeff. *High Life Expectancy on the Island of Paros, Greece*. New York: Philosophical Library, Inc., 1976.

——. "Biological Factors in Aging." *Aging in Culture and Society: Comparative Viewpoints and Strategies*, edited by C.L. Fry. New York: J.F. Bergin, 1980.

Beauvoir, Simone de. *The Coming of Age* (Translated by P. O'Brien). New York, N.Y.: Putnam and Sons, 1972.

Bender, A.D. "Pharmacodynamic Principles of Drug Therapy in the Aged." *Journal of the American Geriatrics Society* 22 (1974):296-303.

Benet, Sula. *Abkhasians: The Long-Living People of the Caucasus*. New York: Holt, Rinehart and Winston, 1974.

Bengsten, Vern; Dowd, James; Smith, David; and Inkeles, Alex. "Modernization, Modernity and Perceptions of Aging: A Cross-cultural Study." *Journal of Gerontology* 30 (6) (1975):688-696.

Bennett, Ruth G. "The Meaning of Institutional Life." *The Gerontologist* 3 (1963):117-125.

——. "Social Exchange." *International Encyclopedia of the Social Sciences*. New York: Macmillan 7 (1968):452-457.

Berger, Peter. *The Sacred Canopy: Elements of a Sociological Theory of Religion*. Garden City, New York: Doubleday, 1967.

Bergman, U. *Siedlungsgeographische Untersuchung*. Kahl am Main: Archives, 1974.

Berkner, L.K. "The Stem Family and the Developmental Cycle in the Peasant Household." *American Historical Review* 77 (1972).

Bernardi, Bernardo. "The Age System of the Masai." *Annali Lateranesi* 18 (1955): 257-318.

Bild, B.R. and Havighurst, Robert. "Senior Citizens in Great Cities: The Case of Chicago." *The Gerontologist* 16 (1976):63-69.

Birren, James E. et al, eds. *Human Aging: A Biological and Behavioral Study*, PHS Publication #986 Washington, D.C.: U.S. Government Printing Office, 1963.

Bischofberger, Otto. *The Generation Classes of the Zanaki (Tanzania)*. Fribourg: University Press, 1972.

Blackwell, B.L. "Upper Middle Class Adult Expectations about Entering the Sick Role for Physical and Psychiatric Dysfunctions." *Journal of Health and Social Behavior* 8 (1967):83-95.

Blau, Peter M. *Exchange and Power in Social Life*. New York: Wiley, 1964.

——. "Social Exchange." *International Encyclopedia of the Social Sciences*, Vol. VII, pp. 452-457. New York: Macmillan/Free Press, 1968.

Blauner, Robert. "Death and Social Structure." *Middle Age and Aging*, edited by Bernice L. Neugarten. Chicago, Ill.: University of Chicago Press, 1968, pp. 531-540, 535ff.

Bloom, M. "Social Work and the Aging Family." *The Family Coordinator* 21 (1972):111-118.

Boissevain, Jeremy. "The Place of Non-groups in the Social Sciences." *Man* 3 (1968):542-556.

——. *Friends of Friends*. New York: St. Martins Press, 1974.

Boissevain, Jeremy and Mitchell, J. Clyde. *Network Analysis: Studies in Human Interaction*. The Hague: Mouton, 1973.

Bott, Elizabeth, *Family and Social Networks*. London: Tavistock, 1957.

——. *Family and Social Networks*, 2nd ed. New York: Free Press, 1971.

Boureston, N. and Tars, S. "Alterations in Life Patterns Following Nursing Home Relocation." *The Gerontologist* 14 (1974):506-510.

Bowers, A.W. "Hidatsa Social and Ceremonial Organization." Smithsonian Institution, Bureau of American Ethnology Bulletin 194. Washington, D.C.: U.S. Government Printing Office, 1965.

Bowers, Nancy. "Demographic Problems in Montine New Guinea." *Culture and Population: A Collection of Current Studies,* edited by Steven Polgar. Chapel Hill: Carolina Population Center, 1971.

Boyer, Eunice. "Health Perception in the Elderly: Its Cultural and Social Aspects." *Aging in Culture and Society: Comparative Viewpoints and Strategies,* edited by C.L. Fry. New York: J.F. Bergin, 1980.

Braun, Rudolf. *Industrialisierung und Volksleben.* Zurich: Zurcher Oberland, 1960.

Brim, Orville G., Jr., and Wheeler, Stanton. *Socialization after Childhood.* New York: Wiley, 1966.

Brody, S.J.; Poulshock, S.W.; and Masciocchi, C.F. "The Family Caring Unit: A Major Consideration in Long Term Care." *Journal of Gerontology* 33 (1978).

Brotman, Herman B. *Projections of the Population in the Year 2000.* Administration on Aging. Washington, D.C.: U.S. Government Printing Office, 1973.

———. "Every Tenth American." *Sourcebook on Aging.* Chicago, Ill.: Marquis Academic Media, 1977a.

———. "Life Expectancy: Comparison of National Levels in 1900 and 1974 and Variations in State Levels, 1969-1971." *The Gerontologist* 17 (1) (1977b):12-22

Brown, Paul and Winefield, Gillian. "Some Demographic Measures Applied to Chimbu Census and Field Data." *Oceania* 35 (1965):175-190.

Brownlee, Ann T. *Community, Culture, and Care.* St. Louis: C.V. Mosby, 1978.

Bucher, Rue. "Pathology: A Study of Social Movements within a Profession." *Social Problems* 10 (1962):40-51.

Burch, G.E. "The Special Problems of Heart Disease in Old People." *Geriatrics* 32 (1977):51-54.

Busse, Ewald W. and Pfeiffer, E. *Behavior and Adaptation in Late Life.* Boston, Mass.: Little, Brown & Co., 1969.

Butler, Robert N. *Why Survive: Being Old in America.* San Francisco: Harper and Row, 1975.

Butler, Robert N. and Lewis, Myrna I. *Aging and Mental Health: Positive Psychological Approaches.* St. Louis: C.V. Mosby, 1973.

Byerts, T.O., ed. *Environmental Research and Aging.* Washington, D.C.: Gerontological Society, 1974.

Byrne, Susan. "Arden: An Adult Community." Ph.D. dissertation. University of California, Berkeley, 1971.

Cahalan, Donald, and Cisin, Ira H. "American Drinking Practices: Summary of Findings from a National Probability Sample, I: Extent of Drinking by Population Subgroups." *Quarterly Journal of Studies on Alcohol,* 29 (1968a):130-151.

———. "American Drinking Practices: Summary of Findings from a National Probability Sample, II: Measurement of Massed versus Spaced Drinking." *Quarterly Journal of Studies on Alcohol,* 29 (1968b):642-656.

Cahalan, Donald; Cisin, Ira H.; and Crossley, Helen M. *American Drinking Practices: A National Study of Behavior and Attitudes Related to Alcoholic Beverages.* Washington, D.C.: George Washington University, Social Research Group, 1967.

———. *American Drinking Practices: A National Study of Drinking Behavior and Attitudes.* New Brunswick, N.J.: Rutgers Center of Alcohol Studies, 1969.

Cahalan, Donald; Cisin, Ira H.; Kirsch, A.D.; and Newcomb, C.H. *Behavior and Attitudes Related to Drinking in a Medium-sized Urban Community in New England.* Washington, D.C.: George Washington University, 1965.

Caird, F.T. and Judge, T.G. *Assessment of the Elderly Patient.* Kent, Tenn.: Pilman Publications, 1977.

Camargo, O. and Preston, G.H. "What Happens to Patients Who Are Hospitalized for the First Time When Over Sixty-Five Years of Age?" *American Journal of Psychiatry* 102 (1945):168-173.

Cantor, Marjorie. "Life Space and the Social Support System of the Inner City Elderly of New York." *The Gerontologist* 15 (1975):23-27.

———. "The Configuration and Intensity of the Informal Support System in a New York City Elderly Population: Is Ethnicity a Determining Factor?" Presented at the Annual Gerontological Society Meetings, 1976.

Caplan, Gerald. *Support Systems and Community Mental Health.* New York: Behavioral Publications, 1974.

Carlson, Rick. *The End of Medicine.* New York: John Wiley and Sons, 1975.

Carp, Frances. "The Mobility of Older Slum Dwellers." *The Gerontologist* 12 (1972):56-65.

Carrier, Norman and Hobcraft, John. *Demographic Estimation for Developing Societies: A Manual of Techniques for Detection and Reduction of Errors in Demographic Data.* London: London School of Economics, 1971.

Carruth, Bruce; Williams, Erma Polly; and Heyman, Morton, M. *Alcoholism and Problem Drinking Among Older Persons.* New Brunswick, N.J.: Rutgers Center of Alcohol Studies, 1973.

Cassell, Eric J. "On Educational Changes for the Field of Aging." *The Gerontologist* 12 (1972):251-256.

Chalfont, H.P. and Kwitz, R.A. "Alcoholics and the Sick Role: Assessments by Social Workers." *Journal of Health and Social Behavior* 12 (1971):66-72.

Clark, Margaret. "The Anthropology of Aging, A New Area for Studies of Culture and Personality." *The Gerontologist* 7 (1) (1967a):55-65.

———. "An Anthropological Approach to Aging." In *Culture and Aging,* edited by B.G. Anderson and M. Clark. Springfield: Charles C. Thomas, 1967b.

———. "Patterns of Aging Among the Elderly Poor of the Inner City." *The Gerontologist* 11 (1971):58-66.

———. "An Anthropological View of Retirement." In *Retirement,* edited by Frances M. Carp. New York: Behavioral Publications, 1972a, pp. 117-156.

———. "Cultural Values and Dependency in Later Life." In *Aging and Modernization,* ed. Donald O. Cowgill and Lowell D. Holmes. New York: Appleton-Century-Crofts, 1972b.

———. "Contributions of Cultural Anthropology to the Study of the Aged." In *Cultural Illness and Health: Essays on Human Adaptation,* edited by Laura Nader, and T. Maretzki. Washington, D.C.: American Anthropological Assn., 1973, pp. 78-88.

Clark, Margaret and Anderson, Barbara G. *Culture and Aging: An Anthropological Study of Older Americans.* Springfield: Charles C. Thomas, 1967.

Clark, Margaret and Mendelson, M. "Mexican-American Aged in San Francisco: A Case Description." *The Gerontologist* 9 (1969):90-95.

Coe, Rodney. "Self Conception and Institutionalization." In *Older People and Their Social World,* ed. Arnold Rose and Warren Peterson. Phil.: F.A. Davis, 1965.

———. "Processes in the Development of Established Professions." *Journal of Health and Social Behavior* 11 (1970):59-67.

Cohen, Abner. *Custom and Politics in Urban Africa.* Berkeley: University of California, 1969.

———. *Two-Dimensional Man.* Berkely: University of California Press, 1974.

Collins, Alice and Pancoast, Diane. *Natural Helping Networks.* Washington: National Association of Social Workers, 1976.

Collins, June M. *Valley of the Spirits: The Upper Skagit Indians of Western Washington.* Seattle and London: University of Washington Press, 1974.

Collins, S.D., Trantham, K.S., and Lehman, J.L. *Sickness Experience in Selected Areas of the U.S.: US-HEW-PHS Mono #25.* Washington, D.C.: U.S. Government Printing Office, 1955.

Colson, Elizabeth and Scudder, Thayer. "Elderly Gwembe Tongans." In *Other Ways of Growing Old,* edited by P. Amoss and S. Harrell. Stanford: Stanford University Press, 1981.

Conrad, Peter. "The Discovery of Hyperkinesis: Notes on the Medicalization of Deviant Behavior." *Social Problems* 23 (1976):12-21.

Cool, Linda. "Ethnicity and Aging: Continuity through Change for Elderly Corsicans." In *Aging in Culture and Society: Comparative Viewpoints and Strategies,* edited by C.L. Fry. New York: J.F. Bergin, 1980.

Cooper, J.A.D. "Institutional Response to Expectations for Health Care." *Journal of Medical Education* 44 (1969):31-35.

Costello, J. P. and Tanaka, G. "Mortality and Morbidity in Long-Term Institutional Care of the Aged." *Journal of the American Geriatric Society* 9 (1961):959-963.

Cowgill, Donald O. "A Theoretical Framework for Considerations of Data on Aging." Paper presented to the Society for Applied Anthropology, Miami, Florida, 1971.

———. "Aging in American Society." In *Aging and Modernization,* edited by D.O. Cowgill and L.D. Holmes. New York: Appleton-Century-Crofts, 1972a.

———. "A Theory of Aging in Cross-Cultural Perspective." In *Aging and Modernization,* edited by D.O. Cowgill and L.D. Holmes. New York: Appleton-Century-Crofts, 1972b.

Cowgill, Donald O. and Holmes, Lowell, D., eds. *Aging and Modernization.* New York: Appleton-Century-Crofts, 1972a.

———. "The Theory in Review." In *Aging and Modernization,* edited by D.O. Cowgill and L.D. Holmes. New York: Appleton-Century-Crofts, 1972b.

Critchfield, Richard. "Revolution of the Village." *Human Behavior* 8 (5) (1979):18-27.

Conkhite, L.W. "Control and Regulation of the Health Industry." *Journal of Medical Education* 49 (1974):14-18.

Crowe, Patricia W. *Good Fences Make Good Neighbors: Social Networks at Three Levels of Urbanization in Tirol, Austria.* (Unpublished Ph.D. dissertation). Stanford University: Department of Anthropology, 1978.

Cumming, Elaine and Henry, William E. *Growing Old: The Process of Disengagement.* New York: Basic Book, 1961.

Cutler, Neal E. and Harootyan, R.A. "Demography of the Aged." In *Aging,* eds. Woodruff D.S. and Birren, J. New York: D. Van Nostrand, 1975, pp. 31-69.

Davis, John W., and Gibbin, Marilyn J. "An Areawide Examination of Nursing Home Use, Misuse, and Non-Use." *American Journal of Health* 61 (June 1971):1146-1155.

Davis-Friedman, Deborah, *Old People and Their Families in the People's Republic of China.* Unpublished Ph.D. dissertation. Boston University, 1979.

Delora, J.R. and Moses, D.Y. "Specialty Preferences of Nursing Students." *Nursing Research* 18 (1969):137-144.

Devereaux, Edward C., Jr.; Bronfenbrenner, Urie; and Suci, George J. "Patterns of Parent Behaviour in the United States of America and the Federal Republic of Germany: A Cross-National Comparison." *International Social Sciences Journal* 14 (1962).

Douvenmeuhle, R.H. "Aging Versus Illness." In *Normal Aging II,* edited by E. Palmore. Durham, N.C.: Duke University Press, 1974.

Dowd, James J. "Aging as Exchange: A Preface to Theory." *Journal of Gerontology* 30 (1975):584-595.

Dyson-Hudson, Neville. "The Karimojong Age System." *Ethnology* 2 (1963):353-401.

———. *Karimojong Politics.* London: Oxford University Press, 1966.

Earley, L. William and von Mering, O. "Growing Old the Outpatient Way." *American Journal of Psychiatry* 125 (1969):963-967.

Eckert, J. Kevin. *The Unseen Elderly.* San Diego: Companile Press, 1979a.

———. "Urban Renewal and Redevelopment: High Risk for the Marginally Subsistent Elderly." *The Gerontologist* 19 (1979b):496-502.

Edwards, C.D. "A Candid Look at Health Manpower Problems." *Journal of Medical Education* 49 (1974):19-26.

Ehrenreich, Barbara and Ehrenreich, John. "Health Care and Social Control." *Social Policy* 5 (1974):26-40.

Ehrlich, Phyllis. "Study of the St. Louis 'Invisible' Elderly Needs and Characteristics of Aged 'Single Room Occupancy' Downtwon Hotel Residents." (Revised Report). St. Louis: Institute of Applied Gerontology, St. Louis University, 1976.

Eisdorfer, Carl. "Observations on the Psychopharmacology of the Aged." *Journal of the American Geriatrics Society* 23 (1975):53-57.

Eisenstadt, S.N. "African Age Groups." *Africa* 24 (1954):100-113.

———. *From Generation to Generation: Age Groups and Social Structure.* New York: Free Press, 1956.

Eister, Allan. "A Theory of Cults." *Journal for the Scientific Study of Religion* 11 (1972):310-333.

Ekeh, Peter P. *Social Exchange Theory: The Two Traditions.* Cambridge: Harvard University Press, 1974.

Elder, Glen H., Jr. "Age Differentiation and Life Course." *Annual Review of Sociology*, Vol. 1. Palo Alto: Annual Reviews, Inc., 1975.

Ellinson, D. "Work, Retirement, and the Sick Role." *The Gerontologist* 8 (1968):189-192.

Elmendorf, William W. and Kroeber, A.L. *The Structure of Twona Culture with Notes on Yurok Culture.* Pullman: Washington State University, 1960.

Emerson, Richard M. "Power-Dependence Relations." *American Sociological Review* 27 (1962):37-41.

———. "Exchange Theory, Parts 1 & 2." In *Sociological Theories in Progress,* Vol. II, ed. Joseph Berger, Morris Zelditch, Jr. and Bo Anderson. Boston: Houghton Mifflin, 1972.

Epstein, A.L. "The Network and Urban Social Organization." In *Social Networks in Urban Situations,* edited by J. Clyde Mitchell. Manchester: Manchester University Press, 1969, pp. 77-116.

Erickson, Rosemary and Eckert, Kevin. "The Elderly Poor in Downtown San Diego Hotels." *The Gerontologist* 17 (1977):440-446.

Erikson, Erik. *Identity and the Life Cycle.* New York: International University Press, 1959.

Estes, C.L. "Barriers to Effective Community Planning for the Elderly." *The Gerontologist* 13 (1973):178-183.

Evans-Pritchard. E.E. "The Nuer: Age Sets." *Sudan Notes and Records* 19 (1936):233-269.

———. *The Nuer.* Oxford:·Oxford University Press, 1940.

Fabrega, Horacio, Jr. *Disease and Social Behavior: An Interdisciplinary Perspective.* Cambridge: MIT Press, 1974.

Feeney, Griffith. *Deomographic Concepts and Techniques for the Study of Small Populations.* Honolulu, Hawaii: East West Population Institute Reprint No. 66, East-West Center, 1975.

Fennell, Valerie. "The Hierarchical Aspects of Age Relations in Curlew Point." Unpublished Ph.D. dissertation. University of North Carolina, Chapel Hill, 1974.

———. "Age Relations and Rapid Change in a Small Town." *Gerontologist* 16 (1977):405-411.

Firth, Raymond. "Family and Kinship in Industrial Society." In *Development of Industrial Societies,* edited by Paul Holmos, University of Keele, 1964.

Fischer, David H. *Growing Old in America.* New York: Oxford University Press, 1978.

Fischer, Wolfram. "Rural Industrialization and Population Change." *Comparative Studies in Society and History* 15 (1973).

Fisher, Claude et al. *Networks and Places.* New York: Free Press, 1977.

Foner, Anne. "Ascribed and Achieved Bases of Stratification." In *Annual Review of Sociology,* Vol. 5, edited by Alex Inkeles, James Coleman, and Ralph H. Turner. Palo Alto: Annual Reviews, Inc., 1979, pp. 219-242.

Foner, Anne and Kertzer, David I. "Transitions over the Life Course: Lessons from Age-Set Societies." *American Journal of Sociology* 83 (1978):1081-1104.

———. "Intrinsic and Extrinsic Sources of Change in Life-Course Transitions." In *Aging from Birth to Death,* edited by Matilda White Riley. Boulder: Westview Press, 1979, pp. 121-136.

Food and Drug Administration. *Task Force on Prescription Drugs.* Washington, D.C.: U.S. Government Printing Office, 1968.

Fortes, Meyer. *The Web of Kinship among the Tallensi.* London: Oxford University Press, 1949.

Fosbrooke, H.A. "An Administrative Survey of the Masai Social System." *Tanganyika Notes and Records* 26 (1948):1-50.

Foucault, M. *Madness and Civilization.* New York: Pantheon, 1965.

Fowles, D.G. *Some Prospects for the Future Elderly Population.* U.S. Department of Health and Welfare Publication No. (OHDS) 78-20288. Washington, D.C.: U.S. Government Office, 1978.

Fox, Renee C. "The Medicalization and Demedicalization of American Society." *Daedalus* 106 (1977):9-22.

Friedman, Elizabeth. *Crest Street: A Family/Community Impact Statement.* Durham, N.C.: Duke University Policy Paper, 1978.

Freidson, Elliot. *Profession of Medicine.* New York: Dodd, Mead and Co., 1970.

Fry, Christine L. "The Ages of Adulthood: A Question of Numbers." *Journal of Gerontology* 31 (1976):170-177.

———. "Community at Commodity: The Age Graded Case." *Human Organization* 36 (1977):115-123.

———. "Structural Conditions Affecting Community Foundation among the Aged." In *The Ethnography of Old Age,* ed. J. Keith. Special Issue of *Anthropological Quarterly,* 52 (1) (1979):7-18.

———. "Cultural Dimensions of Age: A Multidimensional Scaling Analysis." In *Aging in Culture and Society: Comparative Viewpoints and Strategies,* edited by C.L. Fry. New York: J.F. Bergin, 1980a.

———. "Toward an Anthropology of Aging." In *Aging in Culture and Society: Comparative Viewpoints and Strategies,* edited by C.L. Fry. New York: J.F. Bergin, 1980b.

Fry, Christine, ed. *Aging in Culture and Society: Comparative Viewpoints and Strategies.* New York: J.F. Bergin, 1980.

Fry. L. "Medical Care Systems: Comparative International Characteristics." *Journal of Medical Education* 48 (12), Part 2 (1973):31-38.

Fuchs, V. *Who Shall Live? Health Economics and Social Change.* New York, N.Y.: Basic Books, 1975.

Fuller, Charles E. "Aging among Southern African Bantu." In *Aging and Modernization,* edited by D.O. Cowgill and L.D. Holmes. New York: Meredith Corporation, 1972.

Geertz, Clifford. "Person, Time and Conduct in Bali; An Essay in Cultural Analysis." *Cultural Report Series,* No. 14. New Haven, Conn.: Yale University South East Asia Studies, 1966.

———. "Ritual and Social Change: A Javanese Example." In *The Interpretation of Cultures: Selected Essays.* New York: Basic Books, 1973.

Gessain, Monique. "Les Classes d'Age chez les Vassari d'Etyolo (Senegal Oriental)." In *Classes et Association d'Age en Afrique de l'ouest,* edited by Denise Paulme. Paris: Plon, 1971, pp. 157-184.

Gillis, Sr. M. "Attitudes of Nursing Personnel Toward the Aged." *Nursing Research* 22 (1973):517-520.

Giraldo, Z.I., and Weatherford, Jack M. *Life Cycle and the American Family.* Durham, N.C.: Duke University Policy Paper, 1978.

Glad, DD. "Attitudes and Experiences of American-Jewish and American-Irish Male Youth as Related to Differences in Adult Rates of Inebriety." *Quarterly Journal of Studies on Alcohol,* 8 (1947):406-472.

Gladne, J.R. "The Role of the Physician in the Nursing Home: Past, Present and Future." *Journal of the American Geriatrics Society* 21 (1973):444-449.

———. *Medical Problems of the Elderly.* Medical Services Administration, U.S. Department of Health, Education and Welfare. Washington, D.C.: U.S. Government Printing Office, 1975.

Glascock, Anthony P. and Feinman, Susan. "A Holocultural Analysis of Old Age." *Comparative Social Research* 3, 1980.

Glaser, B.G. and Strauss, A.L. *Awareness of Dying.* Chicago, Ill.: Aldine Press, 1965.

———. *Theory of Status Passage.* Chicago, Ill.: Aldine Press, 1971.

Glazier, William H. "The Task of Medicine." *Scientific American* 228 (1973):13-17.

Glick, Paul. "The Family Cycle." *American Sociological Review* 12 (1947).

Glick, Paul, and Parke, Robert, Jr. "New Approaches to Studying the Life Cycle of the Family." *Demography* 2 (1965).

Goldsmith, Jack and Goldsmith, Sharon S. "Crime and the Elderly: An Overview." In *Crime and the Elderly: Challenge and Response,* ed. Jack Goldsmith and Sharon S. Goldsmith. Lexington, Mass: D.C. Heath and Co., 1976.

Goldstein, S. "The Biology of Aging." *New England Journal of Medicine* 285 (1971): 1120-1129.

Goodale, Jane. *Tiwi Wives: A Study of the Women of Melville Island North Australia.* Seattle: University of Washington Press, 1971.

Goode, William J. *World Revolution and Family Patterns.* New York: The Free Press of Glencoe, 1963.

Goodwin, Granville, *The Social Organization of the Western Apache.* Chicago, Ill.: University of Chicago, Press, 1942.

Goody, Jack, ed. *The Development Cycle in Domestic Groups.* Chicago: Markham, 1958.

———. "Aging in Non-Industrial Societies." In *Handbook of Aging and the Social Sciences,* edited by R.H. Binstock and E. Shanas. New York: Van Nostrand Reinhold Co., 1976.

Granick, Ruth and Nahemow, Lucille. "Pre-admission Isolation as a Factor in Adjustment to an Old Age Home." In *Psychopathology of Aging,* edited by Paul Hoch and Joseph Zubin. New York: Grune and Stratton, 1961, pp. 285-392.

Granick, S. and Patterson, R.D., eds. *Human Aging II: An 11-year Followup Biomedical and Behavioral Study.* (Publ. # (HSM) 71-9037). Washington, D.C.: U.S. Government Printing Office, 1971.

Greenberg, Selig. *The Quality of Mercy.* New York, N.Y.: Atheneum, 1971.

Griffin, Joyce. "A Cross-Cultural Investigation of Behavioral Changes at Menopause." *Social Science Journal* 14 (2) (1977):49-55.

Gubrium, J.F., ed. *Late Life: Communities and Environmental Policy.* Springfield, Ill.: Charles C. Thomas, 1974.

———. *Living and Dying at Murray Manor.* New York: St. Martins Press, 1975.

Guemple, Lee. "Human Resource Management: The Dilemma of the Aging Eskimo." *Sociological Symposium* 2 (1969):59-74.

Gulliver, P.H. "The Age Set Organization of the Jie Tribe." *Journal of the Royal Anthropological Institute* 83 (1953):147-168.

———. "The Turkana Age Organization." *American Anthropologist* 60 (1958):900-922.

———. *Social Control in an African Society.* London: Routledge and Kegan Paul, 1963.

———. "Age Differentiation." In *International Encyclopedia of the Social Sciences,* edited by David L. Sills, Vol. 1. New York: Macmillan and Free Press, 1968, pp. 157-162.

Gunter, L. "Students' Attitudes Toward Geriatric Nursing." *Nursing Outlook* 19 (1971):466-469.

———. "Biological Aging: An Essentially Normal Process." *JAMA* 230 (1974):1651-1652.

Gunther, Erma. "An Analysis of the First Salmon Ceremony." *American Anthropologist* 28 (1926):605-617.

———. *A Further Analysis of the First Salmon Ceremony.* University of Washington Publications in Anthropology 2 (No. 5):129-73. Seattle: University of Washington Press, 1928.

Gutmann, David L. "An Exploration of Ego Configurations in Middle and Late Life." In *Personality in Middle and Late Life,* edited by B.L. Neugarten. New York: Atherton Press, 1964.

———. "The Country of Old Men: Cross-Cultural Studies in the Psychology of Later Life." In *Occasional Papers in Gerontology,* ed. W. Donahue. Ann Arbor: Institute of Gerontology, University of Michigan, 1969.

———. "Alternatives to Disengagement: Aging among the Highland Druze." In *Culture and Personalities: Contemporary Readings,* edited by Robert LeVine. Chicago, Ill.: University of Chicago, 1976, pp. 232-245.

Hall, G.H. et al. *Guide to Development of Protective Services for Older People.* (National Council on the Aging) Springfield, Ill.: Charles C. Thomas, 1973.

Hall, M.R.P. "Adverse Drug Reaction in the Elderly." *Gerontological Clinica* 16 (1974):144-150.

Hallowell, A. Irving. "Review of Leo Simmons' The Role of the Aged in Primitive Society." *Annals of the American Academy* 244 (1946):229.

Hallpike, C.R. *The Konso of Ethiopia: A Study of the Values of a Cushitic People.* Oxford: Clarendon Press, 1972.

Hamer, John H. "Aging in a Gerontocratic Society. The Sidamo of Southwest Ethiopia." In *Aging and Modernization,* edited by D.O. Cowgill and L.D. Holmes. New York: Appleton-Century-Crofts, 1972.

Hammerman, H. "Health Services: Success and Failure in Reaching Older Adults." *American Journal of Public Health* 64 (1974):253-56.

Harlan, William. "Social Status of the Aged in Indian Villages." *Vita Humana* 7 (1964):239-252.

Hart, C.W.M. and Pilling, Arnold. *The Tiwi of North Australia.* New York: Holt, Reinhart and Winston, 1960.

Hasenfeld, Y., English, R. *Human Service Organizations.* Ann Arbor: University of Michigan Press, 1975.

Hauser, Philip M. "Aging and World-Wide Population Change." In *Handbook of Aging and the Social Sciences,* edited by Robert H. Binstock and Ethel Shanas. New York: Van Nostrand Reinhold, 1976.

Havighurst, Robert J. "The Future Aged: The Use of Time and Money." *The Gerontologist* 15 (1975):10-15.

Havighurst, R.J. and Albrecht, Ruth. *Older People.* New York: Longmans, Green, and Company, 1953.

Hayner, Norman. *Hotel Life.* Chapel Hill: University of North Carolina Press, 1936.

Hemminki, E. "Review of Literature on the Factors affecting Drug Prescribing." *Social Science and Medicine* 9 (1975):111-115.

Hendel-Sebestyen, Geselle. "Role Diversity: Toward the Development of Community in a Total Institutional Setting." In *the Ethnography of Old Age,* edited by J. Keith. Special Issue of *Anthropological Quarterly,* 1979.

Henry, Jules. *Culture Against Man.* New York: Random House, 1963.

———. *On Sham, Vulnerability and Other Forms of Self-Destruction.* London: U.K.: Penguin Books, 1973.

Henry, W.E. "The Role of Work in Structuring Life Cycles." *Human Development* 14 (1971).

Hentig, Hans von. *The Criminal and His Victim.* New Haven: Yale University Press, 1948.

Hertz, E. and Hutheesing, O. "At the Edge of Society: The Nominal Culture of Urban Hotel Isolates." *Urban Anthropology* 4 (1975):317-332.

Hess, Beth. "Friendship." In *Aging and Society: A Sociology of Age of Stratification,* edited by Matilda Riley, Marilyn Johnson, and Anne Foner, Vol. 3. New York: Russell Sage Foundation, 1972.

Hess, Thomas. *Puget Salish Dictionary.* Seattle: University of Washington Press, 1976.

Higginson, J. "Disease Priorities in Medical Education." *Journal of Medical Education* 48 (12), Part 2 (1973):95-101.

Hippler, Arthur. "Fusion and Frustration: Dimensions in the Cross-Cultural Ethnopsychology of Suicide." *American Anthropologist* 71 (6) (1969):1074-1087.

Hirschild, Larry. "Social Policy and the Life Cycle." *Social Science Review,* 1977.

Hochschild, Arlie. *The Unexpected Community.* Englewood Cliffs: Prentice-Hall, 1973.

Hodkinson, H.M. "Biomedical Side Effects of Drugs in the Elderly." *Gerontological Clinica* 16 (1974):175-178.

Holding, E.M. "Some Preliminary Notes on Meru Age-Grades." *Man* 42 (31) (1942):58-65.

Holmberg, Allan. *Nomads of the Long Bow: The Siriono of Eastern Bolivia.* Garden City: Natural History Press, 1969.

Holmes, Lowell D. "The Role and Status of the Aged in a Changing Samoa." In *Aging and Modernization,* edited by D.O. Cowgill and L.D. Holmes. New York: Appleton-Century-Crofts, 1972.

———. "Trends in Anthropological Gerontology: From Simmons to the Seventies." *International Journal of Aging and Human Development* 7 (3) (1976):211-220.

———. "Anthropology and Age: An Assessment." In *Aging in Culture and Society: Comparative Viewpoints and Strategies,* edited by C.L. Fry. New York: J.F. Bergin, 1980.

Holmes, Thomas H., and Rahe, Richard H. "The Social Readjustment Rating Scale." *Journal of Psychosomatic Research* 2 (1967):213-218.

Homans, George C. *Social Behavior: Its Elementary Forms.* New York: Harcourt, 1961.

Howell, Nancy. "Toward a Uniformitarian Theory of Human Paleodemography." In *The Demographic Evolution of Human Populations,* edited by R.H. Ward and Kenneth M. Weiss, London: Academic Press, 1976.

Huntingford, G.W.B. *The Nandi of Kenya.* London: Routledge and Kegan Paul, 1953.

Ikels, Charlotte. "The Coming of Age in Chinese Society: Traditional Patterns and Contemporary Hong Kong." In *Aging in Culture and Society: Comparative Viewpoints and Strategies,* edited by C.L. Fry. New York: J.F. Bergin, 1980.

Illich, Ivan. *Medical Nemesis: The Expropriation of Health.* New York: Pantheon, 1976.

Institute of Gerontology. "No Longer Young: The Older Woman in America." Workgroup Reports, 26th Conference on Aging. Ann Arbor: University of Michigan, 1974.

Jackson, Jacqueline J. "Negro Aged: Toward Needed Research in Social Gerontology." *The Gerontologist II* 2 (1971):52-57.

Jacobs, Alan H. "Masai Age-Groups and Some Functional Tasks." Proceedings of Conference held at the East African Institute of Social Research, 1958, Makerere College, Kampala, Uganda.

Jacobs, Jerry. "Fun City, An Ethnographic Study of a Retirement Community." New York: Holt, Rinehart and Winston, Inc., 1974.

Jaeger, Dorothea and Simmons, Leo W. *The Aged Ill: Coping with Problems in Geriatric Care.* New York: Appleton-Century-Crofts, 1970.

Jeffers, Frances, C. "You and the Aging in Your Community." *The Gerontologist* 10 (1970):57-59.

Jellinek, E.M. "Death from Alcoholism in the United States in 1940: A Statistical Analysis." *Quarterly Journal of Studies on Alcohol* 3 (1942):465-494.

Jessor, R.T.; Graves, T.; Hanson, R.; and Jessor, S.L. *Society, Personality and Deviant Behavior: A Study of a Tri-Ethnic Community.* New York: Holt, Rinehart, and Winston, Inc., 1968.

Jilek, Wolfgang. *Salish Indian Mental Health and Culture Change.* Toronto and Montreal: Holt, Rinehart and Winston of Canada, 1974.

Johnson, L.A., and Goodrich, C.H. *Use of Alcohol by Persons 65 Years and Over, Upper-East Side of Manhattan.* Report to the National Institute on Alcohol Abuse and Alcoholism, 1974.

Johnson, Sheila. *Idle Haven: Community Building Among the Working-Class Retired.* Berkeley: University of California Press, 1971.

Jonas, Karen. "Factors in Development of Community in Age-Segregated Housing." In the *Ethnography of Old Age,* edited by J. Keith. Special Issue of *Anthropological Quarterly,* 52 (1) (1979).

Jonas, Karen and Wellin, Edward. "Dependency and Reciprocity: Home Health Aid in An Elderly Population." In *Aging in Culture and Society: Comparative Viewpoints and Strategies,* edited by C.L. Fry. New York: Praeger J.F. Bergin, 1980.

Jones, G.I. "Ibo Age Organization, with Special Reference to the Cross River and Northeastern Ibo." *Journal of the Royal Anthropological Institute of Great Britain and Ireland* 92 (1962):191-211.

Kagan, Dianne. "Activity and Aging in a Columbian Peasant Village." In *Aging in Culture and Society: Comparative Viewpoints and Strategies,* edited by C.L. Fry. New York: J.F. Bergin, 1980.

Kahana, Eva. "The Humane Treatment of Old People in Institutions." *The Gerontologist* 13 (1973):282-289.

Kahn, R. "Excess Disabilities in the Aged." In *Readings in Aging and Death: Contemporary Perspectives,* edited by S. Zarit. New York: Harper and Row (1977): 228-229.

Kahn, R.L. "The Mental Health System and the Future Aged." *The Gerontologist* 15 (February 1975 Supplement):24-31.

Kalish, R.A. and Yuen, S. "Americans of East Asian Ancestry: Aging and the Aged." *The Gerontologist II* 2 (1971):36-47.

Kandel, Randy F. and Heider, Marion. "Friendship and Factionalism in a Triethnic Housing Complex in North Miami." In *The Ethnography of Old Age,* edited by J. Keith. Special Issue of *Anthropological Quarterly* (52) (1) (1979).

Kane, Robert L. and Kane, Rosalie A. *Long-Term Care in Six Countries: Implications for the United States.* Washington, D.C.: U.S. Department of Health, Education, and Welfare Public Health Service, National Institutes of Health, No. (NIH) 76-1207, 1976.

Kastenbaum, L. and Aisenburg, R. *The Psychology of Death.* New York: Springer, Inc., 1972.

Kastenbaum, Robert, and Candy, Sandra E. "The Four Percent Fallacy: A Methodological and Empirical Critique of Extended Care Facility Population Statistics." *Aging and Human Development* 4 (Winter 1973):15-21.

Keith, Jennie. See also Ross, Jennie Keith.

Keith, Jennie. "The Ethnography of Old Age: Introduction." *Anthropological Quarterly* 52 (1979):1-6.

———. "Old Age and Community Creation." In *Aging in Culture and Society: Comparative Viewpoints and Strategies,* edited by C.L. Fry. New York: J.F. Bergin, 1980a.

———. " 'The Best is Yet to Be': Towards an Anthropology of Age." In *Annual Review of Anthropology, Vol. 9.* Edited by B. J. Siegel. Palo Alto: Annual Reviews, Inc. 1980b.

Keith, Jennie, ed. "The Ethnography of Old Age." *Anthropological Quarterly* 52 (1) (1979).

Kent, Donald P. "The Elderly in Minority Groups: Variant Patterns of Aging." *The Gerontologist II* 2 (1971):48-51.

Kenyatta, Jomo. *Facing Mount Kenya: The Tribal Life of the Gikuyu.* London: Secker and Warburg, 1938.

Kerns, Virginia. Daughters Bring In: Ceremonial and Social Organization of the Black Carib of Belize. Unpublished Ph.D. dissertation. University of Illinois, Urbana, 1977.

———. "Aging and Mutual Support Relations among the Black Carib." In *Aging in Culture and Society: Comparative Viewpoints and Strategies,* edited by C.L. Fry. New York: J.F. Bergin, 1980.

Kertzer, David I. "Theoretical Developments in the Study of the Age-Group Systems." *American Ethnologist* 5 (1978):368-374.

Kertzer, David I., and Madison, Oker B.B. "African Age-Set Systems and Political Organization: The Latuka of Southern Sudan." *Uomo,* forthcoming.

Kew, J.E.M. "Coast Salish Ceremonial Life: Status and Identity in a Modern Village." Ph.D. dissertation. University of Washington, 1970.

Kiefer, C.W. "Notes on Anthropology and the Minority Elderly." *The Gerontologist* 11 (1971):94-98, Part 2.

———. "Lessons from the Issei." In *Late Life: Communities and Environmental Policy,* edited by J. Gubrium. Springfield: Charles C. Thomas, 1974a.

———. *Changing Cuptures, Changing Lives.* San Francisco: Jossey-Bass, 1974.

Killian, Eldon C. "Effect of Geriatric Transfers on Mortality Rates." *Social Work* 15 (1970):19-26.

Killworth, Peter and Bernard, H. Russell. "Informant Accuracy in Social Network Data." *Human Organization* 35 (1976):35-41.

Kinkade, Dale, Personal Communication, 1976.

Kirk, Lorraine and Burton, Michael. "Meaning and Context: A Study of Contextual Shifts in Meaning of Masai Personality Descriptions." *American Ethnologist* 4 (1977):734-761.

Kittrie, N. *The Right To Be Different.* Baltimore: Johns Hopkins Press, 1971.

Kleemeier, R. "Moosehaven: Congregate Living in a Community of the Retired." *American Journal of Sociology* 59 (1954):347-51.

Kleh, J. "When to Institutionalize the Elderly." *Hospital Practice* 12 (1977):121-134.

Knowles, J.H. "The World of Health and the American Physician." *Journal of Medical Education* 49 (1974):50-56.

———. "Introduction." In *Daedalus: Journal of the American Academy of Arts and Science* 106 (Winter 1977):1-7.

Knowles, John H., ed. *Doing Better and Feeling Worse.* New York: Norton, 1977.

Knupfer, Genevieve, and Room, Rubin. "Age, Sex and Social Class as Factors in the Amount of Drinking in a Metropolitan Community." *Social Forces* 12 (1964):224-240.

Komorovsky, Myra. *Blue Collar Marriage.* New York: Random House, 1964.

Kosberg, J.I. "Differences in Proprietary Institutions Caring for Affluent and Nonaffluent Elderly." *The Gerontologist* 13 (1973):299-304.

Kovar, M.O. "Health of the Elderly and Use of Health Services." *Public Health Reports* 92 (1977):9-17.

Kramer, M., et al. "Patterns of Use of Psychiatric Facilities by the Aged: Past, Present and Future." In *Psychology of Adult Development and Aging,* edited by Eisdorfer, Carl. Washington, D.C.: American Psychological Assoc., 1973.

Krasner, M. and Muller, C. "Manpower in Obstetrics-Gynecology in a Period of Declining Birth Rate." *Medical Care* 12 (1974):1031-1037.

Kuhn, Thomas S. *The Structure of Scientific Revolutions.* Chicago: University of Chicago Press, 1970.

Kurth, Suzanne B. "Friendship and Friendly Relations." In *Social Relationships,* edited by George J. McCall et al. Chicago: Aldine Publishing Co., 1970.

Kurtzman, J. and Gordon, P. *No More Dying.* New York: Dell, 1976.

La Fontaine, J.S., ed. *Sex and Age As Principles of Social Differentiation.* New York: Academic Press, 1978.

Lally, Maureen et al. "Older Women in Single Room Occupant (SRO) Hotels: A Seattle Profile." *The Gerontologist* 19 (1979): 67-73.

Lambert, H.E. "The Use of Indigenous Authorities in Tribal Administration: Studies of the Meru of Kenya Colony." Communication #16, School of African Studies, University of Capetown, 1947.

———. *Kikuyu Social and Political Institutions.* London: Oxford University Press, 1956.

Lomouse, Annette. "Family Roles of Women: A German Example." *Journal of Marriage and the Family* 31 (1969).

Lamy, P.P. and Kitter, M.F. "The Geriatric Patient: Age-Dependent Physiologic and Pathologic Changes." *Journal of the American Geriatric Society,* 1971.

Laslett, Peter. *Family Life and Illicit Love in Earlier Generations.* New York: Cambridge University Press, 1977.

Laughlin, Charles D., Jr. and Laughlin, Elizabeth R. "Age Generations and Political Process in So." *Africa* 44 (1974): 266-279.

Lawton, A.H. "The Role of Medical Education in Gerontology." *Journal of the American Geriatrics Society* 17 (1969): 230-234.

Lawton, M. Powell. "Social Ecology and the Health of Older People." *American Journal of Public Health.* 64 (1974): 257-60.

Lawton, M. Powell and Kleban, Morton. "The Aged Resident of the Inner City." *The Gerontologist* (1971): 277-283.

Lawton, M. Powell, Kleban, Morton, and Singer, Maurice. "The Aged Jewish Person and the Slum Environment." *Journal of Gerontology* 26 (1971): 231-239.

Learoyd, B.M. "Psychotropic Drugs and the Elderly Patient." *Medical Journal of Australia* 1 (1972): 1131-1133.

Legesse, Asmarom. *Gada.* New York: Free Press, 1973.

———. "Age Sets and Retirement Communities." In the *Ethnography of Old Age,* edited by J. Keith. Special Issue of *Anthropological Quarterly* 52 (1): (1979).

Lemon, Bruce, Bengston, Vern and Peterson, James. "An Exploration of the Activity Theory of Aging: Activity Types and Life Satisfaction Among In-Movers to a Retirement Community." *Journal of Gerontology* 27 (1972): 511-523.

Leonard, O.E. "The Older Rural Spanish-Speaking People of the Southwest." In *Older Rural Americans: A Sociological Perspective,* edited by E.G. Youmans. Lexington: University of Kentucky Press, 1967.

Levin, G. and Roberts, E. *The Dynamics of Human Service Delivery.* Cambridge, Mass.: Ballinger Publishing Co., 1976.

LeVine, Robert. "Intergenerational Tensions and Extended Family Structure in Africa." In *Social Structure and the Family,* edited by E. Shanas and G. Streib. Englewood Cliffs: Prentice Hall, 1965.

———. "Adulthood and Aging in Cross-Cultural Perspective." *Items* 31/32 (1978): 1-5.

Levinson Gerontological Policy Institute. *Alternatives to Nursing Home Care: A Proposal.* Washington, D.C.: Government Printing Office, 1971.

Levi-Strauss, Claude. *The Raw and the Cooked.* New York and Evanston: Harper and Row, 1970.

Levy, J.E. "The Older American Indian." In *Older Rural Americans: A Sociological Perspective,* edited by E.G. Youmans. Lexington: University of Kentucky Press, 1967.

Linton, Ralph. "Age and Sex Categories." *American Sociological Review* 7 (1942): 589-603.

Lipman, A. and Sterne, R.S. "Aging in the United States: Ascription of a Terminal Sick Role. *Sociology and Social Research* 53 (1968): 194-203.

Litman, T.J. "Health Care and the Family: A Three Generational Study." *Health Care* 9 (1971): 67-81.

Lomax, Allan and Arensberg, Conrad. "A Worldwide Evolutionary Classification of Cultures by Subsistence Systems." *Current Anthropology* 18 (1977): 659-708.

Loomis, A.L. "The Climate and Environment Best Suited to Old Age in Health and Disease." *The Medical News* 53 (1888): 345-348.

Lopata, Helena Z. "Role Changes in Widowhood: A World Perspective." In *Aging and Modernization,* edited by D.O. Cowgill and L.D. Holmes. New York: Appleton-Century-Crofts, 1972.

———. *Widowhood in An American City.* Cambridge: Schenkman Publishing Co., 1973.

———. "Support Systems of Elderly: Chicago of the 1970's." *The Gerontologist* 15 (1975): 35-41.

Losch, C. "Aging in a Culture without a Future." *Hastings Center Report* 5 (1977): 42-44.

Lowenthal, Marjorie. "Social Isolation and Mental Illness in Old Age." *American Sociological Review* 29 (1964): 54-70.

———. *Four Stages of Life.* San Francisco: Jossey-Bass, 1975.

Lowenthal, Marjorie and Haven, Clayton. "Interaction and Adaptation, Intimacy: A Critical Variable." *American Sociological Review* 33 (1968): 20-50.

Lowenthal, Marjorie and Robinson, Betsy. "Social Networks and Isolation." In *Handbook of Aging and the Social Sciences,* edited by Robert Binstock and Ethel Shanas. New York: Van Nostrand Reinhold, (1976): 432-456.

Lowie, Robert. "Plains Indians Age-Societies." New York American Museum of Natural History Anthropological Papers, 1916.

Lowy, Louis. "Models for Organization of Services to the Aging." *Aging and Human Development* 1 (1970): 21-36.

Lozier, John and Althouse, R. "Social Enforcement of Behavior Toward Elders in an Appalachian Mountain Settlement." *The Gerontologist* 14 (1974): 69-80.

Luft, H.S., Hershey, J.C., and Morrell, J. "Factors Affecting the Use of Physician Services in the Rural Community." *American Journal of Public Health* 66 (1976): 865-871.

Lupri, Eugen. "Contemporary Authority Patterns in the West German Family: A Study in Cross-National Validation." *Journal of Marriage and Family* 31 (1969).

Maduro, Renaldo. "Artistic Creativity and Aging in India." *International Journal of Aging and Human Development* 5 (1974): 303-329.

Malinowski, Bronislaw. *Argonauts of the Western Pacific.* London: Routledge and Kegan Paul, 1922.

Manard, Barbara B., Kart, Cary S., and van Gils, Dirk W.L. *Old Age Institutions.* Lexington, Mass.: Lexington Books, 1975.

Markson, Elizabeth. "A Hiding Place to Die." *Transaction* 21 (1971): 1-5.

Mauss, Marcel. *The Gift: Forms and Functions of Exchange in Archaic Societies.* Glencoe, Ill.: Free Press, 1925.

Maxwell, Milton. "Drinking Behavior in the State of Washington." *Quarterly Journal of Studies on Alcohol* 13 (1952): 219-239.

Maxwell, Robert J. "The Changing Status of Elderly in Polynesian Society." *Aging and Human Development* 1 (1970): 127-46.

Maxwell, Robert J. and Silverman, Phillip. "Information and Esteem." *Aging and Human Development* 1 (1970a): 361-392.

———. "Information and Esteem: Cultural Considerations in the Treatment of the Aged." In *Human Aging and Dying,* edited by R.J. Maxwell and W.H. Watson. New York: St. Martin's Press. 1970b.

Mayer, A.J. "Graying America." *Newsweek* 89 (1977): 50-63.

McGough, James P. *Marriage and Adoption in Chinese Society with Special Reference to Customary Law.* Unpublished Ph.d. dissertation. Michigan State University, 1976.

McKain, Warner C. "The Aged in the U.S.S.R." In *Aging and Modernization,* edited by D.O. Cowgill and L.D. Holmes. New York: Appleton-Century-Crofts, 1972.

McKinlay, John B. "The Sick Role—Illness and Pregnancy." *Social Science and Medicine* 6 (1972): 561-572.

McMullen, J.J. "The Prevention and Management of Disability in General Practice." *J. Royal College General Practitioners* 17 (1979): 80-90.

Mechanic, David. *Medical Sociology,* 2nd edition. New York: Free Press, 1978.

Mendelson, M.A. *Tender Loving Greed.* New York: Alfred A. Knopf, 1974.

Merkin, D.H. *Pregnancy as a Disease: The Pill in Society.* Port Washington, N.Y. Kennikot Press, 1976.

Michigan Office of Services to the Aging. *Substance Abuse among Michigan's Senior*

Citizens: Current Issues and Future Directions. Report to the Seniors and Substance Abuse Task Force, Lansing, Michigan, 1979. Lansing, Mich.: Office of Services to the Aging.

Middleton, John. *The Kiduyu and Kamba of Kenya.* London: International African Institute, 1953.

Mihalick, M. and Fisch, C. "Should ECG Criteria Be Modified for Geriatric Patients." *Geriatrics* 32 (1977): 65-72.

Mitchel, J. Clyde. *Social Networks in Urban Situations.* Manchester: University of Manchester Press, 1969.

Molinaro, R.P.L. "Appunti circa gli Usi,Costumi e Idee Religiose dei Lotuko dell' Uganda." *Anthropos* 35-36 (1940-1941): 166-201.

Monroe, R.T. "How Well Are Older People?" *Journal of the Michigan State Medical Society* 59 (1960): 748-751.

Moore, Alexander. *Life Cycles in Atchatlan: The Diverse Careers of Certain Guatemalans.* New York: Teacher's College, Columbia University, 1973.

Moore, Joan W. "Mexican Americans." *The Gerontologist II* 2 (19 Ma): 20-25.

Moore, Lorna G., Van Arsdale, Peter W., Glittenberg, JoAnn E., and Aldrich, Robert A. *The Biocultural Basis of Health: Expanding Views of Medical Anthropology* (with a foreword by Jonas Salk). St. Louis: C.V. Mosby, 1980.

Morton, E.V.B. "Advances in Geriatrics." *Practitioner* 203 (1969): 525-534.

Moses, D. "Older Patients in the General Hospital." *Nursing Clinics of North America* 2 (1967): 705-14.

Moss, Frank and Hallamandaris, V.J. *Too Old Too Sick Too Bad: Nursing Homes in America.* Germantown, Md.: Aspen Systems Corp., 1977.

Mulford, Harold A. "The Prevalence and Extent of Drinking in Iowa, 1961: A Replication and Evaluation of Methods." *Quarterly Journal of Studies on Alcohol* 24 (1963): 39-53.

Mulford, Harold A. and Miller, Donald E. "Drinking in Iowa, II. The Extent of Drinking and Selected Sociocultural Categories." *Quarterly Journal of Studies on Alcohol* 21 (1960a): 26-39.

––––. "Drinking in Iowa, III. A Scale of Definitions of Alcohol Related to Drinking Behavior." *Quarterly Journal of Studies on Alcohol* 21 (1960b): 267-278.

––––. "Drinking in Iowa, IV. Preoccupation with Alcohol and Definition of Alcohol, Heavy Drinking and Trouble Due to Drinking." *Quarterly Journal of Studies on Alcohol* 21 (1960c): 279-291.

Mumford,Lewis. "For Older People: Not Segregation, But Integration." *Archtectural Record* 119 (1956): 191-194.

Mumsell, Marvin R. "Functions of the Aged among Salt River Pima." In *Aging and Modernization,* edited by D.O. Cowgill and L.D. Holmes. New York: Meredity Corporation, 1972.

Muratori, C. "Lomoro Xujang (1853-1912): A Lotuxo chief, Tirrangore." *Sudan Notes and Records* 30 (1949): 107-109.

––––. "A Case of Magical Poisoning in a Lotuko Village." *Sudan Notes and Records* 31 (1950): 133-136.

––––. "Ikang, Queen of Tirrangore." *Sudan Notes and Records* 35 (1954): 144-147.

Murdock, George P. *Outline of Cultural Materials.* New Haven: HRAF, Inc., 1961.

––––. "Ethnographic Atlas: A Summary." *Ethnology* 6 (2) (1967).

––––. "World Sampling Provinces." *Ethnology* 7 (1968): 305-326.

––––. *Outline of World Cultures.* New Haven: HRAF, Inc., 1975.

Murdock, George P. and White, Douglas R. "Standard Cross-Cultural Sample." *Ethnology* 8 (1969): 329-369.

Myerhoff, B. *Number Our Days.* New York: E.P. Dutton, 1978,

Myerhoff, Barbara and Simic, Andre. *Life's Career-Aging: Cross-Cultural Studies in Growing Old.* Beverly Hills: Sage Publications, Inc. 1977.

Nahimow, Nina and Adams, Bert N. "Old Age among the Baganda: Continuity and Change." In *Late Life: Communities and Environmental Policy,* edited by J. Gubrium, Springfield: Charles C. Thomas, 1974.

Naroll, Raoul. "What Have We Learned from Cross-Cultural Surveys?" *American Anthropologist* 72 (1970): 1227-1288.

———. "Holocultural Theory Tests." In *Main Currents in Cultural Anthropology,* edited by Raoul Naroll and Frada Naroll. New York: Appleton-Century-Crofts, 1973.

Naroll, Raoul, et al. "Standard Ethnographic Sample." *Current Anthropology* 11 (1970): 235-248.

Naroll, Raoul, Michik, Gary, and Naroll, Frada. "Hologeistic Theory Testing." In *Comparative Studies by Harold E. Drivers and Essays in His Honor,* edited by Joseph E. Jorgenson. New Haven: HRAF Press, 1974.

———. *Worldwide Theory Testing.* New Haven: HRAF Press, 1976.

National Committee on Maternal Health. *Doctors and Family Planning.* Publication Number 19. New York: National Committee on Maternal Health, 1963.

National Council on the Aging. *The Myth and Reality of Aging in America.* Washington, D.C: National Council on the Aging, 1977.

National Disease and Therapeutic Index. "The Political Economy of Medical Care." *International Journal of Health Services* 5 (1975): 65-94.

National Institute on Alcohol Abuse and Alcoholism. "Economic Costs of Alcohol Related Problems." *Alcohol and Health: New Knowledge.* Second Special Report to the Congress, Washington, D.C., 1974. Washington, D.C.: U.S. Government Printing Office.

Navarro, Vincente. "The Political Economy of Medical Care: An Explanation of the Composition, Nature, and Functioning of the Present Health System of the United States." *International Journal of Health Services* 5 (1975): 65-94.

Needham, Rodney. "Introduction." In *Rethinking Kinship and Marriage.* R. Needham, ed. London: Tavistock Publications, 1971.

———. "Age, Category and Descent." In *Remarks and Inventions,* edited by Rodney Needham. London: Tavistock, 1974.

Neugarten, Bernice L. "The Awarness of Middle Age." In *Middle Age,* edited by Owen, R. London: BBC, 1967.

———. "Adult Personality." In *Middle Age and Aging, A Reader in Social Psychology,* edited by Bernice Neugarten. Chicago: University of Chicago Press, 1968.

———. "Age Groups in American Society and the Rise of the Young-Old." *Annals American Academy Political and Social Sciences,* (Sept., 1974): 187-198.

———. "The Future and the Young-Old." The *Gerontologist* 15 (Part II, 1975): 2-9.

Neugarten, Bernice L. and Datan, Nancy. "Sociological Pespectives on the Life Cycle." In *Life Span Developmental Psychology,* edited by B.P. Baltes and K.W. Schaie. New York: Academic Press, 1973.

Neugarten, Bernice, and Hagestad, Gunhild. "Age and The Life Course." In *Handbook of Aging and the Social Sciences,* edited by R. Binstock and E. Shanas. New York: Van Nostrand Reinhold, 1976.

Neugarten, Bernice, Havighurst, Robert, and Tobin, Sheldon. "The Measurement of Life Satisfaction." *Journal of Gerontology* 16 (1961): 134-143.

———. "Personality and Patterns of Aging." In *Middle Age and Aging,* edited by B. Neugarten. Chicago: University of Chicago Press, 1968.

Neugarten, Bernice L. and Moore, Joan W. "The Changing Age Status System." In *Middle Age and Aging,* edited by B.L. Neugarten. Chicago: University of Chicago Press, 1968.

Neugarten, Bernice, Moore, Joan, and Lowie, John. "Age Norms, Age Constraints, and Adult Socilaization." *American Journal of Sociology* 70 (1965): 710-715.

Nie, N.H., Hull, C.H., Jenkins, J.G., Stienbrenner, K, and Bent, D.H. *SPSS Statistical Package for the Social Science.* New York: McGraw-Hill Book Company, 1970.

Nithman, C.J., Parkhurst, Y.E., and Sommers, E.B. "Physicians' Prescribing Habits: Effects of Medicare." *Journal of the American Medical Association* 217 (1971): 585-587.

Norbeck, Edward. "Age Grading in Japan." *American Anthropologist* 55 (1953): 373-383.

Nusberg, Charlotte. "Implications for Aging of World Demographic Trends." *Ageing International* 6 (3) (1979): 3.

Oosterwal, Gottfried. "Messianic Movement." *Philippine Sociological Review* 16 (1-2) (1968): 40-50.

Opler, Morris E. "An Interpretation of Ambivalence of Two American Indian Tribes." In *Reader In Comparative Religion,* edited by William Lessa and Evan Vogt. New York: Harper and Row (1965): 468-478.

Oppenheimer, Valerie K. "The Life-Cycle Squeeze: The Interaction of Men's Occupational and Family Cycles." *Demography* 11 (1974).

Ortner, Sherry. "Is Female to Male as Nature Is to Culture?" In *Woman, Culture and Society,* edited by Michelle Z. Rosaldo and Louise Lamphere. Stanford: Stanford University Press (1974): 65-87.

Ottenberg, Simon. *Leadership and Authority in an African Society: The Afikpo Vilalge-Group.* Seattle: University of Washington Press, 1971.

Palmore, Erdman B. "Medical Care Needs of the Aged." *Postgraduate Medicine* 51 (May 1972a): 194-200.

———. "Medical Care Needs of the Aged." *Postgraduate Medicine* 51 (June 1972b): 139-142.

———. *Normal Aging.* Durham, N.C.: Duke University Press, 1974.

———. *The Honorable Elders: A Cross-Cultural Analysis of Aging in Japan.* Durham, N.C.: Duke University Press, 1975.

———. "Total Chance of Institutionalization among the Aged." *The Gerontologist* 16 (1976): 504-507.

Parsons, Talcott. "Age and Sex in the Social Structure of the United States." *American Sociological Review* 7 (1942): 604-616.

———. "The Kinship System of the Contemporary United States." *American Anthropologist* 45 (1943).

———. *The Social System.* New York: Free Press, 1951.

———. "The Sick Role and the Role of the Physician Reconsidered." *Health and Society,* (Summer 1975): 257-278.

Parsons, Talcott and Fox, Renee. "Illness, Therapy, and the Modern Urban American Family." *Journal of Social Issues* 13 (1952): 31-44.

Pattison, E. Mansell. "A Theoretical-Empirical Base for Social System Therapy." In *Current Perspectives in Cultural Psychiatry,* edited by E.F. Foulks et al. New York: Spectrum Press (1977): 217-254.

Pelto, Pertti J. *Anthropological Research: The Structure of Inquiry.* New York: Harper & Row, 1970.

Peristiany, J.G. *The Social Institutions of the Kipsigis.* London: George Routledge & Sons, 1939.

———. "The Age Set System of the Pastoral Pokot." *Africa* 21 (1951): 188-206.

Petersdorf, Robert. "Medical Care for the Aged." *Journal of Chronic Diseases* 26 (1973): 197-199.

Peterson, E.T. "The Import of Adolescent Illness on Parental Relationships." *Journal of Health and Social Behavior* 13 (1972): 429-436.

Peterson, Osler L. "Geriatrics: The Need for Science and Policy." *Annals of Internal Medicine* 89 (1978): 279-281.

Petrin, A. "The Fate of Drugs in the Organism in Advanced Age." *International Journal of Clinical Pharmacology* 9 (1974): 157-159.

Pierce, Robert C.; Clark, Margaret; and Kaufman, Sharon. "Generation and Ethnic Identity." *International Journal of Aging and Human Development* 9 (1978): 19-29.

Pihlblad, C.T., Beverfelt, Eva and Helland, Haktor. "Status and Role of the Aged in Norwegian Society." In *Aging and Modernization,* edited by D.O. Cowgill and L.D. Holmes. New York: Appleton-Century-Crofts, 1972.

Pino, C.J.; Rosica, L.M.; and Carter, T.J. "The Differential Effects of Relocation on Nursing Home Patients." *The Gerontologist* 18 (1978): 167-172.

Pitts, J. "Social Control: The Concept." In *International Encyclopedia of the Social Sciences,* Vol. 14. New York: Macmillan, 1968.

Plath, David W. "Japan: The After Years." In *Aging and Modernization,* edited by D.O. Cowgill and L.D. Holmes. New York: Meredith Corporation, 1972.

———. "Ecstasy Years—Old Age in Japan." *Pacific Affairs* 46 (3) (1973): 421-430.

Pospisil, Leo. *Kapauku Papuans and Their Law.* New Haven: Human Relations Area File Press, 1971.

Press, Irwin and McKool, Mike, Jr. "Social Structure and Status of the Aged: Toward Some Valid Cross-Cultural Generalizations." *Aging and Human Development* 3 (1972): 297-306.

Prins, A.H.J. *East African Age-Class System: An Inquiry into the Social Order of Galla, Kipsigis, and Kikuyu.* Westport, Conn.: Negro University Press, 1970 (1953).

Radcliffe-Brown, A.R. "Age Organization Terminology." *Man* 29 (1929): 21.

Rahe, Richard H.; Meyer, Merle; Smith, Michael; Kjaer, George; and Holmes, Thomas H. "Social Stress and Illness Onset." *Journal of Psychosomatic Research* 8 (1964): 35-44.

Rainwater, Lee. "Social Status Differences in the Family Relationships of German Men." *Marriage and Family Living* 24 (1962).

Rappaport, Roy A. *Pigs for the Ancestors: Rituals in the Ecology of a New Guinea People.* New Haven: Yale University Press, 1968.

Rathborne-McCune, Eloise; Lohn, Harold, Levenson, Julia; and Hsu, James. *Community Survey of Aged Alcoholics and Problem Drinkers.* Report to the National Institute on Alcohol Abuse and Alcoholism, Washington, D.C., 1976. Baltimore: Levindale Geriatric Research Center.

Reichard, Suzanne; Livson, Florine; and Peterson, Paul G. *Aging and Personality.* New York: Wiley, 1962.

Reiman, Jeffrey H. "Aging as Victimization: Relfections on the American Way of (Ending) life." In *Crime and the Elderly,* ed. Jack Goldsmith and Sharon S. Goldsmith. Lexington, Ma.: D.C. Heath and Co., 1976.

Richen, Marilyn C. "Legitimacy and the Resolution of Conflict in an Indian Church." Ph.D. dissertation, University of Oregon, 1974.

Riesman, David. "Some Clinical and Cultural Aspects of the Aging Process." In *Individualism Reconsidered,* edited by David Riesman, Encino, Ca.: Glencoe Free Press (1954): 484-492.

Riley, J.W., and Marden, C.F. "The Social Pattern of Alcoholic Drinkers." *Quarterly Journal of Studies on Alcohol* 9 (1948): 353-362.

Riley, Matilda W., et al. *Aging and Society, Vol. 1, An Inventory of Research Findings.* New York: Russell Sage Foundation, 1968.

Riley, Matilda White, ed. *Aging from Birth to Death.* AAAS Selected Symposium 30. Boulder: Westview Press, 1979.

Riley, Mathilda W.; Johnson, Marilyn E.; and Foner, Anne; editors. *Aging and Society: A Sociology of Age Stratification.* New York: Russell Sage Foundation, 1972.

Riley, Matilda W. and Waring, Joan. "Age and Aging." In *Contemporary Social Problems,* 4th ed., edited by Robert K. Merton and Robert Nisbet. New York: Harcourt Brace Janovich, 1976.

Rodstein, M. "The ECG in Old Age: Implications for Diagnosis, Therapy and Prognosis." *Geriatrics* 32 (1977): 76-79.

Rohner, Ronald P. "Advantages of the Comparative Method of Anthropology." *Behavior Science Research* 12 (1977a): 117-144.

———. "Why Cross-Cultural Research?" In *Issues in Cross-Cultural Research,* edited by Leonore Loeb Adler. New York: New York Academy of Sciences, 1977b.

Rohner, Ronald P., et al. "Guidelines for Holocultural Research." *Current Anthropology* 19 (1) (1978): 128-129.

Roman, P.M. and Trice, H.N. "The Sick Role, Labelling Theory, and the Deviant Drinker." *International Journal of Social Psychiatry* 14 (1968): 245-251.

Rose, Arnold M. "The Subculture of Aging." In *Older People and Their Social World,* edited by Arnold M. Rose and Warren K. Petersen. Philadelphia: F.A. Davis, 1965.

Rosen, George. "The Evolution of Social Medicine." In *Handbook of Medical Sociology,* eds. Howard E. Freeman; Sol Levine; and Leo Reeder. Englewood Cliffs, N.J.: Prentice Hall (1972): 30-60.

———. *Preventive Medicine in the United States: 1900-1975.* New York: Prodist, 1976.

Rosenfeld, Albert. *Prolongevity.* New York: Avon, 1976.

Rosengren, William R. "The Sick Role during Pregnancy: A Note on Research in Progress." *Journal of Health and Social Behavior* 3 (1962a): 213-218.

———. "Social Instability and Attitudes towards Pregnancy as a Social Role." *Social Problems* 9 (1962b): 371-378.

Rosenmayr, Leopold. "The Elderly in Austrian Society." In *Aging and Modernization,* edited by D.O. Cowgill and L.D. Holmes. New York: Appleton-Century-Crofts, 1972.

————. "The Family—A Source of Help for the Elderly?" In *Family, Bureaucracy and the Elderly,* edited by Ethel Shanas and Marvin Sussman. Durham: Duke University Press, 1977.

Rosin, A.J. and Glatt, M.M. "Alcohol Excess in the Elderly." *Quarterly Journal of Studies on Alcohol* 32 (1971): 53-59.

Rosow, Irving. "Retirement Housing and Social Integration." *The Gerontologist* 1 (1961): 85-91.

————. "And Then We Were Old." *Transaction* 2 (2) (1965): 20-26.

————. *Social Integration of the Aged.* New York: Free Press, 1967.

————. "Old People: Their Friends and Neighbors." *American Behaviorial Scientist* 14 (1970): 59-69.

————. *Socialization to Old Age.* Berkeley: University of California Press. 1974.

Ross, Jennie Keith. See also Jennie Keith.

Ross, Jennie Keith. "Learning to be Retired: Socialization into a French Retirement Residence." *Journal of Gerontology* 29 (2) (1974a): 211-223.

————. "Life Goes On: Social Organization in a French Retirement Residence." In *Late Life: Communities and Environmental Policy,* edited by J. Gubrium. Springfield: Charles C. Thomas (1974b): 99-120.

————. "Successful Aging in a French Retirement Residence." In *Successful Aging,* edited by E. Pfeiffer. Durham: Duke University Press, 1974c.

————. *Old People, New Lives, Community Creation in a Retirement Residence.* Chicago: University of Chicago Press, 1977.

Ross, Jennie Keith and Ross, Marc Howard. "Participant Observation in Political Research." *Political Methodology,* Winter 1974.

Rothstein, W.G. "Professionalization and Employer Demands: The Causes of Homeopathy and Psychoanalysis in the United States." In *Professionalization and Social Change,* ed. Paul Holmes, Kelle Staffordshire: The University of Keele (1973): 159-178.

Ruel, J.J. "Kuria Generation Sets." Proceedings of Conference held at the East African Institute of Social Research, Makerere College, Kampala, Uganda, 1958.

Ryan, William. *Blaming the Victim.* New York: Vintage, 1970.

Sahlins, Marshall D. "Poor Man, Rich Man, Big Man, Chief: Political Types in Melanisia and Polyonesia." In *Peoples and Cultures of the Pacific,* edited by Andrew P. Vayda. Garden City: Natural History Press, 1968.

Sangree, Walter H. "The Bantu Tiriki of Western Kenya." In *Peoples of Africa,* edited by James L. Gibbs, Jr. New York: Holt, Rinehart and Winston (1965): 41-80.

————. *Age, Prayer, and Politics in Tiriki, Kenya.* New York: Oxford University Press, 1966.

Sanjek, Roger. "A Network Method and Its Use in Urban Ethnography." *Human Organization* 37 (1978): 257-269.

Sankar, Andrea P. "The Evolution of the Sisterhood in Traditional Chinese Society: From Village Girl's House to Chai T'angs in Hong Kong." Unpublished Ph.D. dissertation. University of Michigan.

Saward, E.W. "National Considerations.' *Journal of Medical Education* 48, Part 2 (1973): 105-110.

Schneider, David M. *American Kinship: A Cultural Account.* Englewood Cliffs: Prentice-Hall, Inc., 1968.

Schneider, David and Smith, R. *Class Differences and Sex Roles in American Kinship and Family Structure.* New York: Prentice-Hall, 1973.

Schonfield, A.E.D. "Training Practitioners for Work with the Aged." *Canadian Mental Health* (Sept.-Oct. 1973): 9-11.

Schultz, Carol M. "Age, Sex and Death Anxiety in a Middle Class American Community." In *Aging in Culture and Society: Comparative Viewpoints and Strategies,* edited by C.L. Fry. New York: J.F. Bergin, 1980.

Schurtz, Heinrich. *Altersklassen und Mannerbunde.* Berlin: Georg Reimer, 1902.

Scott, Joan and Tilly, Louise A. "Woman's Work and the Family in Nineteenth-Century Europe." *Comparative Studies in Society and History* 17 (1975).

Seidel, Victor. "Can Physicians Be Attracted to Ghetto Practice." In *Medicine in the Ghetto,* edited by John C. Norman. New York: Appleton-Century-Crofts (1969): 175-179.

Seligman, C.G. "Some Little-Known Tribes of the Southern Sudan." *Journal of the Royal Anthropological Institute* 55 (1925): 15-35.

Seligman, C.G. and Seligman, Brenda Z. "The Social Organization of the Latuka." *Sudan Notes and Records* 8 (1926): 1-45.

―――. *Pagan Tribes of the Nilotic Sudan.* London: Routledge and Kegan Paul, 1932.

Shanas, Ethel. "The Unmarried Old Person in the United States: Living Arrangements and Care in Illness, Myth and Fact." Paper prepared for the International Social Science Seminar in Gerontology, 1963, Markanyd, Sweden.

―――. "Sociological Factors of Aging Significant to the Clinician." *Journal of the American Geriatrics Society* 17 (1969): 284-288.

―――. "Measuring the Home Health Needs of the Aged in Five Countries." *Journal of Gerontology* 26 (1971): 35-45.

―――. "Family Kin Networks and Aging in Cross-Cultural Perspective." *Journal of Marriage and the Family* 35 (3) (1973): 505-511.

―――. "Health Status of Older People." *American Journal of Public Health* 64 (1974): 261-264.

―――. "Gerontology and the Social and Behavorial Sciences: Where Do We Go from Here?" *The Gerontologist* 15 (6) (1975): 499-502.

―――. "The Family as a Social Support System in Old Age." *The Gerontologist* 19 (1979): 169-174.

Shanas, Ethel and Maddox, George L. "Aging Health and the Organization of Health Resources." In *Handbook of Aging and the Social Sciences,* edited by R. Binstock and E. Shanas. New York: Van Nostrand Reinhold Co. (1976): 592-618.

Shanas, Ethel and Streib, Gordon F., eds. *Social Structure and the Family: Generational Relations.* Englewood Cliffs: Prentice-Hall, Inc., 1965.

Shanas, Ethel; Townsend, Peter, Wedderburn, Dorothy; Frus, Henning; Milhoj, Poul; and Stenhouwer, Jan. *Old People in Three Industrial Societies.* New York: Atherton Press, 1968.

Shannon, G.W. and Dever, G.E.A. *Health Care Delivery: Spatial Perspectives.* New York: McGraw-Hill, 1974.

Shapiro, Joan. *Communities of the Alone: Working with Single-Room Occupants in the City.* New York: Association Press, 1971.

Sharma, K.L. "A Cross-Cultural Comparison of Stereotypes towards Older Persons." *Indian Journal of Social Work* 32 (3) (1971): 315-320.

Shaughnessy, M.E. "The Role of the Medical Director in the Nursing Home." *Journal of the American Geriatrics Society* 21 (1973): 569-571.

Sheehan, Tom. "Senior Esteem as a Factor of Societal Economic Complexity." *The Gerontologist* 16 (5) (1976): 433-440.

Shelton, Austin J. "Igbo Aging and Eldership: Notes for Gerontologists and Others." *The Gerontologist* 5 (1965): 2-23.

―――. "Igbo Child-rearing Eldership and Dependence: Further Notes for Gerontologists and Others." *The Gerontologist* 7 (1967): 236-241.

―――. "The Ages and Eldership among the Igbo." In *Aging and Modernization,* edited by D.O. Cowgill and L.D. Holmes. New York: Appleton-Century-Crofts, 1972.

Sheuring, B. *Ortskunde von Kahl am Main.* Wurzburg: Erziehungswissenschaftliche Fakultat, 1972.

Siegel, Harvey. *Outposts of the Forgotten, New York City's Welfare Hotels and Single Room Occupancy Tenements.* Edison: Transaction Books, 1977.

Siegel, Jacob S. "Demographic Aspects of Aging and the Older Population in the United States." *Current Population Reports.* Special Studies, Series P-23, No. 59, Washington, D.C.: U.S. Bureau of the Census, 1978.

Siemaszko, Maria. "Kin Relations of the Aged: Possible Consequences to Social Service Planning." In *Aging in Culture and Society: Comparative Viewpoints and Strategies,* edited by C.L. Fry. New York: J.F. Bergin, 1980.

Silverman, Philip and Maxwell, Robert J. "An Informational Approach to the Treatment of the Aged." Paper presented to the Gerontological Society, Houston, 1971a.

―――. "Models of Aging." Paper presented to the meetings of the American Anthropological Association, New York, 1971b.

————. "An Anthropological Approach to the Study of the Aged." Paper presented to the Gerontological Society, San Juan, P.R., 1972.

————. "Empirical Issues in the Anthropology of Aging." Paper presented to the American Anthropological Association, Washington, D.C., 1976.

————. "How Do I Respect Thee? Let Me Count the Ways: Deference towards Elderly Men and Women." *Behavior Science Research* 13 (2) (1978):91-108.

————. "Bakersfield Study Schedule." Unpublished manuscript, n.d.

Simmons, Leo. *The Role of the Aged in Primitive Society.* New Haven: Yale University Press, 1945a.

————. "A Prospectus for Field Research in the Position and Treatment of the Aged in Primitive and Other Societies." *American Anthropologist* 47 (1945b):433-438.

————. "Attitudes toward Aging and the Aged: Primitive Societies." *Journal of Gerontology* 1 (1946):41-47.

————. "Aging in Modern Society." In *Toward a Better Understanding of the Aging.* Seminar on Aging, Aspen, Colorado, Sept. 8-13, 1958. New York: Council on Social Work Education, 1959.

————. "Aging in Pre-industrial Societies." In *Handbook of Social Gerontology*, edited by C. Tibbitts. Chicago: University of Chicago Press, 1960.

————. *The Role of the Aged in Primitive Society.* New Haven: Archon Books, 1945a, 1970.

Skinner, E. "Intergenerational Conflict among the Mossi." *Journal of Conflict Resolution* 5 (1961):55-60.

Slater, Philip. "Cross-Cultural Views of the Aged." In *New Thoughts on Old Age,* edited by R. Kastenbaum. New York: Springer, 1964.

Smith, Marian. *The Puyallup-Nisqually.* New York: Columbia University Press, 1940.

Smith, Robert, et al. "Cultural Differences in the Life Cycle and the Concept of Time." In *Aging and Leisure,* edited by R. Kleemeir. New York: Oxford University Press, 1961.

Sokolovsky, Jay, et al. "Personal Networks of Ex-Mental Patients in a Manhattan SRO Hotel." *Human Organization* 37 (1978):5-15.

Sokolovsky, Jay and Cohen, Carl. "The Cultural Meaning of Personal Networks for the Inner-City Elderly." *Urban Anthropology* 7 (1978):323-343.

————. "Measuring Social Interaction of Aging and Elderly: A Methodological Synthesis." *International Journal of Aging and Human Development.* (In Press.)

Solomon, Sonya A. "Family Bounds and Friendship Bonds: Japan and West Germany." *Journal of Marriage and Family* (1977).

Solon, J. and Greenwalt, L. "Physicians' Participation in Nursing Homes." *Medical Care* 12 (1974):486-497.

Somerset, F.R.R. (Lord Raglan.) "The Lotuko." *Sudan Notes and Records* 1 (1918):153-159.

————. "The Lotuko Language." *Bulletin of the School of Oriental Studies.* University of London 2 (1921-1923):267-296.

Sorokin, Pitirim. *Social and Cultural Dynamics,* 3 Vols. New York: American Book, 1937.

Sowada, Alphonse. "New Guinea's Fierce Asmat: A Heritage of Head-hunting." In *Vanishing Peoples of the Earth,* edited by Robert L. Breeden. Washington: National Geographic Society, 1978.

Sparks, D.E. "The Still Rebirth: Retirement and Role Discontinuity." *Journal of Asian and African Studies* 10 (1975):64-74.

Spence, D.L., et al. "Medical Student Attitudes toward the Geriatric Patient." *Journal of American Geriatric Society* 16 (1968):976-983.

Spencer, Paul. *The Samburu: A Study of Gerontocracy in a Nomadic Tribe.* Berkeley: University of California Press, 1965.

————. *Nomads in Alliance: Symbiosis and Growth among the Rendille and Samburu of Kenya.* London: Oxford University Press, 1973.

Spencer, Robert. "Notes on a Bachelor House in the South China Area." *American Anthropologist* (second series) 50 (1948):3.

Spier, Leslie. "The Prophet Dance of the Northwest and Its Derivatives: The Source of the Ghost Dance." *General Series in Anthropology,* No. 1. Menasha, Wisc.: George Banta Publishing Co., 1935.

Spindler, George D. *Urbanization and Identity in a German Village.* New York: Holt, Rinehart, & Winston, 1973.

Spradley, James P. *The Ethnographic Interview.* New York: Holt, Rinehart, and Winston, 1979.

Sprague, C.C. "National Health Policy: Objectives and Strategy." *Journal of Medical Education* 49 (1974):3-13.

Stack, Carol. *All Our Kin.* New York: Harper & Row, 1974.

Stenning, Derrick J. "Household Viability among the Pastoral Fulani." In *The Developmental Cycle in Domestic Groups,* edited by J. Goody. Cambridge: Cambridge University Press, 1971.

Stephens, Joyce. *Loners, Losers and Lovers: A Sociological Study of the Aged Tenants of a Slum Hotel.* Seattle: University of Washington Press, 1976.

Stevens, Rosemary. "Trends in Medical Specialization in the United States." *Inquiry* 8 (1971):9-17.

Stewart, Frank H. *Fundamentals of Age-Group Systems.* New York: Academic Press, 1977.

Straus, Robert, and Bacon, Stanley. *Drinking in College.* New Haven: Yale University Press, 1953.

Streib, Gordon A. "Old Age in Ireland: Demographic and Sociological Aspects." In *Aging and Modernization,* edited by D.O. Cowgill and L.D. Holmes. New York: Meredith Corporation, 1972.

Streib, Gordon F. and Schneider, C.J. *Retirement in American Society: Impact and Process.* Ithaca, N.Y.: Cornell University Press, 1971.

Stroman, D.F. *The Medical Establishment and Social Responsibility.* Port Washington, N.Y.: Kennikot Press, 1976.

Sudnow, David. *Passing On: The Social Organization of Dying.* Englewood Cliffs, N.J.: Prentice-Hall, 1967.

Sumner, William Graham, *Folkways.* New York: The New American Library, 1940.

Sussman, Marvin, and Burchinal, Lee. "Kinship Family Network: Unheralded Structure in Current Conceptualization of Family Functioning." *Journal of Marriage and Family Living* 24 (1962):231-240.

Suttles, Gerald D. "Friendship As a Social Institution." In *Social Relationships,* edited by George J. McCall, et al. Chicago: Aldine Publishing Co., 1970.

Suttles, Wayne. "The Plateau Prophet Dance among Coast Salish." *Southwestern Journal of Anthropology* 13 (4) (1957):352-396.

Syme, S.L., and Berkman, Lisa F. "Social Class, Susceptibility, and Sickness."*American Journal of Epidemiology* 104 (1976).

Szasz, Thomas. *The Manufacture of Madness.* New York: Harper & Row, 1970.

Taeuber, Irene. "The Families of Chinese Farmers." In *Family and Kinship in Chinese Society,* edited by Maurice Freedman. Stanford: Stanford University Press, 1970.

Terri, G., and Franzini, C. "General Considerations on Drug Therapy in the Elderly." *Clinical Gerontology* 20 (1972):474-477.

Thomas, Lewis. "Aspects of Biomedical Science Policy." Address to the Institute of Medicine, Fall Meeting, Nov. 9, 1972, Washington, D.C.

Timiras, P.S. *Developmental Physiology and Aging.* New York: Macmillan, 1972.

Tissue, Thomas. "Old Age, Poverty, and the Central City." *International Journal of Aging and Human Development* 2 (1971):235-248.

Tivin, M.D. "Older Americans: Special Handling Required." Washington, D.C.: National Council on Aging, 1971.

Tobin, S.S. "Social and Health Services for the Future Aged." *The Gerontologist* 15 (Feb. 1975 Supplement):32-37.

Tobin, Sheldon S., and Lieberman, M.A. *Last Home for the Aged.* San Francisco: Jossey-Bass, 1976.

Topley, Marjorie. "The Great Way of Heaven: A Group of Chinese Secret Religious Sects." *Bulletin of the School of Oriental and African Studies* 26 (1963): 2.

———. "Marriage Resistance in Rural Kwangtung." In *Women in Chinese Society,* edited by Marjory Wolf and Roxanne Witkee. California: Stanford University Press, 1975.

Towsend, Claire. *Old Age: The Last Segregation.* New York: Grossman, 1971.

Townsend, Peter *The Family Life of Old People, and Inquiry in East London.* London: Routledge and Kegan Paul, 1957.

———. *The Last Refuge.* London: Routledge and Kegan Paul, 1962.

———. "Isolation, Desolation and Loneliness." In *Old People in Three Industrial Societies,* edited by Ethel Shanas, et al. New York: Atherton Press (1968): 258-287.

———. "The Place of Older People in Different Societies." In *Age with a Future.* Proceedings of the Sixth International Congress of Gerontology. Philadelphia: F.A. David, Co., 1973.

Tuckman, Jacob, and Lorge, Irving. "Attitudes toward Old People." *Journal of Social Psychology* 37 (1953): 249-260.

Tunstall, Jeremy. *Old and Alone.* London: Routledge and Kegan Paul, Ltd., 1966.

Turnbull, Colin. *Wayward Servants.* London: Eyer & Spottis Woode, 1975.

Tylor, Stephen. *Cognitive Anthropology.* New York: Holt, Rinehart and Winston, 1969.

Underwood, Jane H. "The Reappearing Elderly?" mimeo. n.d.

United States Department of Commerce. Bureau of the Census. *Subject Report, 1970: Marital Status.* Washington, D.C.: Government Printing Office, 1970a.

———. Bureau of the Census. *Subject Report, 1970: Persons in Institutions and Other Group Quarters.* Washington, D.C.: Government Printing Office, 1970b.

———. *Social Indicators.* Washington, D.C.: Government Printing Office, 1973.

United States Department of Health, Education and Welfare. "Some Demographic Aspects of Aging in the U.S." Series P-23, *Current Population Reports,* No. 43 (February). Washington, D.C.: U.S. Government Printing Office, 1973.

———. *Facts About Older Americans 1976.* U.S. Department of Health, Education, and Welfare Publication No. (OHD) 77-20006, 1976.

———. Current Estimates from the Health Interview Survey: U.S.-1977. Publication No. (PHS) 78-1554. Washington, D.C.: U.S. Government Printing Office, 1978.

United States Department of Health, Education and Welfare. Bureau of Public Assistance. Social Security Administration. *Recipients of Old Age Assistance in Early 1953, Part 1-State Data.* Public Assistance Report No. 26. Washington, D.C.: Government Printing Office, 1955.

United States Department of Health, Education, and Welfare, National Center for Health Statistics. *Characteristics of Patients of Selected Types of Medical Specialists and Practitioners: U.S. July 1963-June 1964.* (USPHS Publ. No. 1000, Series 10, No. 28). Washington, D.C.: U.S. Government Printing Office, 1966.

———. *Age Patterns in Medical Care, Illness and Disability: U.S. July 1963-June 1965.* (USPHS Publ. No. 1000, Series 10, No. 32). Washington, D.C.: U.S. Government Printing Office, 1966.

———. *Measures of Chronic Illness Among Residents of Nursing Homes, United States, June-August, 1969.* Vital and Health Statistics Series 12, No. 24. Washington, D.C.: Government Printing Office, 1974a.

———. *Vital Statistics of the U.S., Vol. 2, Life Tables, Section 5.* Washington, D.C.: Government Printing Office, 1974b.

———. *Provisional Statistics, Annual Summary for the United States 1975, Births, Deaths, Marriage, Divorces.* Washington, D.C.: Government Printing Offices, 1975.

United States Department of Health, Education and Welfare, Health Resources Administration. *Determining Health Manpower Requirements: An Overview of Planning Agencies' Decisions and Methods.* Publication No. (PHS) 79-14003. Washington, D.C.: U.S. Printing Office, 1979.

United States Department of Health, Education and Welfare. Public Health Service. Office of Nursing Home Affairs. *Long-Term Care Facility Improvement Study.* Pub. No. 76-50021. Washington, D.C.: Government Printing Office, 1975.

United States Department of Health, Education and Welfare, Surgeon General Office. *Healthy People* (GPO #071-001-00416-2). Washington, D.C.: U.S. Government Printing Office, 1979.

United States Senate Hearing. *Medicine and Aging: An Assessment of Opportunities and Neglect.* Washington, D.C.: U.S. Government Printing Office, 1976.

United States Senate-Special Committee on Aging. *Developments in Aging, 1970.* Washington, D.C.: U.S. Government Printing Office, 1971.

———. *Home Health Care Services in the United States.* 92nd Congress, 2nd Session. Washington, D.C.: U.S. Government Printing Office, 1972.

Vail, David J. *Dehumanization and the Institutional Career.* Springfield, Ill.: Charles C. Thomas, 1966.

Van Amelsvoort, V.F.P.M. *Early Introduction of Integrated Rural Health into a Primitive Society.* Assen: Van Gorcum, 1964.

Van Arsdale,Peter W. *Perspectives on Development in Asmat* (Vol. 5 of The Asmat Sketch Book Series, ed. by Frank A Trenkenschuh). Agats, Irian Jaya: Asmat Museum, 1975.

———. "Population Dynamics among Asmat Hunter-Gatherers of New Guinea: Data, Methods, Comparisons." *Human Ecology* 6 (4) (1978a): 435-467.

———. "Activity Patterns of Asmat Hunter-Gatherers: A Time Budget Analysis." *Mankind* 11 (1978b): 453-460.

Van Arsdale, Peter W. and Gallus, David. "The 'Lord of the Earth' Cult among the Asmat: Prestige, Power and Politics in a Transitional Society." *Irian: Bulletin of Irian Jaya Development* 3 (2) (1974): 1-31.

Van Gennep, Arnold. *Rites of Passage.* Paris: Emile Nourry, 1909. (English translation by Monika B. Vizedom and Gabrielle L. Caffee, Routledge and Kegan Paul, 1960).

Vatuk, Sylvia. "The Aging Woman in India: Self-Perceptions and Changing Roles." In *Woman in Contemporary India,* edited by A. De Souza. Delhi: Manohar, 1975.

———. "Withdrawal and Disengagement as a Cultural Response to Aging in India." In *Aging in Culture and Society: Comparative Viewpoints and Strategies,* edited by C.L. Fry. New York: J.F. Bergin, 1980.

Veatch, Robert. "Generalization of Expertise." *Hastings Center Studies* 1 (1973): 29-40.

von Mering, Otto. "An Anthropo-Medical Profile of Aging: Retirement from Life in Active Ill Health." *Journal of Geriatric Psychiatry* 3 (1969): 61-89.

———. "Anthropology in Medicine and Psychiatry. *Anthropology and the Behavorial and Health Sciences,* edited by von Mering, O. and Kasdan, L. Pittsburgh: University of Pittsburgh Press, 1970.

———. "The Diffuse Health AberrationSyndrome: A Bio-Behavioral Study of the Perennial Out-Patient." *Psychosomatics* 8 (1972): 293-303.

von Mering, Otto and Earley, L. William. "Major Changes in the Western Medical Environment." *Archives of General Psychiatry* 13 (1965): 195-201.

———. "The Diagnosis of Problem Patients." *Human Organization* 25 (1966): 20-23.

———. "The Ambulatory Problem Patient: A Unique Teaching Resource." *American Journal of Psychiatry* 126 (1969): 108-112.

von Mering, Otto and Schiff, S. "The Intermittent Patient: His Reference Groups and Intergroup Tensions." *Archives of General Psychiatry* 18 (1968): 400-404.

von Mering, Otto; Shannon, Gary; Deal, William; and Fischer, Pamela. "A Long Day's Journey to Health Care." *Human Organization* 35 (1976): 381-389.

von Mering, Otto and Weniger, F.L. "Sociocultural Background of the Aging Individual," edited by J.E. Birren. Chicago, Ill.: University of Chicago Press (1959): 279-335.

Waldron, J. "Increased Prescribing of Valium, Librium and Other Drugs—An Example of the Influence of Economic and Social Factors on the Practice of Medicine." *International Journal of Health Services* 7 (1977): 37-62.

Wallace, Anthony. "Revitalization Movements." *American Anthropologist* 58 (1956): 264-281.

Warren, RichardL *Education in Rebhausen.* New York: Rinehart & Winston, 1967.

Weatherford, Jack M. *Family Culture, Behavior and Emotion in a Working-Class German Town,* (unpublished Ph.D. dissertation). University of California, San Diego: Department of Anthropology, 1977.

———. "Deutsche Kultur, amerikanisch betrachtet." In *Deutschland: Das Kind mit den zwei Kopfen,* edited by Hans Christoph Buch. Berlin: Verlag Klaus Wagenbach, 1978.

———. "A Millenium of Modernization." In *Village Viability in Modern Society,* edited by Priscilla Reining and Barbara Lenkerd. Washington, D.C.: American Association for the Advancement of Science, 1980.

Weiss, Kenneth M. "Demographic Models for Anthropology. Memoirs of the Society for American Archaeology." No. 27. *American Antiquity* 38 (2, pt. 2) (1973a.).

———. "A Method for Approximating Age-Specific Fertility in the Construction of Life Tables for Anthropological Populations." *Human Biology* 45 (2) (1973b): 195-210.

Wershow, Harold J. "The Four Percent Fallacy; Some Further Evidence and Policy Implications." *The Gerontologist* 16 (1976): 52-55.

Whiteman, J. "The Function of Food in Society." *Nutrition* 20 (1966): 4-8.

Whiting, Beatrice B. and John W.M. Whiting. *Children of Six Cultures.* Cambridge: Harvard University Press.

Williams, Gerry C. "Warriors No More; A Study of the Indian Elderly." In *Aging in Culture and Society: Comparative Perspectives and Strategies,* edited by Christine Fry. New York: J.F. Bergin, (1980): 101-111.

Wilson, Monica. *Good Company: A Study of Nyakyusa Age Villages.* Boston: Beacon Press, 1963 (1941).

―――. "Nyakyusa Age-Villages." *Journal of the Royal Anthropological Institute* 79 (1960 [1949]): 21-25.

Wolstenholme, G.E.W. and O'Connor, M., eds. In *Ethics in Medical Process.* Boston: Little, Brown and Co., 1966.

Yang, C.K. *Chinese Communist Society: The Family and the Village.* Cambridge: The MIT Press, 1959.

Zegwaard, Gerard A. "Headhunting Practices of the Asmat of West New Guinea." In *Melanesia: Readings on a Culture Area,* edited by L.L. Langness and John C. Weschler. Scranton: Chandler, 1971.

Zhorowski, Mark, "Cultural Components in Response to Pain." In *Patients, Physicians and Illness,* ed. E.F. Jost. New York: The Free Press of Glencoe (1958): 256-268.

Zinberg, Sheldon. "The Elderly Alcoholic." The *Gerontologist* 14 (1974): 221-224.

Zola, Irving. "Medicine as an Institution of Social Control." *Sociological Review* 20 (1972): 487-504.

Zorbaugh, Harvey. *The Gold Coast and the Slum: A Sociological Study of Chicago's Near North Side.* Chicago: University of Chicago, Press, 1929.

Author Index

Subject Index

List of Contributors

Amoss, Pamela T., University of Washington
Arluke, Arnold, Northeastern University
Bainton, Barry, University of Arizona
Bohannon, Paul, University of California, Santa Barbara
Cohen, Carl, New York University Medical Center
Faulwell, Margaret, Chicago State University
Feinman, Susan L., University of Wyoming
Fennell, Valerie, Georgia State University
Francis, Doris Goist, Case Western Reserve University
Fry, Christine L., Loyola University of Chicago
Glascock, Anthony P., University of Wyoming
Kayser-Jones, Jeanie, University of California, San Francisco
Keith, Jennie, Swarthmore College
Kertzer, David I., Bowdoin College
Lopata, Helen Znaniecka, Loyola University of Chicago
Madison, Oker B.B., University of Denver
Nydegger, Corinne N., University of California, San Francisco
O'Rand, Angela, Duke University
Peterson, John M., Hebrew Rehabilitation Center for the Aged, Boston
Pomerantz, Rhoda, S., Johnston R. Bowman Health Center
Sankar, Andrea, University of California, San Francisco
Sokolovsky, Jay, University of Maryland, Baltimore County
Van Arsdale, Peter W., University of Denver
Von Mering, Otto, University of Florida
Weatherford, Jack M., AAAS Congressional Fellow